Contract and Tort Law for Paralegals

Nora Rock

Laurence M. Olivo

Jean Fitzgerald

emp

2013
Emond Montgomery Publications
Toronto, Canada

Emond Montgomery Publications Limited
60 Shaftesbury Avenue
Toronto ON M4T 1A3
http://www.emp.ca/highered

Printed in Canada.

We acknowledge the financial support of the Government of Canada through the Canada Book Fund for our publishing activities.

Acquisitions editor: Bernard Sandler
Developmental editor: Sarah Gleadow
Assistant developmental editor: Francine Geraci
Marketing manager: Christine Davidson
Director, sales and marketing, higher education: Kevin Smulan
Supervising editor: Jim Lyons
Copy editor: Diane Gula
Production editor: Nancy Ennis
Proofreader: David Handelsman
Text designer and typesetter: Shani Sohn
Indexer: Paula Pike
Cover image: Tara Wells

Library and Archives Canada Cataloguing in Publication
Rock, Nora, 1968-
    Contract and tort law for paralegals / Nora Rock, Laurence M. Olivo, Jean Fitzgerald.

Includes index.
ISBN 978-1-55239-468-7

    1. Contracts—Canada—Textbooks.   2. Torts—Canada—Textbooks.
3. Legal assistants—Canada.   I. Olivo, Laurence M., 1946-
II. Fitzgerald, Jean   III. Title.

KE850.R63 2012   346.7102   C2012-903129-1
KF801.Z9R63 2012

Contents

Contracts and Torts: Establishing Context

1

OVERVIEW

LEARNING OUTCOMES

After completing this chapter, you should be able to:

- Define "contract" and "tort" and explain the difference between the two.

- Summarize the basic history of contract law and tort law.

- Distinguish criminal law and civil law.

- Distinguish statute law and common law and explain the interplay between the two.

- List two statutes with roots in contract law.

- List two statutes with roots in tort law.

INTRODUCTION

If you are reading this text, it's likely because you have just embarked on a course of study that requires you to develop a working familiarity with Canadian law. For students new to the law, that requirement can seem very daunting at first. However, it's unlikely that you are new to learning itself. If you have successfully mastered any other doctrine before (consider English grammar, for instance), you have learned that all doctrines are *systems*, and all systems have familiar elements: a structure, general rules, specific rules, and exceptions. You can take comfort in knowing that the law is a system like any other, and that you will be able to understand it by using the same learning strategies you have been perfecting since birth.

When striving to understand a system, it is useful to start with an analysis of the system's structure. That basic structural analysis is the purpose of this chapter.

Where Are We?

This is a text about contracts and torts. A **contract** is an agreement between two or more parties; a **tort** is a wrong that occurs between two or more parties. Contracts and torts are the two main disciplines (subsystems) at the heart of the **common law**, which is one of two major components of Canadian law. The other major component is **statute law**.

The common law/statute law division is actually one of two ways in which Canadian law is typically partitioned; the other partition is based on the distinction between criminal law and **civil law**. Contracts and torts are both civil law disciplines.

By the end of this chapter, you should understand both major partitions: between the common law and statute law, and between the criminal law and civil law. With that understanding in place, you will be able to consider contracts and torts in context; that is, you will understand how these two important doctrines fit within the overall system of Canadian law. First, however, here is a brief overview of the historical roots of contracts, torts, **crimes**, and statutes.

HISTORICAL ROOTS AND DEVELOPMENT

As you may know, the concepts of law and justice are very ancient, and law in some form has been relied upon in every known human society.

The idea that the law should be administered by a government is not as universal. In many early societies, legal problems were solved through the use of **self-help remedies**, for example, duels or **distress**. (To use the self-help remedy of distress usually means to take or retain possession of something that is not yours in satisfaction of a debt.) In some societies, tribal elders were considered to have the authority to resolve disputes. In more modern contexts—for example, the US "Wild West" of the late 19th and early 20th centuries—the combination of a large undeveloped territory needing governing and a fledgling government sometimes created a renewed, though temporary, emphasis on the importance of self-help remedies.

contract
an agreement between private parties or between a private party and the state

tort
a wrong between private parties or between a party and the state

common law
a type of law developed in England, based on previous judicial decisions and common to all the people of a country

statute law
laws passed by legislatures

civil law
individuals' responsibility for pursuing remedies for harms between them

crime
an act or omission that is an offence under criminal law

self-help remedy
a remedy exercised by a wronged party without recourse to a formal system of justice

distress
a traditional remedy under which a person in possession of the goods of another can seize and/or sell those goods as compensation for a wrong

History suggests that the longer a civilization flourishes and grows, the more organized its legal system tends to become and, eventually, it becomes important for the government to administer not only the criminal law (usually the first priority), but also contract and tort disputes.

The development of contract types and uses has historically not been driven by governments but, rather, by ingenious individuals looking for effective solutions to business problems. Contract law is the older of the two common-law disciplines, most likely because societies need commerce to flourish, and commerce requires reliable contracts. Complex contract concepts—like bills of exchange, sureties, guarantees, and commodity futures contracts—have been around for centuries, invented because circumstances required them. Where courts were available, the legal decisions issued about the enforceability of these contracts helped influence their modern form.

The evolution of tort concepts into a form we would recognize is considerably more recent. Before that could happen, a clear distinction had to emerge between tort and crime. In modern society, we tend to view a crime as a wrong against society as a whole (and against the government), and a tort as a "private wrong" between individuals, between corporations, or between an individual and a corporation. This distinction is, however, fairly contemporary. Also, self-help remedies (shooting trespassers; taking an eye for an eye) were more satisfactory for dealing with tort problems than they were for dealing with contract disputes. Governments and courts have been slower to intervene in tort situations, and have tended to do so primarily to bring order to a might-is-right state.

Negligence, now the most important of all tort doctrines, was particularly late to emerge. The recognition that we may owe a **duty of care** to others in the absence of a contract—which is the idea at the heart of negligence—was not fully endorsed by case law until the 1932 British decision in *Donoghue v. Stevenson*.[1]

At the same time as the concepts of contract, tort, and crime were developing, various societies grappled with the issue of how to organize the emerging legal principles. In some societies, including ancient Rome and 19th-century France, comprehensive **legal codes** of laws were created and put into writing. The rationale for a written code was that it made the law objective and, also, accessible to anyone willing to take the time to read it.

However, legal codes have some drawbacks: for example, they can severely limit the evolution of legal concepts. Also, as a society grows more complex, the code needed to record its laws may become so long and unwieldy that the benefit of accessibility is undermined: navigating the complex code eventually requires expert knowledge.

For this reason, many societies, including all of Canada except Quebec, have taken a different approach: while written documents (called statutes) have been used to organize certain areas of the law, the bulk of the law has been left to develop through the **accretion** of court decisions, guided by the concept of **precedent**. The Canadian version of this system, called "the common law," originated in Brit-

---

1. *McAlister (Donoghue) v. Stevenson*, [1932] A.C. 562 (H.L.).

negligence
an act committed without intention to cause harm, but which a reasonable person would anticipate might cause harm

duty of care
a legal obligation imposed on an individual to take reasonable care to avoid causing harm to another who might reasonably be affected and who ought to be in the individual's contemplation

legal codes
formal (usually written) collections of legal provisions

accretion
slow accumulation over time

precedent
a legal decision that is taken as a guide in subsequent cases; an essential doctrine of common law that requires judges to follow the rule in a previously decided case when that case deals with similar facts or issues to the case currently being decided and that case was decided by a higher court in the same jurisdiction or by the Supreme Court of Canada

ain and was exported to British territories around the world. Now that many of those territories are nations independent of Britain, the common law continues to evolve within them, often growing in different directions depending on the jurisdiction.

Modern Canadian law is now a system comprising many different components: case-based common law (in most jurisdictions), law based on a civil code (in Quebec, because of the province's historical ties to France), a **constitution** that has precedence over and helps to organize the law, and principles and provisions contained in a myriad of separate statutes.

constitution
written and unwritten laws that set out how a country will be governed

Where do contracts and torts fit in? These doctrines have retained their common-law basis, and most of the new developments in contract and tort emerge as common-law concepts. However, primarily for accessibility and public policy reasons, some contract and tort concepts (for example, implied terms in a commercial sales contract or the consequences of contaminating the environment) eventually become **codified** in statutes.

codified
written down and organized into topics

Ours is a structurally complex legal system. Some of that complexity relates to the way the law has developed over centuries. However, the partitions and distinctions in our system are not merely historical quirks or holdovers. They remain because they serve a purpose: for example, to allow the law to grow with the times or to isolate issues requiring government management (for example, through a statute and regulations).

We now turn to the Canadian Constitution and the framework it provides for administering the law within Canada.

THE CONSTITUTION AND THE CHARTER

The Constitutional Context

A traditional aspect of the birth of a new state is the creation of a constitution. Canada's Constitution (which, when passed, was named the *British North America Act*) was introduced in 1867.[2]

Because Canada is a federation—a political unit that includes both a national government and several smaller political units (in our case, provincial and territorial governments)—one issue that received considerable attention in the creation of its Constitution was the division of regulatory power between the federal and provincial/territorial governments. Establishing this basic division of powers prevents overlapping or inconsistent laws and allows each tier of government to collect taxes to fund and administer a logical share of government activity.

The division of powers within the Canadian federation is set out in ss. 91 and 92 of the Constitution. A detailed analysis of that division is not necessary for the purpose of this book; however, you should know that some of the most important spheres of regulation reserved to the provincial governments include:

---

2. *Constitution Act, 1867* (U.K.), 30 & 31 Vict., c. 3, reprinted in R.S.C. 1985, App. II, No. 5.

- property and civil rights,
- local commerce,
- provincial justice, and
- "matters of a local and private Nature."

Legal disputes based on contracts or torts are private in nature; in other words, even if one of the parties happens to be a government agency—which sometimes happens—the dispute is triggered not by government action or policies, but rather by wrongs alleged to have been committed between individuals, between corporations, or between an individual and a corporation. Many contract and tort disputes involve disputes over or intrusions on private property; many others involve problems that have arisen in the course of (local) commerce. All these elements illustrate that contract and tort disputes arise most commonly within the provincial regulatory sphere, are tried in provincial courts, and, to the extent that they are shaped by legislation (for example, by statutes that set out limitation periods within which lawsuits must be brought), are most often governed by provincial legislation.

Application of the Charter

The *Canadian Charter of Rights and Freedoms*[3] is, like the 1867 Constitution, a very important source of Canadian law. The Charter, passed in 1982, is not a separate statute but rather an addendum to the *Constitution Act, 1982*.

The Charter was the product of the Canadian government's effort to give constitutional status to certain essential human rights and freedoms. As a constitutional document, it ensures that the protection of those rights and freedoms is given precedence over other government legislative and administrative objectives.

The guarantees provided in the Charter do not have universal application. Rather, they apply to government legislation (both federal and provincial/territorial) and government action. This means that any law passed by the federal or a provincial or territorial legislature (parliament) is subject to the application of the Charter, and the provisions of that law cannot be contrary to the guarantees provided in the Charter. For example, in the 1990s, a number of legal challenges were brought under (relying on) the Charter by people seeking to have the definition of "spouse" in various laws interpreted or changed to include same-sex spouses. It is now usual for a statute mentioning spouses to incorporate a definition that includes same-sex spouses.

The question what constitutes "government action" for the purpose of determining the Charter's application is more complicated. Because Canadian governments involve themselves in a wide range of activities using a wide range of means, drawing a line between where government activity ends and private activity begins is a challenge. For example, if a government offers a grant to an arts organization, and the grant permits the organization to hold an art exhibition, is the exhibition

---

3. *Canadian Charter of Rights and Freedoms*, Part I of the *Constitution Act, 1982*, being Schedule B to the *Canada Act 1982* (U.K.), 1982, c. 11 [Charter].

"government activity" governed by the Charter? The answer to this question is almost certainly "no"; however, there are cases that are less clear-cut. For example, in the wake of the 2010 Vancouver Olympics, a Charter challenge based on the Vancouver Organizing Committee's (VANOC's) decision not to include women's ski jumping went all the way to the British Columbia Court of Appeal before being ultimately resolved (the answer to the question about whether VANOC's decision was government action was "no").[4]

Does the Charter ever apply in contract or tort cases? It certainly does. Canadian governments frequently enter into contracts with private parties; in doing so, the governments are bound by the Charter to protect the rights and freedoms of those affected. Where a government is alleged to have committed a tort, the government's actions may, if the circumstances warrant, be deemed to be both **tortious** and **unconstitutional**. For these reasons, whenever a **plaintiff** commences a contract or tort lawsuit against a government body, the plaintiff should consider whether the Charter is "engaged" (involved, triggered), so that the appropriate arguments can be made in the **statement of claim**, and so that certain special additional pre-trial procedures are followed.

tortious
actionable in tort

unconstitutional
in contravention of
a constitution

plaintiff
in civil law, the party
bringing the suit

statement of claim
a document prepared and
filed by a plaintiff in a lawsuit
that initiates the court action

UNDERSTANDING THE CIVIL/CRIMINAL PARTITION AND DISTINGUISHING TORTS FROM CRIMES

Historical Development

The second major partition in Canadian law is the distinction between civil law and criminal law. In the modern context, this distinction is very clear both in intellectual and procedural terms, but this was not always the case. In many ancient societies, including some of those from which modern Canadian law draws its roots, there were times when the lines between crime and tort were blurred.

This blurring related to the development of the concept of government, which was quite different—for example, in medieval Europe—than it is in modern Canada. In nations or nation-states ruled by monarchs (kings, queens, emperors), there was *some* perceived difference between the wrongs committed between individuals and the wrongs committed against the monarch and his or her court, but the notion that a wrong against the monarch was a wrong against the public good was still emerging. When you consider that many of these monarchies were highly autocratic, with a great gulf in wealth between the monarchy and the common people, it's quite understandable that people had not yet come to associate the undemocratic "government" with the public good. In many of these early societies, the monarchy doled out harsh "criminal" punishment against those who wronged the king, but left the general citizenry to its own devices to sort out the wrongs among themselves.

---

4. *Sagen v. Vancouver Organizing Committee for the 2010 Olympic and Paralympic Winter Games*, 2009 BCCA 522 (CanLII); 2009 BCSC 942 (CanLII).

Eventually, in most early nations, pressure by individuals or the inconvenience of a violent "self-help" society (or both) prompted the creation of a monarch-sponsored police force and the establishment of penalties for offences between commoners. A system of criminal justice typically grew up around these initiatives, and the concept of crime, once reserved for wrongs against the monarch, was extended to apply to wrongs between individuals—and so the criminal law was born.

In modern Canadian society (and in many other societies around the world), the criminal law evolved as a separate branch of the law, with its own rules and procedures. Canadian criminal law is now statute-based, with the primary (but not only) relevant statute being the *Criminal Code*.[5] The *Criminal Code* established not only the **substantive criminal law** (the crimes themselves; called "offences"), but also the procedure for prosecuting those offences, which is different from the **civil procedure** and often takes place in separate courts.

substantive criminal law
also called "offences," the crimes themselves

civil procedure
established steps, rules, and procedures used to administer civil (non-criminal) justice

As the criminal law developed, it became increasingly clear that there were distinctions between wrongs and that not all interpersonal wrongs merited the same penalty. First, not all wrongs had the potential to disrupt the social order: only serious or violent wrongs were properly viewed as being against the general public good. Because government budgets (even in medieval times) were limited, it made sense to dedicate government resources to the prosecution of only those wrongs that threatened the broader community. Lists of public-order wrongs were drawn up, and only the wrongs that made the list became crimes that the government would prosecute. (The rest became private wrongs or, in other words, torts.) The partition between the criminal law (the state's responsibility for prosecution of wrongs against the public good) and the civil law[6] (individuals' responsibility for pursuing remedies for harms between them) was born.

Second, in some cases, the need for compensation for victims was a more important issue than the need to deter the wrongdoing, especially when the harm done was accidental. (The notion that wrongs should be compensated with money is actually older than the concept of crime, and many societies already had a system in place for obtaining the government's backing for compensation orders.) The obvious moral and practical distinctions between wrongs became the basis for the idea that, when determining whether a wrong deserved a criminal penalty or a compensation order, the focus of the analysis should be on the wrongdoer's **intent**. Did the person act maliciously, with the intent to cause harm, or was the harm the result of carelessness or accident? Only the former—an act performed with a "guilty mind"—was deemed to be deserving of criminal consequences. The Roman concept of **mens rea**, which means "guilty mind" and is traceable back to about 400 BCE, is still prominent in the criminal law today.

intent
the mental state (conscious action, malice, carelessness, etc.) at the time of the act of the person who committed the act

mens rea
(Latin) "guilty mind"; the blameworthy mental element in a criminal offence

But what of harm done without *mens rea*? How were these wrongs to be addressed? Unintentional wrongs formed the basis of negligence, which is the modern heart of the law of tort. However, as you will learn in Part II of this book,

---

5. *Criminal Code*, R.S.C. 1985, c. C-46.
6. Note that the term "civil law" used in this context is not to be confused with the law made under the *Civil Code of Québec* (L.R.Q., c. C-1991), also described as "civil law."

tort law has also made a place for certain intentional wrongs, to allow victims to seek compensation for the losses that flow from those wrongs.

Modern Implications of the Civil/Criminal Partition

defendant
in civil law, the party being sued; in criminal law, the party charged with the offence

As you progress through this text, reading about contract and tort law scenarios, you may find yourself wondering on occasion, "Isn't this **defendant**'s behaviour (also) a crime?" In many cases, you will be right.

Criminal culpability and civil liability overlap every time one person intentionally does something (or neglects to do something) that harms another person or another person's property. How the wrong will be redressed is up to the parties involved. The decision about whether a criminal investigation and prosecution will follow a wrongful act is up to the **Crown** (the provincial or federal government). The police (not the victim, though his or her opinion may be influential) will decide whether an alleged wrongdoer will be charged, and the Crown attorney (interchangeably called "the Crown prosecutor" or just "the Crown") will decide whether the crime charged will be prosecuted. On the other hand, the decision about whether a civil suit will be brought in tort or in contract is up to the victim—called the plaintiff in a civil case—who must decide whether the odds of succeeding in court and being compensated (or obtaining a settlement through threat of court) merit the costs of taking the case to trial.

Crown
the provincial or federal government

Many factors guide the choices of these two decision-makers (Crown and plaintiff), including: How serious was the wrong? How easy will it be to prove? How substantial were the damages? Are there any reasons besides damages or punishment of moral guilt (for example, protection of the public or, in a civil case, public vindication of being "in the right") that would make going to court worthwhile?

Depending on the existence and strength of these factors, *both* a criminal prosecution and a contract or tort lawsuit may be warranted. A familiar example is the O.J. Simpson matter, in which defendant O.J. Simpson was tried criminally (and acquitted) and sued civilly (and found liable) for two murders in the early 1990s.[7] A more typical example occurs in the context of serious **fraud**. When one party defrauds another, the state may see the need for criminal punishment and deterrence and will charge the defendant with criminal fraud; the plaintiff (whoever lost the money) may see the benefit in suing for compensation under the law of contract or tort, depending on the specific facts.

fraud
a tort and/or crime based on deception for the purpose of profit

Where appropriate in this book, the criminal consequences of acts that form the basis of contract or tort disputes will be pointed out, so that you can understand how the criminal and civil law intersect.

---

7. Criminal trial: *People v. Simpson*, No. BA097211, 1995 W.L. 704381, at *2 (Cal. Super. Ct. October 3, 1995). Civil trials: *Rufo v. Simpson*, No. SC031947, *Goldman v. Simpson*, No. SC036340, and *Brown v. Simpson*, No. SC036876, 1997 W.L. 53038 (Cal. Super. Ct. February 10, 1997).

LAW IN PRACTICE
Civil and Criminal Standards of Proof

Canadian law reserves different sets of procedures for the management of criminal and civil cases. Also different, in the two separate systems, are some of the rules with respect to evidence. Evidence law has both procedural components (for example, rules prescribe the order in which the parties' evidence is presented) and substantive components. Substantive evidence law deals with issues that go beyond the orderly conduct of the hearing and that may significantly influence the outcome of the case; for example, an evidence rule restricts the extent to which evidence of a defendant's involvement in acts similar to the act that forms the basis of the offence may be introduced in support of the defendant's alleged guilt.

The evidence rule with the most significant impact on the outcome of criminal matters is the rule with respect to standard of proof. In all court cases—whether civil or criminal—the primary task of each side is to prove certain facts that support either the charge or the defence. Proof is, however, almost never absolute. The best that most parties can hope for is to influence the **trier of fact**'s—the judge or **jury**'s—level of belief in the accuracy of what is being alleged.

The term "standard of proof" describes the degree to which the trier of fact must be convinced of the validity of the essential evidence in the case before he or she can find in favour of the party presenting that evidence. The standard of proof required for a successful criminal case is very high: the trier of fact must be convinced "beyond a reasonable doubt" of the accused's guilt. The civil standard of proof is much lower: the plaintiff need only establish the truth of the facts forming the basis of its case "on a balance of probabilities"; in other words, the plaintiff must succeed in rendering the trier of fact at least 51 percent convinced.

The high standard of proof required in criminal cases is considered to be an essential protection of individual liberty. It also means that the prosecution's evidence, in a criminal case, must be significantly stronger than what would be required in a civil lawsuit based on the same facts. In summary:

- Criminal standard of proof: beyond a reasonable doubt.
- Civil standard of proof: on a balance of probabilities.

trier of fact
the judge or jury in a trial

jury
a group of 12 (in criminal cases) or 6 (in civil cases) citizens over the age of majority who are convened to hear evidence, make findings of fact, and deliver a verdict in a trial

TORTS AND CONTRACT CONCEPTS IN STATUTE LAW

Introduction

As noted earlier in this chapter, both tort and contract have long roots in the common law, and the two doctrines continue to evolve according to common-law principles like ***stare decisis*** (judges' practice of looking to precedents for guidance in deciding later cases).

stare decisis
(Latin) "to stand by the decision"; judges' practice of looking to precedent for guidance in deciding later cases

Typically with common-law doctrines, as the case law has built up and become more complex and detailed, "branches" have formed within both contract and tort. Each branch so formed eventually fills out to form a subtopic within the general sphere of the main doctrine. For example, within tort law, there is a major division between "intentional torts" (which, like criminal law, rely on conscious intent) and the law of negligence. The intentional tort branch can be further subdivided, depending on the focus of analysis, into further categories: intentional torts against the physical person, intentional torts against property, and intentional torts affecting commerce or business relations. The Law in Practice feature on mind maps (Chapter 9, page 187) provides one possible illustration of this process of subdivision.

In some cases, as particular sub-branches of tort or contract law have evolved and become increasingly specialized, they have attracted the attention of government, and this attention has led to the codification of the sub-branch into statute form. A number of factors influence the codification of a branch of the common law:

1. The branch deals with an area characterized by heavy government involvement—that is, the government wishes to control the evolution of the law (for example, environmental law or food safety).

2. The branch lends itself naturally or traditionally to government support and enforcement, so it makes sense that the rules are government-created (for example, trespass to property).

3. The rules within the sub-branch have become so detailed that it has become burdensome to cite the common law to apply them, and business efficiency demands a clear code (for example, sale-of-goods law).

4. There has been a shift or evolution in societal values and government priorities with respect to a topic, and the common law cannot evolve quickly enough to keep up (for example, with respect to the privacy protection of electronic records, now managed under statutes like the Canadian *Personal Information Protection and Electronic Documents Act*[8]).

5. The common law has evolved inelegantly or poorly, with internal contradictions, entrenched ambiguities, or other flaws that made a "scrap and redo" approach attractive (for example, the Ontario *Occupiers' Liability Act*[9]).

6. The law has evolved in a direction that is contrary to current government policy, and the government has decided to "overrule" it through codification (for example, the Ontario *Business Regulation Reform Act, 1994*[10]).

7. The further development of the branch requires technical expertise, and so may be better handled by subject experts than by generalist judges (for example, the Alberta *Electronic Transactions Act*[11]).

---

8. *Personal Information Protection and Electronic Documents Act*, S.C. 2000, c. 5.
9. *Occupiers' Liability Act*, R.S.O. 1990, c. O.2.
10. *Business Regulation Reform Act, 1994*, S.O. 1994, c. 32.
11. *Electronic Transactions Act*, S.A. 2001, c. E-5.5.

The emergence of one or more of these factors tends to stimulate political will to legislate in the area, and the common-law "branch" is ultimately converted into statute law.

Interplay Between Common Law and Statutes

The process noted in the previous section demonstrates how statutes grow out of the common law; it is, however, important to remember that the codification of a branch of the law does not eliminate the further influence of judicial decisions on the doctrine.

A statute is a less flexible tool than a common-law rule: it may be amended at intervals, but it does not have the capacity, the way a common-law rule does, to immediately expand to adapt to novel fact scenarios.

Consider the following example: occupiers' liability statutes, in force in all provinces, regulate the imposition of tort-style liability on parties who have control of property and who fail to prevent harm happening to visitors to that property. In the 1997 case of *Olinski v. Johnson*,[12] the victims of a brawl between rival lacrosse players brought a lawsuit under the Ontario *Occupiers' Liability Act*, alleging that the occupier of the arena in which the lacrosse match was held failed to protect them from being attacked by the rival players in an arena corridor beyond the playing surface. The occupier, in this case, was found to be the lacrosse team that rented the arena for the purpose of hosting the match.

While the provisions of the *Occupiers' Liability Act* could be relied upon to establish the duty of the hosting team, as occupier, to provide adequate policing and supervision of events on the playing field, the issue in the case was the status of the corridor. Did the hosting team have to provide supervision in the corridor? The provisions of the *Occupiers' Liability Act* were silent about exactly where the area of "occupation" begins and ends for an occupier in these circumstances (an occupier who is renting an arena). The parties had no choice but to take their dispute about the corridor to court—first the trial court, then the Ontario Court of Appeal—for a final answer about whether an arena occupier must police arena corridors (the answer was "yes"). As a consequence of the operation of common-law precedent, it is now settled Ontario law that an occupier of an arena is an occupier not only of the playing field but of the associated corridors, even though there is no mention of arena corridors in the *Occupiers' Liability Act*.

This example demonstrates that not only do common-law rules often provide the foundation for statutes but, through the process of judicial interpretation of statutes, they also build upon, refine, and inform the meaning of statutory provisions.

Contract Principles in Statute Law

A contract, you will learn, can be as simple as a one-sentence verbal agreement sealed with only a handshake. However, at the opposite end of the spectrum, con-

---

12. *Olinski v. Johnson*, 1997 CanLII 603, 32 O.R. (3d) 653 (C.A.).

tracts can be extremely complex and detailed (consider, for example, international treaties like the free trade agreements that govern certain aspects of international trade between Canada and foreign countries or the contracts that govern nuclear disarmament).

Where an area of trade or negotiation lends itself to complex contracts, it can become burdensome to have to research and cite numerous common-law cases when choosing or defending contract terms. For this reason, certain areas of contract have become codified into statute. The supporting statute establishes certain key terms or **conventions** (for example, rules of interpretation), so that the contract parties need not elaborate—or sometimes even include—those terms or conventions: they are simply "read in" should the contract ever have to be interpreted. Good examples of statutes that create implied substantive terms are the provincial sale-of-goods acts.[13] An example of a statute that governs the interpretation of contracts is the federal *Interpretation Act*.[14]

While the statutes just mentioned help streamline the contract drafting and interpretation process, there is another purpose behind the codification of certain kinds of contract terms. The making of contracts is, at its heart, private-sphere activity between individuals; however, certain areas of commerce have the potential to operate unfairly against the consumer, particularly against unsophisticated consumers or consumers with few economic resources. To offset the potential for exploitation, governments have stepped in to regulate consumer contracts in these areas by passing statutes that impose certain limits on the **freedom of contract** that would normally prevail between private parties. A familiar example is the context of residential tenancies, the contracts for which must comply with the terms of landlord and tenant statutes, such as the Ontario *Residential Tenancies Act, 2006*.[15] Similar statutes exist in other provinces. Another context in which consumer contracts are heavily regulated is in insurance: statutes regulate insurance contracts at both the provincial and federal levels.

Table 1.1 provides a few other examples of statutes that regulate the making of contracts.

conventions
ways of doing something that have been accepted for so long that they amount to unwritten rules

freedom of contract
the freedom of parties to decide contract terms of their own choosing

Tort Principles in Statute Law

Tort law, as you will learn in the chapters to come, has several internal divisions: some torts are based on injury to the person, others on injury to property or to business relations. Increasingly important in the tort field are claims against professionals for professional negligence, claims against manufacturers for problems related to products, claims arising from environmental harm, and claims against property owners for injuries sustained on public and private property.

As in the case with contracts, tort concepts are sometimes codified as statutes. This tends to happen for one of two reasons:

---

13. For example, the Ontario *Sale of Goods Act*, R.S.O. 1990, c. S.1, and provincial equivalents.
14. *Interpretation Act*, R.S.C. 1985, c. I-21.
15. *Residential Tenancies Act, 2006*, S.O. 2006, c. 17.

1. a government chooses to regulate an activity (for example, driving on public roads) that is the source of tort claims; or
2. the common-law rules regulating an area of the (tort) law require systematic updating or reconciliation (for example, the law relating to the liability of the occupiers of property).

In a few areas—notably, environmental law—legislation and regulations have almost completely replaced the common law; but because human beings find new ways to harm each other every day, the general common-law principle of negligence continues to be relevant and to provide a foundation for litigation.

Table 1.2 provides examples of statutes that codify tort principles.

TABLE 1.1 Examples of Statutes in Contract Law

Federal Statutes	Provincial Statutes
• *Divorce Act*	• Provincial family law statutes that regulate contracts about, e.g., the division of family property
• Statutes that regulate international trade—e.g., the *International Sale of Goods Contracts Convention Act*	• Statutes that regulate sales and marketing of farming products—e.g., milk, eggs
• *Bankruptcy and Insolvency Act*	• Statutes that regulate bulk sales—e.g., sale of inventory and goods in the context of insolvency

TABLE 1.2 Examples of Statutes in Tort Law

Federal Statutes	Provincial Statutes
• Federal environmental legislation, such as the *Canadian Environmental Protection Act, 1999* • Federal food and drug safety legislation • Legislation related to the protection of wild animals and sea life • Legislation governing safety in aviation • Legislation for the management of firearms and other weapons • Legislation for the protection of intellectual property—e.g., the *Copyright Act*	• Trespass to property statutes • Occupiers' liability statutes • Provincial negligence acts • Provincial environmental protection acts • Statutes that regulate traffic and traffic accidents • Statutes that regulate health and safety in the workplace and compensation for workplace injuries • Provincial product and food safety statutes and regulations

Tort/Contract Hybrids in Statute Law

In some contexts, contract and tort issues exist side by side. Consider, for example, employment law. The rules that govern how an employment relationship can legally be terminated have traditionally been established through the contract of employment that exists between the employer and the employee. However, when an employment relationship goes wrong, there may not be only a breach of the employment contract; there may also be torts committed by one party against the other. For example, a departing employee may injure the business interests of his or her ex-employer by sharing trade secrets or customer lists with a new employer; or an employer may harm the psychological well-being of the employee by dismissing him or her in an insensitive, abusive, or humiliating way. Because it would be cumbersome to have two separate statutes regulating employment relationships (one for contract aspects, one for tort), employment statutes like the federal *Canada Labour Code*[16] or provincial statutes like the Yukon *Employment Standards Act*[17] typically address both classes of issues.

Other examples of types of statutes that regulate both contract and tort aspects of subject areas include territorial treaties, such as the *International Boundary Waters Treaty Act*;[18] statutes that regulate natural resource exploitation, like the *Great Lakes Fisheries Convention Act*;[19] and statutes that regulate professions, like the Nova Scotia *Chartered Accountants Act*.[20]

HOW THIS TEXT IS ORGANIZED

Following this introductory chapter, the remainder of this book is divided into two parts.

Part I, which contains Chapters 2 through 8, covers contract law. Those chapters provide an introduction to basic elements required to create a valid contract, followed by further detail about the doctrines of offer and acceptance, consideration, legality, writing requirements, and capacity to contract. Chapter 5 examines problems with contracts, including those relating to misrepresentation, duress, undue influence, unconscionability, and mistake. Chapter 6 deals with the exercise of contract rights, Chapter 7 with contract interpretation, and Chapter 8 with breach of contract and legal remedies for breach.

Part II of the text covers the law of torts. In Chapter 9, the three essential elements of tort are introduced, followed by a discussion of the basic classification system of torts into the following categories: intentional tort; nuisance; negligence; and strict, vicarious, and absolute liability. Chapters 10 through 14 expand on each of these categories, incorporating discussion of defences to tort and remedies.

---

16. *Canada Labour Code*, R.S.C. 1985, c. L-2.
17. *Employment Standards Act*, R.S.Y. 2002, c. 72.
18. *International Boundary Waters Treaty Act*, R.S.C. 1985, c. I-17.
19. *Great Lakes Fisheries Convention Act*, R.S.C. 1985, c. F-17.
20. *Chartered Accountants Act*, S.N.S. 1900, c. 154.

The choice to cover contracts first and torts second reflects the development of the doctrines in the common law. Most core contract principles are centuries old; by contrast, some of the key aspects of negligence law (a subcategory of tort) have emerged only in the last several decades. A second reason for this organization is that it is not uncommon, in litigation, for a plaintiff to base his or her cause of action in contract, but to add a tort component (whether in addition to the contract claim or as a "plan B") in an effort to recover additional damages or damages of a type not recognized in contract litigation. To understand these kinds of claims, it is important to learn about contracts first.

Throughout Parts I and II, special features are included in the text to support your learning. They include definitions of legal terms (shown in the margins and also in the Glossary at the end of this book); figures, tables, and other visual features; short topical features (for example, the Law in Practice feature on standards of proof that appears on page 9 of this chapter); and case studies (Case in Point features). Each chapter concludes with a Chapter Summary, followed by a selection of review questions designed to help test your understanding of the material.

CHAPTER SUMMARY

This is a book about contracts (agreements between private parties, or between a private party and the state) and torts (wrongs between private parties or between a party and the state). Contracts and torts are the two most important Canadian common-law disciplines. This chapter discusses torts and contracts and the common law in general in the broader context of Canadian law, which, besides common-law principles, also comprises statute law and a constitution that is paramount over all other legislation, and that incorporates the *Canadian Charter of Rights and Freedoms*.

Besides the general distinction between the common law and statute law, there is another essential distinction: that between civil law and criminal law. The criminal law differs from tort law in that it addresses wrongs between individuals and the state (the state, in this context, also represents the interests of the public at large). Many torts also differ from crimes in that the level of guilty intent seen in tort defendants falls short of criminal intent (*mens rea*). Further, the objectives of criminal prosecutions—typically, punishment and protection of society—are quite different from the objectives of tort lawsuits, which are characteristically pursued with the goal of obtaining compensation for the harm suffered by the plaintiff. In a few cases, a wrong by one person against another leads to both a criminal prosecution and a tort lawsuit.

Though the common law and statute law are contrasted in this chapter, it is important to recognize that the two are far from separate. Common-law concepts are regularly "codified" into statute form. Reasons for codification of common-law sub-branches include legal complexity, technical complexity, and conflict between the common law and government policy objectives. Once statutes are created, common-law decisions that interpret their provisions allow those statutes to adapt and extend to novel fact situations. Statutes that incorporate contract concepts include provincial sale-of-goods legislation and residential tenancies law. Tort-based statutes include those that regulate occupiers' liability, product liability, environmental law, and trespassing. Finally, there are statutes that include aspects of both tort and contract, including those that govern international boundaries or the exploitation of natural resources and those that regulate professions.

KEY TERMS

accretion

civil law

civil procedure

codified

common law

constitution

contract

conventions

crime

Crown

defendant

distress

duty of care

fraud

freedom of contract

intent

jury

legal codes

mens rea

negligence

plaintiff

precedent

self-help remedy

stare decisis

statement of claim

statute law

substantive criminal law

tort

tortious

trier of fact

unconstitutional

BIBLIOGRAPHY

Encyclopedia Britannica, online: <http://www.britannica.com>.

Clarence Ray Jeffery, "The Development of Crime in Early English Society" (1957) 47:6 Jour. Crim. Law, Criminol. and Pol. Sci. 647, online: <http://www.jstor.org/stable/1140057>.

Margaret Kerr, JoAnn Kurtz & Laurence M. Olivo, *Canadian Tort Law in a Nutshell*, 3d ed. (Toronto: Carswell, 2009).

REVIEW QUESTIONS

True or False?

_____ 1. Common-law case decisions can affect the interpretation of statute law.

__T__ 2. The *Canadian Charter of Rights and Freedoms* governs the terms of contracts made between private parties.

__F__ 3. In early societies, the distinction between torts and crimes has always been clearly defined.

_____ 4. A statutory provision is less flexible than a common-law rule when it comes to adapting to novel fact scenarios.

_____ 5. The development of contract types and usages has historically been driven by individuals looking for solutions to business needs.

_____ 6. Statutes that regulate the practice of professions often incorporate both tort and contract principles.

_____ 7. The penalty for a criminal offence is damages designed to compensate the victim.

_____ 8. Negligence law emerged later than the law of contracts.

_____ 9. Originally, only wrongs against the monarchy were viewed as crimes.

_____ 10. The standard of proof in a criminal case is lower than the standard of proof in a civil case.

Fill in the Blanks

1. The only Canadian province that does not have a common law based legal system is _____.

2. In a criminal case, the parties are the _____ and the _____.

3. The Latin term that describes the rule that new cases should be decided consistently with decided cases is _____ _____.

4. *Mens rea* refers to the _____ aspect of a crime.

5. A tort is a _____ that occurs between two or more parties.

6. Statute law is also known as _____.

7. Environmental law initially evolved as a branch of _____ law.

8. _____ _____ is the body of rules that governs how a criminal trial will be conducted.

9. In order for a plaintiff to succeed in a civil trial, his or her case must be proved on a balance of _____.

10. The Canadian Constitution provides that _____ have jurisdiction over the regulation of local commerce.

Short Answer

1. Why have certain societies chosen to organize their legal rules in the form of a comprehensive written code?

2. If the Charter does not apply to contracts between private individuals, why must we learn about it in a book about contracts and torts?

3. List at least three reasons that have led individual branches of contract or tort law to be codified into statute form.

4. How do common-law case decisions influence statute law?

5. Why is the common law different in various common-law jurisdictions— for example, why does the Canadian common law differ in some ways from the British common law?

6. What factors does the Crown typically consider when deciding whether or not to charge and prosecute an offence?

7. What factors does a plaintiff typically consider when deciding whether or not to sue in tort over harm suffered?

8. How do statutes that govern contracts streamline and simplify the contract-making process?

9. Why do certain statutes seek to impose limits on freedom of contract?

10. Why do some statutes contain provisions that govern both contract and tort issues?

EXERCISES

1. Locate an online version of a statute that regulates the practice of a profession in your province or territory. Read the statute, and identify (a) at least one provision that relates to the making of contracts or the content of a contract, and (b) at least one provision that regulates or prohibits an action that might cause harm (tort-avoidance provision).

PART I

CONTRACT LAW

Introduction to the Law of Contracts

2

OVERVIEW

LEARNING OUTCOMES

After completing this chapter, you should be able to:

- Provide a definition of "contract."

- Discuss intention and agreement as prerequisites for a contract.

- List three features that are essential in most contracts.

- Discuss whether a court will enforce an agreement for which there is mutual intention, but no agreed terms.

- Explain "capacity" and "consideration."

- Compare and contrast positivism and judicial interventionism as approaches to contract interpretation.

WHAT IS A CONTRACT?

Contracts are agreements made between two or more persons that the law recognizes and will enforce. "Persons," for the purpose of this definition, includes not only human beings, but also corporations that have the necessary status to be treated as legal entities in their own right.

Contracts are not simply long documents written in legalese and covered in ribbons and seals. They are part of everyday life in our society, where economic exchange is an essential part of getting things done. For example, buying a bus token, paying a parking fee, buying a cup of coffee, using a credit card to buy a jacket, leasing an apartment, and buying this textbook all involve agreements between you and someone else where you agree to do something (pay money) in exchange for the other person's doing something (giving you a parking space for your car, a cup of coffee, or a book). These common, everyday contracts can be in writing or they can be oral; they can be explicit, like an apartment lease that spells out in writing the details of what was agreed to; or they can be implicit, like buying a cup of coffee where you serve yourself and hand over money, and no one exchanges a word.

FEATURES OF LEGALLY ENFORCEABLE CONTRACTS

Not all agreements are recognized by the law as contracts. For example, if you invite me to dinner and I agree to come but then fail to show up, I have breached the rules of good manners, but not the law. The law defines our agreement as a social agreement rather than as an enforceable contract, primarily because certain things that make an agreement a contract appear to be missing. For example, an intention to create legally binding relations is missing, as is a promise from me to do something for you of legally recognizable value in exchange for the invitation, other than just showing up and eating your food.[1]

---

1. Where parties promise to exchange something of recognizable value, there is said to be *valuable consideration*. Because of the commercial origins of contract law, the courts look for an exchange of promises involving things of monetary cost or value, although consideration need not be money or even be reduced to a specific amount in dollars and cents. Consideration is discussed in more detail in Chapter 3, Formation of a Contract.

LAW IN PRACTICE
Some Basic Terms

- The terms **contract** and **agreement** are used interchangeably to refer to the same thing: a binding contract.
- A party to a contract or agreement who undertakes to do something is sometimes referred to as a **promisor**. The party who receives the benefit of the promise made by the promisor is sometimes referred to as the **promisee**.
- In the bargaining process that precedes making the contract or agreement, the promisor may be referred to as the **offeror**, and the person to whom the offer is made may be referred to as the **offeree**.

Agreements that the law recognizes as contracts have certain features in common, described below.

Offer and Acceptance of the Offer

For a contract to be created, one party must offer to do something, and the other party must promise to accept that offer. This exchange of promises in contract law is referred to as **offer** and **acceptance**. To constitute an agreement, the mutual exchange of promises that includes an offer and an acceptance must relate to acts that are performed at the time the agreement is made, or acts to be performed in the future. However, an offer may be followed by a counteroffer rather than acceptance. This exchange, or bargaining behaviour, may go on for some time until the parties reach an agreement. When the parties have reached an agreement there is said to be, in the words of older cases, *consensus ad idem* (a "meeting of the minds"), and the parties may be referred to as being *ad idem*. The concepts of offer and acceptance and agreement are discussed in more detail in Chapter 3, Formation of a Contract.

Intention to Create Legally Binding Relations

The parties to an agreement must intend that the promises each makes to the other will be legally binding. This means that if one party breaks a promise, the other may ask the courts to enforce the contract by providing a remedy for the breach. Generally, the courts have held that social agreements (such as a dinner invitation), agreements between family members, and moral vows (such as a vow to join a religious order or to give to charity) are not legally enforceable because an intention to create legally binding relations is missing. But in other types of agreements, uncertainty about parties' intentions can arise, as the Case in Point feature below illustrates.

In deciding whether an agreement is legally binding, the courts have taken two different approaches. In some cases, the courts have taken a subjective approach,

contract/agreement
an agreement made between two or more persons that the law recognizes and will enforce; a binding contract

promisor
the party to a contract who undertakes to do something

promisee
the party to a contract who receives the benefit of a promise made by another party to the contract

offeror
a person who, during the bargaining process that precedes making a contract, agrees to do something for the other party; once the offer is accepted, the bargain is concluded and the parties have made an agreement

offeree
a person to whom an offer is made during the bargaining process

offer
a promise to do something or give something of value to another person; if the other accepts the offer, a binding contract exists

acceptance
when there has been acceptance of an offer made by one party in the bargaining process, the parties are assumed to have reached an agreement on contract terms, and a binding contract exists from that time

consensus ad idem
when there has been acceptance by the offeree of an offer, the parties have reached an agreement on terms, and they have an intention to be bound by those terms; they are said to have reached a *consensus ad idem* (a "meeting of the minds"); sometimes a shorter form is used, and the parties are said to be *ad idem*

unjust enrichment
a legal doctrine by which the courts sometimes award compensation to a party in the absence of a contract, or where the compensation is not contemplated by the contract because it is equitable to compensate the party who has enriched the other party with the expectation of, but not the receipt of, financial reward

examining the evidence of what the parties actually thought they were doing or said they were doing to determine whether they intended to create legally binding rules to govern their behaviour. In other cases, the courts have taken an objective approach, determining the intention of the parties not by what they thought they said they intended, but by what a "reasonable person" would think they intended, considering the surrounding social context. Much of the case law on this issue uses the objective method, which has resulted in an approach where a fictional "reasonable person" relying on an understanding of social norms and values in our society would simply "know" that a dinner invitation was a social agreement and outside the law of contract.

CASE IN POINT

Courts Rely on Doctrine of Unjust Enrichment to Charge Defendant for Services Even Though Contract Never Completed

From: *Skibinski v. Community Living British Columbia*, [2010] B.C.J. No. 2076 (S.C.).

The following case illustrates the kinds of problems and issues that may arise in determining whether the parties intended to form contractual relations.

Ms. Savone, a 48-year-old woman with severe mental and physical disabilities, came into the care of an organization called Community Living British Columbia, the defendant in this case. Community Living became responsible for caring for Ms. Savone, but did not have the necessary arrangements in place. The plaintiff Skibinski, who had a long career caring for people with mental disabilities and a good reputation for the delivery of services to the mentally disabled, came forward and took Ms. Savone into her home on an emergency basis in July 2007. Ms. Skibinski had other clients of Community Living British Columbia under her care in her home, and the defendant paid for her care of the clients. But at the time she took Ms. Savone home, she did not have a contract for the additional client.

Because Skibinski did not have the necessary licence to care for Ms. Savone, negotiations between the plaintiff and defendant broke down, and the defendant refused to pay for Ms. Savone's care. The dispute went to court.

The plaintiff alleged that the defendant had agreed that it would retain her services with an implied term that they would negotiate for fair compensation. Alternatively, she sought compensation based on **unjust enrichment** in that she had provided services for which the defendant was responsible and for which the defendant had paid nothing. The defendant denied that it was liable in con-

tract because, it said, there was no contract. It argued that the plaintiff's actions constituted an officious intervention or meddling, and amounted to no more than the acts of a volunteer acting gratuitously. Accordingly, the plaintiff's actions released the defendant from any obligation to pay her for her services.

The court granted judgment to the plaintiff on the ground of unjust enrichment, despite the absence of a formal contractual agreement between the parties, based on a finding that the plaintiff did work and incurred expenses for which the defendant was responsible, in circumstances where the defendant did not or could not otherwise carry out its responsibilities.

The defendant reasonably would likely have been willing to pay had negotiations continued. The plaintiff's prompt intervention in July 2007 was in the public interest. Savone's needs were great; the plaintiff was ready, willing, and able; and suitable alternatives were not readily available at that time. Under these circumstances, it was fair and just for the defendant to have to pay for the services the plaintiff had provided.

The court concluded that the compensation ought to reflect the amounts that one could reasonably infer that the defendant would agree to pay for services provided by the plaintiff. The plaintiff was entitled to compensation from July 11, 2007 to the judgment date, for a total amount of $334,308. The plaintiff also claimed damages for mental distress caused by the defendant, but the court denied this part of her claim.

> ## PRACTICE TIP
>
> If you are acting gratuitously (without compensation) in an emergency, generally you will have some difficulty later claiming compensation. For that reason, those who make a living dealing with emergencies, such as tow truck operators, should either get paid up front, or have simple written agreements covering compensation and other terms covering the assistance they render. Be careful, however, not to create detailed contracts with lots of fine print. Such contracts may cover all the terms to your advantage; however, in cases where the other party is under pressure, courts may well find that the party was under duress and may disallow parts or all of such contracts. These issues are discussed in Chapter 5, Contractual Defects.

Exchange of Valuable Consideration

Although there are some exceptions, to be enforceable, most contracts require that each party promise something of value to the other. Usually this takes the form of payment or giving something of value in exchange for some goods or services of value. For example, when you park your car in a parking lot, the lot owner is promising a parking space for your car as valuable consideration, and you accept the offer by promising to pay an agreed price for the space. What constitutes valuable consideration is discussed in more detail in Chapter 3, Formation of a Contract.

Legal Capacity to Contract

Not everyone is eligible to enter into a contract. Generally, for a contract to be enforceable, the parties are assumed to be roughly equivalent in bargaining power and must meet minimum standards of intelligence, rationality, and maturity. More important, they must meet these standards to have the contract enforced against them if they fail to keep the promises they made. For this reason, minors and persons with certain types of mental disability may not have to honour their contractual obligations in whole or in part. This topic is discussed in more detail in Chapter 4, Legality, Formalities, and Capacity.

Compliance with Legal Formality Requirements

Not every agreement in which the parties possess the capacity to enter into a contract, have agreed to enter into legal relations, and have given valuable consideration will result in a legally binding contract. An agreement may meet all these requirements and still be deemed unenforceable because it fails to meet formality requirements. While many contracts may be based on an exchange of oral promises, some contracts—such as contracts for the sale of land—must be in writing. Others must be in writing *and* be witnessed, have seals attached, or meet other formal requirements to be enforceable. Formality requirements are discussed in more detail in Chapter 4, Legality, Formalities, and Capacity.

FIGURE 2.1
Components of an Enforceable Contract

1. Capacity of all parties (precondition)

+

2. Intention on the part of two or more parties to create legal relations

+

3. A mutual agreement

+

4. A benefit (consideration) flowing to each side

+

5. Compliance with formal requirements (required only in certain cases; signature, seal, etc.)

Figure 2.1 summarizes the components of an enforceable contract.

HOW CONTRACT LAW DEVELOPED

You may wonder why some agreements are recognized as binding contracts while others are not, why some people are eligible to enter into contracts but others are not, or why there must be valuable consideration for an agreement to be a valid contract. An understanding of how contract law developed can help answer some of these questions.

Canadian contract law outside Quebec is based on English common law. Although there are some minor differences in contract law in England and Canada, the main elements are derived from English law. Before the 16th century, there was no law of contracts as we now know it in England and Canada. However, from the late Middle Ages on, there did exist the tort of owing a debt and failing to repay it.[2] The law focused on the wrongful act of failing to repay money owed on a debt. An agreement that involved an exchange of services or goods was not enforceable under this rule of law.

The lack of a modern law of contract was not important as long as commercial transactions were primarily simple and local. But in the early modern period, trade and commerce expanded and became more complex, and a national economy began to develop. As commercial transactions became more complex, the law evolved to permit merchants and others to enter into complex legal arrangements to govern their activities and to provide remedies when parties found themselves in a commercial dispute. In *Slade's Case*[3] in 1602, the law finally broke away from enforcing only monetary debts to enforcing other kinds of commercial promises. From this point, the common law began to enforce all kinds of commercial bargains where there was valuable consideration, and began to evolve on a case-by-case basis to the kind of contract law we have now.

---

2. For a more detailed discussion on the tort origin of contract law, see G.H.L. Fridman, *The Law of Contract in Canada*, 5th ed. (Toronto: Carswell, 2006), c. 1.

3. *Slade's Case* (1602), 4 Co. Rep. 91 (K.B.).

CASE IN POINT

Slade's Case: The Beginnings of Modern Contract Law

From: *Slade's Case*, (1602) Trinity Term, 44 Elizabeth I In the Court of King's Bench, first published in (1602), 4 Co. Rep. 91.

John Slade contracted with Humphrey Morley to sell grain he was growing to Morley for £16. The day for payment came, but Morley reneged on the deal and refused to pay. Slade was entitled to sue in *assumpsit* for the tort of failing to pay a debt (though this was still a novel and controversial approach), but his lawsuit also involved an action on the case. This was a special form of pleading that allowed Slade to recover not only the contract price based on *assumpsit*, but also compensation for other additional damage suffered by Slade as a result of Morley's failure to honour his obligation.

Slade was represented by Francis Bacon, a prominent lawyer as well as a Renaissance scholar and writer. Morley was represented by Sir Edward Coke, a famous lawyer

and later chief justice of England, whose commentaries on the common law were a staple of legal training for two centuries.

The courts were initially divided over whether the action could succeed, but when the argument was brought before the whole bench of all the courts of England, the King's Bench found that a person harmed by another's breach of a contract was not limited to suing only for non-payment of the debt but could also seek compensation for all the damages sustained that resulted from the contract breach. After *Slade's Case*, the law recognized virtually any kind of contractual breach, not just breach by failure to pay a contract price. Contract law as we know it was born.

Positivism Versus Judicial Interventionism

A factor that contributes to difficulties in interpreting case law on contract issues is the tension in the courts between two points of view about how the law should be interpreted. Under the **positivist** approach, judges take the position that it is not up to them to impose their own interpretation of a contract on the parties. Judges who take this view try to give a dictionary or literal meaning to the words used in a contract, regardless of the outcome. These judges assume that parties to the contract have equal bargaining power and are free to bargain as they wish without the court's meddling in the process. Judges often say that it is not their job to remake a bad bargain or rewrite a badly written contract. Underlying this view is the idea that governments in general, and courts in particular, should not interfere in private persons' economic affairs.

Under the **judicial interventionist** approach, judges may look at the economic forces surrounding the making of a contract, at notions of fundamental fairness, and at other contextual facts as a background to interpreting the language of a contract. This approach is more likely to be used when there is an inequality of bargaining power between the parties—for example, in consumer contracts. However, some judges take this interpretive approach when the parties have equal bargaining power but, in the judge's view, the likely outcome is socially or economically undesirable.

The positivist approach has been the principal, and older, approach to interpreting contract law in England, Canada, and the rest of the common-law world up to

positivism
an approach to the interpretation of law that states that the meaning to be given to the words in legal rules should be the ordinary, dictionary meaning without resorting to social, economic, or political values to aid in interpretation

judicial interventionism
an approach to the interpretation of law that draws on social, economic, and political values in interpreting the meaning and application of legal rules and principles

the mid-20th century. As judicial interventionism or judicial activism has become more commonly used in Canadian courts in general, it has also had an increasing impact on modern contract law. To some extent, this approach is the source of some of the differences in contract law between Canada and England today, because Canadian courts tend to be more interventionist than English courts. However, the differences should not be overstressed. The basic law of contract is very similar in both jurisdictions, and Canadian judges have tended to be sparing in their use of interventionism in contract law.

CHAPTER SUMMARY

Contracts are agreements between two or more persons that the law will recognize and enforce. However, not all contracts are enforceable. For a contract to be enforceable by the courts, it must have certain key features:

1. The parties must have come to a mutual agreement on certain terms: a contract cannot be based on one party's wishes that have not been accepted by the other.
2. The parties must have had an intention to create an enforceable legal relationship that the law will recognize.
3. With some exceptions, there must be an exchange of valuable consideration: each party must receive some benefit from the other (for example, one party receives goods or services and the other party receives payment).
4. The parties must have the capacity to contract. Parties who are unable to fully understand the implications of a contract are considered *not* to have the capacity to contract.
5. For certain kinds of contracts, legal formality requirements must be met (for example, in Canada, a contract for the sale of land must be in writing).

These various elements of an enforceable contract will be further elaborated in the next few chapters.

Contract law developed from tort law and evolved into modern contract law in the 17th century. It developed from case law as judges tried to adapt contract law to modern business practices.

The extent to which courts should draw inferences about contracts and the intentions of the parties who create them has always been a source of tension within the law. The positivist approach to contracts involves passing judgment based on a narrow and literal meaning of the contract terms. Proponents of the judicial interventionist approach are more likely to investigate or speculate about the true intentions of the parties, and to interpret the contract according to those intentions, even if they are not explicitly communicated in the provisions of the contract.

KEY TERMS

acceptance

agreement

consensus ad idem

contract

judicial interventionism

offer

offeree

offeror

positivism

promisee

promisor

unjust enrichment

REVIEW QUESTIONS

True or False?

_____ 1. With some exceptions, a valid contract requires the exchange of something of value by each of the parties.

_____ 2. Any oral contract is enforceable.

_____ 3. Where contracts are governed by statute law, Parliament may intervene to protect weaker parties or to rationalize the common law.

_____ 4. A corporation can be a party to a contract.

_____ 5. The consideration offered in exchange for a promise is invalid unless it constitutes objectively reasonable compensation for the promise.

_____ 6. The judicial interventionist approach to contracts involves giving a dictionary or literal meaning to the words used in a contract.

_____ 7. *Slade's Case* expanded contract law to include commercial obligations other than simply the duty to pay debts.

_____ 8. A contract can come into being if at least one party has the intention to create a legally binding relation with the other party.

Fill in the Blanks

1. The _____ is the party to whom an offer is made.

2. When one party promises to do something for another without expectation of anything in return, this is often called a _____ promise.

3. A person with a serious cognitive deficit may lack the ability to make a valid contract because she does not have _____ _____.

4. When contract parties have reached an agreement, they are said to be ____ _____.

5. Two examples of contract formalities are the requirements that the contract ____ ____ _____ and ____ _____.

6. The payment or other benefit one party receives from the other in exchange for discharging his or her obligations is called _____.

7. A contract is created when one party makes an _____ and the other party gives her _____.

8. The judicial interventionist approach to contract interpretation is often used to redress an imbalance in _____ _____.

Short Answer

1. What is a contract?
2. What is the difference between a contract and an agreement?
3. What main features must a contract have to be binding?
4. What does it mean for the parties to an agreement to be *ad idem*?
5. What is the difference between a subjective and an objective approach to legal interpretation?
6. Explain what is meant by the term "valuable consideration."
7. Why do we limit the contractual rights of minors and persons who have certain types of mental disabilities?
8. Give an example of a formality requirement in contract law, and explain its purpose.

EXERCISES

1. Explain whether, in the following fact situations, you could sue for breach of contract. Give the rationale for your answers.

    a. You invite me to dinner. I agree to come, but fail to show up.
    b. Your sister promises to lend you some money because you are in debt, but later changes her mind and refuses to do so.
    c. You invite me to dinner and agree to pay me an amount of money if I praise an invention of yours to another dinner guest who is interested in investing in your invention. I agree to attend, but I fail to show up, and the other guest decides not to invest in your invention.

2. Read *Skibinski v. Community Living British Columbia*, the Case in Point feature on page 24. Was this case decided based on the objective standard of a "reasonable person," or on a subjective reading of the evidence about what the parties thought they were doing?
3. Explain why the law does not enforce all agreements.
4. How has the positivist interpretation of contract law led to increased reliance on statutes as a basis for contract law?
5. Contract law has been described as a practical response to the development of a more complex modern economy. Explain how contract law changed and developed to meet the needs of a changing economy.

Formation of a Contract 3

LEARNING OUTCOMES

After completing this chapter, you should be able to:

- Explain the "reasonable person" test for determining whether a party intended to be legally bound by his or her promise.

- Describe the features of a valid offer, counteroffer, and acceptance and explain how the effective timing of an offer and acceptance is determined.

- Understand how an offer can effectively be revoked and how an offer can lapse.

- Define "consideration" and describe the qualities of valid consideration.

- Explain how consideration is treated in debtor–creditor relationships, under circumstances where a party gratuitously promises to make a charitable donation, and where the parties have not explicitly defined the quantum of payment for a service.

- Define "estoppel" and explain how the doctrine of estoppel is relevant to contract law.

- Understand the current state of the law with respect to e-commerce and the matters that parties engaged in e-commerce may need to consider.

ELEMENTS OF A VALID CONTRACT

As discussed in Chapter 2, for an agreement to be a valid, binding, and enforceable contract, certain elements must be present. If any of these elements are missing or defective, the courts will not enforce the rights and duties created by that agreement. An unenforceable or defective contract is also known as a **void contract**. A void contract is no contract at all, because it has no legal force or binding effect. The parties to a void contract may have gone through some form of making a contract, but because one or more of the necessary elements were missing, no contract came into being. Hence, a void contract is one that may be "avoided" by one or both parties.

void contract
a contract that does not exist at law because one or more essential elements of the contract are lacking; an unenforceable contract

The essential elements of a contract are:

- the intention to create a legal relationship;
- offer and acceptance of the offer;
- an exchange of something of value, usually referred to as consideration; and
- legality.

INTENTION TO CREATE A LEGAL RELATIONSHIP

The parties to a contract must have intended from the beginning of their negotiations that legal obligations would result from their agreement. This assumption is based on the premise that the contract will be the result of a meeting of the parties' minds, or *consensus ad idem*, on the terms and conditions that will form the contract.

The first requirement of a contract is the intention of the promisor to be bound by the promise he or she made. All agreements contain some kind of a promise, either to do something or to refrain from doing something. Although all contracts contain promises, not all promises become contracts. Some promises carry with them a moral obligation, but only a valid contract carries with it a legal obligation.

presumption of law
an inference in favour of a particular fact; a rule of law whereby a finding of a basic fact gives rise to the existence of a presumed fact or state of affairs unless the presumption can be rebutted, or proven false, by the party seeking to deny the presumed fact

Because examining intention requires finding out what was in the promisor's mind at the time the promise was made, proving intention can be difficult. As a result, the courts rely on a **presumption of law** that promisors intend to be bound by the promises they make. Once this presumption has been made, the **onus**, or burden of proof, shifts to the promisor to prove that the intention did not exist. The courts look to evidence, such as the conduct of the parties at the time the promise was made, the circumstances surrounding the making of the promise, the statements made by the parties, and the relationship between the parties. The test to be applied is: "Would a reasonable person hearing the promise assume that the promisor intended to be bound?"

onus
the burden of responsibility or proof

LAW IN PRACTICE
Example of "Reasonable Person" Test

In the US case of *Higgins v. Lessig*,[1] a farmer who had a $15 harness stolen from him angrily exclaimed in front of several people, "I will give $100 to any man who will find out who the thief is!" Immediately, one of the people present named the thief and claimed the reward. The farmer refused to pay, and the informer sued for the $100. The court held that the statement was "the extravagant exclamation of an angry man" and that a reasonable person would not assume that the farmer intended to be bound.

The relationship between the parties is an important factor to be considered. If the promise occurs in an **arm's-length transaction** in which the parties are "strangers" to each other or unrelated, or in commercial or business dealings, the courts assume that the promise is binding unless one or both parties can convince the court that there was no intention.

However, the courts also recognize that promises made between people who are not at arm's length may not be intended to be binding. Promises made between family members and in social situations are usually not assumed to be binding. In addition, the courts assume that promises to donate money to charity or to join a religious order are generally not intended to create a binding contract.

arm's-length transaction
a transaction negotiated by unrelated parties, each acting in his or her own independent self-interest; "unrelated" in this context usually means not related as family members by birth or marriage, and not related by business interests

Example of a Non-Arm's-Length Transaction

Your sister promises to come to your daughter's ballet recital. You buy her a ticket but she does not show up, nor does she pay you for the ticket. It is unlikely that the courts would presume that your sister intended to be legally bound by her promise.

Example of an Arm's-Length Transaction

You are selling tickets to your daughter's ballet recital to help raise funds for a new dance studio. A company promises to buy a block of tickets from you but never pays for them. The courts would be more likely to presume that the company intended to be legally bound by its promise, because it is at arm's length.

---

1. *Higgins v. Lessig*, 49 Ill. App. 459 (1893).

Did Mom and Daughter Have a Deal?

From: *Jones v. Padavatton*, [1969] 2 All E.R. 616 (C.A.).

In this case, a mother and daughter agreed that the mother would pay an allowance to her daughter if the daughter would leave her current employment and study for the bar in England. Relying on this arrangement, the daughter quit her job and started her legal studies. Mom paid the allowance as agreed. Because the daughter could not find suitable housing, they altered the agreement, with the mother providing a house for the daughter to live in. Mother and daughter then had a dispute, and the mother began proceedings to evict the daughter. The daughter argued that a deal is a deal, and that this was a contractual arrangement that the mother was required to honour.

All the judges agreed that there was some kind of arrangement, with some elements of flexibility owing to unforeseeable circumstances. The subsequent arrangement to provide a house for the daughter was an adaptation to circumstances and was an amendment to the original agreement. But was it a contract?

The majority of the court held that this was merely a family arrangement made in good faith and was not intended as a rigid, binding agreement. Consequently, it was not an enforceable contract. Lord Justice Salmon stated that the daughter was not a youngster, had a good job, and was well established. By accepting the mother's offer, she was setting aside her career and prospects, uprooting herself and her child and moving to England for the possibility of becoming a barrister, something that would please the mother. The daughter did this with some sense of unease, but was induced by the mother's promise of financial assistance, later confirmed by the mother's solicitor. Looking at all the circumstances, and applying an objective test of what a reasonable person would think, Salmon L.J. held that there was sufficient evidence to support a serious intention on the part of both parties. The arrangement was therefore a contract and enforceable by the daughter, even though some of its terms were uncertain. The judge held that the daughter had no right to stay in the house on the grounds that the time for completing legal studies had elapsed and, with it, the right to remain in the house. Thus the contract, while enforceable, was discharged by the passage of time.

Advertisers also often make statements that they do not intend to be legally binding. The courts allow advertisers some latitude in their advertisements as long as they do not mislead the public. The courts sometimes accept exaggeration as an indication that the advertiser did not intend to be bound (for example, "Come to Joe's Diner for the best Wiener schnitzel in the world!"). As a general rule, the courts view advertisements as "invitations to do business" (sometimes referred to as "invitations to treat" in older cases) rather than promises to the public at large. So if you sued Joe's Diner because its Wiener schnitzel was not the best in the world, a court would be unlikely to find that Joe's Diner intended to be held to its promise.

However, although advertisers are not generally subject to the presumption that they intend to be bound by their promises, the courts will enforce those promises if the party seeking to rely on the promise can convince the court that the advertiser intended to be bound. To find this intent, the courts examine the advertisement carefully, applying the "reasonable person" test.

"Mere Puffery" or an Intention to Be Bound?

From: *Carlill v. Carbolic Smoke Ball Co.*, [1893] 1 Q.B. 256 (C.A.).

This is an example of the factors that the courts examine in determining intention to be bound by a promise made in the form of an advertisement. In this English case, the Carbolic Smoke Ball Co. manufactured and advertised a product that it claimed would cure or prevent influenza. In fact, the company went so far as to advertise that it would pay £100 to anyone who used its product and contracted influenza. The advertisement also stated that the company intended to be bound by its promise and, as a sign of good faith, it had deposited £100 with a bank to be used for this purpose. Mrs. Carlill purchased the product, used it according to the company's instructions, and contracted influenza. The company refused to pay her the £100, claiming that it never intended to be bound by its promise and that the advertisement was a "mere puff."

The court found that the words of the advertisement clearly expressed the intention to be bound and ordered the company to pay the £100 to Mrs. Carlill.

OFFER AND ACCEPTANCE

Nature of an Offer

A valid contract does not come into existence until one party, the offeror, has made an offer and the other party, the offeree, has accepted it. An offer is normally conditional—that is, the offeree must do something or give some promise in exchange. The initial offer is tentative. Once an offeree accepts and agrees to fulfill the conditions contained in the offer, the contract is formed and the promise becomes binding. To be valid, an offer must contain all the terms of the contract, either expressly or impliedly (implicitly).

> **Example of an Offer**
>
> I offer to sell you my car for $5,000. My offer is conditional on your agreeing to fulfill the condition in my offer—paying me $5,000. Once you accept my offer by agreeing to fulfill the condition, our mutual promises become binding. I must sell you my car, and you must pay me $5,000.

An invitation to do business by displaying goods for sale or by advertising these goods does not constitute an offer. For example, a business that uses a newspaper advertisement to sell goods for a certain price is not making an offer because the business does not intend to sell its goods to every person who reads the advertisement. The supply of those goods is likely to be limited. If the advertisement were an offer, the business would be bound to sell the goods to every person who saw it and accepted the offer by agreeing to pay the price. The purpose of the advertisement is to attract potential customers. Those customers might make an offer to purchase the goods, which the merchant can accept, or the merchant can make an offer to customers once the customers express an interest in the goods, which the customers can accept. The advertisement is simply a way to start the negotiation process.

However, some advertisements have been found to be offers. For example, an advertisement stating that a store will sell a television set at a greatly reduced price to the first 10 people who arrive at the store on a certain date ("a gate-crasher special") can be interpreted as an offer. The offer of a reward for information or for the return of a lost item made to the public at large can be interpreted as an offer. However, these types of advertisements are the exception to the rule that advertisements are not offers but merely invitations to do business.

Communication of an Offer

There is no particular format in which the offer must be made, as long as it is understood by the offeree to be an offer. Offers can be made verbally, in writing, or through gestures (for example, raising your hand to make a bid at an auction). A general rule is that the offer must be communicated by the offeror to the offeree before it is capable of being accepted.

This condition may seem self-evident, but it becomes important when offers are not made face to face. For example, if an offer was made by letter, telegram, fax, email, or other method, it is vital to know when the offeree became aware of the offer, because the offer is not valid until it is received by the offeree, and the offeror is not bound by the offer until it has been accepted. No person can accept an offer of which he or she was unaware.

Example of Lack of Communication of an Offer

A person posts a notice on his office bulletin board offering a reward of $100 for the return of his lost briefcase. A co-worker finds his briefcase and, unaware of the reward, returns it to him. If she later sees the notice, she cannot go back and demand the reward. Because she was not aware of the offer when she returned the briefcase, she cannot later accept the offer. No contract was created.

Another general rule is that only the person to whom an offer is made may accept the offer, even if others are aware of it. This rule prevents offerors from being forced to enter into contracts with persons not of their own choosing. However, if an offer is made to the public at large, it is assumed that the offeror is implying that the identity of the offeree is unimportant to the contract, and anyone may accept the offer.

Example of Lack of Communication of an Offer

You leave a note for your neighbour in his mailbox that you will pay him $200 if he will cut down a tree on your property. Before he sees the note, another neighbour takes it and cuts down the tree in your absence. Upon your return, the second neighbour demands payment of the $200. You are not obligated to pay him the $200, even though you benefited from his labour. The offer was not made to him, and therefore was not capable of being accepted by him. No contract was formed.

Acceptance of an Offer

Acceptance of an offer may be made verbally or in writing, or it may be inferred from the conduct of the parties. However, certain rules must be complied with before acceptance of an offer is valid.

First, acceptance must be communicated by the offeree to the offeror in the manner requested by or implied in the offer. Second, the acceptance must be clear, unequivocal, and unconditional.

Communication of the Acceptance

Communication of the acceptance is simple if the offer states the method of acceptance. An offer might state that the offer may be accepted only in writing or in person. In that case, the acceptance must be communicated in the stated manner.

However, the offer may not contain such a precise stipulation. The courts look at a number of variables to determine what may constitute a valid form of communication of an acceptance. For example, they look at the form in which the offer was made, the usual and ordinary way of doing business in a particular industry, and the history of dealings between the parties to determine whether the method of communication was valid.

Although the form of acceptance must generally be positive in nature, even silence can be a valid form of acceptance if the parties have agreed in advance that silence is sufficient or the parties have habitually used this method in previous transactions.

Example of Silence as Acceptance

You belong to a music club. Each month the club mails you a notice advising that it will send you that month's selection of CDs unless you mail back the notice stating that you do not want them. The agreement you have with the club states that failure to send back the notice constitutes acceptance of the CDs. In this case, then, silence constitutes acceptance.

If a person's conduct, though silent, leads the offeror to believe that the offeree has accepted the offer, especially where the person receives some benefit from the offeror, and knows that the offeror expects to be compensated for the services or goods supplied, the courts may find that a contract has been formed.

Example of Silence as Acceptance

In the case of *Saint John Tug Boat Co. Ltd. v. Irving Refining Ltd.*,[2] the plaintiff made its tugboat available for use by the defendant. The terms of the rental of the tug were never agreed on in writing, but a verbal agreement was made and extended twice. No formal authorization was made for a further extension, but the defendant continued to make use of the tug. The defendant

---

2. *Saint John Tug Boat Co. Ltd. v. Irving Refining Ltd.*, [1964] S.C.R. 614.

then tried to deny liability for all charges arising from the continued use of the tug. The court stated:

1. Liabilities are not to be forced upon people behind their backs any more than you can confer a benefit upon a man against his will.

2. But if a person knows that the consideration is being rendered for his benefit with an expectation that he will pay for it, then if he acquiesces in its being done, taking the benefit of it when done, he will be taken impliedly to have requested its being done: and that will import a promise to pay for it.

PRACTICE TIP

In a case like *Saint John Tug Boat*, it is always a good idea to reduce verbal agreements to writing, confirming the verbal terms by letter or email, not only to make the contract enforceable, but also to make the terms clear and explicit.

There is consumer legislation to deal with the situation that arises when sellers send unsolicited goods to members of the public. For example, the Ontario *Consumer Protection Act, 2002*[3] provides a "cooling-off" period for a consumer who accepts unsolicited goods or services. In this case, the supplier shall refund a payment received from a consumer in respect of unsolicited goods or services within 15 days after the day the consumer demands the refund.

In some cases, performance of the terms of the offer may constitute acceptance. In those cases, acceptance is complete when the offeree performs all the terms contained in the offer. In such a case, notifying the offeror of the acceptance is unnecessary.

Example of Acceptance by Performance

You send a letter to a mail-order company offering to purchase some of the items in its catalogue. The mail-order company does not write back to you but responds by sending you the items requested. In this case, performance of the terms of the offer (sending you the items) can constitute acceptance.

The issue of communication of an acceptance was raised in the case of *Carlill v. Carbolic Smoke Ball Co.*, discussed above. The company raised the argument that Mrs. Carlill had not communicated her acceptance of its offer before using its product, so no contract was formed. The court did not accept this argument, holding that the offer implied that notification of acceptance was not necessary. The company had asked that its customers buy and use the product, and performance of these terms was sufficient acceptance of the offer, without communication to the company.

---

3. *Consumer Protection Act, 2002*, S.O. 2002, c. 30, Sched. A, s. 21, as amended.

Rules for Determining Communication of the Acceptance

The moment of acceptance can be important, and rules have been established to determine when communication of an acceptance takes place.

If acceptance is to be made verbally, acceptance takes place when the words are spoken, either by telephone or in person.

If acceptance may be made in writing, the "postal acceptance rule" applies. Using the mail to make and accept offers has been so common that the courts have established a rule that states that when acceptance of an offer may be validly made by mail, acceptance takes place when the properly addressed and stamped letter of acceptance is placed in the mailbox. The contract is formed at the time of mailing, even though the offeror may not be aware of the acceptance until several days later. Even if the letter is then lost or is delivered late, the contract is valid. The reasoning is that offerees who use the mail to accept an offer have done everything they must do at that point. While it can be argued that it may be harsh to expect offerors to be bound by contracts if they have no knowledge of the acceptance, an offeror who invited acceptance by mail must be prepared to accept the risk that the acceptance may be delivered late or go astray. However, an offeror may stipulate in the offer that acceptance by mail is acceptable but will be binding only when the letter is actually received by the offeror. Such a specific term in the offer overrides the postal acceptance rule.

While the general fallback rule is that an offer is accepted when it is received, the development in the late 20th century of email, fax, voice messaging, and interactive websites has complicated the determination of when an offer or acceptance has been communicated.

PRACTICE TIP

As a result of the evolution of the law on acceptance resulting from developments in e-commerce, it is wise to spell out, in the contract, how acceptance is to be communicated and when acceptance is deemed to occur.

Counteroffers and Inquiries

If the acceptance of an offer is not clear, unequivocal, and unconditional, it is not an acceptance but may be a counteroffer or an inquiry. If a person, upon receiving an offer, states that he or she "thinks it is a great deal but would like to think about it," there is no acceptance because it is not clear and unequivocal. If he or she agrees to some of the terms but not others or wants to add or vary terms, there is no acceptance because it is conditional. Until an offer is accepted without qualification, no contract is formed.

Offers, counteroffers, and inquiries are common in most negotiations. However, it can sometimes be difficult to determine what was an offer, what was a counteroffer, and what was an inquiry in the midst of negotiations.

counteroffer
a response to an offer by
an offeree that does not
unconditionally accept
the terms of the offer
but proposes to add to
or modify the terms

A **counteroffer** is a response by the offeree that does not unconditionally accept the terms of the offer but proposes to add to or modify the terms of the offer. By making a counteroffer, the offeree rejects the original offer and puts a new offer on the table. Note that by rejecting the original offer by making a counteroffer, the offeree cannot then go back and accept the original offer unless the offeror makes the original offer again.

inquiry
questioning by the offeree
as to whether the offeror
will consider other terms
or is willing to modify
the terms of the offer; an
inquiry does not constitute
a counteroffer and is not a
rejection of the original offer

An **inquiry** by the offeree as to whether the offeror will consider other terms or is willing to modify the terms of the offer does not constitute a counteroffer and will not result in rejection of the original offer. In this case, the offeree can still accept the original offer.

Examples of a Counteroffer and an Inquiry

Michelle: I will sell you my motorcycle for $4,500. (*offer*)

Sanjay: I can pay you $3,500 for it. (*rejection and counteroffer*)

Michelle: I could lower the price to $4,200, just for you. (*rejection and counteroffer*)

Sanjay: Would you consider $3,800? (*inquiry*)

Michelle: Not a chance! (*answer to inquiry*)

Sanjay: I will accept your offer to sell for $4,200, but I'll need three months to pay you. (*rejection and counteroffer*)

Michelle: I need the money now. Forget it. I can sell it to someone else. (*rejection*)

Sanjay: Don't be so hasty. I'll pay you the $4,200 now. (*fresh offer*)

In this case, no contract has been formed. Even though Sanjay's last counteroffer only added a term to Michelle's last offer (payment over time), it constituted a rejection of Michelle's offer. Once Sanjay rejected Michelle's offer, he was unable to go back and accept it. Even though he was willing to accept the terms of Michelle's last offer, his intervening counteroffer took it "off the table," and Michelle was under no obligation to accept Sanjay's fresh offer.

Lapse and Revocation of an Offer

lapse
the termination or failure
of an offer through the
neglect to accept it within
some time limit or through
failure of some contingency

An offer may **lapse** or it may be **revoked**, rendering the offer a **nullity** and not capable of being accepted.

An offer may lapse under any of four conditions:

revoke
to annul or make void by
recalling or taking back;
to cancel or rescind

1. Either of the parties dies, declares bankruptcy, or is declared insane prior to acceptance of the offer.

2. The offeree rejects the offer or makes a counteroffer.

nullity
nothing; something that
has no legal force or effect

3. The offeree fails to accept the offer within the time period specified in the terms of the offer.

4. No time period is specified in the terms of the offer, and the offeree fails to accept the offer within a reasonable time period.

PRACTICE TIP

To avoid "reasonable time" problems, consider setting out how acceptance is to be communicated and the length of time the offer is open before it lapses. To avoid having a contract lapse owing to bankruptcy, death, or insanity of a party, consider including wording that ensures the contract will survive those changes in status.

Once an offer has lapsed, it cannot be accepted even if the offeree was unaware of the lapse.

Determining a "reasonable time period" where no time period has been specified in the terms of the offer depends on the circumstances in each case and the nature of the anticipated contract. An offer to sell a crop of tomatoes will have a much shorter reasonable time period for acceptance than an offer to sell concrete blocks.

The offeror may revoke the offer at any time prior to acceptance. The revocation must be communicated to the offeree before the offeree accepts the offer. Generally, the offeror must communicate the revocation directly to the offeree. For direct communication, the revocation is effective when it is received by the offeree. How-

CASE IN POINT

What Is a Reasonable Time for Acceptance?

From: *Barrick v. Clark*, [1951] S.C.R. 177, [1950] 4 D.L.R. 529 (S.C.C.).

In this Supreme Court of Canada case, Barrick wrote to Clark on November 15, offering to sell his farm to Clark for $150,000. The letter stated that the deal could close immediately and title would be transferred on January 1. In the letter, Barrick stated, "trusting to hear from you as soon as possible." Clark was away when the letter arrived and did not accept the offer until December 10. In the meantime, Barrick sold the farm to a third party. Both the third party and Clark claimed they had a valid contract with Barrick.

The Supreme Court of Canada ruled that Clark's acceptance was valid; because the offer did not set out a specific time period, it was reasonable to determine how long the offer should remain open from the surrounding circumstances. In particular, the court stated:

> Farm lands . . . are not subject to frequent or sudden changes or fluctuations in price and, therefore . . . a reasonable time for the acceptance of an offer would be longer than that with respect to such commodities as shares of stock upon an established trading market. It would also be longer than in respect to goods of a perishable character.

ever, the offer can also be revoked indirectly. If the offeree has actual knowledge (from a reliable source) of the revocation of the offer or of circumstances in which it would be unreasonable for the offeree to expect the offeror to stand by the offer, this knowledge may prevent the offeree from accepting the offer. The onus of proving that the offeree had this knowledge rests on the offeror.

Such circumstances might be the sale of the offered goods to another party or the loss or destruction of the goods. However, an offeror who sells goods without revoking an outstanding offer runs the risk of the first offeree accepting the offer and thus becomes liable for **breach of contract** with the first offeree.

breach of contract
failure, without legal excuse, to perform any promise that forms part of a contract

Examples of Breach of Contract and Revocation

Dawn offers to sell her horse to Maria. Maria says she needs time to think about it, and Dawn says she will keep the offer open until the end of the week. The next day, Dawn sells the horse to Miguel without revoking her offer to Maria first. The following day, Maria communicates her acceptance of Dawn's offer.

If Maria is unaware of the sale to Miguel, she is still entitled to accept Dawn's offer and a contract is formed. Dawn, of course, will be unable to fulfill the terms of the contract (delivering the horse to Maria) and will be in breach of contract.

If Maria hears from a reliable source that Dawn sold the horse to Miguel, Dawn may be able to argue that this was a form of indirect communication of the revocation of the offer and that Maria was no longer able to accept the offer once she had this information.

CONSIDERATION

gratuitous promise
a promise made by someone who does not receive consideration for it

consideration
the price, which must be something of value, paid in return for a promise

The law makes a distinction between a **gratuitous promise** and a contract. In a gratuitous promise, one party agrees to do something for free or without reward. In contrast, a contract is essentially a bargain in which each party gets something in return for his or her promise to perform the obligations in the contract. The price paid in return for the promise is called **consideration**. Without consideration there is no contract.

Consideration can take many forms. Most commonly, of course, consideration is the payment of money. However, consideration can also be the exchange of goods or services, an agreement to refrain from doing something, or the relinquishment of a right. Where a party has made a statement or a promise relinquishing a right, or refraining from doing something, the party may be **estopped** (stopped or prevented) from later repudiating the statement or promise, if the other party relied on it in good faith. Factual and promissory estoppel are discussed later in this section.

estopped
stopped or prevented

The consideration in a contract must also be legal. If the consideration is illegal (for example, paying a sum of money to a person to murder someone else), the consideration fails and the contract is unenforceable. The legality of contracts will be discussed in detail later in this chapter.

Gratuitous Promises

In most circumstances, the courts will not enforce gratuitous promises. Because they lack consideration, gratuitous promises are not contracts. However, there are some exceptions to this rule.

The promise of a donation to a charity is a gratuitous promise. The promisor who pledges to donate a sum of money to a charity receives nothing in return apart from the thanks of the charity and the knowledge of a good deed done (and possibly a tax receipt). Most people do honour their pledges to charities, and most charities would not consider legal action to try to enforce a subscriber's pledge. However, there are cases in which the courts have upheld the promise of a donation to a charity on the basis that the subscribers pledged to donate funds for a specific undertaking.

Note that if the pledge constitutes only a small part of the total funds needed for the undertaking, the courts are unlikely to enforce the promise. The pledge must constitute a substantial portion of the funds needed. In addition, if the moneys are pledged not for a specific project or undertaking but for the day-to-day expenses of the charity, the courts will not enforce the promise.

A gratuitous promise that is made **under seal** will be enforced even without consideration. Originally, a seal was used on a document to prove its authenticity and to substitute for a signature at a time when few people were literate. The seal was usually wax, and a signet ring was impressed into the wax. Over time, gummed wafers were substituted, or impressions were made directly onto the paper. Even the word "seal" or "LS" (short for *locus sigilli* or "the place of the seal") can constitute a seal. To properly execute a document under seal, the promisor must sign the document and affix the seal at the time of signature. A document under seal is called a **deed**.

A promise made under seal does not require consideration to make it binding. The courts have traditionally viewed the seal on a document as an indication that the promisor understands the significance of his or her act and intends to be bound by the promise contained in the document.

under seal
bearing an impression made in wax or directly on paper, or affixed with a gummed paper wafer, to guarantee authenticity

deed
a written contract, made under seal by the promisor(s); also called a formal contract

CASE IN POINT

An Enforceable Gratuitous Promise?

From: *Sargent v. Nicholson* (1915), 9 W.W.R. 883 (Man. C.A.) and *YMCA v. Rankin* (1916), 10 W.W.R. 482 (B.C.C.A.).

In these cases, the charity (the YMCA in both cases), relying on the pledges received from its subscribers, committed itself to constructing new buildings. When the subscribers refused to honour their pledges, the court held that there was an implied request from the subscribers that the charity undertake the project as the "price" for the pledge. The court held that this was sufficient consideration.

Estoppel Based on Fact

When one person asserts as true a certain statement of fact and another relies on that statement to his or her detriment, the maker of the statement will be estopped from denying the truth of the original statement in a court of law, even if it turns out to have been untrue.

Example of Estoppel Based on Fact

Alberto leased a retail shop from Ewalina. Alberto wanted to get rid of furniture at the back of the shop but believed that it belonged to Ewalina. She told Alberto it had belonged to the previous tenant but it came with the lease and Alberto could do what he wanted with it. Alberto sold the furniture for a profit. Subsequently, Ewalina realized that her husband had inherited the furniture from his mother. Ewalina sued Alberto for the value of the furniture, but was unsuccessful. Ewalina was estopped from denying the truth of her statement to Alberto when they negotiated the lease, that he could do as he liked with the furniture, even though the statement was untrue. Because Alberto relied on her statement, he should not have to suffer detrimental consequences because he acted in good faith on what Ewalina had told him.

Promissory Estoppel

promissory estoppel
a rule whereby a person is prevented from denying the truth of a statement of fact made by him or her where another person has relied on that statement and acted accordingly

Another exception to the rule that most gratuitous promises cannot be enforced occurs in cases involving **promissory estoppel** (also known as equitable estoppel). Once a party makes a promise or representation to the other party, and the other party relies on this statement of fact to his or her detriment, the statement or promise cannot later be denied. The party is estopped from denying the promise previously made. In other words, the party who relied on the promise can "raise estoppel" against the party who made the statement to ensure that he or she fulfills the promise.

Five elements must be present to constitute promissory estoppel:

1. There must be an existing legal relationship between the parties at the time the statement on which the estoppel is founded was made.
2. There must be a clear promise or representation made by the party against whom the estoppel is raised, establishing his or her intent to be bound by what he or she has said.
3. There must have been reliance, by the party raising the estoppel, on the statement or conduct of the party against whom the estoppel is raised.
4. The party to whom the representation was made must have acted on it to his or her detriment.
5. The promisee must have acted equitably.

Promissory estoppel usually involves an assurance by one party that it will not enforce its legal rights with the intention that the assurance be relied on and acted on by the other party.

CASE IN POINT

When Is a Gratuitous Statement Enforceable?

From: *Central London Property Trust, Ltd. v. High Trees House, Ltd.*, [1947] K.B. 130.

In this English case, a landlord gratuitously promised to reduce the rent on a long-term lease because of the difficulties the tenant was experiencing due to the war. After the war, the landlord's representative sued the tenant for the full amount of the rent owing. Clearly, no consideration passed from the tenant to the landlord in exchange for the promise to reduce the rent. However, the tenant relied on the promise to his detriment. The court stated:

> [A] promise was made which was intended to create legal relations and which, to the knowledge of the person making the promise, was going to be acted on by the person to whom it was made, and which in fact was so acted on. In such cases the courts have said that the promise must be honoured.

PRACTICE TIP

Promissory estoppel is hard to prove, because you need reliable evidence. If the promises relied on are oral it is a good idea to send a letter or an email confirming what was promised. Documentary evidence made at the time of the event is much more credible evidence than oral "he said, she said" recollections long after the event.

Adequacy of Consideration

The courts insist that the consideration exchanged have some value to the parties, but will not examine the adequacy of the consideration to determine whether the promise and the consideration are of equal value. The adequacy of the consideration is a matter of personal judgment. As long as consideration is present, the requirement is satisfied. The consideration may be as little as one dollar or even one cent, or may take the form of an item, such as a book or a photograph, that has value or significance to no one apart from the parties to the contract.

If a party agrees to a contract in which he or she receives grossly inadequate consideration for his or her promise, the courts will nevertheless enforce the contract. However, this lack of interference occurs only where both parties are equally capable of looking after their own interests and there is no evidence of **fraud**, undue influence, or duress. If one party can prove that the consideration in the contract was grossly inadequate *and* can prove the existence of some form of fraud, undue influence, or duress, the court may hold that the contract is unenforceable. This situation is dealt with in more detail in Chapter 5, Contractual Defects.

fraud
false or misleading allegations for the purpose of inducing another to part with something valuable or to give up some legal right

Past Consideration

Consideration must be something that is to be received at the instant the promise is made (*present consideration*) or at a later date (*future consideration*). It cannot be something that the person received before the promise was made (**past consideration**). Even if a person promises to reward another who has previously done an act gratuitously, the promise is not binding because past consideration is no consideration at all. To be a valid and an enforceable contract, the promise and the consideration must be exchanged for each other. This is not the case when the act is done first and the promise is made later.

past consideration
an act done or something given before a contract is made, which by itself is not consideration for the contract

Examples of Present, Future, and Past Consideration

- Fazil purchases a book from Margaret. Margaret gives him the book and Fazil pays the money immediately. The act (Margaret's giving Fazil the book) and the promise (Fazil's payment for the book) occur at the same time. This is *present consideration*.
- Fazil purchases a book from Margaret on credit and agrees to pay her for it in a month. The act (Margaret's giving Fazil the book) occurs in the present and the promise (Fazil's payment for the book) is made at the same time as the act, although the payment will occur at a later date. This is *future consideration*.
- Margaret gives Fazil a book as a gift (a gratuitous act). A few months later, Fazil finds out that it is a valuable first edition and offers to pay Margaret for it, but later changes his mind and refuses to pay. The act (Margaret's giving Fazil the book) occurred before the promise was made (Fazil's promising to pay for the book). This is *past consideration*, and Fazil's promise to pay Margaret cannot be enforced.

Existing Legal Obligation

The promise to do something that a party is already obligated to do under another contract or under a statute cannot be consideration. If an existing contract obligates one party to perform a certain act for another party, that same act cannot form the consideration for another contract. There must be *fresh consideration* for a new promise. Otherwise, the promise is gratuitous.

Example of an Existing Legal Obligation

Bruce and Patrice enter into a contract whereby Bruce agrees to build a backyard deck for Patrice. Patrice needs to have the deck completed by a certain date, and Bruce agrees to this term. However, Bruce later finds that he cannot complete the deck on time without hiring extra workers. He tells Patrice that he will need an additional $5,000 if she wants the deck completed by the date specified. Patrice agrees to pay the extra $5,000, and Bruce then completes the deck on time. However, Patrice refuses to pay Bruce the additional $5,000.

Bruce cannot enforce Patrice's promise to pay the additional $5,000 because Patrice received no consideration for her promise to pay. The only thing Bruce offered her in exchange for the additional $5,000 was the completion of the deck by a certain date, something he was already obligated to do in the original contract. Patrice received no fresh consideration for her promise. However, if Bruce had offered her fresh consideration (such as offering to stain the deck as well), Patrice's promise to pay would have been enforceable because it would have been supported by consideration. Bruce could also have had the agreement to pay the additional $5,000 executed under seal, which would have made fresh consideration for the promise to pay the additional $5,000 unnecessary.

Similarly, if a party has an obligation under a statute to perform certain duties, agreeing to perform those duties cannot be consideration for another contract. This applies to persons who have obligations to perform public duties, such as police officers.

More recently, starting in England, courts have begun to reconsider the idea that the modification of an existing contract always requires fresh consideration. In *Williams v. Roffey Bros. and Nicholls (Contractors) Ltd.*,[4] the English Court of Appeal held that the requirement of fresh consideration could be relaxed to make enforceable a gratuitous promise (one made without fresh consideration) to pay more, so long as:

- the promisor obtains some benefit or advantage from the new arrangement, and
- the promise was not made under duress—for example, a refusal to carry out essential parts of an existing contract unless further payment is made.

PRACTICE TIP

Proof of whether there were post-contractual modifications with or without coercion often depends not on the contract language, but on collateral communications. It is best if these collateral communications, even if oral, be reduced to writing at some point in the form of letters, emails, or memoranda. For emails, preserve the meta data (information about when something was sent, who sent it, and to whom it was sent), because timing of these communications may be important.

Debtor–Creditor Relationships

Although the requirement for fresh consideration for a promise makes good sense in most instances, it can lead to unfair results in others, particularly in debtor–creditor relationships. In a debtor–creditor relationship, the debtor is obligated to pay to the creditor a certain sum of money. The debtor's obligations are discharged when the full amount of the debt is paid in accordance with the terms

---

4. *Williams v. Roffey Bros. and Nicholls (Contractors) Ltd.*, [1989] E.W.C.A. Civ. 5.

CASE IN POINT

When Is the Modification of an Existing Contract Enforceable?

From: *NAV Canada v. Greater Fredericton Airport Authority Inc.*, 2008 NBCA 28, 229 N.B.R. (2d) 238, 290 D.L.R. (4th) 405.

Nav Canada was responsible for providing aviation services and equipment to the airport. There was a contract between the parties covering these services. Subsequently, the airport authority decided to extend one of its runways. It asked Nav Canada to relocate the instrument landing system. Nav Canada concluded that part of that system should be replaced and upgraded as part of the relocation. The cost of the new piece of equipment was $223,000. Nav Canada, however, refused to make provision in its budget for the new equipment unless the airport authority agreed to pay the cost. The airport authority stated that it was not contractually required to do this, but would pay under protest. Nav Canada relied on this statement and ordered the equipment. The airport authority then refused to pay for it.

The dispute went to arbitration. The arbitrator ruled that Nav Canada had the exclusive right to decide whether or not to replace equipment, but that there was nothing in the existing contract that permitted Nav Canada to make the airport authority pay for it. However, the arbitrator ruled that the subsequent exchange of correspondence about who was to pay constituted a new and separate contract that was supported by considera-

tion (the airport authority got new equipment that would make the use of its new runway more effective). The use of the term "under protest" was not in itself enough to negate the airport authority's obligation to pay Nav Canada.

In the Court of Appeal, the court examined the consideration doctrine at some length, and while the fresh consideration doctrine was not abandoned by the court, in this case the court held that it was unsatisfactory because it was both overinclusive and underinclusive. It was overinclusive in that it accepted renegotiations induced by coercion so long as there was fresh consideration, and it was underinclusive in that it rejected voluntary agreements where there is no consideration, but also no coercion. The court noted with approval *Williams v. Roffey Bros. et al.*[5] Here, the court recognized that the doctrine of consideration that developed in the 19th century might not be entirely relevant in every modern situation. Consequently, on an incremental, case-by-case basis, the court should be prepared to accept as valid and binding post-contractual modifications unsupported by additional consideration provided there is no coercion. This case, the court held, was such a case.

of the contract (loan, credit card, financing agreement, and so on). However, it is common practice for debtors and creditors to enter into an agreement to allow the debtor to pay a lesser amount than the total owed, especially where a debtor has defaulted in payment.

For example, Marcel, a debtor, owes $10,000 and offers to pay $9,000. The creditor, Su Mei, agrees to accept the sum of $9,000 in full and final settlement of the $10,000 debt. For many reasons, Su Mei may find that it is to her benefit to accept the lesser amount rather than to pursue Marcel through the courts for the full amount. In addition, Marcel ought to be able to rely on Su Mei's promise that she will take the lesser amount in full satisfaction of the debt. However, the requirement of fresh consideration makes the agreement to accept the lesser amount unenforceable. Because Marcel was already obligated to pay that sum of money (and more), Su Mei received no fresh consideration for the promise to pay the

5.   *Williams v. Roffey Bros. et al.*, [1991] 1 Q.B. 1.

lesser amount. Su Mei would then be free to sue Marcel for the outstanding sum of $1,000.

To address this problem and to allow debtors and creditors to enter into such arrangements with the knowledge that they are enforceable, many provinces in Canada have passed legislation that states that a creditor who accepts a lesser sum in satisfaction of a debt will not later be allowed to claim the balance. In Ontario, such a provision is found in the *Mercantile Law Amendment Act*.[6] However, where the creditor agrees to accept a lesser amount, he or she can change his or her mind at any point before receiving the lesser sum.

Quantum Meruit

It is not unusual for one party to request goods or services from another and for that person to deliver such goods or services without a price being discussed. This is not a situation of a gratuitous promise. Even though the consideration is not specifically mentioned in the request, an agreement of this type will not fail for lack of consideration. The law will imply a promise to pay in a request for goods or services.

Quantum meruit is a concept that is relied on by someone whose occupation is to provide services or goods in a situation where payment is understood and expected.

Where there is no mention of price, the implied promise is for payment of what the services are reasonably worth, or payment for *quantum meruit*. Parties who have negotiated a contract that specifies the price to be paid for the goods or services cannot later rely on the doctrine of *quantum meruit* to get a better price. *Quantum meruit* can be relied on only when the contract is silent as to the amount (or *quantum*) of the consideration, in circumstances where payment is clearly required.

In determining the reasonable worth of goods or services, the courts look to the prices charged by similar suppliers and fix the contract price accordingly. *Quantum meruit* also applies to situations where there has been substantial performance, although performance is not complete. To prevent one party from getting some benefit for the work done without having to pay would be unfair. Where there has been substantial performance, the court therefore will try to determine the value of the work that has been done and award compensation for that work. *Quantum meruit* in connection with substantial performance is discussed in more detail in Chapter 8, Breach of Contract and Remedies.

> **quantum meruit**
> an equitable doctrine that states that no one should unjustly benefit from the labour and materials of another; under those circumstances, the law implies a promise to pay a reasonable amount, even in the absence of a contractual term for price

ELECTRONIC COMMERCE

The ability to transact business over the Internet—that is, to participate in electronic commerce (e-commerce)—is a significant and relatively recent development. E-commerce brings together buyers and sellers from all over the world and provides unprecedented opportunities for the exchange of goods, services, and ideas.

Traditional contract law applies to Internet transactions. However, the Internet also introduces many new legal issues and risks. Some of these risks are being

---

6. *Mercantile Law Amendment Act*, R.S.O. 1990, c. M.10.

addressed with legislation, such as the federal *Personal Information Protection and Electronic Documents Act*[7] (PIPEDA, mentioned in Chapter 10), the Ontario *Consumer Protection Act, 2002,*[8] and the Alberta *Electronic Transactions Act.*[9] However, the law governing e-commerce is currently in a state of flux as businesses, consumers, citizens, and governments negotiate the rules of this new context.

Contract parties engaged in e-commerce may need to concern themselves with some of the following matters:

- the authenticity of electronic documents and signatures, and whether these signatures are binding;
- the place to resolve a dispute when the parties to a contract are from different regions;
- the laws that apply when contracting parties from different countries, with different laws, are involved;
- the time that the contract is created; and
- access to parties' personal information (for example, credit card numbers).

Authenticity of Documents and Electronic Signatures

Although there is no legal necessity that a contract be in writing to be enforceable, a written agreement certainly makes the existence of a contract and its specifics much easier to prove. How can parties achieve contractual certainty on the Internet, where documents may be readily altered, and where it is easy to assume a false identity?

PIPEDA, a federal statute, and provincial electronic commerce statutes address this concern by recognizing electronic documents and "signature equivalents" that are protected by password or encryption. Any contract that can be entered into in writing and on paper can be entered into electronically. Electronic documents and signatures are the equivalent of written contracts signed by hand.

Place for Dispute Resolution

The international reach of e-commerce can create problems where the contracting parties are located in different countries or jurisdictions. Imagine, for example, a dispute arising among an Internet service provider located in the United States, a vendor in Canada, and a purchaser in Spain. If there is a contractual dispute, where will it be resolved? Each of the parties may have legitimate reasons for arguing that the dispute should be resolved in its own jurisdiction.

Some Internet contracts have tried to create predictability about the place where disputes will be resolved by specifying the place for resolution in the contract. A party who uses the Internet to sell goods to international customers would be wise to include a term in its standard contract that provides that any contractual dis-

---

7. *Personal Information Protection and Electronic Documents Act*, S.C. 2000, c. 5.
8. *Consumer Protection Act, 2002*, S.O. 2002, c. 30, Sched. A.
9. *Electronic Transactions Act*, S.A. 2001, c. E-5.5.

agreements are to be heard in its own jurisdiction. Rather than running the risk of expensive and lengthy litigation, parties may also include clauses requiring disputes to be submitted to binding arbitration.

Applicable Law for Dispute Resolution

While basic common-law contract principles, such as offer and acceptance, are similar in most parts of the world, the details of contract law are not. Statutes governing consumer protection, fraud, sales tax, and illegal commercial activity (such as gambling) override the common law and vary widely among countries. Businesses that buy and sell over the Internet risk running afoul of the laws and regulations of other jurisdictions. It is nearly impossible to ensure absolute compliance with the laws of every jurisdiction; however, businesses that are extensively engaged in e-commerce should seek legal advice to minimize their risks.

Buyers and sellers may include a clause in their contracts that specifies the law that will govern their disputes. This is known as a *governing law clause*. Courts generally respect the choices that the parties have expressed in their contracts, unless there are public policy concerns, such as tax avoidance or criminality.

Timing of Formation of Contract

Most business contracts are created when one party makes an offer and the other party communicates her acceptance of this offer. With e-commerce, this process can occur very quickly, and it is sometimes difficult to determine when an offer is made or accepted. The timing of an offer and the acceptance of it can be of critical importance in some circumstances. For example, consider an offer that expires after 24 hours. When does the clock start running: when the email is sent, when the email is received, or when the email is opened and read? If acceptance is not communicated within the correct 24-hour time period, a contract does not exist.

Statutes such as Ontario's *Electronic Commerce Act, 2000*[10] (ECA) have adopted the rule that unless the parties specify otherwise, an offer exists as soon as the party making the offer hits the "send" button, and acceptance occurs when the acceptance message is received, whether or not the message is opened and read. The Ontario ECA provides that the offer and the acceptance may be made by means of electronic communication, such as sending an email or clicking an icon.

Protection of Privacy

There are a number of security measures that may be taken to preserve the confidentiality of credit card numbers and personal identifying information exchanged over the Internet.

Federal and provincial legislation concerning e-commerce establishes standards for protection of the privacy of information exchanged electronically. Most commercial websites post privacy policies, have secure transaction logos, and use encryption to prevent credit card information from being intercepted.

---

10.   *Electronic Commerce Act, 2000*, S.O. 2000, c. 17.

Since January 1, 2004, PIPEDA has applied to all businesses in Canada that collect, use, or disclose personal information in the course of commercial activities. It explicitly extends protection to information that businesses have built up over time before the passage of the Act.

CHAPTER SUMMARY

A contract is an agreement that is enforceable at law. A contract that is not enforceable is a void contract.

For a contract to be enforceable, the essential elements of a contract must be present. Some of the elements of an essential contract—intention, offer and acceptance, and consideration—are explained in this chapter. Three additional elements—legality, formal requirements, and capacity—are discussed in Chapter 4.

The first element of a valid contract is intention: each of the parties must have the intent to create an agreement that is legally binding. Where a party disputes the presence of this element, the court will need to consider evidence in support of (and against) intention. When examining this evidence, the court considers the facts from the perspective of a reasonable person in the same situation and decides whether or not that imaginary reasonable person would have expected the agreement to be legally binding.

The second essential element is an offer—or a promise—made by the offeror and communicated to the offeree. An offer is distinct from an "invitation to treat," which is essentially an invitation for the *other* party to make an offer. (For example, in general, a store's display of goods in a shop window is an invitation to treat, not an offer.)

An offer can be communicated in various ways: not only verbally, but by letter, fax, email, and so on. There are special rules to determine the timing of an offer made in this way.

An offer can be revoked (withdrawn) by the offeror at any time prior to acceptance, but not afterward. An offer can also lapse (expire), either because it was specifically time-sensitive and the time for acceptance ran out, or because of undue delay. The length of the delay that will cause an offer to lapse depends on the circumstances. Once an offer has been revoked or has lapsed, it cannot be validly accepted.

For a contract to be created, the offeree must communicate his or her unequivocal acceptance to the offeror. The method of acceptance, like the method of offer, can vary, and there are special rules for determining the timing of acceptances by mail, fax, email, and so on. If, instead of unequivocally accepting an offer, the offeree proposes different terms (a lower price, for example, or a different mode of payment), the response is not an acceptance, but rather, a counteroffer. The counteroffer must now be unequivocally accepted by the original offeror before a contract is created. A counteroffer, like an offer, can be revoked or can lapse.

The contract must include consideration, or an exchange of something of value between the parties. While each party must receive some benefit from the contract, the courts will not disturb a contract based on apparent inequality in the benefit received. For example, a telephone company may offer a customer a new cellphone for one cent in exchange for the customer's willingness to enter into a telephone contract, which the court will permit, or a father may offer to sell his old car to his daughter in exchange for a dollar.

Consideration must be delivered at the time the contract is made (present consideration) or in the future (future consideration). An offer to buy a friend lunch because last week that friend helped you move to a new apartment is not legally binding, because the consideration for your offer was exchanged in the past (before the lunch was offered or contemplated).

At one time, payment of (all or part of) a debt already owed was not deemed sufficient consideration for the creditor to discharge the debt. This rule has since been changed to permit debtors in default to negotiate new payment terms under some circumstances.

Charitable pledges sometimes pose contract problems, because it can be hard to identify the consideration received by the proposed donor. In general, charities do not seek to enforce broken promises to donate funds. However, where the charity relied on the pledge in incurring a specific expense (for example, $4 million was promised, and the charity built a community centre and named it after the proposed donor), courts may enforce the contract based on equitable principles or by ruling that the naming constituted good consideration.

An agreement without consideration is a gratuitous contract and will not be enforced unless it is under seal.

Electronic commerce represents a comparatively recent development in contract law. Although traditional contract law applies to Internet transactions, e-commerce includes certain risks that do not exist in the case of written agreements on paper (including concerns about document authenticity and privacy) and additional rules (for example, when an offer is considered to be made and accepted). The law in this area is in a state of flux and will continue to develop over time.

KEY TERMS

arm's-length transaction	nullity
breach of contract	onus
consideration	past consideration
counteroffer	presumption of law
deed	promissory estoppel
estopped	*quantum meruit*
fraud	revoke
gratuitous promise	under seal
inquiry	void contract
lapse	

REVIEW QUESTIONS

True or False?

_____ 1. A counteroffer terminates an offer such that it can no longer be accepted.

_____ 2. An offer can be accepted without being communicated.

_____ 3. Where a debtor is required by contract to pay the balance of a loan on April 15, but advises the lender on March 31 that she will pay on April 1, and then doesn't, the lender can sue for breach of contract even though there is no fresh consideration for the change in terms.

_____ 4. The postal acceptance rule provides that an offer is accepted when the addressee receives the letter containing the acceptance.

_____ 5. Past consideration is not valid consideration for a contract.

_____ 6. Where a contract is made by parties at arm's length to each other, there is a presumption that the parties intended to create legal relations.

_____ 7. Past consideration can be valid consideration.

_____ 8. To be valid, an offer must contain all of the terms of the contract, whether expressly or by implication.

_____ 9. Where the original offeror rejects a counteroffer, the initial offer becomes valid again.

_____ 10. An offer can be communicated by silence under certain circumstances.

_____ 11. Not all contracts that can be entered into on paper can be entered into electronically.

Fill in the Blanks

1. An advertisement is generally viewed by the court not as an offer, but as an _____ _____ _____ _____.

2. When the offeror withdraws or terminates an offer, the offer is said to be _____.

3. Promissory _____ prevents a party who has made a promise from breaching it to another party's detriment.

4. When an offer is time-limited and the offeree fails to accept it before the time runs out, the offer is said to have _____.

5. To be valid, a modification to a contract must generally be supported by _____ consideration.

6. A gratuitous promise is one made without _____.

7. The principle of _____ _____ may be applied to quantify consideration where the contract is silent as to the amount payable.

8. An unenforceable or defective contract is also known as a _____ contract.
9. A gratuitous promise may be enforceable if made under _____.
10. The _____ _____ _____ determines the timing of the creation of a contract accepted by mail.
11. Contract parties engaged in e-commerce may be concerned about the _____ of electronic documents and whether _____ are binding.

Short Answer

1. How do the courts determine whether the parties to an agreement intended to create a legal relationship?
2. When does an offer lapse?
3. How may an acceptance be communicated? When does silence constitute acceptance?
4. Consider whether acceptance has been communicated and a contract formed in the following examples:
   a. Allan emails Betty on Monday and offers to sell her his car for $3,000. She emails him back the same day and accepts his offer. Allan does not check his email.
   b. Allan phones Betty and offers to sell her his car for $3,000. She tells him that she will get back to him. She emails him the same day, accepting his offer. He only uses his email for work and doesn't check it. Betty doesn't phone him back, so he sells the car to Charles.
   c. Allan meets Betty and offers to sell her his car for $3,000. She cannot decide immediately, so Allan tells her to email him before Wednesday, although he usually uses his email address only for work. On Tuesday, Betty emails him her acceptance.
5. What distinguishes a counteroffer from an inquiry?
6. How may an offer be revoked, and when is such revocation effective?
7. "The courts are not concerned with the adequacy of consideration." What does this mean? Give an exception to this statement.
8. Under what conditions will a court enforce a gratuitous promise?
9. Explain the differences among past, present, and future consideration.
10. What conditions must be present for the courts to enforce a claim of *quantum meruit*?

EXERCISES

1. Willie the electrician receives a telephone call late at night from Colin. Colin explains that he has just come home and his house has no power. Colin insists that Willie come over immediately because it is the middle of winter and he is without heat. Willie explains that he charges extra for emergency calls, but no actual price is ever discussed over the phone. Willie arrives at Colin's house. He finds that the house has no power because Colin tripped the main circuit breaker by plugging in too many appliances. Willie simply turns the main circuit breaker back on and leaves. He sends a bill to Colin for $400. Is Colin obliged to pay this amount? Explain.

2. Sharri places an advertisement in the paper offering to sell her piano for $4,000. Aaron writes to Sharri in response to the advertisement and offers to buy her piano for $3,000. Sharri receives Aaron's offer on January 3 and telephones him to ask whether he will consider increasing his offer. Aaron tells her he will think about it. Mary writes to Sharri, offering to buy her piano for $3,200. Sharri receives the letter on January 5. She writes to Mary the same day and tells her she will sell the piano for $3,500. Mary receives the letter on January 7, and writes back the same day advising Sharri that she accepts the offer to buy the piano for $3,500. Unfortunately, the letter is lost in the mail, and Sharri never receives it. Aaron writes to Sharri on January 5 stating that he will pay her $4,000 for her piano by paying her $3,000 now and $1,000 in one month. Sharri receives Aaron's letter on January 8 and telephones Aaron the same day to confirm that the payment terms are acceptable. Sharri then receives a telephone call from Mary on January 9 in which she learns of Mary's acceptance by letter dated January 7. Sharri then tells Mary she now wants $4,000 for the piano. Is Sharri bound to sell her piano to either Mary or Aaron? Why or why not?

3. Sara needs her car repaired before she leaves for a business trip on December 15. She takes it to Speedy Repair, where she agrees to pay $500, and Speedy Repair agrees to have her car ready for December 14. On December 12, Speedy Repair telephones Sara to tell her that the repairs are behind schedule and it does not think it can have the car ready by December 14 as promised. Sara is frantic and offers them an additional $500 to have the car ready for December 14. Speedy Repair agrees and offers to throw in a car wash and wax "for good business relations." Speedy Repair's mechanics work overtime and the car is ready by December 14, as well as being shiny and clean. Sara then refuses to pay the extra $500. Is Speedy Repair entitled to the additional $500? Explain.

4. Upon his death, Phillippe left his entire fortune in trust to his daughter, Danielle. Because she was a child when he died, Elizabeth was appointed Danielle's guardian. When Danielle turns 21, she is entitled to her inheritance. However, under the terms of the trust, Danielle cannot access the trust moneys until then. Elizabeth spends a great deal of money on Danielle's education, sending her to expensive private schools and to

university. Elizabeth incurs personal debt as a result of Danielle's educational costs. When Danielle turns 21, she gets her inheritance and promises to repay Elizabeth for the money Elizabeth spent on her education. Danielle fails to repay Elizabeth. Can Elizabeth enforce Danielle's promise? Why or why not?

5. The Parliament of Canada, after many years of staying out of the bedrooms of the nation, passed a statute "prohibiting anyone from selling post-coital contraceptive medication, otherwise known as the 'morning-after pill.'" Cheapo Pharmacy put up a poster by the prescription drop-off, advertising the Cheapo Morning-After Pill for only $10. Cheapo is charged with violating the statute.

   Would Cheapo likely be convicted? If not, what would Parliament have to do to ensure a conviction in this case? Explain your answer.

Legality, Formalities, and Capacity

4

OVERVIEW

LEARNING OUTCOMES

After completing this chapter, you should be able to:

- List at least three illegal purposes that can affect the validity of a contract.

- Explain the difference between an unlawful and an illegal contract, and describe the impact on the remedy available to the parties in the event of a breach.

- Describe the difference between a simple contract and a formal contract.

- Describe at least two contract "formalities" and understand how to comply with a requirement for formalities.

- Understand why the law requires that contract parties have capacity.

- Explain at least three factors that may limit a party's capacity.

- Understand the legal status of a minor's contract.

INTRODUCTION

In Chapter 3, you learned that the validity of a contract requires that the parties had an intention to be legally bound, that one party made an offer that the other accepted, and that there was an exchange of consideration.

In this chapter, we examine three additional contract elements: legality, formalities, and capacity. A contract's legality is essential to its validity. In general (with very narrow exceptions), it is also essential that the parties to a contract have the capacity to contract at the time the contract is made.

As you will learn in this chapter, the requirement of writing applies only to certain well-defined categories of contracts.

LEGALITY

In order to be binding and enforceable on the parties, a contract must have a legal purpose. To have a legal purpose, a contract cannot violate any statute, and it cannot violate public policy. If, for either reason, the contract is found to have an unlawful purpose, the courts will not enforce it and will declare it to be void, or illegal, or both.

The distinction between a contract that is merely void for having an unlawful purpose and one that has an unlawful purpose and is also illegal is important. If the contract is merely void for being unlawful, the court may grant some remedies to the parties who entered into it by attempting to restore them to their original positions. For example, if money and goods have changed hands but the contract is unlawful, the court may order the goods and the money returned.

However, if the contract is not only unlawful but also illegal, the court will not grant any remedies to any party who knowingly entered into it. Remedies are discussed in more detail in Chapter 8, Breach of Contract and Remedies.

Example of Effects of Illegality

In the case of *Archbolds (Freightage) Ltd. v. S. Spanglett Ltd.*,[1] the court stated:

> The effect of illegality upon a contract may be threefold. If at the time of making the contract there is an intent to perform it in an unlawful way, the contract, although it remains alive, is unenforceable at the suit of the party having that intent; if the intent is held in common, it is not enforceable at all. Another effect of illegality is to prevent a plaintiff from recovering under a contract if in order to prove his rights under it he has to rely upon his own illegal act. . . . The third effect of illegality is to avoid the contract *ab initio* [void from the time it is made] and that arises if the making of the contract is expressly or impliedly prohibited by statute or is otherwise contrary to public policy.

---

1. *Archbolds (Freightage) Ltd. v. S. Spanglett Ltd.*, [1961] 1 Q.B. 374, at 388 (C.A.).

Contracts That Violate Statute Law

It is important to look closely at the wording of the statute in question to determine whether a contract that violates the statute is void or void and illegal.

- Some statutes expressly prohibit certain activities and may describe contracts that provide for such activities, and the activities themselves, as "unlawful" and "illegal" and may impose criminal penalties, such as a fine or imprisonment. Such contracts have an unlawful purpose and may be illegal as well.
- Some statutes prohibit certain kinds of agreements; only a few will be discussed here.
- Some statutes impose requirements on certain activities. A contract that provides for activities that do not comply with those requirements has an unlawful purpose by implication.

A contract to commit any act prohibited by the *Criminal Code*[2] is both void and illegal. This includes, for example, any agreement to commit murder, rob, assault, or kidnap. The courts will not enforce such a contract and will not provide any remedies to parties who enter into it. Because conspiring to commit a crime is a criminal offence, entering into a contract to commit a crime is a form of conspiracy and a crime in itself. Even if the crime is not carried out, the parties to the illegal contract can be charged with conspiracy. The *Customs Act*[3] prohibits contracts to smuggle, and such contracts are both void and illegal.

Some contracts prohibit activities that are contrary to the public interest. The *Competition Act*[4] prohibits business practices that unduly restrict business, such as an agreement to fix prices, eliminate competition, allocate markets, or create monopolies. Such business practices represent forms of **restraint of trade**. The Act renders illegal any contract entered into whose purpose is to engage in the prohibited practices. It is possible to obtain governmental approval to enter into contracts to engage in such practices (such as for mergers) to avoid violating the Act. However, without approval, such contracts are void and illegal.

The *Workplace Safety and Insurance Act, 1997*[5] prohibits any agreement between employers and employees that attempts to deprive employees of the protection of the Act. For example, a contract in which an employee agrees not to make any workplace injury claims if he or she is injured on the job is void, although it is not illegal. Contracts to sell land that violate the provisions of the *Planning Act*,[6] and in which the parties do not obtain approval from the government, are void but not illegal. The *Bankruptcy and Insolvency Act*[7] renders void, but not illegal, any contract a person enters into in which that person transfers property either as a gift or for inadequate compensation within one year before declaring bankruptcy.

restraint of trade
practices that are designed to artificially maintain prices, eliminate competition, create a monopoly, or otherwise obstruct the course of trade and commerce

2. *Criminal Code*, R.S.C. 1985, c. C-46.
3. *Customs Act*, R.S.C. 1985, c. 1 (2d Supp.).
4. *Competition Act*, R.S.C. 1985, c. C-34.
5. *Workplace Safety and Insurance Act, 1997*, S.O. 1997, c. 16, Sched. A.
6. *Planning Act*, R.S.O. 1990, c. P.13.
7. *Bankruptcy and Insolvency Act*, R.S.C. 1985, c. B-3.

Various statutes and bylaws require tradespeople and professionals to be licensed before they can offer services to the public. If an unlicensed tradesperson or professional enters into a contract for services that he or she is not licensed to provide, such a contract is void but not illegal. However, this law generally applies only to the services provided, not to any goods provided. An unlicensed plumber, then, could not enforce that part of the contract for payment for the work he or she did, but could enforce that part of the contract that provided for the supply of goods, such as pipes and fittings. However, this issue cannot be raised as a defence by the unlicensed tradesperson to the enforcement of the contract by the other party. If the unlicensed plumber did shoddy work and caused damage, the plumber could be sued for breach of contract by the customer. The plumber could not then claim that he or she incurred no liability under the contract because he or she was unlicensed. This is an application of the general principle that a party may not rely on his or her own wrongdoing to gain an advantage in court.

Table 4.1 summarizes the kinds of contracts that violate statute law and their legal status.

Contracts That Violate Public Policy

Contracts that violate public policy are void and may be illegal as well. These contracts are contrary to the public good.

Such contracts include those designed to interfere with the administration of justice (for example, paying a witness to give a certain kind of evidence in court), injure the public service (for example, giving "kickbacks" to a public official), promote unnecessary litigation (for example, paying someone to start a lawsuit to generate publicity), or suppress evidence of a crime (for example, entering into an agreement not to report a theft if the wrongdoer pays back the money).

Other contracts may be void because they involve an agreement to commit a dishonest or immoral act. For instance, contracts for loans that charge an unconscionably high rate of interest are void. Contracts for loans that charge an interest rate higher than 60 percent are also illegal. Contracts that involve prostitution are void. Some contracts that involve gambling are void. However, societal mores

TABLE 4.1   Contracts That Violate Statute Law

Category	Type of Contract	Legal Status
1. Prohibited activities	Agreements to commit any act prohibited by the *Criminal Code*	Void and illegal
2. Prohibited agreements	Agreements not in the public interest—e.g., agreements that restrain competition or deprive people of their rights	Void but not necessarily illegal—e.g., legal if government approval is obtained
3. Activities with statutory requirements	Agreements for service between unlicensed professionals and consumers, where the professional is required to be licensed to deliver services to the public	Void but not illegal

change, and some acts that may once have been considered immoral by the courts are no longer illegal.

Example of Change in Societal Mores

In the case of *Prokop v. Kohut*,[8] the court stated that it would not enforce an agreement made between a man and a woman that granted the woman a half-interest in the man's estate based on the couple's commitment to live together as a married couple although they were not married. Despite the fact that the couple lived together for 16 years, the court dismissed the woman's claim, stating that any such contract would be "void as having been made for an illegal consideration and the plaintiff can recover nothing." However, the more recent case of *Chrispen v. Topham*[9] dismissed the traditional approach, with the judge stating, "In my opinion, it cannot be argued that the [cohabitation agreement] between the plaintiff and the defendant was made for an immoral purpose, and therefore, [is] illegal and unenforceable. Present day social acceptance of common-law living counters that argument."

Business contracts can be challenged as void for containing **restrictive covenants** that constitute a restraint of trade. While these contracts may not violate the *Competition Act*, discussed above, they nonetheless may be void for violating public policy. There is a presumption at law that all restrictive covenants that constitute a restraint of trade are void. However, this presumption can be rebutted if the party wishing to enforce the contract can show that the restrictive covenant did not generally restrain trade.

> **restrictive covenant**
> a provision in a contract that prohibits certain activities or uses of property

When a business is sold, the purchasers usually want to ensure that the vendors do not engage in a business that would compete with them. The parties often include a restrictive covenant in the sale agreement that the vendors will not open a competing business for a certain period of time within a certain geographical area. If the time period and the geographical area of restriction are reasonable, the courts will uphold the contract. However, if they are unreasonable, the courts will find that the restrictive covenant is a restraint of trade and will not enforce it. What is "reasonable" depends on the circumstances of each case and the standards of the industry or business in question.

Example of a Restrictive Covenant

Newco Ltd. buys a dry-cleaning business in Toronto from Oldco Ltd. In the sale agreement, Newco states that it does not want Oldco opening a dry-cleaning business anywhere in the province of Ontario for a period of 25 years. The courts would likely find that such a restrictive covenant is contrary to public policy and is therefore void. However, if the covenant stated that the restricted area was within a 10-kilometre radius from the business site and for a period of four years, the courts would likely uphold it.

---

8. *Prokop v. Kohut* (1965), 54 D.L.R. (2d) 717 (B.C.S.C.).
9. *Chrispen v. Topham* (1986), 28 D.L.R. (4th) 754 (Sask. Q.B.); aff'd 39 D.L.R. (4th) 637 (Sask. C.A.).

Contracts between employers and employees that unreasonably restrict the employee's right to compete with the employer or to work for a competitor after the employment agreement terminates can also be void for restraint of trade. However, if the time period and geographical area are reasonable, the courts may enforce the contract. It is harder to enforce a contract of this nature than a contract for the sale of a business, because the courts are reluctant to restrict an individual from earning a living. However, if the restraint is reasonable and necessary, it will not offend the public interest and will be enforced.

Restitution: A More Modern Approach to Legality Issues

Modern commentators have been highly critical of the courts' refusal to soften the impact resulting from a contract found to be void because it is illegal. There is a tendency in some recent court decisions to look beyond an automatic and rigid response to a finding that a contract is illegal and to mitigate the impact of such a finding in circumstances where the illegality is a technicality or one of the parties was innocent of illegal intent. In such cases courts have severed illegal parts of a contract, or introduced a concept of notional severance, in effect rewriting parts of a contract that had made it illegal.[10] A more recent trend has been to develop the law of restitution to put a party back in the position he or she should have been in had the contract not been illegal. The cases so far, as the example that follows illustrates, may permit restitution in cases where:

- a contract is illegal and granting relief is clearly not contrary to public policy, or
- a party acted in good faith or in justifiable ignorance of whether the contract was legal or illegal.

PRACTICE TIP

Where the subject matter involves a regulated activity, such as a consumer transaction, an extension of credit, or an activity requiring licensing, it may be wise to obtain legal advice about legal limits on the activity prior to entering into a contract. While the court may forgive an unwitting innocent straying into an area of illegality (see the Case in Point feature below), it will still impose a "reasonable person" test, and a reasonable person might well be expected to obtain legal advice, particularly in commercial transactions subject to regulation.

10. *Transport North American Express Inc. v. New Solutions Financial Corp.*, 2004 SCC 7, [2004] 1 S.C.R. 249; *William E. Thomson Associates Inc. v. Carpenter* (1989), 61 D.L.R. (4th) 1 (Ont. C.A.).

CASE IN POINT

Can a Party Obtain Relief When a Contract Is Held to Be Illegal?

From: *Still v. M.N.R. (C.A.)*, [1998] 1 F.C. 549.

In this case, Still had married a Canadian citizen and immigrated to Canada to join her husband. Having applied for permanent resident status, she was provided with a document that stated she would be granted permanent resident status and that the document declared her eligible to apply for employment and/or student status. Still assumed this meant that she could work without needing to do anything further, and she did so from May to October 1993, when she was laid off. In September, she received her permanent resident status. In October after she was laid off, she applied for employment insurance. Her claim was denied on the ground that her employment contract was void because she was not technically a permanent resident until September. Although her employment contract from September to its termination was valid, it was not a long enough period to support a claim for employment insurance.

Still appealed this decision to the Tax Court, and then to the Federal Court of Appeal. The latter court noted that the classic model, in which the contract is strictly unenforceable, was no longer persuasive as it was far too rigid and ill-suited for solving the problem at hand. The court favoured the following principle, to be applied on a case-by-case basis: "where a contract is expressly or impliedly prohibited by statute, a court may refuse to grant relief to a party when, in all of the circumstances of the case, including regard to the object and purposes of the statutory prohibition, it would be contrary to public policy, reflected in the relief claimed, to do so." Consequently, the court should look to those "policy considerations which outweigh the applicant's *prima facie* right to unemployment insurance benefits." The court then went on to find that Still had acted in good faith without stealth or deception. Nor was there a penalty for her breach of the *Immigration Act*. Last, the court found that the deprivation of employment insurance benefits was disproportionate to the breach of statute and ordered restitution in the form of payment of employment insurance benefits.

FORM AND WRITING REQUIREMENTS

Formal and Simple Contracts

Contracts can be classified as either **formal contracts** or **simple contracts**. Formal contracts, also called deeds, are in writing and sealed by the promisor.

Deeds were the first type of contract to be recognized as valid, enforceable contracts. The early common law did not recognize most promises, whatever the form, for the purpose of enforcement. However, if a contract was written and sealed by the promisor, the formal act of applying a seal to the document was seen as evidence of a serious intention to make and keep a promise. Contracts under seal were the first to be enforced by the courts.

formal contract
a contract that is in writing and sealed by any party who is a promisor (which may be one or both parties); formal contracts are also called "deeds," and in English law are sometimes referred to as "covenants"

simple contract
a contract that can be oral or in writing and that is not a formal contract

---

LAW IN PRACTICE
Types of Contracts

Formal contracts (*deeds*) must be in writing and under seal. A seal is required to enforce a promise made if there is no consideration. For example, if I promise to give you my car as a gift, there is no consideration, because you are not required to do anything to obtain the car. For this gift to be enforceable by you, I must make the gift in writing and under seal. This type of contract is enforceable because of its form, regardless of its contents.

Simple contracts:

- *May* be oral agreements.
- *May* be in writing.
- If required by the *Statute of Frauds* or other legislation, *must* be in writing and signed by the parties who have made promises that are meant to be enforced if breached.

Contracts that are not formal contracts are called simple contracts. "Simple" does not refer to the complexity of the contract. A simple contract can be very complicated and may go on for pages. It may be oral or in writing. In the medieval period, the common-law courts would not recognize simple contracts as worthy of enforcement.

However, by the end of the 17th century, the law was well on its way to enforcing all simple contracts and abandoning prescribed formality requirements altogether. Today, simple contracts do not depend on any particular ceremony or prescribed form to be enforceable. However, there are some areas of contract law where enforceability depends on meeting some formality requirements.

As you will learn in this chapter, contracts of certain types that cover certain subject matter must be in writing and signed by the party or parties to be bound to be valid and enforceable. As well, when a contractual promise is made by one party to another without any valuable consideration, a seal is required. In the absence of consideration, the seal is still seen as evidence of a serious intention to create legal relations.

The Statute of Frauds

The *Statute of Frauds (An Act for the Prevention of Frauds and Perjuries)*[11] was enacted in England in 1677. It was originally passed in the wake of the English civil war and other upheavals that began in 1640 and was designed to introduce order and stability to the law, particularly with respect to fraudulent claims concerning long-term leases and other land rights (which had required deeds or formal contracts). The Statute was adopted during the colonial period in Canada and

---

11. *Statute of Frauds (An Act for the Prevention of Frauds and Perjuries)* (1677), 29 Car. II, c. 3.

the United States. It has long been regarded as an anachronism and has been repealed in England, but ss. 1-4 are still relevant to the law of contract today in most parts of Canada, except for British Columbia, Quebec, and Manitoba.

The *Statute of Frauds* requires that certain types of contracts be in writing and be signed by the parties who are to be bound by their promises. Such contracts do not necessarily have to be made under seal unless there is an absence of consideration. The Statute also covered certain situations that are now dealt with by simple contracts. Because of the Statute, these contracts must be in writing.

Table 4.2 lists the kinds of contracts under the Ontario *Statute of Frauds*[12] that must be in writing and signed. They are explained in detail in the sections that follow.

Contracts by a Trustee of an Estate to Pay Estate Debts

If the trustees of an estate decide to pay the debts of the estate out of their own personal funds, their promise to do so must be put in writing if they are to claim from the estate what they paid out to third parties. This might happen if an estate debt is pressing and a penalty may be imposed or interest is accumulating on the debt. The estate trustee might pay the debt out of personal funds to prevent the estate from losing money. Then, when estate funds later become available, he or she may claim from the estate the amount paid.

Contracts to Assume the Liabilities of Another

Contracts where a third party promises to perform the obligation of another person must, under the Statute, be in writing and be signed by the third party. If the promise is not in writing, it cannot be enforced against the third party. The Statute describes two contractual situations where third parties agree to assume another's liability: guarantees and assumed liability for torts.

Guaranteeing debt: A **guarantee** arises where the **guarantor** promises to pay the debt of another person if that other person fails to pay the debt when it is due.

> ### Example of a Guarantee of a Debt
>
> Johann wants to borrow money from the Caring Bank. The bank manager knows that Johann does not have a full-time job, has few assets, and is a poor credit risk. The bank manager says the bank will lend Johann the money if Johann can find someone to guarantee the loan. Johann asks his friend Antonio to act as guarantor. Antonio goes to the bank and gives his guarantee in writing, signing the guarantee. A few weeks later, Johann misses a payment installment. On default, the manager calls Antonio and tells him that the bank is looking to him to repay the loan and will be relying on the signed guarantee to enforce Antonio's obligation.

TABLE 4.2 Contracts That Must Be in Writing and Signed

Under the Ontario *Statute of Frauds*, certain types of contracts must be in writing and signed by the person to be bound:

- contracts by an executor of an estate to pay debts of the estate from personal funds (s. 4)
- contracts by a person to guarantee the debts of another or to be responsible for the tort obligations of another (s. 4)
- contracts for the sale of land or affecting any interest in land except for leases of less than three years (ss. 3 and 4)
- contracts made after attaining the age of majority to ratify debt obligations incurred as a minor (s. 7)

guarantee
a promise by a third party to pay the debt of another person if that person fails to pay the debt when it is due

guarantor
a third party who gives a guarantee to the creditor of another person

---

12. *Statute of Frauds*, R.S.O. 1990, c. S.19.

Assuming responsibility for a tort: If a third party promises to pay the damages that may be found to be owing by another person to a tort victim, the third party must give this promise in writing and sign the document if he or she is to be held liable for the torts of another. If there is no signed, written document, a mere oral promise is unenforceable.

Example of Assuming Responsibility for Another's Tort

Jocasta's son Oedipus drove his car into Tiresias's parked van. Jocasta, who owns the insurance policy on her son's car, does not want to pay a higher insurance premium as a result of the accident. She promises Tiresias that she will pay for the damage to his van out of her own pocket if he agrees not to notify the insurance company. Tiresias, having read this textbook, insists that she set out her promise in writing and place her signature on it so that he can enforce the agreement if she tries to back out of it.

Contracts for the Sale of Land or That Affect Any Interest in Land

Contracts in which one person gives an interest in land to another must be in writing under the terms of the Statute. In addition, in various jurisdictions in Canada, transfers of interests in land must meet other formality requirements, including the use of a prescribed form, seals, and other mandatory information.

The rules requiring written agreements for transfers of interests in land have given rise to two problems. First, the courts have had great difficulty in determining what kinds of agreements are concerned primarily with land and nothing else. Second, where an agreement is unenforceable because it is not in writing, the courts have had to decide what remedies can be provided where one person performed his or her part of the bargain, relying on the agreement, and the other was using the technical requirements of the Statute to unfairly get out of the deal by getting the benefit of the other's part performance without having to do anything in return.

The English *Statute of Frauds* and most other statutes of frauds modelled after it (for example, the Ontario *Statute of Frauds*) contain vague wording with respect to the application of the legislation: the Ontario statute purports to apply to "any interest . . . concerning [land]";[13] this has caused great confusion in the case law. The courts have had to develop some principles by which they can sort claims into two categories: contracts that are concerned primarily with the sale of land or the transfer of some interest in land, and contracts that may have involved a transfer of an interest in land but are also concerned with other things. The Statute requires contracts that are concerned primarily with land transfers to be in writing to be enforceable; contracts that are about land but also about something else may not have to be in writing.

Example of a Contract Concerned with a Transfer of an Interest in Land

Cain promises to sell Canaan to Abel for $10. For Abel to enforce this agreement, it must be in writing and signed by Cain because it is primarily concerned with the transfer of an interest in land.

---

13. Ibid., s. 4.

Example of a Contract Concerned with a Transfer of an Interest in Land and Something Else

Vivaldi wishes to hire Offenbach to play in his orchestra. Vivaldi offers Offenbach a large salary and promises that if Offenbach stays with the orchestra Vivaldi will also transfer a parcel of land to him. The contract may not need to be in writing to be enforceable by Offenbach because it is primarily about something other than the transfer of a parcel of land.

Contracts Made After Attaining the Age of Majority to Ratify Debt Obligations Incurred as a Minor

If a minor incurs a debt before reaching the age of majority, and the debt is not related to necessities, the contract cannot be enforced against the minor once he or she has reached the age of majority unless the individual ratifies the contract in writing. The effect of minority status on contract enforcement is discussed below under the heading "Protecting Weaker Parties."

Technical Requirements for Written Contracts

The *Statute of Frauds* requires that an agreement be in writing. Whether required by the Statute or generally, the following considerations apply. A formal document drafted by lawyers is not necessarily required. The contract can consist of written notes on the back of a menu or on a restaurant tablecloth or an exchange of letters, faxes, or emails. Whatever the form, a written agreement, whether it is one document or several letters between the parties, should:

- identify the parties to the contract by name or by description;
- identify the terms of the contract, including the offer that has been accepted and the consideration to be given;
- be signed by the party whose promise is being enforced (it is not necessary to have other parties' signatures if the agreement is not being enforced against them); and
- include a printed or stamped signature, which may suffice in place of an actual signature. An actual signature is preferable if there is an issue about whether a party actually "signed" an agreement.

PRACTICE TIP

If you have to draft or review written contracts, keep a checklist like the one above, but customize it to your own specific requirements. Use it to see that all necessary elements are present.

Formal contracts (deeds) must be in writing and under seal, which means that the document should be signed by the persons being bound, with a gummed paper seal or a wax impression attached next to the signature. Drawing a circle next to the signature and labelling it "LS" (*locus sigilli* or "the place of the seal") is sufficient evidence that the document is meant to be under seal. It is also usual for the document to be signed by the person who witnessed the promisor signing and affixing the seal to the document.

Signatures are not legally required in theory, but are invariably present because seals are usually gummed and do not by themselves identify the person to be bound. When contract law was developing, seals were usually made by impressing a signet ring with a person's identifying sign or coat of arms into hot wax applied to the document. This is obviously no longer done, because most people do not have coats of arms, signet rings, or seals, or carry around hot wax.

PRACTICE TIP

Don't have a seal? Draw a circle on the page where the seal would be affixed, and write "LS" inside the circle. This may be evidence that the document was intended to be under seal. As an alternative, you can also write, where the seal would be affixed, "This document is, and is intended to be, under seal."

The existence of the seal indicates that the party signing the document intends to be bound by the agreement even when he or she receives no consideration from other parties, as in cases where the promisor is promising a gift to someone. This can be important if, as in tax cases, it matters that a conveyance of something is meant to be seen as a gift and not something else.

Must the seal be affixed for the contract to be enforceable? The fact that a person has gone to the trouble of affixing a seal is, in theory, evidence of serious intent, so that validity and enforceability arise from the solemn form of the agreement itself. In most cases, evidence that the document was intended to be sealed will suffice to make it a deed and have it enforced as if it were a deed. However, there are still cases where some evidence that seals were affixed (even if they later fell off) is required.

If a corporation or other legal "person" who is not an individual, such as a government department, is a signatory to a contract, it usually will execute an agreement using a corporate seal that identifies the corporation by name. Some statutes require that a signing officer of the corporation sign his or her name next to the seal. Often, the seal alone or the signature of a corporate officer is sufficient. Legislation governing business corporations in many jurisdictions no longer requires a corporation to have and use a seal.

affidavit of execution
a sworn statement in writing, signed by the witness to a contract, stating that the witness was present and saw the person signing the contract actually sign it; the affidavit can be used to prove that a party to a contract actually signed it

Generally, most contracts need not be witnessed unless there is some statutory requirement. But it is a good idea to have the signatures witnessed so that if proof of a signature on a contract is required it can be more readily obtained. For some deeds, witnesses are required, and an **affidavit of execution** by the witness may also be required in which the witness swears that he or she was present and saw the party sign the document. In this situation, the affidavit of execution itself becomes evidence that a party to the contract signed it.

PROTECTING WEAKER PARTIES

From the 17th century on, the development of modern contract law was driven by the needs of an expanding trading, manufacturing, and banking economy. These needs included a legal system that would enforce commercial agreements without interfering with the bargaining process that led to them. The common law met these needs by interpreting commercial agreements and enforcing them. The courts rarely inquired into the process that led to forming a contract; they assumed that in commercial agreements, business people were roughly equal in bargaining power and could look after themselves. If a party made a bad bargain because he or she was not as sharp or clever as the other party, that was his or her misfortune.

Although this "hands-off" approach is the one usually taken in contract law, the courts do sometimes intervene where parties are clearly unable to protect themselves in the bargaining process. This can occur because one party lacks the intellectual capacity to protect himself or herself, or the other party acts dishonestly during the bargaining process or takes advantage of a position of trust, or the other party has expert knowledge of the subject matter of the contract that the weaker party cannot have and takes unfair advantage of that knowledge. The sections that follow explore some of the circumstances in which the courts protect weaker parties where the capacity of a party to enter into a contract is at issue.

LEGAL CAPACITY TO CONTRACT

Not everyone is legally entitled to enter into contracts. Some persons, by their status, are presumed not to have the ability to enter into contracts or have limited rights to contract. The purpose here is to protect the weaker party from the stronger and more able party. This class of persons who lack or have limited capacity to contract includes **minors** and **persons under mental disability**.

MINORS

The general rule is that contracts with minors are not enforceable against the minor. At common law, a minor is an individual who is under 21 years of age. The common-law definition of age has been replaced by statutory definitions in most provinces and territories, where, as in Ontario, the age of majority is now 18 for the purposes of entering into contracts.[14] Because minors are presumed to be naive, inexperienced, and easily taken advantage of, some protection is required.

Contract Rights and Obligations Generally

While the general rule is that contracts with minors are not enforceable against minors, contracts for "necessaries of life" made by a minor are enforceable, but

minor
at common law, an individual under the age of 21; minority status has also been defined by statute law, lowering the age of majority to 18 or 19 in most provinces

persons under mental disability
a general term that includes persons who are delusional and insane so as to be a danger to themselves and others, and those who, while not insane and dangerous, lack the ability to manage their own affairs

---

14. In some provinces the age of majority is 19. There are also other statutes that grant rights on the basis of age. For example, an individual in Ontario can enter into contracts as someone of full age and capacity at 18 but cannot buy alcoholic beverages until the age of 19. See *Age of Majority and Accountability Act*, R.S.O. 1990, c. A.7.

other contracts are not *if* the minor repudiates them. The reason for enforcing contracts for necessaries is that some minors may have to meet some of their basic needs themselves. If a seller could not enforce a contract against a minor in these circumstances, the seller would have a disincentive to contract with minors, a situation that might hinder a minor's ability to purchase food or shelter.

A minor contracting for things that are *not* necessaries is another matter. When a minor makes a contract for something that is not a necessity, the law classifies the contract into one of two types:

- contracts that are void *ab initio*, or
- contracts that are voidable at the option of the minor.

Because minors may be taken advantage of, the law creates various opportunities for them to treat contracts for non-necessaries that provide some benefit as **voidable** by allowing minors to repudiate them, in some cases even after the age of majority has been reached. However, if the contract is prejudicial or of no benefit, it may be treated by the courts as **void *ab initio***, which means that the court will treat the contract as invalid from the beginning and of no force or effect. No rights can ever arise under such a contract, and the minor gets no choice as to whether it is enforceable against him or her.

If the contract is voidable, the minor may enforce it if he or she chooses, or repudiate it and recover money paid under it, or the minor may use it as a defence to enforcement by the other party. However, until the minor does what is required to treat the contract as voidable, unless the contract is void *ab initio*, it is presumed to be valid and enforceable.

voidable contract
a contract that may be avoided or declared void at the option of one party to the contract; once it is declared invalid no further rights can be obtained under it, but benefits obtained before the declaration are not forfeit

void *ab initio*
invalid from the beginning; no rights can arise under a contract that is void *ab initio*

Enforceable Contracts: Purchases of Necessaries

As in most provinces, the Ontario *Sale of Goods Act*[15] provides that a minor is liable to pay a reasonable price for goods that are necessaries that have been sold and delivered to the minor. Section 3(2) states that "necessaries" are "goods suitable to the conditions in life of the minor . . . at the time of the sale and delivery."

As to what goods are actually necessaries, the case law indicates that the context determines what is suitable given the minor's "conditions in life" or social and economic class. The necessaries for a minor from a wealthy family may be luxuries for a minor from a less wealthy family. How goods are used may also determine whether they are necessaries. If a minor buys clothes so that he or she will be "cool," they may be seen as non-necessaries, but if the minor buys clothes, even expensive ones, to be properly dressed at work, they may be classed as necessaries because they are used in connection with earning a living.

Even where a contract is binding because it is for necessaries, the law will not make the minor pay more than a reasonable price. Thus, a merchant suing a minor on a contract for necessaries may find recovery of the purchase price limited to what the court thinks is a reasonable price.

---

15. *Sale of Goods Act*, R.S.O. 1990, c. S.1.

It is also clear that contracts for necessary services are binding on a minor. Medical and dental services and, in some cases, contracts for training for employment have been classed as necessaries.

Example of Contracts for Necessaries

Tamar, aged 17, moves into a dormitory at school because she is far from home. She signs a rental contract. She also decides to rent a TV. A month later, Tamar decides to move back home and tries to repudiate both contracts. She may be held to the dorm rental contract, since this was for necessary services. The TV is arguably not a necessary; she may be able to avoid this contract by pleading her minority status and get her money back and be relieved of future rental charges. She will also have to return the TV.

Enforceable Contracts: Employment

Generally, minors who enter into employment contracts, formal or informal, are bound by their terms unless the terms are not beneficial to the minor. Presumably, minors accept employment to meet their needs, so an employment contract could be viewed as a contract for necessaries. However, just as an article of clothing can be a luxury or a necessity, depending on what it is for, a job can also be classed that way. A minor who works because his or her needs would not be met otherwise is in a different position from a minor who works to acquire spending money for luxuries. However, the case law does not focus on whether work is a necessity; rather, it accepts a service contract as enforceable by both parties unless the contract does not benefit the minor. "Benefit" has been held by the courts to include

CASE IN POINT

When Is a Waistcoat an Extravagance?

From: *Nash v. Inman*, [1908] 2 K.B. 1 (C.A.).

An action was brought by a tailor for clothes supplied to the defendant while the latter was an undergraduate at Cambridge University. The defendant was a minor at the time of the sale and delivery of the goods. He was the son of well-to-do parents. The clothing supplied included, among other things, 11 expensive waistcoats. The only evidence for the plaintiff was that of its travelling salesperson—that he visited Cambridge to solicit business and had heard that the defendant was a big spender. The plaintiff rested his claim on the grounds that the defendant was a minor and that the goods were necessaries. The defendant argued that there was no evidence that the goods were necessaries, in which case the contract could not be enforced against him. The judge agreed and dismissed the case. The plaintiff appealed. The Court of Appeal held that the defendant had proved both his minority status and that the purchases were extravagant in the circumstances; therefore, the contract could hardly be described as one for the purchase of necessaries.

an appropriate salary, but also may include consideration of whether there was a general advantage for the minor in acquiring skills and satisfying aims or desires, and whether the minor was taken advantage of. It has also been suggested that the test of "benefit" may be whether a "prudent and informed parent" would have approved this contract for his or her minor child.[16]

> ### Example of Minors' Employment Contracts
>
> Arturo, aged 16, is hired to work in a factory. He is paid less than the minimum wage and has to sign a form that he will not make a workers' compensation claim if he is injured on the job. He quits without notice and repudiates the contract. The employer will have difficulty enforcing the contract because these conditions appear to be detrimental to Arturo, and a prudent and informed parent would not likely permit a child to work under these conditions.

CASE IN POINT

No Benefit, No Contract

From: *Toronto Marlboro Major Junior "A" Hockey Club et al. v. Tonelli et al.* (1979), 23 O.R. (2d) 193 (C.A.).

John Tonelli was a young hockey player of exceptional ability. When he was 17 he entered into a contract with the Toronto Marlboro Junior A Hockey Club (the Marlies), an amateur club from which professional hockey players were normally recruited. Tonelli agreed to play hockey only for the Marlies for a period of three or, at the plaintiff's option, four years for minimal salary and to pay to the plaintiff 20 percent of his earnings during his first three years as a professional hockey player. The contract contained other terms highly unfavourable to Tonelli. On attaining the age of 18, Tonelli repudiated the agreement and entered into an agreement with a professional hockey club in Houston, Texas at a professional's salary. An action for damages against Tonelli for breach of the contract and against Tonelli's agent for breach of contract was dismissed on the ground that the contract, not being on the whole beneficial to Tonelli, was voidable at his option. On appeal by the Marlies club to the Ontario Court of Appeal, Zuber J.A., dissenting, held that the appeal should be dismissed.

Justices Arnup and Blair said that a contract of service is enforceable against a minor only if it was for his or her benefit when made, the onus being on the adult party to establish the benefit. In the circumstances, considering Tonelli's exceptional ability and the terms of the contract, it could not be said that the contract was beneficial; in fact, it could be considered very onerous and one-sided. Consequently, Tonelli could not be liable.

Mr. Justice Zuber, dissenting, said that the test should be whether a prudent and informed parent would approve the minor's contract. In this case, a parent would have done so because the alternative was exclusion from the junior league, which would not have been in Tonelli's best long-term professional interest.

---

16. *Toronto Marlboro Major Junior "A" Hockey Club et al. v. Tonelli et al.* (1979), 23 O.R. (2d) 193 (C.A.).

Contracts for Non-Necessaries

When a minor has entered into a contract for non-necessaries, the contract is always enforceable by the minor, but the minor may be able to avoid enforcement of the contract against him or her in some circumstances.

If the contract is not fully executed, the minor may avoid the contract. If the minor as a buyer repudiates the contract, he or she must return the goods, whatever state they are in. He or she will not be liable for the wear and tear to the goods but may be liable for damage to them that goes beyond reasonable wear and tear. If the minor is the seller, he or she must be able to return the money if the minor wishes to repudiate and have the goods returned to him or her.

If the contract for non-necessaries has been fully executed so that goods and money have changed hands, the contract cannot be set aside. However, the court may order a refund to the minor of the difference between the price actually paid and a court-determined price, as would be the case for necessaries.

If the contract is ongoing, as, for example, if the minor joined a monthly CD or book club, he or she can repudiate any future liability but cannot recover money spent for benefits already received.

If the creditor has loaned money for non-necessaries to a minor, the creditor cannot recover the debt if the minor chooses not to pay.

Effect of Reaching the Age of Majority on Minors' Contracts

Where a contract is for necessaries, the liability continues. However, if the contract is for non-necessaries and has not been repudiated by the minor during his or her minority, the contract has to be classified as to type. For this purpose there are two types:

1. *Contracts for non-necessaries that are valid unless the minor repudiates them.* These are contracts that confer ongoing or continuous benefits that are made while an individual is a minor and which carry on after the age of majority has been reached. The contract will continue to bind the individual unless he or she, before or shortly after reaching the age of majority, does something that constitutes repudiation of the agreement.

2. *Contracts for non-necessaries that are invalid unless ratified by the minor.* These are contracts that confer a one-time benefit, for example, where goods are ordered while the individual is a minor but are not to be delivered to complete contract performance until the minor has reached the age of majority. These contracts must be ratified in writing by the minor during his or her minority or shortly thereafter. If the minor does not ratify the contract, the seller must return the deposit. These two types of contracts are discussed below.

Voidable Ongoing Benefit Contracts for Non-Necessaries: Valid Unless Repudiated

Where a minor acquires by contract permanent property that carries some obligations for the minor, the contract is presumed to be valid and enforceable unless the minor repudiates it during his or her minority or shortly after reaching the age of majority. "Shortly after" appears to be measured in weeks or months rather than years.[17] The classes of contracts affected are contracts that transfer shares to a minor, partnership agreements, and marriage contracts. If the minor, after reaching the age of majority, acts to accept the contract, he or she cannot repudiate it.[18] If he or she does repudiate it, no special form of repudiation is required.[19] It can be written, oral, or inferred from an act. Repudiation is an all-or-nothing affair: the minor cannot repudiate the non-beneficial parts of the contract and hold the other party to the rest of the agreement.[20]

Table 4.3 lists the consequences of repudiation.

Example of a Contract That Is Valid Until Repudiated

Luc bought 80 shares in a private company when he was a minor. He paid $8,000, and a further $2,000 is due when he is 22 years old. Two days after reaching the age of majority, Luc considers repudiating the contract. Luc would be able to repudiate this contract because it is in a contract category—share transfers—that permits repudiation while he is a minor or shortly thereafter; two days is certainly "shortly thereafter." However, suppose that a dividend cheque arrives that same day and he cashes it. Because Luc has engaged in an act that affirms his acceptance of the contract by cashing the dividend cheque, he may now be barred from repudiating the contract.

TABLE 4.3   Consequences of Repudiation by a Minor

- Contracts are enforceable and effective until they are repudiated.
- The minor, on repudiating the contract, is relieved of future obligations and accrued but undischarged obligations.
- Money paid by the minor before repudiation may not be recoverable if the adult party performed his or her obligations under the contract before repudiation by the minor.
- The minor may recover property such as goods after repudiation if the goods have not been consumed and can be restored to the minor.

Voidable One-Time Benefit Contracts for Non-Necessaries: Void Unless Ratified

All other contracts for non-necessaries made by a minor must be ratified when the minor reaches the age of majority or they cease to be valid and enforceable. Such contracts for non-necessaries can also be repudiated by the minor before reaching the age of majority, but are presumed valid unless challenged. Their validity ceases on the age of majority being reached unless they are ratified. In Canada, the ratification must be in writing and signed by the minor.

17. *Foley v. Canada Permanent Loan and Savings Society* (1883), 4 O.R. 38; *Whalls v. Learn* (1888), 15 O.R. 481 (D.C.).
18. *In the Matter of Prudential Life Insurance Co.: Re Paterson*, [1918] 1 W.W.R. 105 (Man. S.C.).
19. *Butterfield v. Sibbit and Nipissing Elec. Supply Co.* (1950), 4 D.L.R. 302 (Ont. H.C.).
20. *Henderson v. Minneapolis Steel & Machinery Co.*, [1930] 3 W.W.R. 613, [1931] 1 D.L.R. 570 (Alta. S.C.).

Table 4.4 lists the consequences of invalidation through failure to ratify.

Example of a Contract That Must Be Ratified to Be Valid

Michelle, aged 17, decides to buy a sailboat. She pays $10,000 as a first installment and will pay the balance in June of next year. She will be 18 in April of next year. Michelle decides she does not want the sailboat and refuses to ratify the contract when she turns 18. Because she must ratify the contract and the sailboat is not a necessary, the contract ceases to be enforceable by the seller and is now void. Michelle is entitled to get her money back because the seller can be restored to his or her previous position.

Void Contracts

In Canada, some minors' contracts have been held to be void *ab initio*. Some cases have held that a contract that is not beneficial is void without the minors having to do anything. The better view is that in order to fall under the void *ab initio* category, a contract has to be more than "not beneficial"—it would have to be clearly prejudicial or harmful, which is a more stringent requirement for holding a contract to be void.

Table 4.5 lists the consequences of void contracts.

Example of Contract Void ab Initio

Henry is a wealthy minor. He is prevailed upon by his cousin Anna to lend her a large sum of money at a very low rate of interest. Anna has been bankrupt three times and is clearly a poor credit risk. Because the interest is unreasonably low and the risk of loss of the money is very high, the contract would be prejudicial to Henry, and it is arguably void *ab initio*.

TABLE 4.4   Consequences of Invalidation Through Minor's Failure to Ratify

- Prior to validation, the minor can enforce the contract against the adult, but not vice versa.
- A third party cannot rely on the invalidity of a contract to escape liability. For example, an adult who agrees to indemnify another for a minor's debt is still bound even if the minor fails to validate the contract by ratifying it.
- If the minor does not ratify, he or she is not liable for future accrued liabilities under the contract.
- If the minor does not ratify, money can be recovered, provided that the minor can restore the adult to his or her pre-contract position. If the minor has paid in part for goods and then refuses to ratify, he or she must return the goods and may lose the deposit, although he or she may recover other moneys paid.

TABLE 4.5   Consequences of Void Minors' Contracts

- The minor is entitled, not being bound, to have all of his or her money or property returned.
- The adult need not be restored to his or her pre-contract position.

PRACTICE TIP

A practical approach for an adult who contracts with a minor is to find another adult to be jointly liable with the minor for the contractual liability. It is not a good idea to have an adult guarantee the obligation as a secondary debtor, because if the minor's contract is made void, the liability on the guarantee is also void, although an agreement by an adult to indemnify a person who contracts with the minor may survive if the minor's contract is found to be void.

Law Affecting Minors in British Columbia

The law affecting minors in British Columbia is somewhat different from the law in other common-law provinces and Quebec. It is summarized as follows.

A minor's contract is unenforceable against the minor unless one of these conditions is met:

- The contract is enforceable under some statute.
- The minor validates the contract on attaining the age of majority.
- The minor wholly or partly performs the contract shortly after attaining the age of majority.
- The contract is not repudiated by the minor within a year of having attained the age of majority.

Where a contract is invalid, the court has broad discretion to provide remedies and may discharge parties from contractual obligations or order restitution or compensation.

CASE IN POINT

No Legal Obligation to Pay?

From: *R. v. Rash* (1923), 53 O.L.R. 245 (C.A.).

The defendant, a minor, was tried under what was then s. 417 of the *Criminal Code* with defrauding his creditors by concealing, removing, or disposing of property. The defendant, while a minor, had purchased groceries at wholesale with the intent of selling them at retail. The argument of the defendant was that he was a minor when he committed the offence, so he could not be found guilty even though he had disposed of his wholesale stocks without paying his creditors.

The magistrate convicted the defendant. On appeal, the Court of Appeal held that the conviction should be set aside. The defendant, as a minor, was under no legal obligation to pay his creditors. During his minority they had no enforceable claim against him and, upon attaining his majority, he had the legal right to repudiate liability, which he did by refusing to pay. Therefore, those who sold him the groceries were not his "creditors" within the meaning of s. 417. The conviction was quashed.

CAPACITY OF PARTIES UNDER IMPAIRMENT AND PERSONS UNDER MENTAL DISABILITY TO CONTRACT

Drunkenness

The law will intervene in some circumstances where someone who is intoxicated enters into an agreement. Intoxication alone is not sufficient, but can be a defence to enforcement by the sober party. The intoxicated party may void the contract on the basis of his or her own intoxication in the following circumstances:

- The intoxicated party, because of the intoxication, did not know what he or she was doing.
- The sober party was aware of the intoxicated state of the other party.
- Upon becoming sober, the intoxicated party moved promptly to repudiate the contract.

The basis for this approach is not that one party is drunk but that the other party might defraud the drunkard. Thus, even where the sober party is not aware of the intoxicated state of the other party, if there is evidence of intoxication so that it may be presumed, the unfairness or one-sidedness of a contract might result in its being voided. This view moves the law toward a position that an unconscionable or markedly unfair agreement permits the court to presume that the sober party had knowledge of the intoxication of the other party where there is evidence of intoxication.

Example of Repudiation for Drunkenness

Melissa has had so much to drink that she cannot stand, her words are slurred, and her conversation makes little sense. Semareh has an old sofa she would like to get rid of. She persuades Melissa to buy the sofa for a price that is almost the price of a new sofa. Melissa sobers up the next morning, realizes what she has done, and calls Semareh to tell her the deal is off. Melissa was clearly very drunk; it would have been hard for Semareh to be unaware of that.

It is doubtful that Melissa was coherent enough to know what she was doing when she bought the sofa. Melissa repudiates at the first reasonable opportunity once she sobers up. She will probably succeed in repudiating the contract.

CASE IN POINT

A Sober Awakening?

From: *Bennet v. Latitude 49 Developments Ltd.*, 1999 CanLII 6513 (B.C.S.C.).

Jack Bangay and his wife were joint shareholders of a company. The company ran a pub that the plaintiffs wished to purchase. The sale documents were for the sale of assets: the pub, its stock in trade, and so on. Bangay maintained that his instructions were to sell the shares, not the assets. When the sale of assets was completed, Bangay attempted to repudiate the sale on the basis of his own intoxication.

The court found that Bangay was indeed an alcoholic with a serious drinking problem. There was evidence, including that of his wife, that when he was drinking, he was very good at concealing its effects so that a stranger might not know that he was intoxicated. The court also noted that the documents for the sale were very clearly for the sale of the pub as an asset and not for the sale of shares.

The plaintiffs' evidence was that the contract was regular on its face as to its terms and that there was no evidence that Bangay was intoxicated when the deal was finally completed. Further, there was ample time beforehand to examine the sale documents.

In the circumstances, the court determined that even if Bangay was intoxicated, the other party could not reasonably have been aware that he was. In all of the circumstances the contract was valid and enforceable.

PRACTICE TIP

If you think there might be an issue of intoxication by one of the parties to an agreement, it is a good idea to meet with the party, observe his or her demeanour, go over the terms and provisions, and then attend to formally signing the contract. Avoid using email or other electronic means to sign the contract. You or another person should take notes on observing the party to rebut possible claims of intoxication as a ground for repudiation. If the party does appear to be intoxicated, it is wise not to proceed with signing the contract at that time.

Mental Disability

Some types of mental disability may be sufficient to allow a person to repudiate a contract in certain circumstances. Generally, the law is concerned with the lack of capacity arising from mental disability. For example, people who have schizophrenia may have delusions, but if they can manage their own daily and business affairs and look after their personal finances, they may have the capacity to enter into some contracts. The mentally disabled persons that the law protects are those who are unable to manage their own affairs or are unable to appreciate the nature and consequences of their actions.

The law deals in the following ways with those who are unable to manage their own affairs:

- Provincial legislation provides that a person can be declared unable to manage his or her affairs. If there has been such a judicial finding, contracts made thereafter are void on the ground that there is a lack of capacity to consent to the provisions of a contract. Contracts made prior to the finding may be voidable, as noted below.
- If a person lacks capacity because he or she is unable to handle his or her affairs, but there has been no judicial finding, the contracts made are voidable at the option of the person who is mentally disabled. If the contracts are not repudiated, they are presumed to be enforceable.

As is the case with drunkenness, for repudiation to succeed where no judicial finding of incapacity has been made, the other party must know of the mental disability. There need not be actual knowledge if there is wilful disregard of the surrounding circumstances from which the mental state could be presumed. Thus, if the non-disabled party suspects from the other's conduct that the other might lack capacity due to mental disability, that may be sufficient knowledge.

The fairness of the contract is also important because there must be evidence that the contract is fair to the mentally disabled party. Some cases go on to require that the contract be unconscionable to be voidable, although that view has been rejected in Canada and England. It follows that if the contract is fair, or the other party is unaware of a mental disability that affects capacity, then the contract is enforceable and not voidable by the person who is mentally disabled.

As with minors, persons with a mental disability are liable to pay a reasonable price for necessaries, and contracts for necessaries cannot be repudiated.

Examples of Mental Disability as a Ground for Avoiding a Contract

- François has been diagnosed with Alzheimer's disease and has been found by a court to be incompetent to handle his own business affairs. After this finding, François contracts to have aluminum siding installed on his house. His brother finds out and tells the contractor. The contractor has no right to proceed, because a contract made by a person found by a court to be incompetent is void *ab initio*.
- François's brother also discovers that François had contracted to have aluminum siding installed by another contractor two weeks before being found incompetent by the court. François has memory problems that are obvious to a casual observer, but the terms of the contract are reasonable. Because the contractor has not taken advantage of François, this contract may be difficult to repudiate. However, if there is already new or adequate aluminum siding on the house, François (through his brother) may be able to argue that the contract is unfair because it is unnecessary, and that, on the whole, the contract is inequitable.

CASE IN POINT

Lack of Capacity, but Dismissal with Cause

From: *Elliott v. Parksville (City)* (1990), 66 D.L.R. (4th) 107, 29 C.C.E.L. 263 (B.C.C.A.).

This was an appeal to the Supreme Court of British Columbia from a decision dismissing an action for wrongful dismissal. Ms. Elliott had been the municipal clerk, having risen through the ranks of municipal employees. She sent two contradictory letters to the municipal council, one resigning her position and a second asking to go on sick leave. There was a known history of mental illness and evidence that she was mentally ill when she sent both letters. The council accepted Elliott's resignation and offered her three months' sick leave. Her work record to this point had been less than satisfactory: she had been late, failed to perform duties as assigned, been insubordinate, had a negative impact on other staff, and had given herself an unauthorized salary increase. She had been told of these deficiencies, and the council considered them when accepting her letter of resignation.

At trial, the judge found that the letters were of no force and effect because the appellant lacked capacity, but she had been properly dismissed for cause. The trial judge's decision was upheld by the appellate court.

PRACTICE TIP

As with parties who may be intoxicated during the formation of a contract, it is wise to deal with anyone who you suspect might be mentally incapacitated in person. If you discover this to be the case, you may inquire whether there is someone who holds power of attorney with authority to enter into a contract with the grantor (the incapacitated person), or whether there is a court order appointing a guardian. If so, you can deal with the guardian or person granted power of attorney (usually referred to as "the attorney," although this does not mean the person is or has to be a lawyer).

CHAPTER SUMMARY

This chapter discussed three issues that can affect the validity of contracts: legality, the presence (or absence) of contract formalities, and the issue of the parties' capacity to contract.

Legality

In order for a contract to be valid, it must not have an unlawful or illegal purpose. A contract with an unlawful or illegal purpose is void (unenforceable) at law.

Although courts will not enforce an unlawful contract, they will in some cases order that the parties be returned to their original positions (for example, by ordering money paid to be returned). If the contract is illegal, however, the courts will not make any attempt to "undo" the breached contract. Apart from contracts that have a purpose that is criminal or obviously immoral (which are illegal), the distinction between an unlawful and an illegal contract is not always obvious. Where a contract is prohibited by statute, the statute will sometimes identify the contract as illegal and void, or as merely void.

The two main ways in which a contract can be unlawful or illegal are (1) by violating the provisions of a statute or (2) by being contrary to public policy. An example of a contract that is unlawful because it violates statute law is a contract between an employer and employee through which the employee promises (perhaps in exchange for a settlement) not to exercise his or her rights under the Ontario *Workplace Safety and Insurance Act, 1997*. An example of a contract that is illegal because it is contrary to public policy is a contract offering a bribe to a public official in exchange for a special privilege that would not otherwise be granted.

Formalities

Contracts can be grouped into two categories: simple contracts and formal contracts. Formal contracts, also called deeds, are in writing and under seal. Simple contracts may be oral or in writing but they are not formal contracts, usually because they are not under seal. Although many oral contracts are enforceable, some contracts must be in writing and in some cases must be under seal as well.

An example of a contract that must be under seal is a contract that promises a benefit without requiring consideration in return (a gratuitous contract). If not under seal, such a contract is not enforceable; however, if made under seal, the contract can be enforced despite the lack of the normally essential requirement of consideration.

The Ontario *Statute of Frauds* requires that certain contracts involving estate debts, guarantees for third parties, and the transfer of interests in land be in writing. To prevent rigid and unfair application of this rule, which requires written contracts, the courts have developed some exceptions where there has been part performance by one party.

Capacity

Although the courts normally do not interfere with the rights of parties to contract, they will in some circumstances intervene to protect a weaker party from a stronger one where it is likely that one side will extract an unfair advantage from the other.

Some parties to a contract are protected on the basis of their status. Protective rules apply to minors, drunkards, and persons with a mental disability. Minors can be held to contracts for necessaries and to beneficial employment contracts. In most instances, contracts for non-necessaries may not be enforced against minors. If the minor accepts the contract and does not repudiate it during his or her minority, the minor may be able to repudiate the contract on reaching the age of majority. In some cases, the contract must be positively ratified or affirmed by the minor on reaching the age of majority. A minor's contract that is prejudicial or harmful may be void *ab initio*.

In the case of drunkards, if intoxication results in the drunkard's not knowing what he or she was doing, but the other party knew it and, on becoming sober, the intoxicated party moves to repudiate the contract, a court may well set the contract aside because of diminished capacity.

In the case of those who have a mental disability, a person found by a court to lack mental capacity is unable to enter into valid contracts except for necessaries; contracts for non-necessaries are void. When the person suffers from a mental disability but has not been so declared by a court, and if the other party to the contract knew or ought to have known of the disability, the mentally disabled party may be able to avoid the contract.

KEY TERMS

affidavit of execution

formal contract

guarantee

guarantor

minor

persons under mental disability

restraint of trade

restrictive covenant

simple contract

void *ab initio*

voidable contract

REVIEW QUESTIONS

True or False?

_____ 1. Ali, aged 15, bought an expensive snowboard, paid for it, and had it delivered. As a minor he can repudiate this contract.

_____ 2. If a contract for non-necessaries made by a minor is not repudiated at or about the time the age of majority is reached, the contract continues in force and is valid.

_____ 3. Every contract that has an unlawful purpose is also illegal.

_____ 4. When its terms are reasonable, a restrictive covenant may be enforceable.

_____ 5. A contract that is made without consideration can be enforceable if it is in the form of a deed.

_____ 6. If a contract is meant to be under seal but the seal has fallen off, the contract will be unenforceable.

_____ 7. All contracts by minors are either void or voidable.

_____ 8. A simple contract can be either oral or in writing.

_____ 9. There are no circumstances whatsoever under which a court will allow a party a remedy under an illegal contract.

_____ 10. Even where a contract is binding on a minor, the minor will never be required, by a court, to pay more than a reasonable price.

Fill in the Blanks

1. By signing a _____, a third party can assume legal responsibility for the obligations of one of the parties to a contract should that party fail to meet his obligations. The third party is known as a _____.

2. The age under which a person is considered a _____ can vary by jurisdiction and by contract purpose.

3. A contract that is written, witnessed, and under seal may be described as a _____ contract.

4. A contract between pork producers by which each signatory agrees not to sell pork below a stated price per pound may be invalid because it is a contract in _____ ____ _____.

5. A contract that is void ____ _____ is void from the moment it is made and can never be rendered valid.

6. Where one or both parties to a contract have the option to challenge its validity due to a defect (but could also choose to honour the contract and have a court enforce it), the contract is said to be _____.

7. A _____ is a formal contract that contains a promise without consideration (for example, a gift).

8. A restrictive _____ can be used to restrict the commercial activities of another party—for example, to prevent a former employee from soliciting the clients of his or her former employer after being fired.

9. The legislation that first prescribed formalities for certain kinds of contracts was called the *Statute* ____ _____.

10. A minor can _____ a contract that would otherwise have been voidable by discharging his or her obligations under it after reaching the age of majority.

Short Answer

1. What is the difference between a contract that has an unlawful purpose and a contract that is illegal?
2. Describe two instances where a contract would be void for violating a statute.
3. Describe two instances where a contract would be void for violating public policy.
4. What is a restrictive covenant?
5. What are the formality requirements for a contract that is a deed?
6. What kinds of contracts does the Ontario *Statute of Frauds* require to be in writing and signed by the parties to be enforceable?
7. Is it a good idea to have a signed contract witnessed? Why or why not?
8. What does the phrase "inequality of bargaining power" mean?
9. In what circumstances can a minor's contract be repudiated if it is not for necessaries and not an employment contract?
10. What are the consequences of repudiating a minor's contract?

EXERCISES

1. Viktor owns a movie theatre that shows unusual and little-known movies. He wants to generate publicity to attract audiences to a movie he is showing that is particularly violent and frightening. He enters into a contract with Louise whereby Louise will come to his theatre and pretend to faint during the movie. She is then to sue him, claiming damages for nervous shock and stress. Viktor agrees to pay her expenses for the lawsuit and an additional $5,000. Louise fulfills her part of the contract. The lawsuit is well publicized, and even though Louise loses her lawsuit, people flock to see the movie in droves. Viktor never pays Louise the $5,000. Can she enforce this contract? Explain.

2. Maupassant Developments obtained planning permission to build a subdivision in Boresville in 1990. As part of the permission process, Maupassant promised to set aside some of the land as parkland or to pay green-space fees to the municipality. This document was required by provincial legislation to be by way of a formal deed. In 2000, the

municipality of Boresville discovered that Maupassant had neither set aside parkland nor paid the green-space fees. The typed document was sealed by the municipality with its municipal seal. Maupassant's name was typed in, but there is no evidence that a seal was ever applied or that he signed it. What is the likelihood of the municipality's being able to enforce this agreement?

3. Greta is 17 and lives with her mother, who does not earn much money. Greta needs to work part time to contribute to the family income while going to school. She gets a job in an office as a receptionist. Because she has few clothes suitable for business purposes, she buys several suits to wear to work. She buys them on sale and gets a good price. After bringing them home, Greta decides she wants to return some of them. The seller says they were sold on sale with no right of return. Can Greta argue her minority status and repudiate this agreement?

4. How can adults who wish to contract with minors protect themselves from repudiation of a contract by a minor? What will work? What will not work?

5. Compare and contrast the rights of drunkards and minors to repudiate contracts. How are their rights similar? How are they different? Do the differences in approach make sense to you? Why or why not?

6. Read the Court of Appeal decision in *Toronto Marlboro Major Junior "A" Hockey Club et al. v. Tonelli et al.* (Case in Point, page 74). Compare the approaches of the majority with that of the dissent by Mr. Justice Zuber. What is the standard adopted by the majority and the minority to "test" a minor's employment contract? Are the differences, if any, significant? Which do you prefer and why?

Contractual Defects

5

OVERVIEW

LEARNING OUTCOMES

After completing this chapter, you should be able to:

- Define "contractual defect" and list at least three examples.

- Explain the distinction between an innocent and a fraudulent misrepresentation.

- Understand which defects render a contract void (void *ab initio*) and which render it merely voidable.

- Distinguish between duress and undue influence.

- Explain what is meant by "unconscionability" in the context of transactions.

- Describe the consequences of various kinds of mistakes on the part of contract parties.

INTRODUCTION

A contractual defect is a defect in one of the elements of a valid contract. In some cases, the contractual defect renders the contract void *ab initio*; in other cases, it renders it voidable. This chapter discusses misrepresentation, duress, undue influence, unconscionability, and mistake—factors that can affect the parties' intention to create a legal contract.

MISREPRESENTATION

Overview

A misrepresentation is a false statement that induces someone to enter into a contract. It is generally part of the bargaining process. For example, you are considering ordering a carload of tomatoes and while you examine them you ask the seller, "Are these grade A tomatoes?" and the seller replies "Yes," then the "Yes" may be a statement made to induce you to enter into the contract. If you enter into the contract because of the answer, then the inducement is a **material inducement**. If the statement is false and the seller is not aware that it is false, it is an **innocent misrepresentation**. If the statement is false and the seller knows it is false, it is a **fraudulent misrepresentation**. If you are aware that the statement is a misrepresentation and enter into the contract anyway, or you are not influenced by the statement to enter into the agreement but do so for other reasons, then you may not **rescind** the contract because of the false statement because you were not induced by it to enter into the contract.

If the misrepresentation induces you to enter into the agreement but it is not related to a material fact that goes to the heart of the contract, then you may not rely on the misrepresentation to rescind the contract. For example, the seller says, "Tomatoes are necessary for health." This general statement about tomatoes may be a misrepresentation (you can enjoy good health and never eat a tomato), but it is not the kind of statement that has anything directly to do with material concerns that affect buying a carload of tomatoes. For an innocent misrepresentation to be material, it must result in a substantial difference between what the party bargained for and what the party obtained from the contract (see, for example, *Alberta North West Lumber Co. v. Lewis*;[1] *Kennedy v. Royal Mail Co. of Panama*[2]).

Usually, failing to say anything does not give rise to rescission. If you ask the seller, "Are these grade A tomatoes?" and the seller says nothing, and the tomatoes turn out not to be grade A, there is no misrepresentation, particularly if you could look at the tomatoes and decide for yourself. However, if the seller has special information that you could not reasonably know, his or her omission may amount to a misrepresentation. Some statutes, in particular those protecting consumers from sophisticated sellers, also permit rescission for an omission by a seller that amounts to a material misrepresentation.

material inducement
a statement made before a contract is struck that influences a party to enter into the contract

innocent misrepresentation
a false statement that the maker of the statement does not know is false, made to induce a party to enter into a contract

fraudulent misrepresentation
a false statement that the maker knows is false, made to induce a party to enter into a contract

rescission
the cancellation, nullification, or revocation of a contract; the "unmaking" of a contract

---

1. *Alberta North West Lumber Co. v. Lewis*, [1917] 3 W.W.R. 1007.
2. *Kennedy v. Royal Mail Co. of Panama* (1867), L.R. 2 Q.B. 580.

A statement that is a misrepresentation must be a statement of fact, not an opinion. The words themselves do not always make it easy to decide whether a statement is a fact or statement of opinion. In our example, the seller's answer "Yes" to a question could be seen as a statement. However, if the seller had instead said, "I *think* these are grade A tomatoes," this would be his or her opinion and no more than that. The cases indicate that an opinion is not seen as sufficient to induce you to enter into a contract, because it lacks the certainty and emphasis of a statement. This may be an impractical and illogical distinction, because the opinion of a knowledgeable seller, though a misrepresentation, might very well induce you to enter into a contract.

A material misrepresentation does not make a contract void *ab initio*. It will make the contract voidable by the party who was misled by the misrepresentation (or material omission). Once the misrepresentation is discovered, the misled party should act as soon as possible to rescind the contract. In doing so, he or she must accept no further benefits under the contract, or he or she may be deemed to have affirmed the contract (demonstrated acceptance of it) despite the misrepresentation and, by doing so, have waived (given up) the right of rescission.

A misrepresentation may not only induce you to enter into a contract; it may also become a term of the contract. For example, the seller may not only make a misrepresentation that the tomatoes are grade A; he or she may also make it a term of the contract by describing the tomatoes as being grade A. In this case, the contract is not subject to rescission for misrepresentation, but is subject to an action for breach of contract because the tomatoes described and promised to you do not meet the description in the contract itself.

Innocent Misrepresentation

Innocent misrepresentation is the misrepresentation of a material fact that the person making it believes to be true, but which is discovered to be false after the contract has been made. If the innocent party can show that he or she was induced by the statement to enter into the contract and that the statement was material, he or she may ask for the equitable remedy of rescission (remedies are discussed in greater detail in Chapter 8). At common law, the party who has suffered a loss cannot obtain a remedy unless the untrue statement can be construed as a term of the contract or the untrue statement was made negligently. If it is a term of the contract, then the victim can sue for breach of what is a perfectly valid contract and obtain damages for whatever losses he or she sustained. If the false statement was negligently made, though the maker thought it was true then, although there is no contractual remedy at common law, the innocent party could sue the other party for negligent misrepresentation in tort, in which case the maker of the statement would be liable for all the foreseeable damage actually sustained. Tort law—including the law of negligence and the specific tort of negligent misrepresentation—is the subject of Part II of this text.

The common law, then, leaves the victim of a "pure" innocent misrepresentation without a remedy. However, the doctrine of equity—a special branch of our law designed to promote fairness by creating exceptions to the unfair application of the strict rules of common law—provides relief in this situation. (For a fuller discussion of equitable principles, see below.) The victim of a pure misrepresentation may request the equitable remedy of rescission. Rescission does not include an award of damages for the victim's losses; it does, however, revoke a voidable contract at the instance of the injured party and, as far as possible, restores the parties to their pre-contract positions. Doing this may mean that the party who suffered the loss may receive his or her money back, but other consequential damages (for example, in a contract for manufacturing supplies, the loss of an opportunity to fill an important order), even in equity, cannot be recovered. This means that of the three types of innocent misrepresentation, the pure type may lead to something less than full recovery of all of the losses causally connected to the contract. Consequently, it is important to classify the innocent misrepresentation further because of the different remedies available.

- An innocent misrepresentation that can be classified as a term of the contract can give rise to an action for breach of the term of the contract.
- An innocent misrepresentation that is made negligently can give rise to an action in tort for negligent misrepresentation.
- An innocent misrepresentation that is classified as "pure" will give rise to revocation of the contract and some indemnification to restore the injured party as much as possible to his or her pre-contract position. This remedy is referred to as **restitution**.

restitution
a remedy by which one seeks to rescind a contract; if granted, restitution restores the party, as far as possible, to a pre-contract position

Examples of Innocent Misrepresentation

- Eduardo wants to buy a vacant lot on which to build a warehouse. He asks Marlene, the seller, if the lot is zoned for a warehouse. Marlene asks the municipality and is told the land is zoned for a warehouse. She tells Eduardo this. Eduardo agrees to purchase the vacant land at an agreed price. After the contract is made but before the property is transferred to Eduardo, Marlene discovers that since she inquired, the city has changed the zoning to residential use only. She tells Eduardo, who states that he is rescinding the contract. In this case, Eduardo wanted to buy vacant land and he obtained it, but the statement about the zoning was a material inducement considering what he wanted to do with the land. The statement probably is not a term of the contract because the sale was for land, not for land zoned commercial. However, as he probably would not have bought the land if the zoning did not meet his needs, it is arguable that Marlene's statement is a "pure" misrepresentation (it is not a term and it was not made negligently, because she made inquiries).
- Suppose instead that when Eduardo asks Marlene whether the lot is zoned for a warehouse, she replies, "Sure." She honestly thinks it is, but she does not check with the municipality to see if she is correct. Because Marlene may be negligent in not checking the zoning before answering the question, she may be held to have made a negligent misrepresentation on which Eduardo relied to his detriment. Eduardo may be able to sue Marlene in tort on the basis of negligent misrepresentation.

- In an unrelated transaction, Eduardo says to Marlene, "I am looking to purchase a truck with a 10-tonne capacity. I am prepared to buy your truck if it can carry 10 tonnes, but not otherwise." Here it could be argued that Eduardo is not just bargaining for a truck but for a truck with specific qualities, which could be seen to be a term of the agreement. In this case, Marlene's misrepresentation, because it leads to a breach of the term of the contract, gives rise to an action for breach of contract rather than an action for rescission.

Fraudulent Misrepresentation

A fraudulent misrepresentation is a misrepresentation in which an apparent statement of fact is made without any belief by the maker that it is true and with the intent that the person to whom it is made will act on it and be induced to enter into the contract.[3] The fact stated must be a positive misstatement of a past or present fact, although in some cases a representation of a future event may be seen as a fact about what is certain to happen rather than an opinion about what might happen.

For example, you invest in a business because you are told that it will expand to all major Canadian cities within two years. The statement is known by the maker to be false, but because it is unqualified and certain in tone, it may be classed as a fraudulent misrepresentation of a fact rather than an opinion. Otherwise, it could be seen as an opinion as to what is expected to happen in the future, which, as mere opinion, could not be held to be a misrepresentation that could give rise to a claim for damages (an "actionable" misrepresentation). If a statement about the future is made and qualified by words such as "likely to happen," "fully expect," or "strongly anticipate," then it is likely, because of the qualifications, to be seen as a statement of opinion, not fact (see, for example, *Allen v. Allen*[4]).

If the statement of fact is one that the intended victim could check, the law normally expects the victim to look after his or her interests and affords no remedy if he or she fails to do so. However, even where the victim could find out, if the statement is made fraudulently the law will step in because, as the Supreme Court explained in its decision in *Sager v. Manitoba Windmill Co.*,[5] eliminating fraud is seen as more important than teaching contracting parties to be careful and alert.

A fraudulent statement about the state of the law, as opposed to a statement of fact, however, cannot amount to a misrepresentation because everyone is presumed to know the law. In practical terms, this makes little sense, because if a person relies on a false statement of the law, that reliance proves that he or she did *not* know the law.

The speaker must make the fraudulent statement with no belief in the truth. This means that the speaker knew the statement was untrue, or the speaker made the statement with reckless disregard as to whether it was true but the speaker

---

3. G.H.L. Fridman, *The Law of Contract in Canada*, 3d ed. (Scarborough, ON: Carswell, 1994), 305-8.
4. *Allen v. Allen* (1976), 15 Nfld. & P.E.I.R. 362 (Nfld. Dist. Ct.).
5. *Sager v. Manitoba Windmill Co.* (1913), 23 D.L.R. 556 (Sask. S.C.).

believed it to be untrue. Where the speaker is reckless in making a statement but believes it to be true, there is no fraudulent statement (*Derry v. Peak*[6]). The statement could, of course, give rise to negligent misrepresentation, for which damages are available.

For an action to succeed, the representation must not only be fraudulent, but it must also be made with the view to having the intended victim act on it. Thus, the statement must be material and must be made to induce the other party to enter into the contract. It must also be made or at least directed at, among others, the person who acts on it. If a knowingly false statement is made to X, who enters into the contract, and X later sells to Y, who knew nothing of the statement, Y cannot sue for fraudulent misrepresentation because the statement was not directed at Y or intended by the speaker to be made to Y, and the statement did not induce Y to enter into the agreement.

Not only must the statement be directed to the victim, it must also influence the victim to enter into the contract. The statement cannot be material if the intended victim is not induced by it to enter into the contract. Reliance on the statement by the victim is something that must be shown. The statement does not have to be the only reason the victim enters into the contract, but it does have to be an important reason.

If the victim is successful in showing that he or she was induced to enter into the agreement by a fraudulent misrepresentation, the following remedies may be available:

- Fraudulent misrepresentation is equivalent to the tort of deceit (sometimes called civil—as contrasted with criminal—fraud) and thus gives rise to a claim in tort for damages.
- Fraudulent misrepresentation results in a contract induced by fraud that is voidable at the option of the victim. It is not, however, void *ab initio*. If rescission is granted, the court will attempt to restore the victim to his or her position before the contract was made. If this cannot be done, the court will award damages. Damages for other losses not covered by rescission may also be available. If damages are awarded, they should put the victim back into the position he or she would have been in had the fraud not occurred. If the injured party wishes to rescind, he or she must not delay in making the claim and must not affirm the contract by accepting any benefits from it once he or she discovers the fraud.

Example of Fraudulent Misrepresentation

Rory has founded a software company and is trying to sell shares to raise capital. His prospectus states that he has secured government support. He knows that in fact he has not done so and has no idea whether he will be

---

6.   *Derry v. Peak* (1889), 14 App. Cas. 337 (H.L.).

successful in getting it. Sonia, smelling a winner (she thinks), buys some shares. Later the government refuses to give Rory's company a cent. Sonia moves to rescind for fraudulent misrepresentation on the grounds that she would not have invested had she known that the government would not support the company and that Rory made a statement that was untrue at the time, so he fraudulently misrepresented the situation. This gives Sonia the right to rescind the contract so that she can be restored to her pre-contract position as far as possible. In the alternative, she may sue him for the tort of deceit and claim damages for the fraudulent misrepresentation.

Misrepresentation by Omission

Although silence usually cannot be interpreted as misrepresentation, in some circumstances a failure to disclose may amount to misrepresentation. If the failure to disclose makes previous statements or disclosures untrue and fraudulent, then it can give rise to an action for fraudulent misrepresentation. Where the failure to disclose results in statements that are true but misleading, there is no fraudulent misrepresentation unless there is a clear duty to inform.

The duty to inform is restricted to a range of contracts where "utmost good faith" is required between the parties (sometimes referred to by the Latin term as *uberrimae fidei* **contracts**). These contracts are characterized by a marked power imbalance between the parties, where one party is in the position of having to trust and rely on the other and has placed confidence and trust in the other. Many family agreements fall into this category, as do trust agreements where a trustee has ownership and control over property that he or she exercises for a beneficiary of that property. Other types of trust agreements include the lawyer–client relationship, doctor–patient relationship, partnership contracts, and corporation–corporate director contracts. Last, insurance contracts require full disclosure. An insurance company is absolutely dependent on the insured party's disclosing all risks before the insurance rate is fixed. The insurance company has no way of knowing some of the risks unless the party who has the knowledge cooperates by providing information about these risks. For all of these "good faith" contracts there is a positive duty to disclose and not to remain silent. A knowing silence may amount to a fraudulent misrepresentation.

uberrimae fidei **contracts** a class of contracts where full disclosure is required because one party must rely on the power and authority of another, who must behave with utmost good faith and not take advantage of the weaker party

Example of Misrepresentation by Omission

Sara is the trustee for her disabled sister Rachel and invests in property for the trust to earn income for Rachel. Sara decides to borrow money from the trust to invest in her own highly risky company. She fails to disclose this to Rachel. Later, Rachel finds out and rescinds the loan contract on the ground that Sara has, as trustee, a duty of the utmost good faith that requires her to disclose to Rachel that she is investing for her own benefit. Sara's omission, where the information is material and where Rachel relies generally on Sara to behave toward her with the utmost good faith, amounts to a misrepresentation that allows Rachel to rescind the contract.

DURESS

duress
an unlawful threat or
coercion used by one
person to induce another
to perform some act
against his or her will

At common law, a party to a contract can ask that it be declared void or can defend against its enforcement on the ground that the party was induced to enter into the contract by actual or threatened physical force or unlawful confinement directed against the party or his or her spouse, children, or near relatives. Because **duress** can be based on threats made to immediate family, the contracting party need not be threatened, but the threat must be the reason that he or she enters into the contract. Because the effect of threats is to negate real consent to enter into the agreement, one can argue that if there is no consent, there can be no contract, and thus the contract is void *ab initio*. However, the law in Canada and England treats duress like fraud by making the contract voidable (see, for example, *Saxon v. Saxon*[7]).

For duress to succeed, it is not always necessary for the person making the threat to be a party to the contract. If a third party threatens one of the contracting parties and the other contracting party knows of the threat and takes advantage of it, there are sufficient grounds for a defence of duress to succeed. However, because the contract is voidable, if there are grounds for a defence based on duress and the threatened party delays taking steps to void the contract or takes steps to affirm and accept the contract, the threatened party loses the right to rescind the agreement.

This doctrine of duress is very narrow and is based on tort and criminal law concepts that are older than the modern law of contract and have simply been carried over to contract law. However, the common law does expand and evolve, and courts have recognized that this narrow concept of duress may be inadequate for contract law situations. Consequently, the concept of duress has been expanded to include physical threats to property as well as to people and also to include economic duress.

For example, in *North Ocean Shipping Co. v. Hyundai Construction Ltd.*,[8] there was a contract to build a ship at a stated price. Owing to currency devaluation, the price became worth less than it had been when the contract was made. The shipbuilder knew that the customer needed the ship to fulfill its own shipping contracts. The shipbuilder refused to complete the ship unless the customer paid more money to cover the losses from currency devaluation. In this situation, the court held that the knowledge of the customer's urgent need of the completed ship was used to pressure the customer into paying more, something it would not otherwise have done. However, no remedy was granted because the customer affirmed the contract by paying the money and accepting the ship when it was completed. The result of this expansion of the law of duress is that the courts now look not so much at the particular form that duress takes but at whether

- there is commercial pressure that amounts to a coercion of the will, which negates contractual consent;
- there are alternative ways of avoiding the coercion; or
- the pressure exerted was legitimate.

---

7. *Saxon v. Saxon*, [1976] 4 W.W.R. 300 (B.C.C.A.).
8. *North Ocean Shipping Co. v. Hyundai Construction Ltd.*, [1979] 3 W.L.R. 419 (Q.B.).

This functional view of duress suggests that a variety of circumstances other than mere physical harm can give rise to the defence of duress. Duress in the form of threats may amount to criminal extortion, which opens up the possibility of criminal remedies as well as civil ones. In this context, however, the threat of civil proceedings to collect a debt is neither extortion nor duress, provided there is a bona fide belief that there is a right to sue to collect the debt.

Example of Duress

Spiro has just been made an offer that he cannot refuse; Mariella has told him that if he does not lend her $10,000 at 0.05 percent interest, he might not live to attend next year's New Year's Eve party. Spiro lends her the money and then moves to rescind the contract on the ground of duress, arguing that threats to his life caused him to enter into this disadvantageous contract.

UNDUE INFLUENCE

The common law of duress depended on a finding of physical duress to persons or property, although it has expanded to include economic duress and could well expand further. **Undue influence** developed under the law of equity to provide remedies for more subtle forms of oppressive behaviour. The doctrine can be applied in two types of contract situations: actual undue influence, which covers contracts, including gifts, where one party actually engages in conduct that results in applying moral or other undue pressure to obtain a desired contractual result; and presumed undue influence, which arises when the relationship between the parties raises a presumption of undue influence at or before the time the contract was made.

> **undue influence**
> persuasion, pressure, or influence short of actual force that overpowers a weaker party's judgment and free will and imposes the will of the stronger party

In both situations the court is concerned with the same thing—the domination of one party by another so as to prevent the latter from making an independent decision. The difference between the two situations is in the onus of proof. In the case of actual undue influence, the party that is claiming undue influence must prove that the other party used undue influence to compel the first party to enter into the contract. In the case of presumed undue influence, once the relationship is shown to exist, there is a presumption of undue influence, which reverses the evidentiary burden. The person alleged to have resorted to undue influence must prove that the transaction was free of its effects in order to escape liability.

The kinds of relationships that give rise to a presumption of undue influence include, not surprisingly, many of the relationships that give rise to the requirement of utmost good faith in contractual relations: family, solicitor–client, doctor–patient, guardian–ward, and trustee–beneficiary relationships. The Supreme Court of Canada has made it clear that the presumption is not restricted to existing categories but may extend to any other "special" relationships, such as **fiduciary** relationships, confidential relationships, or advisory relationships (see *Geffen v. Goodman Estate*[9]). However, the reasoning behind this expansion is not

> **fiduciary**
> a relationship where one person is in a position of trust to another and has a duty to safeguard the other's interests ahead of his or her own interests

---

9. *Geffen v. Goodman Estate* (1991), 81 D.L.R. (4th) 211 (S.C.C.).

clear. Recent cases have produced concurrent decisions, with different reasons being given by different judges in the same case to explain the development of the concept of "special" relationships. Where a "special" relationship exists, it is not necessary to show that the party affected by undue influence is also disadvantageously affected by the contract.

Where the presumption applies, the transaction is set aside unless the party benefiting from the contract can demonstrate that the party allegedly influenced had independent advice of some kind, often independent legal advice, so that the party allegedly influenced could be said to be entering into the contract with his or her eyes open. Independent legal advice, in particular, may be important. It requires the adviser to do a proper and thorough job and not just go through the motions.

Examples of Undue Influence

- Ian has befriended the elderly Enrique and does various things for him, including running errands, doing chores, and generally being helpful. Enrique has become quite dependent on Ian both for help and for company. One day Ian announces that he needs money to repay a debt and unless Enrique can give him a temporary loan, Ian will have to move away to find other work. Enrique does not want to lose Ian's help and company so, against his better judgment, he lends him the money. Enrique then has misgivings and moves to rescind the loan, arguing that Ian used friendship and the dependent relationship to unduly pressure Enrique into lending him the money. If Enrique can demonstrate this, he may prove undue influence to a degree that is sufficient to void the loan agreement. It may also be a "special relationship" given Enrique's age, needs, and dependence on Ian, so undue influence would be presumed. In this case, Ian could rebut the presumption by showing that Enrique had independent legal advice.
- Assume the same fact situation, but suppose Enrique and Ian are father and son. Here, because the nature of the relationship falls into a category where undue influence is presumed, the burden would be on Ian to demonstrate that Enrique had independent advice sufficient to give Enrique a clear and objective view of what he was doing.

UNCONSCIONABILITY

In some circumstances, the law of equity will relieve a party from the effects of unconscionable conduct by the other contracting party. The focus here is not on conduct that affects consent, as is the case for undue influence or duress. With an unconscionable transaction the focus is on the reasonableness of the contract itself and the way in which the party whose conduct is in question behaved during the bargaining process. This is very broad, and you should appreciate that not every "unfair" contract will result in a court's declaring the transaction to be unconscionable when someone, through stupidity, recklessness, or foolishness, has made a bad bargain. Finding the balance between unconscionability and stupidity is not always easy, and the case law is not particularly helpful because the cases seem to turn on a judge's subjective view of particular facts. However, where an action based on undue influence or duress may fail because pressure on the victim did not interfere too much with consent by the victim, the contract may still be avoided because its terms are unconscionable or the behaviour of the other party was unconscionable.

For example, where one party is illiterate or intellectually disadvantaged and the other party knows this and takes advantage by persuading the disadvantaged party that "this is a good deal" when in fact it is not, if the disadvantaged party is keen to close the deal, there may be no duress or undue influence. In fact, no pressure or coercion may have been necessary. The wrong is in one party's knowing that there was a lack of bargaining power or ability by the other and taking advantage of that fact, leaving the victim with a grossly unfair and inequitable bargain.

Another approach to this issue has developed in England. In *Lloyds Bank v. Bundy*,[10] a father placed a mortgage on his house in order to secure a loan for his son. The son was in financial difficulty, and the father was emotional, upset, and ready to do just about anything to help his son. The majority found that there had been undue influence by the bank regarding the father, its customer, who should have had but did not have independent legal advice before agreeing to what turned out to be a very bad bargain. However, Lord Denning arrived at the same result by a different route: he combined undue influence and other equitable doctrines to develop a ground for rescinding contracts on the basis of "inequality of bargaining power." This approach includes undue influence and possibly duress where there is a lack of independent consent to the terms of the contract, as well as unconscionability, where the nature of the bargain and the state of mind of the victim in entering into the contract are relevant. Where, in the circumstances, the bargain—because of its contents, the behaviour of the advantaged party, and the state of mind of the disadvantaged party—is grossly one-sided, there may be sufficient evidence of inequality of bargaining power to warrant court interference.

Whether the English "inequality of bargaining power" approach or the Canadian "unconscionability" approach is taken, the result may be the same: overturning immoral and inequitable bargains. What the case law has not developed so far is a methodology for identifying inequitable bargains that would cause the court to interfere with an individual's freedom to contract.

Example of Unconscionable Contracts

Derek, who has a hearing disability, thinks it would be "cool" to have a good sound system. He wears a hearing aid and reads lips. It is obvious to anyone talking to Derek that he is hearing impaired and that the better sound in a high-quality system would be useless to him. Derek walks into Sam's Electronics and tells Sam that he wants a sound system that is really cool. Sam notices that Derek is hearing impaired and realizes that the quality of a high-priced system would be useless to him, but he tells Derek he has a "good deal" on a cool system for $8,000. This is in fact an extremely high price. Derek eagerly puts his money down but later changes his mind and moves to rescind on the ground that the transaction is unconscionable. Because Sam

---

10.   *Lloyds Bank v. Bundy*, [1974] 3 All E.R. 757 (Q.B.).

CASE IN POINT

Insurance Adjusters: Not on Your Side!

From: *Jones v. Jenkins*, 2011 ONSC 1426 (CanLII).

In October 2005, Brandon Jones was seriously hurt in a motorcycle accident. He made a claim against the defendant driver and the driver's insurance company, ING.

Jones dealt with ING through Paul Smith, an insurance adjuster. To move the case along, Smith instructed Jones to make a proposal for settlement. Jones offered to settle for approximately $240,000.

At the time, Jones was not yet fully recovered, but he was anxious to return to work. He had $15,000 in debt, was living out of his car, was relying on food banks for food, and his third child was on the way. In his efforts to get back to work, he had physical examinations as part of his application for accident benefits. While Jones himself did not see the results of these examinations, Smith, the adjuster, did. The results revealed that Jones's injury was more serious and more permanent than the details in Jones's offer of settlement reflected.

Smith came back to Jones with a counteroffer of about $19,000. Smith's rationale for the low counteroffer was that there was a $30,000 "deductible" on claims, and that Jones was 75 percent at fault in the accident. Neither rationale was true. The policy had no deductible on claims over $100,000, and the allegation that Jones was 75 percent at fault was based on Smith's reliance on the at-fault rules that govern negotiations between insurance companies—rules that do not apply between private parties.

Jones, however, desperate for money, accepted the offer and signed a document releasing the defendant and ING from liability. A year later, after receiving legal advice, he brought a claim against ING and argued that the release should be found void based on unconscionability.

The court acknowledged that not every ill-considered release is "unconscionable." Madam Justice W.L. MacPherson went on to analyze the case on its facts. She applied a three-part test established in *Woods v. Hubley*[11] and *Coleman v. Bishop*,[12] which stands for the principle that a contract is unconscionable if it can be proved:

1. that there is an inequality of bargaining power arising out of ignorance, need, or distress of the weaker party;
2. that the stronger party has unconscientiously used the position of power to achieve an advantage; and
3. that the agreement reached is substantially unfair to the weaker party or is sufficiently divergent from community standards of commercial morality that it should be set aside.

In this case, the evidence reflected that Jones was a man with very poor literacy who had been under the mistaken belief that Smith, the adjuster, was committed to acting in his best interests. Jones was also in serious financial difficulty, which made him vulnerable.

Justice MacPherson also noted that Smith withheld information about Jones's own injury from him, misrepresented the "deductible," and wrongly relied on insurance fault determination rules that had no application to the case to suggest that Jones was 75 percent at fault.

Justice MacPherson found that, considered together, all these factors led to an unconscionable result. That result was sufficiently unfair as to diverge from community standards of commercial morality. The release Jones signed in 2006 was void, and his suit against the defendant was allowed to proceed.

---

11. *Woods v. Hubley*, [1995] N.S.J. No. 459 (C.A.).
12. *Coleman v. Bishop* (1991), 103 N.S.R. (2d) 265 (T.D.).

knew Derek could not derive any substantial benefit from a high-quality sound system, it may be shown that the bargain is such a poor one for Derek that it is unconscionable. The fact that the price is unduly high may be further evidence of unconscionability, but there is no evidence that Derek's disability affects his bargaining power on price: this may simply be a bad bargain and will not attract court interference. However, the fact that the price was represented as a good price when Sam knew it was not may be a fraudulent misrepresentation, which would void the contract apart from the outcome on the unconscionability issue.

Unconscionability Legislation

Legislatures in common-law jurisdictions have often passed legislation to protect certain classes of persons from unconscionable transactions where duress and undue influence would not necessarily offer protection, and where the application of the unconscionability principle is uncertain. This type of legislation usually tries to define unconscionability and then turns the matter over to the courts for adjudication. There are two types of such legislation in the Canadian provinces, discussed below.

Unconscionable Transaction Legislation

All provinces have legislation that permits a court to interfere with the terms of a loan where the contract is harsh and oppressive and the cost of the loan is excessive (see, for example, the *Unconscionable Transactions Relief Act*[13]). The legislation does not add significantly to the common law, except that it clearly brings loans within the reach of unconscionability doctrines.

A loan is excessively expensive if it can be obtained elsewhere at a lesser rate, but this is not reliable as a test because the rate can be based on a variety of risk factors that make comparisons difficult or impossible. This is particularly so with high-risk loans, where interest rates are high, the pool of comparable lenders is small, and risk assessment is somewhat subjective. A very high interest rate will attract attention if there is an element of unfairness about the loan—for example, if the borrower is desperate and the lender knows it, a statutory remedy might be provided. By way of remedy, the court can reopen the loan and make the lender accept a fair amount, order the lender to repay any overcharges, or cancel or alter any security given by the borrower to obtain the loan. This is different from the remedies available for duress, undue influence, and unconscionability, for which the usual remedies are rescission and damages.

Some provinces have other legislation (sometimes called "unfair practices" legislation) that goes well beyond the common law in giving individuals remedies where a consumer transaction is unfair. These acts permit consumers who have entered into contracts with business sellers that are based on false, misleading, or deceptive representations to rescind those contracts and obtain damages. In addition to private lawsuits to set aside contracts, an unfair practice may bring administrative

---

13. *Unconscionable Transactions Relief Act*, R.S.O. 1990, c. U.2.

proceedings before a regulatory board to ensure compliance by business sellers with the terms of the statute. The Ontario version of unfair practices legislation—the *Business Practices Act*—was repealed in 2005 and was replaced by the *Consumer Protection Act, 2002*[14] (many of the provisions in this Act did not come into force until the summer of 2005).

MISTAKE

Overview

Parties may negotiate all the terms of a contract and appear to come to a meeting of minds, yet fail to make an enforceable contract because they discover that they did not mean the same thing with respect to an essential element. When this happens the parties are said to be *mistaken*, so that their true intentions about something fundamental and important are not reflected in the contract.

While not every mistake leads to a void or voidable contract, as a result of a mistake, a contract may be declared void *ab initio* at common law. If equitable doctrines are invoked, a contract founded in a mistake may be voidable by either party, rescinded in some cases, or rectified in others.

Traditionally, the courts have been very reluctant to terminate agreements that appear to be complete contracts on the ground that a bargain once made must be kept. A party to a contract who says, "I made a mistake, please let me out of this contract" is likely to meet with the judicial response, "Having made a bargain, you will have to live with it." On the other hand, for some mistakes the courts have ruled that it would be unjust to enforce an agreement if it does not represent what the parties were really bargaining about. What has been difficult for the courts in Canada and England to decide, whether using common-law rules or equitable ones, is where to draw the line between a mistake that leaves a contract unenforceable and a mistake that does not. If you review mistake cases, you may come away with the impression that decisions turn on the court's subjective view of whether enforcement would be unfair or unconscionable rather than on some universal objective test or set of criteria that could be applied to measure the nature and effect of the mistake.

Principles of the Law of Mistake

While predicting whether a mistake will give rise to relief in a particular case is difficult, the courts appear to have applied some principles in analyzing mistake cases.

- If what was offered was offered in error, it may be impossible for the other side to accept an unintended offer. Here it could be said that there was no meeting of minds and no real offer and acceptance from which to create a valid contract.[15]

14. *Consumer Protection Act, 2002*, S.O. 2002, c. 30, Sched. A.
15. Per Estey J. in *R. v. Ron Engineering and Construction Ltd.* (1981), 119 D.L.R. (3d) 267 at 277 (S.C.C.). For a detailed discussion of judicial principles used to analyze mistake cases, see Fridman, supra note 3, at 248-67.

- If the mistake concerns something fundamental in the contract, such as the existence of the thing contracted about or a term of the contract, the contract may be void or voidable or subject to rescission or rectification.[16]
- A mistake in the motive or intention for contracting is likely to be seen as irrelevant.[17]
- Unexpected and exceptional contractual consequences that stem from a mistake may well lead to a contract being declared void, voidable, or subject to rescission or rectification.
- If one party is mistaken, the other knows it and says nothing, and the mistake is about something fundamental, then the contract may be treated as void, voidable, or subject to rescission or rectification.
- If both parties are mistaken about something fundamental, the contract may be treated as void or voidable or subject to rescission or rectification.
- If the mistake was due to one party's carelessness or negligence, that party may have to live with the consequences.
- When dealing with a case of mistake, the courts tend toward upholding agreements, and when they do intervene, they are likely to try to save the contract by creating opportunities for rectification before they grant rescission or declare the contract voidable or void or treat it as voidable.

TREATMENT OF MISTAKE AT COMMON LAW AND EQUITY

The preceding discussion suggests that mistake cases are treated differently under common-law rules from the way they are treated under equitable doctrines. At common law, a contract is valid and exists, or is invalid and does not exist. If it is valid and exists, that is the end of the matter. Equity, which is designed to introduce flexible responses to common-law rigidity, takes a different approach: a contract that is not void *ab initio* may still be subjected to equitable remedies if it is inequitable or unconscionable. In equity, a contract could be treated as voidable or be subject to rescission, rectification, or relief from forfeiture. In England, and to a lesser extent in Canada, there has been a trend away from rigid and formalistic application of common-law rules in mistake situations and toward increasing use of equitable doctrines; the focus is more on fairness in outcome and less on enforcing bargains regardless of fairness.

Types of Mistake

Mistake cases can be categorized in terms of mistakes about particulars of the contract and in terms of the effects of the mistakes as determined by which party is mistaken.

---

16.   *Bell v. Lever Brothers Ltd.*, [1931] A.C. 161 (H.L.).

17.   *Ibid.*

Mistakes of Law and Fact

MISTAKE OF LAW

Generally, because everyone is expected to know the law, if either or both parties are mistaken about the law as it affects their contract, the law provides no remedy for the mistake. Because ignorance of the law is no excuse, to be ignorant is to be at the least negligent, and a negligent party cannot ask that his or her mistake, based on that negligence, be corrected. However, practically speaking, courts have often had difficulty in distinguishing between a mistake of fact and one of law.

Suppose, for example, that A sells land to B. A and B assume that A owns the land but both are unaware that C actually owns it. This could be characterized as a mistake of law regarding the legal rights of ownership, or it could be characterized as a mistake of fact where both A and B believe as a fact that A owns the land and are unaware that, in fact, C owns it.

Some jurisdictions have taken steps to counter the effect of the rule by allowing remedies for a mistake in law for contracts that concern the payment of money. The Supreme Court of Canada confronted this issue directly in 1989 in *Air Canada v. British Columbia*,[18] holding that it did not matter whether the mistake was a mistake of fact or of law in determining whether there could be recovery for a mistake. The *Air Canada* case involved the recovery of money paid under a contract where one party claimed that the payment was made on the basis of a mistaken assumption in law that it was owing. There is no clear indication that this case necessarily applies to other types of contract, but there is no logical reason why it should not.

> ### Example of Mistake of Law
>
> Bach and Handel enter into a lease agreement in which Handel rents a house from Bach. At the time, both parties mistakenly believe that a rent control law sets the rent at a lower rate than Bach would otherwise have charged. Bach discovers that the law does not apply and moves to rescind the contract on the ground that both parties were mistaken about the amount of payment required. Depending on how narrowly the *Air Canada* case is applied, Bach may be able to rescind the contract or have it rectified.

MISTAKE OF FACT

Identity of the Subject Matter The focus here is on the subject matter of the contract: what it is about, the obligations involved, or what a term means. "Subject matter" is defined broadly to include the identity of the goods, land, or service; the price to be paid; and the obligations undertaken, provided that these are major or fundamental terms. If the mistake is about a minor matter or collateral term, it cannot cause a contract to be declared void, although it may result in other remedies such as rectification.

The test for determining whether there is a mistake regarding the identity of the subject matter is whether a reasonable person looking at the contract formation

---

18. *Air Canada v. British Columbia*, [1989] 1 S.C.R. 1161, 59 D.L.R. (4th) 161.

process and the resulting contract can determine whether the parties have identified what is fundamental to the agreement.

> ### Example of Mistake as to Identity of the Subject Matter
>
> Simon wanted to buy parcel A. He was induced by an error in the catalogue to buy parcel B, though he thought that he was buying parcel A. On discovering his error, he could sue to rescind the contract on the ground that there was a fundamental misunderstanding between the parties of what they were contracting for.

If there is a mistake, it must be about the identity of the subject matter, not some quality of it, unless the quality is so fundamental that it becomes part of the subject matter. The courts shy away from granting remedies when a mistake about quality is at issue, because this usually affects the value of the contract, which is perceived to raise issues about whether a party has bargained carefully. If a party has not bargained well, the courts are not likely to interfere to remake a bad bargain.

When it has been determined that there is a mistake as to the identity of the subject matter of a contract, because it is fundamental, the parties have failed to reach consensus, so there is no contract, and what appears to be a contract is void *ab initio*.

> ### Example of Mistake as to Identity/Quality of the Subject Matter
>
> Karl wants to buy a carload of winter wheat that is suitable for making bread. He mistakenly believes that Tara has a carload of winter wheat for sale and offers to buy it. Karl says nothing to Tara about the type of wheat he wants, and Tara is unaware that Karl wants winter wheat. The wheat Tara is selling is not winter wheat. Karl completes the purchase and takes delivery. He realizes his mistake and seeks to rescind the contract on the ground that there is a mistake as to the identity of the subject matter: winter wheat versus another type of wheat.
>
> Is this a mistake going to the identity or the quality of the subject matter? If it is the latter, there is no remedy for Karl. To answer this question, the court uses the objective test of a reasonable person analyzing the bargaining process and the final contract. In doing so, a reasonable person is likely to conclude that the parties contracted for the sale of a carload of wheat and that there was no mistake about this. There was nothing apparent in the contract or the bargaining process to indicate that the type of wheat was at issue. There was no objective evidence to alert Tara to what Karl was thinking; Karl never communicated his thoughts, and nothing he did indicated that he was thinking about winter wheat. Karl could be seen to have ideas, motives, or beliefs about the subject matter and reasons for entering into the contract. But he would have to communicate these so that a reasonable person could see and be aware that the type of wheat was fundamental and therefore that the identity of the subject matter included winter wheat, not just wheat. Note that it does not matter whether Tara knew or did not know what Karl wanted—it is what a reasonable person would conclude that counts.

Existence of the Subject Matter   In this situation, the parties intend to contract about the same subject matter and there is no confusion or disagreement about what that subject matter is. However, they may be mistaken about the existence of the subject matter:

- It may never have existed.
- It may have existed but ceased to exist before the parties entered into an agreement.
- Both may think they can contract about it, but it is not something that can be the subject of a contract for legal or other reasons.
- Both may have contemplated the non-existence of the subject matter but may not have reached consensus on how to deal contractually with its non-existence.

If the parties are mistaken about the existence of the subject matter at the time of the contract, then the contract is usually void *ab initio*, and both parties must be returned to their pre-contract positions. The reasoning here is that the parties cannot be *ad idem* (of the same mind) over something that does not exist, so there can be no agreement.

It can also be argued that the existence of the subject matter is a condition precedent to the existence of a valid contract. The application of this approach illustrates a common situation in contract interpretation cases: a fact situation can be analyzed under more than one legal rule or doctrine. How a fact situation is categorized or identified may well determine the outcome of a case.

Example of Mistake in Existence of the Subject Matter

Albert, a grain merchant, contracts to purchase from Bertha a load of grain currently being shipped to London. Unknown to both of them, the grain had spoiled en route and was sold at a distress price by the captain of the ship. In this case, the subject matter of the contract, the load of grain, had ceased to exist when the parties entered into their agreement. Consequently, they cannot reach consensus, and there is no sale.

Suppose that the parties contemplate the possibility of the non-existence of the subject matter of the contract. They may assign the risk for loss or non-existence of the subject matter to one party or the other. Sale of future goods on an executory contract might give rise to this kind of arrangement. A tomato canner, for example, might enter into an agreement in spring for the purchase of field tomatoes that do not now exist but are expected to exist by the end of August. A prudent party would take care to assign risk for goods that do not yet exist and are perishable and fragile. Even where the parties make no specific arrangements to cover destruction before delivery, the courts have occasionally extended the law of mistake as to existence of the subject matter to cover subject matter that did not exist when the contract was made and never existed in the form that could be delivered under the contract. A better approach might be to avoid twisting the law of mistake beyond recognition and to treat this kind of case as a contract that requires a condition precedent—the existence of the subject matter—before the contract can be valid.

Identity of the Party   The common law has long held that a mistake as to the identity of a party to a contract renders the contract void. The basis for this rule is that only the person to whom an offer is made can accept it; another person has no right to the bargain. The rule has a practical basis as can be seen from the cases, many of which arise when a cheat with whom the victim would not ordinarily contract impersonates someone with whom the victim would be prepared to contract.

For example, in *Cundy v. Lindsay*,[19] a person named Blenkarn fraudulently induced the respondents to sell him material. The respondents mistakenly believed that Blenkarn was Blenkiron and Co., a reputable firm with whom they would have contracted. If the respondents had known they were dealing with Blenkarn, they would not have entered into the contract. It was held that the mistake as to identity made by the respondents resulted in there being no contract, because they thought they were contracting with Blenkiron, not Blenkarn. They were not simply mistaken as to Blenkarn's attributes; they were mistaken as to his identity. They believed him to be someone other than whom he was pretending to be. Because no offer was intended to be made to Blenkarn, Blenkarn was not in a position to accept.

While a mistake about identity voids a contract, a mistake about the attributes of a party is likely to have no effect on the contract. However, it can be difficult to determine whether a mistake is about a party's identity or his or her attributes. One eminent English judge called it "a distinction without a difference" (*Lewis v. Averay*[20]).

If Y represents himself as a wealthy man when he is not, and X, who does not know anything about Y other than that he appears to be wealthy, deals with Y in the mistaken belief that Y is wealthy, it could be said that X was mistaken as to the identity of the party because Y was not a wealthy man. Here "wealthy man" is presumed to be the identity. But one could also argue that X thought she was dealing with someone called Y, and she did deal with Y, so there was no mistake about Y's identity, but there was a mistake about one of Y's attributes, his wealth. This is similar to the problem of distinguishing between identity of the subject matter and quality of the subject matter.

Nevertheless, the cases do distinguish between intending to contract with someone who appears to have wealth, a business, or commercial influence where there is a mistake about the person's being wealthy, having a business, or having commercial influence, and intending to contract with someone in the mistaken belief that the person is someone else. But even here, the key appears to be that the mistake in identity is fundamental.

For example, B represents that he has authority to receive bonds from A. In fact, B is a thief and has no authority. A checks on B's identity and, satisfied that B is the person he says he is, delivers the bonds. Here B was who he said he was, and A was contracting with the person she thought she was contracting with. If there is a mistake, it is about B's attribute of being a thief. If there is a solution for A, it may lie in the area of fraudulent misrepresentation, not in mistake as to the identity of

---

19. *Cundy v. Lindsay* (1878), 3 App. Cas. 459 (H.L.).
20. *Lewis v. Averay*, [1971] 3 All E.R. 907 at 911 (C.A.), per Lord Denning.

a party. Mistake as to identity remains limited to situations where offers are accepted by a person for whom the offer was not intended where the identity of the offeree is important or fundamental. This type of mistake can also be treated as a unilateral mistake, where one party is mistaken about something fundamental, and the other party knows it and takes advantage of the mistake. Unilateral mistake is discussed later in this chapter.

> ### Example of Mistake as to Identity of the Party
>
> Ivan the Terrible, seeking to kill off all his enemies without making a fuss, wishes to contract with Lucretia Borgia for the purchase of poisons that do not leave a trace. Lucilla Borgia hears about Ivan's desires and, carrying a nice line of poisons herself, contacts Ivan. Thinking he is dealing with Lucretia, he purchases a variety of poisons from Lucilla. Later, in a fit of remorse after he discovers that Lucilla is not the same person as Lucretia, Ivan demands his money back, saying he was mistaken as to the identity of the person he was contracting with. Because Lucilla and Lucretia are two different people, there is a mistake in identity, not in attributes, because Ivan intended to contract with Lucretia, not Lucilla. Contracting with Lucretia may be seen as important to Ivan and fundamental, because she has a reputation for high-quality poisons, and he would not have contracted with Lucilla had he known he had mistaken her for Lucretia. The fact that Lucilla's poisons were the equal of Lucretia's is not important because this does not affect the formation of Ivan's intent to contract.

Nature of the Contract (Non Est Factum) A party may plead as a defence to an attempt to enforce a contract that he or she made a mistake about the type of contract. For example, a party may think he or she is signing a guarantee for another person's debt when in fact he or she is becoming a principal debtor. This might happen where A is illiterate, blind, or otherwise disabled and is relying on B to prepare the agreement for signature. If B substitutes a document creating primary indebtedness for a guarantee and A signs it, A would say that this was not the type of contract he or she had agreed to. This defence, called the **non est factum** defence, denies that there was consent to the terms of an agreement. If there is no consent, there is no enforceable contract.

The plea of *non est factum* is available only in certain circumstances:

- The party relying on the plea must be illiterate, unable to understand English, blind, or affected by some other disability that prevents the person from reading and sufficiently understanding the document, at least to the extent of understanding the difference between the document the party signed and the document he or she thought he or she was signing (see *Saunders v. Anglia Building Society*[21]).

non est factum
(Latin) "I did not make this"; a defence used by one who appears to be a party to a contract but who did not intend to enter into this type of contract; in effect, the party is denying that he or she consented to this contract

---

21. *Saunders v. Anglia Building Society*, [1971] A.C. 1039 (H.L.).

- The party must not be careless or negligent in signing the document. Blindness or other disability alone is not enough. The party must make some effort to determine what the document is or to obtain assistance before signing it. The effort does not necessarily have to be successful or effective.
- The party must be entirely mistaken as to the type of transaction or contract that he or she is signing. Ignorance of the terms or confusion about the effects of the contract is not sufficient for a successful plea.
- The party relying on the plea must prove that he or she was mistaken as to the type of contract, that he or she was not negligent or careless in signing, and that he or she had a disability that prevented the party from appreciating that the document was entirely different from what he or she thought it was.
- The party relying on the plea need not prove fraud, misrepresentation, or fault by the other party.

The trend in the case law in Canada and England is to narrow this defence, in particular by confining it to situations where the document signed is completely different from the one the party thought he or she was signing. Further, while the courts have been inclusive as to the types of disability that might underlie a plea of *non est factum*, they have required that the mistake go to the nature of the contract itself and that the party show some effort to try to understand the nature of the contract.

Example of Mistake as to Nature of the Contract

Allen is an illiterate farmer. Larissa negotiates a contract to lease 40 hectares of land from Allen. Allen goes to Larissa's lawyer's office to sign the lease. He tells the lawyer he has come to sign the lease. At Allen's request, the lawyer goes over the terms with him, but by mistake the lawyer gives Allen the lease with an option to purchase attached. When Allen discovers what happened, he seeks to negate the contract and pleads *non est factum*. He may be successful, because he has a disability that prevented him from determining the true nature of the document. Allen was not careless: he asked for and received assistance. The mistake was not due to fraud or intentional misrepresentation, but that is not something Allen has to show to succeed with the plea.

The Mistaken Party

So far, we have examined mistakes about particulars of the contract, chiefly mistakes of law and fact. We now turn to an analysis of the doctrine of mistake in the context of who makes a mistake and what the consequences of the mistake are.

Unilateral Mistake

Unilateral mistake occurs when one party to a contract is mistaken about some fundamental element of the contract. What follows from such a mistake depends on whether the unmistaken party knew or ought to have known about the mistake.

unilateral mistake
one party to a contract is mistaken about a fundamental element of the contract

OTHER PARTY IS UNAWARE OF THE MISTAKE

If one party makes a mistake and the other is unaware of it and could not have reasonably been expected to know of it, then the contract is valid and cannot be rescinded or nullified. This result may be explained in terms of the law that requires the mistaken party to bear the cost of his or her own negligence or carelessness. At common law, the test of the unmistaken party's knowledge is objective: what would a reasonable person who is looking at the bargaining process and contract think the unmistaken party knew or ought to have known? The equitable approach is more subjective, because it looks at the intentions of the parties.

Example of Unilateral Mistake: Other Party Is Unaware

Ravi has leased a car from 4 Wheels Ltd. He wants to buy the car at the end of the lease period. He asks 4 Wheels to quote him a buyout price, and 4 Wheels does so. Ravi agrees to the price, unaware that 4 Wheels has made a mistake and quoted a lower price than it intended. Ravi does not have the knowledge or background to know that a pricing mistake has been made and in fact has no real idea of what the market price is. Consequently, it could not be said that he knows or ought to know that 4 Wheels made a mistake, and the contract is binding on 4 Wheels.

OTHER PARTY SHOULD HAVE BEEN AWARE OF THE MISTAKE

If one party makes a mistake and the other is unaware of it but in all of the circumstances should have been aware of it, then the unmistaken party cannot rely on enforcing the contract. Although the contract may or may not be void *ab initio* at common law, it is voidable and could be rescinded in equity at the option of the party who made the mistake on the ground that it would be unconscionable to permit the unmistaken party from taking advantage of an error in offering or accepting the terms of an agreement.

Example of Unilateral Mistake: Other Party Should Have Been Aware

Marek has seen an invitation to tender on a contract to provide fuel to Elizavetta's business. He submits a tender in which he mistakenly miscalculates the unit price. Elizavetta, seeing that the price is very low, accepts the tender immediately. She suspects that Marek has made an error, but she does not know what it is and does not inquire further. Even if she does not know that there is a mistake, a reasonable person would be expected to know that the price was low and would expect the buyer to be aware of an error.

OTHER PARTY IS AWARE OF THE MISTAKE

If one party makes a mistake and the other is aware of it and snaps up the bargain, the contract is voidable by the mistaken party. There is no requirement to show that the unmistaken party misled or deceived the mistaken party, and the results are the same as they would be for a situation where the unmistaken party did not know of the mistake but should have known about it. Where the unmistaken party knows of the mistake, the test is subjective, and the courts will hear evidence from the mistaken party as to what he or she actually intended to do.

Example of Unilateral Mistake: Other Party Is Aware

In the above example, if Marek's calculation error was easily evident on the face of the tender, then Elizavetta either would have had actual knowledge of the miscalculation or ought to have known of the miscalculation.

REMEDIES

The law is not entirely clear on what remedies are available in cases of unilateral mistake. In Canada, it appears that the mistaken party has a choice between rectification of the contract and rescission. If rectification is chosen, the contract is rewritten to correct the mistake. If rescission is chosen, the contract is voided and the parties are returned to their pre-contract positions (see *Devald v. Zigeuner*[22]). This solution has been rejected in England, where rectification is the only remedy. With unilateral mistake, the courts are inclined to resort to the law of equity, which allows for flexible remedies that maximize opportunities for keeping the contract alive.

Mutual Mistake

A **mutual mistake** arises where both parties are mistaken, but they each make a different mistake. The test of whether mistakes have been made is objective. If a reasonable person is of the view that the parties appear to be in agreement on the terms of the contract, then there is apparent assent to the terms of the contract, making the contract valid. As one case put it, "[m]utual assent is not required . . . only apparent manifestation of assent is required" (*Walton v. Landstock Investments Ltd.*[23]). The subjective, inward secret beliefs of a mistaken party are considered to be irrelevant, which prevents the doctrine from being exploited to undo what in effect is a bad bargain by either party.

mutual mistake
both parties to a contract are mistaken but each makes a different mistake

Example of Mutual Mistake

Farid is selling a second-hand mountain bike. Marsha indicates that she would like to buy it. She is looking for a new bike and thinks that Farid's, which is clean and shiny, is new. Farid is unaware that Marsha thinks she is buying a new bike—he thinks she wants to buy a second-hand one. The objective view of the reasonable person might be that the condition of the bike might provide reasonable support for the mistake Marsha made, and that there was no evidence to prevent Farid from being mistaken about Marsha's intent. If so, it might be argued that the parties did not reach consensus and there was no contract.

---

22. *Devald v. Zigeuner* (1958), 16 D.L.R. (2d) 285 (Ont. C.A.).
23. *Walton v. Landstock Investments Ltd.* (1976), 13 O.R. (2d) 693 (C.A.).

Mutual Mistake on Price Not Fatal to Contract

From: *St. James Volkswagen v. Sibbald*, 2004 MBQB 289 (CanLII).

The defendant went shopping for a new car. She had her existing car available for trade-in. She met with a salesperson who worked for the plaintiff car dealer. The "sticker price" on the new car, before the parties began negotiating, was approximately $28,000.

After some discussion, the parties agreed that the dealer would offer the defendant a $4,500 credit for her trade-in.

The parties then began haggling, and many factors affecting price were discussed, including the addition of a spoiler to the car, taxes, and so forth. The defendant made a final offer of $23,000 and then left.

The defendant returned to the dealership on a different day, and was presented with documentation, drafted by the plaintiff dealer, citing a total price of $23,000. The salesperson made the necessary adjustments to subtract the trade-in of $4,500, and to add GST and PST. These calculations resulted in a purchase price of $21,090, which the defendant paid. She then drove off in the car.

A few days later, the plaintiff dealer called to advise her there had been a mistake in the contract, and that she had to return the car.

She refused.

The plaintiff alleged that when a supervisor reviewed the transaction, he noticed that the salesperson had made an error: the $23,000 offer made to the defendant was intended to be *after* trade-in, not before.

The defendant purchaser advised that she accepted the offer as it was described to her: $23,000 before trade-in. She asserted that had she been quoted a higher price, she would not have bought the car.

The court reviewed the facts and found that this was a case of innocent mutual mistake: the salesperson had miscalculated his offer, and the purchaser had accepted it, not aware of the miscalculation.

The court refused to void the contract. In so refusing, the judge explained that the plaintiff dealer was in the best position to avoid the mistake, the purchaser had not intentionally taken advantage of the mistake, and that putting the parties back into their original positions would not correct the situation: the new car would have depreciated, and the dealer had already disposed of the trade-in.

Common Mistake

common mistake
both parties to a contract are mistaken and make the same mistake

A **common mistake** occurs when both parties are mistaken and make the same mistake. They have not reached consensus on essential terms, and there is no enforceable contract. Not every common mistake yields these results—there must be a fundamental common mistake about the subject matter or a term of the contract. Fact situations that give rise to analysis using the doctrine of common mistake can also be analyzed in terms of mistake as to identity, quality, and existence of the subject matter. In the end, using any of these analytic approaches, the contract may be avoided if the mistake is about something fundamental and the party appears to have received far less than what he or she had apparently contracted for.

Example of Common Mistake

Millicent wants to sell her fur coat, which she thinks is mink. Emily agrees to buy it; she too thinks it is mink. Both intend the transaction to be about a mink coat. In fact, both are mistaken—the coat is made of some other kind of fur dyed to look like mink and is worth far less than a mink coat. Assuming that neither Millicent nor Emily is careless in failing to find the true quality on examining the coat, it appears that both have made a common mistake. Because a mink coat is perceived to be different from other kinds of coats, the mistake could be said to be fundamental and to give rise to rescission. Note that on these facts, this could also be seen as a mistake about the identity or quality of the subject matter.

CHAPTER SUMMARY

Where one party makes a statement that is a misrepresentation and induces another to enter into a contract based on the misrepresentation, the law will intervene, depending on whether the statement was a term of the contract or an inducement to enter into it, and whether the misrepresentation was innocently made, negligently made, or made with the intent to defraud or deceive. Depending on the nature of misrepresentation, it can give rise to damages for breach of contract or to rescission of the contract where the contract is voided.

The courts also will void a contract on the ground that one party was induced by duress or undue influence to enter into a contract that he or she would otherwise not have entered into. In other circumstances, where there is no apparent undue influence or duress, the court may intervene on the ground that the contract in its terms is so unfair that it is unconscionable.

When a party makes a mistake, the courts examine the situation carefully in deciding whether a party should be let out of his or her contractual responsibilities. If the mistake is fundamental and concerns the identity or existence of the subject matter, a term of the contract, or the nature of the contract itself, the court will often allow for rescission, rectification, or termination of the contract. The basis for these remedies is that the parties were not really in agreement about essential terms and that a reasonable person would assume that it was reasonable in the circumstances for the party or parties to have made the mistake in question.

The courts also examine mistake from the perspective of who makes the mistake and what the consequences are or should be for the mistaken party. If one party makes a unilateral mistake about a fundamental element of the contract, what happens depends on whether the other party knew or ought to have known of the mistake. One cannot take advantage of a reasonable mistake by the other party. If both parties make a mistake and it is the same one, it is a common mistake. If the mistake is fundamental, then the parties are not *ad idem* and there is no valid contract. If both parties make a mistake, but each party's mistake is different, they have made a mutual mistake. If the result is that they are not *ad idem* about something fundamental, then the contract may be avoided.

KEY TERMS

common mistake
duress
fiduciary
fraudulent misrepresentation
innocent misrepresentation
material inducement
mutual mistake

non est factum
rescission
restitution
uberrimae fidei contracts
undue influence
unilateral mistake

REVIEW QUESTIONS

True or False?

1. The common law provides a remedy for an innocent misrepresentation about a non-material term of a contract.
2. A contract can be unconscionable even if neither party exerted undue influence over the other.
3. Where parties have relied on a mutual mistaken belief about the state of the law when entering into a contract, the court will always uphold the contract regardless of the mistake.
4. Where one party to a contract has made a misrepresentation negligently but unintentionally, the other party may have a remedy in tort.
5. It is possible for a party to successfully prove *non est factum* in a situation where her signature appears on a contract.
6. All contractual defects render contracts void *ab initio*.
7. Intentional dishonesty in presenting what amounts to a material inducement to contract generally renders the contract voidable.
8. Unilateral mistake always renders a contract voidable.
9. It is possible to make a fraudulent misrepresentation by omitting important information about an issue material to a contract.
10. Duress rendering a contract voidable can be based on a threat to a third party, not just the party to the contract.

Fill in the Blanks

1. Where a person who appears to be a party to a contract denies having signed or consented to the contract (for example, alleging he was tricked into signing), the party may raise the defence of ____ ____ _____.
2. In a _____ relationship, one party is in a position of special trust with respect to another party, such that she must protect the other's interests ahead of her own.

3. The _____ _____ rule acts as a bar to the introduction of evidence that is inconsistent with the clear (written) wording of a contract.

4. When, due to a defect, a contract is set aside and the court seeks to return the parties to their pre-contract positions, any refund or repayment made to accomplish this is described as _____.

5. When a party owes a fiduciary duty to another, her contracts with that party must be in _____ _____ _____.

6. A situation in which one party influences another into entering into a contract by threatening to cause significant harm to that party's financial interests can be characterized as _____ duress.

7. If a party continues to accept benefits under a contract after discovering that he was misled into entering it, he may thereby_____ his right to rescind the contract.

8. Certain relationships between parties can create a presumption of _____ _____, which can lead courts to overturn contracts unfavourable to the more vulnerable party.

9. A misrepresentation is _____ when it is made with the intention that the other party act on it, and the other party does so.

10. The law of _____ can sometimes provide a remedy for an unjust contract even if the contract cannot be challenged under the common law.

Short Answer

1. How does an innocent misrepresentation differ from a negligent misrepresentation?
2. What determines whether a misrepresentation is material?
3. Can an omission be a misrepresentation? If so, in what circumstances?
4. In what circumstances can duress be used to rescind a contract?
5. How does undue influence differ from duress in terms of circumstances where it can be used, and in terms of remedies?
6. How does unconscionability differ from duress and undue influence?
7. Why are courts reluctant to terminate or rectify a contract when a party claims that there was a mistake?
8. If one party makes a mistake about the subject matter of the contract and the mistake is not central or material, should a remedy be granted to the mistaken party? Why or why not?
9. Describe the role of the law of equity in dealing with cases of mistake.
10. What are the consequences if a party makes a mistake in the identity of the subject matter of a contract? How are the consequences different from those where the mistake is about the quality of the subject matter? Is the distinction meaningful? Why or why not?

EXERCISES

1. Compare and contrast the various remedies available for different types of misrepresentation. Comment on why some remedies are likely to be more effective for the injured party than others.

2. Puccini bids on a load of Edam cheese being sold by Rossini. Puccini is bidding on and requires regular Edam for his gourmet shop. Rossini has dealt with Puccini before and knows the nature of Puccini's business. Rossini is also told how to package the cheese, but he is not told precisely what grade of Edam Puccini wants. Rossini sells and delivers it. The price is quite a bit lower than the usual price for a load of Edam. On delivery, Puccini discovers that it is a grade of Edam suitable only for processing into a cheese spread. Puccini seeks to rescind the contract and get his money back on the ground that there was a mistake as to the identity of the subject matter.

   Develop and present arguments to support Puccini's position and arguments to support Rossini's position. You may wish to share this exercise with another student, with one of you taking Rossini's position and one of you taking Puccini's.

3. Charlie, a fruit merchant, contracts with Camille to purchase from her a load of mangoes currently being shipped to Vancouver. Charlie and Camille are unaware that the mangoes spoiled along the way and were sold off very cheaply by the captain of the ship. The subject matter of the contract, the load of mangoes, ceased to exist before the parties entered into their agreement and there can be no contract. Would it make a difference if the mangoes spoiled *after* the contract was entered into? What remedies might be available to the parties in this situation? Is the law on mistake of any help here? Consider remedies for breach of contract.

Issues in Contractual Rights: Privity, Assignment, and Discharge

6

LEARNING OUTCOMES

After completing this chapter, you should be able to:

- Explain the principle of privity of contract and describe at least two doctrines that permit third parties to enforce rights under a contract.

- Define "trust" and distinguish between express and constructive trusts.

- Distinguish novation and assignment, as they relate to contracts.

- List at least three ways in which a contract can be discharged.

- Explain how parties can terminate a contract without performing the obligations set out under it.

- Define "condition precedent" and explain how it affects the operation of a contract.

- Understand how some contracts are discharged or terminated by the operation of law.

INTRODUCTION

privity
the relationship that
exists between the
parties to a contract

In this chapter, you will be introduced to the principle of **privity** of contract and to exceptions to the principle. In other words, you will learn about situations in which parties who were not party to the original contract can gain rights to enforce the contract.

You will also learn about how contracts are discharged and how the obligations under a contract are extinguished or wound up. In some cases, the parties may disagree about which actions will effectively discharge contract obligations, about whether the rights under a contract have in fact been extinguished, or both. Common problems with contract discharge are discussed below.

PRIVITY OF CONTRACT

As the term suggests, privity involves being privy to, or a party to, a contract. Only the parties to a contract may claim the benefits of the contract or incur any liability under it. This may seem self-evident, but some contracts purport to confer benefits on third parties, or third parties may wish to be substituted for one of the parties. In those cases, the third parties may wish to enforce the contract.

The general rule is that a third party who is a "stranger" to the contract may not claim any benefits or incur any liability under the contract because of the lack of privity.

Examples of Lack of Privity

- Connor and Julian own adjoining properties. Connor enters into a contract with Maya whereby Maya agrees to rent Connor's property and build a motel on it. Julian would greatly benefit from this, because he owns and operates a restaurant on the adjoining property. However, Maya fails to fulfill the contract and does not build the motel. Despite the fact that Julian will suffer as a result of Maya's breach of contract, he cannot enforce the contract because he is not a party to it—he lacks privity. Only Connor can enforce the contract.
- The homeowners in a certain neighbourhood decide they want to form a residents' association. All of them enter into a contract that states that if any of the homeowners in the neighbourhood fails to cut his or her grass and lets it grow past a certain length, then any other member of the group may cut the grass and the offending homeowner will be obligated to pay a fee of $100 to the member who cut it. Some time after the contract is formed, Brian buys a house and moves into the neighbourhood. Brian does not cut his grass, and Raffi goes over one Saturday morning and cuts it for him. Raffi then sends a bill to Brian for $100. Brian is not obligated to pay the $100 because he was never a party to the contract and cannot incur any liability under it.

The doctrine of privity can be rationalized in terms of the lack of consideration. The third party paid or received no consideration for the contract, and therefore he or she cannot enforce it, nor is bound by it. However, certain statutes can impose liability or confer benefits on third parties despite the lack of consideration, and certain common-law doctrines create exceptions to the principle of privity. A few examples of these exceptions follow.

- The law of partnership (created by statute in most jurisdictions) states that a partner may enter into a contract on behalf of the partnership, and that contract will impose liability on all the partners.
- In some jurisdictions in real property law—which is based on both common-law rules and statutory provisions—contracts that impose restrictions on the use of real property are binding, not just on the parties to the contract, but also on all subsequent owners of the property, even though they were never parties to the original contract, provided that these interests are registered on title. Such restrictions might be the granting of a right of way or a restriction on the height of any building constructed on the property.
- The parties to an insurance contract are the policyholder and the insurance company. However, many insurance contracts, or policies, such as those for life insurance, name a third party as a **beneficiary**. If the insurance company will not honour the policy, it may be enforced by the beneficiary. This right is provided for under insurance legislation[1] and in the case law that has interpreted insurance contracts.

beneficiary
a person who is entitled to the benefits of an agreement entered into between two or more other parties

Apart from established exceptions to the general rule, there are a number of other means by which third parties may assert rights under a contract. These include novation, vicarious performance, and trusts.

Novation

A third party may replace one of the parties to a contract by forming a new contract. The result of **novation** is the termination of the old contract and the substitution of the new contract. The new party has the benefits and liabilities of the contract, and the old party no longer has any rights or obligations. There is no difficulty with privity of contract with novation, because the third party becomes a contracting party. The requirements of novation are as follows:

novation
a requirement that the parties to a contract agree to substitute a new contract for an existing one, thereby terminating the existing contract

- The new party must assume complete liability.
- The other party must accept the new party *in substitution for* the old party, not *in addition to* the old party.
- The other party must accept the new contract in substitution for the old contract.
- The other party must accept that the new contract terminates the old contract.
- The new contract must be made with the consent of the old party.

---

1. See, for example, s. 195 of the *Insurance Act*, R.S.O. 1990, c. I.8.

Example of Novation

Busy Bees Cleaners Inc. agrees to provide office cleaning services to Sharif, Wasserman, and Powell under a long-term contract. The owners of Busy Bees decide to retire and close down the business before the end of the contract. However, they recommend another company, Action Clean Ltd., to replace them. After negotiations, Sharif, Wasserman, and Powell enter into a new contract with Action Clean under the same terms and conditions as their contract with Busy Bees. In doing so, there has been novation. Busy Bees is released from its obligations under the old contract, and the new contract with Action Clean is substituted for the old contract.

Vicarious Performance

As a general rule, a party to a contract must perform his or her obligations under that contract. He or she cannot get a third party to perform those obligations without the consent of the other party. Nevertheless, there are situations in which a party might wish to have a third party do some or all of the work under a contract. This is called **vicarious performance**, which is permissible in limited circumstances.

vicarious performance
the performance of obligations under a contract by a third party in circumstances in which the original party remains responsible for proper performance

A party may employ a third party to perform his or her obligations when the performance required is not of a personal nature. If the work could be performed equally well by another person, the party may "contract out" the work. However, the original party to the contract remains responsible if the work is not done properly. If the work to be done is of a personal nature, the party may not hire another to perform the contract.

It is important to look at the common practices in the business or industry in question to determine whether vicarious performance is acceptable. Vicarious performance is common in a number of trades and industries, including shipping, building construction, dry cleaning, transportation, repair of goods, and manufacturing.

Examples of Vicarious Performance

- Saroj takes her car to Maurice for repair. Maurice agrees to fix her car, which needs engine repair and body work. Maurice does the engine repair himself, but sends the car down the street to Alain for the body work. In this case, vicarious performance is common and acceptable. Saroj needs the work done; presumably she does not care who does it. However, when Saroj gets her car back, she finds that the body work was not done properly. Because Maurice is the original party to the contract, he is responsible for the poorly done body work even though he did not do it himself. Saroj may sue him for breach of contract. Maurice may then in turn sue Alain for breach of contract.
- Glass Hammer Productions Ltd. hires Roberto Forte, a famous opera singer, for a concert. Roberto is feeling poorly on the day of the performance, so he sends his protégé, Bruno Pelizzari, to sing in his stead. In this case, the nature of the performance of the contract is personal, and vicarious performance is not acceptable. Glass Hammer Productions is not required to accept a substitute for the performer it hired.

Trusts

A strict rule that only the parties to an agreement can enforce it has the potential to lead to unfair results. Consider, for example, family law contracts that govern the payment of child support to one parent by the other. The contract is between the parents, but the objective of the contract is to benefit the children (third parties to the contract).

Under the basic rules of contracts, where a contract confers a benefit on a third party, and the parties to the agreement are unwilling to enforce it, the third party is prohibited from enforcing the agreement. The law of trusts developed to deal with this situation.

A **trust** is the result of a contract in which property is transferred from one person to another for the benefit of a third party. The law of trusts allows the person who is to receive the benefit of the contract, the beneficiary, to enforce the contract against the person who is to administer the property for his or her benefit, the **trustee**. A trust that is declared in clear and unequivocal terms, usually in writing, is called an **express trust**.

> ### Example of an Express Trust
>
> Gwyn wants to create a trust for her son, Sean, in case she dies before he turns 18 years of age. In her will, she directs that all of her estate is to be invested for the benefit of Sean until he is 18 years old, and she names her sister Bethan as the trustee. After Gwyn dies, the property is transferred to Bethan. However, instead of administering the trust for the benefit of Sean, Bethan spends the money on herself.
>
> Sean is not a party to the trust agreement—Gwyn and Bethan are the only parties. However, the law of trusts allows Sean to enforce the agreement because he is the beneficiary of the trust.

In other cases, the parties to a contract may create a benefit for a third party without expressly calling it a trust or without using language in the contract that would allow the third party to enforce the contract. In those cases, the third party must argue that a trust was created by inference or implication. The courts will examine the terms of the contract and the acts of the parties to determine whether the true intent of the contract was to create a trust. This can be a difficult argument to make because the courts are reluctant to impose a trust unless there is clear evidence that the parties intended to create one. When the courts find that a trust can be inferred from the contract, it is called a **constructive trust**. The beneficiary of a constructive trust may enforce the terms of the trust.

> ### Example of a Constructive Trust
>
> Natasha and Evelyn form a partnership. The partnership agreement states that if either of them should die, then her share of the profits of the partnership should be paid to her husband. Evelyn dies, and Natasha refuses to pay the profits to Evelyn's husband, Luis. Luis is not a party to the partnership agreement. The partnership agreement did not set up an express trust. He

trust
a legal entity created by a grantor for a beneficiary whereby the grantor transfers property to a trustee to manage for the benefit of the beneficiary

trustee
a person who holds property in trust for, or for the benefit of, another person

express trust
a trust that arises as a result of an agreement, usually in writing, that is created in express terms

constructive trust
a trust created by the operation of law, as distinguished from an express trust

would have to argue that it is a constructive trust that had been created in his favour. If successful, Luis would be able to obtain a share of the profits.

ASSIGNMENT OF A CONTRACT

In a commercial context, a contract is a thing of value that can be treated as an asset. For instance, a contract for the lease of equipment is common. Such a lease allows a customer to finance the acquisition of new equipment, and it allows the vendor to gain extra income in the way of interest charges over and above the sale price for the equipment. Because income is generated over the term of the lease, the lease is an asset, or a **chose in action** or **thing in action**, that the vendor can sell, or assign, to a third party such as a financing company.

The vendor, the **assignor**, assigns his or her rights under the lease to the financing company, the **assignee**. The assignee collects the moneys owing under the lease from the customer, the party to be charged. This **assignment** differs from novation because no new contract is formed, and the consent of the party to be charged is not required.

Although assignments are now common business transactions, at one time the courts would not recognize them. The assignee gained no rights under the contract because of the lack of privity and, therefore, could not enforce the contract. However, the courts now recognize equitable and statutory assignments. They still do not recognize the assignment of contracts for personal services, which may not be vicariously performed or assigned to a third party.

Equitable Assignments

To avoid the privity-of-contract rule in dealing with assignments, the concept of an *equitable assignment* developed. This allows for assigning contractual rights under some circumstances. Equitable assignments have certain characteristics that can make them cumbersome to deal with, but they also have some advantages. An equitable assignment can be verbal or in writing, and it can be a partial assignment of the assignor's rights or a complete and absolute assignment of all of the assignor's rights.

To allow an assignee to enforce a contract by equitable assignment, the following requirements must be met:

- All the parties must be brought before the court. This means that in any action to enforce the contract the assignor must be a party, even if he or she no longer has any interest in or rights under the contract.
- The court must be satisfied that the intention of all parties (but not the party to be charged) is to assign the contractual rights.
- The party to be charged must have notice of the assignment before the assignee can enforce the contract against him or her.

Statutory Assignments

The widespread practice of assigning contracts and the inconvenience of having to make the assignor a party to any actions to enforce the contract led to the development of the statutory assignment. All the common-law provinces have legislation

**chose in action/
thing in action**
an intangible right of ownership in a tangible thing that carries the right to take legal action on it—for example, debts, insurance policies, negotiable instruments, contract rights, patents, and copyrights

assignor
a party who assigns his or her rights under a contract to a third party

assignee
a party to whom rights under a contract have been assigned by way of an assignment

assignment
a transfer by one party of his or her rights under a contract to a third party

that recognizes the assignment of contractual rights. Statutory assignments have different requirements than equitable assignments. They do not replace equitable assignments, so in deciding how to enforce a contract that has been assigned, it is necessary to determine whether it is a statutory or an equitable assignment.

An assignee to a statutory assignment may enforce a contract without involving the assignor if

- the assignment of rights is absolute and unconditional;
- the assignment is in writing and signed by the assignor; and
- express notice of the assignment, in writing, is given to the party to be charged.

Note that the party to be charged does not have to consent to the assignment—he or she must only be given notice of the assignment. The assignment is effective against the party to be charged as of the date that he or she receives the notice. If the assignor has assigned the same contract to two different assignees, either accidentally or fraudulently, the assignee who first gives notice to the party to be charged is entitled to enforce the contract.

CASE IN POINT

What, Precisely, Is Assigned Along with Film Rights?

From: *Simex Inc. v. Imax Corporation*, 2005 CanLII 46629 (Ont. C.A.) (with considerable simplification).

Midland Productions produced some films in Ontario. The rights to those films were owned by related Canadian companies called Ridefilm and IMAX.

Ridefilm/IMAX entered into a contract with SimEx Inc. under which it assigned the rights to certain films to SimEx. SimEx is an Ontario company with a substantial presence in California through its subsidiary.

After the films were assigned to SimEx, certain disputes arose between Midland Productions and IMAX. Midland accused IMAX of failing to pay certain royalties owing under the production contracts for certain films, including some of the films assigned to SimEx.

The dispute between Midland and IMAX went to arbitration in California.

Faced with the claim from Midland, IMAX started a third-party claim against SimEx. IMAX argued that along with the rights assigned to SimEx went the obligations associated with the films, including the obligations to pay royalties. IMAX also argued that because the agreement transferring rights to SimEx contained an arbitration provision establishing Ontario as the jurisdiction in which disputes should be settled, the royalties issue needed to

be arbitrated in Ontario, not in California.

SimEx defended against the claim by arguing that the royalty obligations were *not* assigned to it as part of the assignment of film rights.

SimEx lost its case at the trial level; the trial court judge held that the terms of the assignment of rights transferred "both the burden and the benefits" of the production agreements with Midland to SimEx. SimEx appealed to the Ontario Court of Appeal.

The Court of Appeal overturned the trial judge's decision. Speaking for the court, Rosenberg J.A. held that, in assigning the film rights to SimEx, IMAX did not assign the production agreements for the films, but only ownership of the films that were produced as a result of the production agreements. As a result, SimEx did not become a party to the terms, under those agreements, that related to the payment of royalties and to the forum for resolution of disputes.

SimEx was held to be bound by the transfer agreement between itself and IMAX (which required arbitration of disputes in Ontario) but not by the production agreement between Midland and IMAX.

Defences and Assignments

All assignments, either equitable or statutory, are subject to any "equities" that exist between the original parties to the contract up until the time of notice. These equities might include rights that arise because of fraud, duress, or undue influence on the part of the assignor at the time the contract was entered into.

For example, if the creditor uses duress to force a debtor to enter into a contract, the debtor can use duress as a defence if the creditor tries to enforce the contract. If the creditor assigns the contract to a new creditor, the debtor can claim duress as a defence to payment under the contract in an action by the assignee (the new creditor). Even though it was not the assignee who used duress, the assignee takes the assignment subject to all the conditions that existed between the original parties up until the time notice of the assignment is given to the party to be charged. The assignee can be in no better a position than was the assignor. Defences such as fraud, duress, and undue influence were discussed in more detail in Chapter 5, Contractual Defects.

setoff
in an action for debt, a defence in which the debtor admits that he or she owes a debt to the creditor but also claims that the creditor owes a debt to him or her, and uses this reasoning to cancel or reduce the debt owed to the creditor

Another example of a defence used in assignments law is **setoff**. If the assignor owes money to a party who has financial obligations under this or another contract, the party with the financial obligation can claim the defence of setoff and deduct this debt from the moneys now owed to the assignee under the contract. This creates some risk for the assignee in taking an assignment, and assignees usually require some form of assurance from the assignor that no equities or setoffs exist that would interfere with enforcement of the contract.

Example of Equities

Pierre is employed with Auto Leasing Corp. As part of the terms of his employment, he is entitled to the use of a car. Pierre leases a car from his employer. He signs an agreement that states he is not required to make any lease payments while he is employed with Auto Leasing. If his employment with Auto Leasing ceases for any reason, Pierre must start making the lease payments himself. Auto Leasing experiences business problems and stops paying its employees. In an effort to raise capital, it assigns all its car leases, including Pierre's lease, to United Financing Ltd. At the time of the assignment, it owes Pierre $8,000 in unpaid wages. Auto Leasing then goes out of business. Pierre's employment is terminated, and United Financing wants Pierre to make the payments under the lease. It gives him notice of the assignment and demands payment.

The equities that exist between the original parties, Pierre and Auto Leasing, at the time of the assignment include the wages owed to Pierre. Because United Financing takes the assignment of the lease subject to any equities that exist between the original parties until the time that the notice is given, Pierre can claim a setoff and deduct the $8,000 owed to him by Auto Leasing from the money he owes to United Financing under the lease.

Assignments by Operation of Law

Some assignments occur automatically when certain events occur. These assignments are governed by statutes that set out the duties of the assignor. For example, when a person goes bankrupt, all of his or her contractual rights are assigned to the trustee in bankruptcy. When a person dies, all contractual rights are assigned to the estate trustee with a will (if the person died with a will) or the estate trustee without a will (if the person died without a will). Similar provisions exist for situations where a person becomes incapable of managing his or her affairs because of a mental disability.

DISCHARGE OF CONTRACT

Once a contract has been **discharged**, the obligations under that contract are cancelled, and the contract itself is **null and void**.

Contracts may be discharged:

- by performance,
- by agreement,
- as of right,
- by operation of law,
- by frustration, or
- by breach.

Frustration will be discussed in Chapter 7, Contract Interpretation, and breach is discussed in Chapter 8, Breach of Contract and Remedies.

Discharge by Performance

The most common way to discharge a contract is by performing the obligations under the contract. Performance may consist of performing services, paying money, delivering goods, and so on. Offering to perform the obligations under a contract is called **tender of performance**. For the contract to be discharged, both parties must tender performance. However, if one party tenders performance and the other party does not accept it, the refusing party is in breach of contract unless he or she has a valid and lawful reason. At that point, the party who tendered performance need not attempt to tender performance again and may sue the other party for breach of contract. In addition, one party must not interfere with, hinder, or prevent the other party from tendering performance. Any hindrance can be treated by the tendering party as refusal and breach of contract.

> ### Example of Tender of Performance and Refusal
> Susan and Tanya have a contract whereby Tanya has agreed to buy Susan's crop of tomatoes for an agreed-upon price. However, when the crop is ready, the price of tomatoes has dropped and Tanya no longer wants to buy Susan's tomatoes. She now wants to buy her tomatoes at a lower price from another farmer. Susan delivers the tomatoes to Tanya, but Tanya refuses to accept them. Susan has tendered performance, but Tanya has refused to accept it. Tanya is in breach of contract.

Note that tender of performance must be within the exact terms of the contract. If the performance tendered does not comply with the terms of the contract in any way, the other party need not accept it. Performance must be exactly as specified in the contract and must occur on the right date, at the right time, and in the right place.

discharged
released, extinguished; a discharge of a contract occurs when the parties have complied with their obligations, or other events have occurred that release one or both parties from performing their obligations

null and void
of no force, validity, or effect

tender of performance
offering to perform that which the contracted party is obligated to perform under a contract

Did "Excessive" Release and Tax Deduction Negate Tender of Performance of a Settlement Contract?

From: *Fieguth v. Acklands Ltd.*, 1989 CanLII 2744 (B.C.C.A.).

The plaintiff Fieguth was fired by the defendant Acklands and saw a lawyer about bringing a wrongful dismissal claim. The lawyer worked with the defendant's lawyers and negotiated a wrongful dismissal settlement in the amount of $5,015.92, in exchange for the plaintiff's release of his wrongful dismissal claim against Acklands.

When the time came to comply with the terms of the settlement, Acklands sent the plaintiff's lawyer, in trust, a cheque for $4,012.74 and a release.

When questioned about the amount of the cheque, the defendant explained that it had deducted 20 percent income tax, as required by the *Income Tax Act*.[2] The plaintiff's lawyer asserted that the settlement was not subject to tax.

The plaintiff's lawyer also complained about the terms of release. Upon reviewing the release at trial, the judge agreed that it was "an unusual one containing covenants and indemnities that were excessive and unnecessary."

The plaintiff and his lawyer considered the reduced payment and unusual release to be a failure, on the part of the defendant, to tender performance under the terms of the settlement contract. They went to court.

At trial, the court agreed that Acklands had failed to tender performance. The court awarded the plaintiff damages for wrongful dismissal of over $14,000. Acklands appealed.

The Court of Appeal overturned the judgment, and held that Acklands' tender of $4,012.74 and the "unusual" release *did* constitute good tender of performance, and that the plaintiff was the one who was in breach. As a result, the plaintiff did not have the right to bring a claim against Acklands in court.

In support of the court's decision, McEachern C.J.B.C. held that the defendant had tendered correctly because:

- according to tax law, the settlement was taxable; and
- the general practice of settlement-making includes the expectation that a release will be granted in exchange for the payment. It is not normal practice for the precise terms of the release to be hammered out before the settlement is accepted.

Even though the release in this case was much stricter than normal, the court held that

[i]t should not be thought that every disagreement over documentation consequent upon a settlement, even if insisted upon, amounts to a repudiation of a settlement. Many such settlements are very complicated, such as structured settlements, and the deal is usually struck before the documentation can be completed. In such cases the settlement will be binding if there is agreement on the essential terms.

Example of Non-Complying Performance

Willem and Thomas have a contract whereby Thomas has agreed to buy 1,200 litres of molasses from Willem. The contract states that the molasses must be delivered in 80 15-litre containers. Willem delivers the molasses in 100 12-litre containers. Because the tender of performance does not comply with the terms of the contract, Thomas is not obligated to accept it. Even though the total amount of molasses delivered (1,200 litres) is correct, Willem did not perform his obligations and is in breach of contract.

2. *Income Tax Act*, R.S.C. 1985, c. 1 (5th Supp.).

Tender of payment occurs where the performance required of a party is the payment of money. The precision required for the tender of performance also extends to the tender of payment. To comply with the terms of the contract, payment must be tendered either in **legal tender** or in the method specified in the contract, if any. If the contract states that payment must be made by way of certified cheque, delivery of an uncertified cheque will not constitute performance, and the receiving party need not accept it. If the contract does not specify a form of payment, legal tender must be used. The *Currency Act*[3] states that legal tender consists of notes (also called bank notes or bills) issued by the Bank of Canada and coins issued by the Royal Canadian Mint.

legal tender
notes (bills) issued by the Bank of Canada and coins issued by the Royal Canadian Mint, subject to certain restrictions

To avoid serious inconvenience to payees, the *Currency Act* establishes some limits relating to the legality of payment with large volumes of coins. Paying a debt with a truckload of pennies is not performance and need not be accepted by the creditor. However, unless the contract states otherwise, payment in Canadian notes is always legal tender. The amount tendered must also be the exact amount, as a party is not obligated to make change. Therefore, offering a $1,000 bill to pay a $10 debt (especially when the party knows that the other will not be able to make change) is not proper tender of payment.

In the business world, large sums of money are rarely paid in cash. Cheques and electronic transfers of funds are the preferred forms of payment. Using cash is inconvenient and creates potential security problems. Despite the common practice of using forms of payment other than legal tender, it is important to remember that unless the contract states otherwise, a party to a contract is not obligated to accept any form of payment except legal tender. This fact can be used by unscrupulous parties to get out of a contract to which they would otherwise be bound. Such situations can be avoided by specifying in the contract how tender of payment is to be made or by using cash.

Example of Tender of Payment

Paolo agrees to sell his kayak to Allison for $2,500. They agree that Allison will pick up the kayak the following day. Later the same day, Paolo gets an offer of $2,900 from Renée. Paolo wants to sell the kayak to Renée instead. Allison hears about this and shows up at Paolo's the next day with payment in cash. Paolo cannot refuse the tender of payment. However, if Allison had arrived with a cheque, even a certified one, Paolo would be able to refuse payment because a cheque is not legal tender.

If a debtor tenders payment in the correct form, on the right date, and at the right time and place but the creditor refuses it, the debtor still has the obligation to pay the creditor.

Of course, it would be foolish for a party to refuse a reasonable form of payment for the sole reason that the form was wrong, apart from any other lawful reason for refusing the tender of payment. If a debtor tries to make payment in the form of a

---

3. *Currency Act*, R.S.C. 1985, c. C-52.

certified cheque and the creditor refuses it because it is not legal tender, the creditor is within his or her rights, and the debtor still has the obligation to pay the creditor. However, the creditor might still be prohibited from charging interest on the debt after the date of tender; if the creditor tried to sue the debtor for payment, he or she might face the same cost consequences.

Discharge by Agreement

The parties to a contract may agree between themselves not to proceed with the contract before its terms are fully performed. This is a **waiver**, and it discharges the contract. By agreeing to a waiver, neither party can insist on the performance of the other party's obligations.

waiver
a voluntary agreement to relinquish a right, such as a right under a contract

If, at the time of waiver, neither party to the contract has performed any of the terms of the contract, then there is a mutual release of the parties from their obligations. This mutual release constitutes consideration for the waiver, and it is enforceable. If one of the parties has performed his or her obligations but the other has not, then the waiver lacks consideration, because the party who has completed his or her obligations gains nothing from the waiver. For a waiver to be enforceable under these circumstances, other consideration should be present, or the waiver should be in writing and under seal. A waiver must be voluntary and cannot be imposed by one party on another.

> ### Example of Waiver
>
> Margit agrees to build a garage for Ramesh for $5,000. Before Margit begins construction, Ramesh tells her that he has changed his mind and does not want a new garage after all. At this point, if both Margit and Ramesh agree, they can each waive the other's obligations under the contract and the contract is discharged. Margit is under no obligation to agree but may do so voluntarily if she wishes. The consideration for the waiver is the mutual release of their obligations: Margit from her obligation to build the garage, and Ramesh from his obligation to pay $5,000. Such a waiver would be enforceable. If Margit has already built the garage and Ramesh then states that he no longer wants it, then any agreement by Margit to forgo payment would be without consideration and unenforceable.

material alteration
a change in a contract that changes its legal meaning and effect; a change that goes to the heart or purpose of the contract

The parties to a contract may voluntarily decide to alter or amend its terms. If they change only minor terms, the contract itself remains intact. However, if the changes amount to a **material alteration** of the contract's terms, the original contract is discharged and a new one (the altered contract) is substituted. It is often difficult to determine whether the terms that have been altered are only minor, material, or substantial terms. To make this decision requires an examination of the effect of the alterations. If the alterations change the effect, meaning, or purpose of the contract, they may be material alterations. The alterations must go to the heart or root of the contract. If so, the original contract is discharged, and a new contract has been substituted for the original.

Example of Material Alteration

In November, Ibrahim orders a camper from Bayshore RV Ltd. The camper is to be of a certain size, have a custom layout, and have various custom luxury fittings for the interior. The contract states that the camper will be ready no later than the following May. Over the next few months, Ibrahim keeps changing his mind about what he wants. He changes the fittings, the size of the camper, and the layout. When Bayshore finally has the camper ready, it is nearly July, two months after it was supposed to be ready. Ibrahim refuses to take delivery, claiming that Bayshore is in breach of contract.

Bayshore argues that the changes made to the original contract were not just cosmetic: Ibrahim ordered a different-sized camper with a different layout. Therefore, the alterations were material, the original contract had been discharged, and a new contract had been substituted. The new contract makes no mention of a delivery date, so Bayshore is not in breach of contract.

The parties to a contract may also agree that a new contract will be substituted for an existing contract. If the new contract is between the existing parties, it is a *substituted agreement*. If the new contract involves the substitution of a new party, it is novation, which was discussed above in the context of privity of contract. In either case, the original contract is discharged.

In some cases, a party to a contract may find that he or she is unwilling or unable to fulfill his or her obligations under the contract and wants to terminate it. The other party may be willing to allow the contract to be terminated upon the payment of a sum of money or some other compensation. For example, if a supplier of goods finds that it cannot deliver the goods requested by a buyer, it may offer to substitute other goods. If a party who had agreed to supply services finds that he or she cannot complete the job, the other party may be willing to accept payment of money as compensation for the delay and expense of finding someone else to complete the work. This form of compromise is called **accord and satisfaction**. There is a distinction between accord and satisfaction and the material alteration of terms or a substituted agreement, which is found in the intent of the parties. With accord and satisfaction, the primary intent of the parties is to discharge the existing contract. In the case of a material alteration of terms or a substituted agreement, the primary intent of the parties is to form a new contract.

In the case of *British Russian Gazette & Trade Outlook Ltd. v. Associated Newspapers Ltd.*,[4] the court stated:

> Accord and satisfaction is the purchase of a release from an obligation arising under contract . . . by means of any valuable consideration, not being the actual performance of the obligation itself. The accord is the agreement by which the obligation is discharged. The satisfaction is the consideration which makes the agreement operative.

accord and satisfaction
a means of discharging a contract whereby the parties agree to accept some form of compromise or settlement instead of performance of the original terms of the contract

---

4. *British Russian Gazette & Trade Outlook Ltd. v. Associated Newspapers Ltd.*, [1933] 2 K.B. 616 at 644 (C.A.).

merger
the discharge of one contract by its replacement with, or absorption into, an identical contract

Parties may also discharge a contract by **merger**. If the parties enter into a verbal agreement that they later commit to writing, they have actually formed two contracts. The first is the verbal contract, and the second is the written contract. If the terms of the contract are identical, the first contract is merged with or absorbed into the second contract. The first contract is thereby discharged. If the terms of the contracts are not identical, then either novation or the material substitution of terms has occurred.

Discharge as of Right

The terms of a contract can allow one or both parties to discharge or terminate the contract. This is an **option to terminate**. This is also a form of discharge by agreement, because the option is included in the contract by the agreement of the parties.

option to terminate
a term in a contract that allows one or both parties to discharge or terminate the contract before performance has been fully completed

Ordinarily, the option must be exercised before the complete performance of the contract, and exercising the option is usually subject to certain terms. For example, a contract of employment may be terminated by the employer upon reasonable notice to the employee. A mortgage may be terminated by the mortgagor upon payment of the outstanding principal, plus an interest penalty, to the mortgagee. The exercise of the option to terminate does not depend on any event: the party with such a right may exercise it at will.

condition precedent
an event (or non-event) that must occur (or not occur) before a contract can be enforced

A contract may provide that one or both parties have the right to terminate the contract if some event in the future does or does not occur. This is called a **condition precedent**. For example, someone buying a house may make the agreement to purchase conditional upon obtaining financing. If the financing is not obtained, he or she is not required to purchase the house. Someone buying a business may make the purchase conditional upon receiving a favourable audit of the financial statements of the business. If the auditor's report is negative, the purchase need not be completed. If a certain area of land is currently being considered for rezoning, a land developer may wish to purchase the property only if the rezoning application is *not* approved. If the rezoning application is approved, the developer has no obligation to purchase the property.

These are all conditions precedent that may be included in the terms of the contract. The contract does not come into existence before the fulfillment of the condition precedent. The parties cannot withdraw their offer and acceptance, but they incur no obligation to perform the contract until the condition is fulfilled. The obligation to perform is, in effect, postponed. However, if one of the parties decides to terminate the contract before the fulfillment of the condition, he or she is in breach of contract.

condition subsequent
an event that, if it occurs, may terminate an existing contract

A condition precedent must be distinguished from a **condition subsequent**, which is a future event that, if it occurs, terminates or discharges an existing contract. In the case of the condition precedent, the contract does not come into existence until the event occurs. With a condition subsequent, the contract exists and performance is required, but the contract may be discharged if the event occurs. For example, a contract to attend an outdoor concert may contain a term that states that the ticket price is refundable if the concert is cancelled owing to bad weather. In a contract to construct a building, the building plans may be subject to approval by the owner at various stages throughout construction. Failure to obtain approval from the owner, or the withholding of approval by the owner, will terminate the contract.

A contract may also provide that in the event of a natural disaster or "act of God," strike or lockout, war, or insurrection, the contract is terminated. This kind of a condition subsequent, when written into a contract, is often referred to as a *force majeure* clause and is commonly found in contracts for the transport of goods and for construction. To rely on a *force majeure* clause, the events in question must be beyond the control of the parties to the contract and not able to be avoided through the exercise of **due diligence**.

due diligence
the attention and care that a reasonable person would exercise with respect to his or her concerns; the obligation to make every reasonable effort to meet one's obligations

DISCHARGE OR TERMINATION BY OPERATION OF LAW

The *Bankruptcy and Insolvency Act*[5] provides that upon being released or discharged from bankruptcy, all the contracts under which the bankrupt had any obligations are discharged. There are some exceptions to this rule, including obligations to pay child support and to repay student loans.

All provinces have statutes of limitations that limit the time period within which actions to enforce contractual rights may be commenced. The Ontario *Limitations Act, 2002*,[6] for example, states that a proceeding shall not be commenced in respect of a claim after two years from the date the claim was discovered. The time limits imposed by these statutes are inflexible—it is impossible to enforce a contract if the action is brought outside these time limits.

This does not actually discharge the contract, which remains valid and binding. However, the obligations under the contract can no longer be enforced, so that the effect is the same as if the contract had been discharged.

The time limits imposed by the various limitations statutes are a statute codification of the common-law **doctrine of laches**, which is based on the premise that failure to bring an action for the enforcement of contractual rights within a reasonable time may result in prejudice to the other party. If this is the case, the action will be barred, and the courts will refuse to hear the action or enforce the contract. The *Limitations Act* does not replace the doctrine of laches. The difference between the two is that the limitations statutes impose specific time limits, while the doctrine of laches relies on the concept of a "reasonable" time limit. Therefore, it is theoretically possible to bring an action within the time limits imposed by the limitations statutes but still be barred by the doctrine of laches if the court thinks that a reasonable time limit is shorter than that specified in the statute.

The doctrine of laches simply bars the enforcement of the contract; it does not discharge it. However, the effect is the same as with the limitations statutes. If the contract is unenforceable, it is the same as if it had been discharged.

doctrine of laches
a common-law doctrine that states that the neglect or failure to institute an action or lawsuit within a reasonable time period, together with prejudice suffered by the other party as a result of the delay, will result in the barring of the action

---

5. *Bankruptcy and Insolvency Act*, R.S.C. 1985, c. B-3.
6. *Limitations Act, 2002*, S.O. 2002, c. 24, Sched. B, s. 4.

CHAPTER SUMMARY

As a general rule, a third party who is not a party to a contract cannot incur any liability or claim any benefit under it owing to lack of privity of contract. However, some statutes and common-law doctrines provide an exception to this rule, as in contracts of insurance or contracts that involve partnerships.

A third party may gain rights under a contract by novation, where the third party is substituted for one of the parties, and a new contract is formed. Contracts that do not require personal services may be vicariously performed by a third party. Parties to a contract may create a trust, which expressly confers a benefit on, and may be enforced by, a third party. Parties may also enter into a contract that confers a benefit on a third party by implication or inference, and that the third party can argue is a constructive trust.

Third parties may also acquire rights and liabilities under a contract by way of an equitable assignment or a statutory assignment. Assignments are subject to the equities that existed between the original parties to the contract.

Once a contract is discharged, it is null and void. Contracts are most commonly discharged through performance of the contractual obligations. Performance usually takes one of two forms: performing an action (for example, delivering goods or performing services) or paying money. The act of offering to perform the obligations under a contract is called tender of performance or tender of payment. The performance must comply exactly with the terms of the contract, or the tender need not be accepted by the other party. Once all obligations are performed, the contract is discharged.

Parties to a contract may also agree to discharge it. If the discharge occurs before performance of the contract, it is called a waiver, and the contract is discharged. If the parties agree to materially alter the terms of the contract, a new contract is formed and the original contract is discharged. If the parties agree that the terms of the contract will not be fulfilled and a compromise or settlement is reached instead (called accord and satisfaction), the original contract is discharged. If the parties enter into a verbal contract that is later put in writing, the original verbal contract merges with the written contract and is thereby discharged.

The terms of a contract may also provide that one or both parties have the option to terminate or discharge the contract, usually upon terms such as notice or the payment of money. The terms of a contract may also include a condition precedent, the occurrence of which is necessary before the contract becomes enforceable. If the condition precedent is not fulfilled, the contract is discharged. Another term of a contract may be a condition subsequent, the occurrence of which may discharge the contract.

A contract may be discharged by the operation of law, such as through the operation of the *Bankruptcy and Insolvency Act*, or be in effect discharged, such as through the operation of the *Limitations Act* or the doctrine of laches.

KEY TERMS

accord and satisfaction

assignee

assignment

assignor

beneficiary

chose in action/thing in action

condition precedent

condition subsequent

constructive trust

discharged

doctrine of laches

due diligence

express trust

legal tender

material alteration

merger

novation

null and void

option to terminate

privity

setoff

tender of performance

trust

trustee

vicarious performance

waiver

REVIEW QUESTIONS

True or False?

_____ 1. A certified cheque is legal tender.

_____ 2. Tender of performance can establish breach by the other party if he or she does not accept the performance.

_____ 3. Where both parties mutually agree not to require performance under a contract before the contract is performed by either one, the contract is discharged.

_____ 4. If an assignee takes assignment of a contract and later learns that the assignor owed the other contract party money, the assignee may be required to reduce its bill under the contract by the debt, even though the debt was created by the assignor.

_____ 5. Where a contract includes a condition precedent, the contract obligations (and therefore the contract itself) do not become binding until the condition is met.

_____ 6. Novation can occur automatically, by operation of law.

_____ 7. A condition subsequent is an event that, if it occurs, may discharge an existing contract.

_____ 8. A party waives a contract right when he or she suffers prejudice due to the other party's failure to comply with a contract obligation.

_____ 9. When a material alteration to a contract is requested by one party, the other party will often be justified in demanding consideration or compensation for the change.

_____ 10. The main reason a party may tender performance is to demonstrate that he or she has waived a contract term.

Fill in the Blanks

1. When a party transfers her rights under a contract to another party, the contract is said to be _____.

2. A person who is negatively affected by a contract between two other parties, but who is not a party himself, is likely blocked from suing under the contract because of a lack of _____.

3. Aziza hires Monica, a renowned psychic, to provide palm-reading services at a bridal shower. Monica likely cannot send her cousin Stephen to provide these services in her place, because this is not a contract capable of _____ performance.

4. A _____ is one who holds property for the benefit of another, who is called the _____.

5. When a contract is terminated and replaced by another contract, this is not assignment, but rather _____.

6. Examples of _____ ____ _____ include contract rights, the right to collect a debt, patent rights, and negotiable instruments.

7. When a trust is created on purpose by the parties, it is called an _____ trust.

8. When a trust is created by operation of law (and is not set up by the parties), it is called a _____ trust.

9. When a contract is assigned, the person who gives up the rights is the ____ and the person who obtains those rights is the _____.

10. Where a debtor's obligation to a creditor is reduced by the creditor's obligation to a debtor, this is known as a _____.

Short Answer

1. Explain the doctrine of privity of contract. What is the rationale for its existence?

2. What are the requirements of novation?

3. Describe the difference between a novation and an assignment of a contract.

4. Under what circumstances do assignments occur as an operation of law?

5. What is a setoff, and when may it be used?

6. In what ways can a contract be discharged? What is the effect of discharging a contract?

7. For what reasons might a party legitimately refuse to accept tender of performance?

8. If a creditor refuses to accept tender of payment, is the debtor freed from the obligation to pay? Explain. What might be the effect of a creditor's refusing tender of payment?

9. Define a "waiver." What is the consideration for a waiver? What should you do in a case where there is no consideration for a waiver?

10. Define "condition subsequent."

EXERCISES

1. Sturdy Tires Ltd. manufactures tires and sells them to wholesalers. Sturdy Tires has an agreement with all its wholesalers that they will not sell the tires for less than the list price except where they are selling to approved dealers. In that case, the wholesalers may sell at a reduced price as long as they obtain an agreement in writing from the dealers that the dealers will not sell the tires below the list price.

   Sturdy Tires sells tires to Selkirk & Sons Inc., a wholesaler. Selkirk & Sons then sells the tires at a reduced price to Doucet Auto Limited, an approved dealer. Despite the agreement with Selkirk & Sons, Doucet holds a promotion and sells the tires for less than list price. Sturdy Tires then brings an action to prevent Doucet from selling its tires for less than list price. Will Sturdy Tires be successful in its action? Why or why not?

2. Dead Poodles is a famous rock band. The lead singer is Wendy Leather. The popularity of the band is based almost solely on the vocals of the lead singer. The band is engaged by Rock Promotions Inc. to give a concert on Canada Day on Parliament Hill in Ottawa to an expected crowd of 100,000. The day before the concert, Rock Promotions receives a fax from Wendy stating that she will not be attending the concert because she is getting married that day. Wendy sends her sister, Candy Leather, to sing in her place. The concert is a big success. Even though the crowd is disappointed not to hear Wendy, they love Candy. Can Rock Promotions sue the Dead Poodles for breach of contract?

3. Dixon & Flagel Ltd. manufactures chemicals. Calder's Chemical Supply Inc. is one of its customers. To finance the purchase of its chemical inventory, Calder's enters into inventory financing agreements with Dixon & Flagel for each order of chemicals. On February 1, Dixon & Flagel delivers an order to Calder's. Under the inventory financing agreement, Calder's is to pay Dixon & Flagel the sum of $14,000 over a period of six months for the chemicals.

   On February 10, Calder's discovers that some of the chemicals are defective and demands a refund in the amount of $6,500. On March 1, Dixon & Flagel assigns the contract to Capital Financing Corp. Capital Financing gives Calder's notice in writing of the assignment on March 5. On March 15, Dixon & Flagel delivers another order of chemicals to Calder's. The cost of the second order is $8,000, to be paid over six months. While delivering the second order, Dixon & Flagel damages Calder's loading dock, which costs Calder's $1,500 to repair. Calder's refuses to pay for any of the chemicals until Dixon & Flagel pays the demanded refund and pays for the damage to the loading dock. What options do the parties in this situation have?

4. Creative Designers Ltd. agrees to redecorate Carmen's home for the sum of $20,000. The services are to include completely redecorating the living room, den, and dining room. The work is to start on May 1 and be completed no later than August 1. After work begins, Carmen changes her mind about the colour of the paint she wants in the den and the type of carpet she wants in the living room. She also wants Creative Designers to redecorate the hall and the foyer. Creative Designers agrees to make all the changes. However, the work is not complete on August 1. Carmen claims that Creative Designers is in breach of contract. What arguments may Creative Designers make?

Contract Interpretation

7

OVERVIEW

LEARNING OUTCOMES

After completing this chapter, you should be able to:

- Describe the goal of contract interpretation.

- Distinguish among representations, terms, conditions, and warranties.

- Explain the parol evidence rule.

- Understand the legal rules relating to exclusion and penalty clauses.

- Explain the concept of frustration as it relates to contracts, and distinguish between frustration and impossibility.

THE GOAL OF INTERPRETATION: MAKING THE CONTRACT WORK

Every contract case that comes to court does so either because one party disagrees with the other about what the contract provisions mean, or because he or she knows very well what the provisions mean and seeks to escape the consequences of that meaning. In either situation, the outcome will turn on the court's interpretation of the language of the agreement. Over the centuries, the courts have established rules about classifying contract provisions to determine their consequences, resolving ambiguity or uncertainty, and determining the consequences of attempts to use language to limit the negative consequences of a contract for a party.

The primary aim of the court is to interpret contracts so as to find and give effect to the intention of the parties.

In examining intention, the court may pay some attention to commercial realities, but generally will not use the rules of interpretation to remake a bad bargain. Instead, it will try to interpret a contract to salvage it, in whole or in part, and make it work as it thinks the parties intended. Where a provision is found to be so incoherent as to be impossible to interpret in a reasonable way, the court may determine it to be void for vagueness but will try to save the balance of the contract. Only as a last resort will the court declare a whole contract void because its meaning and purpose are uncertain, or because the original purpose is impossible to carry out.

This does not mean a court will never intervene to declare a contract to be void or voidable. It may do so where one or both parties have made a major mistake about an important element of the contract. Mistake and its effects were discussed in Chapter 5, Contractual Defects. Where contract performance becomes impossible because of circumstances beyond the control of either party, the court may find that the contract is frustrated and bring it to an end.

Here we will introduce some of the major concepts used by courts to interpret contracts:

- *Classifying contract provisions:* We will examine how the courts classify and interpret representations, terms, conditions, and warranties in a contract in terms of the effect those provisions have on the rights and responsibilities of the parties.
- *Assessing evidence to prove the meaning of a provision:* We will look at the search for certainty and the way in which the courts assess evidence using the parol evidence rule to decide the meaning of unclear terms or provisions.
- *Interpreting exclusion and penalty provisions:* We will examine how the courts interpret exclusion and penalty clauses—provisions that seek to enhance or limit liability and damages under a contract—to determine whether there is a breach.
- *Determining frustration:* Last, we will examine how courts determine when and how a contract may become frustrated so that it has become impossible to perform owing to circumstances beyond the control of either party.

CONTRACT PROVISIONS: REPRESENTATIONS, TERMS, CONDITIONS, AND WARRANTIES

As a contract is being negotiated, the parties may make a number of statements to each other. Some statements will be made in the course of negotiations, and others will be terms agreed to in the contract itself. It is not always clear whether a statement is part of the negotiating process or part of the contract. When we establish that a statement is part of the contract, we have to then determine what the effect of the contract statement means in terms of consequences for the parties, particularly if there is a breach of contract.

We must first consider whether a statement is a **representation** or a term of the contract. If a statement is a representation, it is not a part of the contract that either party has agreed to. Instead, it is classified as a statement made by one party during negotiation of the contract.

Representations are important in contract law because some misrepresentations may permit the party who is misled to avoid the contract. To have this effect, a representation must be a statement of fact, not opinion, and must be material; that is, a **material representation** is one that induced the other party to enter into the contract. Misrepresentation was discussed in more detail in Chapter 5, Contractual Defects.

representation
a statement made to induce someone to enter into a contract

material representation
a statement of fact, not opinion, made by one party, of sufficient weight to induce the other party to enter into a contract

> ### Example of a Representation
> Alphonse is looking for a load of Freestone peaches for his jam factory. Freestone peaches have the right texture, and it is crucial that the peaches be of that type. Bertrand has a warehouse full of peaches he wants to sell. Alphonse asks Bertrand, "Are these Freestone peaches?" If Bertrand says "yes," that is a material representation. If Bertrand says, "I think so," that is merely his opinion and not a material representation. If Bertrand says, "Peaches have lots of vitamins," that is not a material representation, because the presence or absence of vitamins is not important to Alphonse in making peach jam. It would not influence him in deciding whether to enter into a contract with Bertrand.

PRACTICE TIP
If you make representations, you may avoid being bound by them if you make them conditional. Phrases such as "to the best of my knowledge," "as far as I can tell," and "so far as I know" may assist the representer, assuming there was some attempt to inform the other party and the representations were not fraudulent. Also, putting disclaimers in large type and simple language in a written contract can help support an argument that the representing party brought the matter to the other party's attention.

CASE IN POINT

The Bad Hair Day

From: *Hirsch v. duBrule*, [2006] A.J. No. 1712 (Prov. Ct.).

The plaintiff was a young woman with thinning hair. She decided to purchase a hair replacement system from the defendant. In the course of discussions with the defendant's representative, the defendant represented to her that he would be able to match her hair or, even if he could not exactly match her hair, he would provide her with a hair replacement system she would be happy with. The court found that this was a pre-contract representation that strongly influenced the plaintiff to have the defendant do the work. The contract itself, however, contained, among other clauses, the following two:

- 10. I [the Plaintiff] acknowledge that the Company's literature and consultation were, and are, intended to familiarize me with the basic methods of hair replacement available today and, in particular, the unique attributes of the Company's method. I realize that the Company's statements describing the benefits and attributes of the System using the method are accurate when related to the average client but are not necessarily accurate with respect to each individual client. . . .

- 14. This document alone contains my entire agreement with the Company. Any promises, inducements, or agreements not set forth in this agreement, whether oral or written, shall have no force or effect.

The court found that the hair replacement was not a good match, and that it failed to meet the promise in the pre-contract representations. The question then was whether the two clauses overrode any representations made. On their face, they clearly did. The court held that where a disclaimer clause in a contract clearly contradicts a pre-contract representation, the disclaimer clause or any clause limiting liability must be clearly brought to the attention of the other party. If it is not, then the contract provision is of no effect. In this case, the clauses limiting liability were *not* clearly brought to the attention of the plaintiff. Consequently, the plaintiff was entitled to rescission of the contract and the return of the price paid.

---

term
a provision of a contract; terms are either conditions or warranties

If a statement related to a contract is not a representation, it may be a **term**. A term is part of the contract itself, an element of what one party or the other has promised.

Terms fall into two categories.

1. If the term of the contract is essential or goes to the root of a contract, it is called a **condition**.

condition
an essential term of a contract, the breach of which denies the innocent party the benefit of the contract, or defeats the purpose of the contract

2. If the term is a minor or subsidiary term of the contract, it is called a **warranty**.

Whether a term is a condition or a warranty determines what the effect will be if it is breached. A breach of condition is considered so serious as to destroy the value of the contract for the victim of the breach so that he or she is deprived of most or all of the contract's value. If the breach is one of warranty only, it is adjudged less serious, and the remedies may be more restricted than would be the case for breach of condition. Determining whether a term is a condition or a warranty is not always easy. You have to examine the contract as a whole, as well as the context in which the agreement was made, including all representations and state-

warranty
a minor term of a contract, the breach of which does not defeat the contract's purpose

ments that the parties made during negotiations. What may be a breach of condition in one case may be a breach of warranty in another, depending on the circumstances. The effects of breach of condition and breach of warranty are discussed in more detail in Chapter 8, Breach of Contract and Remedies.

Examples of Conditions and Warranties

Mai Ling signed an agreement to purchase the latest model of a Zephyr sports car. The model she chose was fast and manoeuvrable, which was important because she drove from Toronto to Montreal every weekend to visit her boyfriend. She chose green for the exterior colour. The car that was delivered was a different model from what she ordered, although it was green. This would be a breach of condition because the car itself, the subject matter of the contract, was quite different from what she bargained for. Had the right model been delivered but in the wrong colour, the colour would likely have been a breach of warranty, because the colour was not her primary concern.

If Mai Ling had contracted to have her house painted and chose green, and the house was painted purple, the difference in colour would amount to a breach of condition. Here, colour would be a key and essential part of the contract, rather than a subsidiary consideration.

CASE IN POINT

Breach of Condition or Warranty?

From: *Herron v. Hunting Chase Inc.*, 2001 ABQB 1134 (CanLII), 2003 ABCA 219 (CanLII).

The plaintiffs agreed to sell shares of Chase Manufacturing. The defendant Hunting agreed to purchase the plaintiffs' shares in Chase. The agreement provided that the plaintiffs' retained earnings would be $200,000 at the time of closing, and that Hunting would pay the plaintiffs certain bonuses.

At closing, the retained earnings did not total $200,000, and Hunting did not pay the bonuses. The plaintiffs sued, seeking payment of the bonuses pursuant to the agreement. Hunting argued that the fact that the plaintiffs had failed to retain the $200,000 excused it from having to pay the bonuses. The trial judge agreed. He found that Herron's failure with respect to the retained earnings was a breach of an essential condition, not a mere breach of warranty, which entitled Chase to repudiate or rescind the contract, not just sue for damages. The plaintiffs appealed.

The appeal was allowed on several grounds. On the issue whether the breach was one of condition or warranty, the appeal court held that it was a breach of warranty. As a result, the breach of the retained earnings provision was not one that entitled the defendants to repudiate the contract. That being the case, as the contract was not void, on the separate issue of the bonuses, Hunting should have paid the bonuses, and Hunting was therefore liable to the plaintiffs for the amounts of the bonuses.

THE SEARCH FOR CERTAINTY: THE PAROL EVIDENCE RULE, ITS EXCEPTIONS, AND RECTIFICATION

Where an oral contract exists, you can imagine how the parties might get into a disagreement about the terms, each party relying on his or her memory as to what was agreed to and remembering the terms of the contract differently. However, when the contract is in writing, it is reasonable to expect that a dispute about its terms can be settled by looking at what is written, and by giving the language used in the contract its plain and ordinary meaning when interpreting the terms. It is also reasonable to say that if the contract is in writing, the parties should not be able to drag in other evidence, oral or written, to contradict the written terms of the agreement.

parol evidence rule
if a contract is in writing and is clear, no other written or oral evidence is admissible to contradict, vary, or interpret the agreement

This is the approach that the common law takes in interpreting written contracts. The approach is expressed in the **parol evidence rule**, which states that if the contract is in writing and the language of the written agreement is clear and unambiguous, then no other oral or written evidence can be used to interpret, vary, or contradict the terms of the written agreement. The court interprets the agreement by looking only at its written terms, and does not consider other evidence because it is not relevant to determining what the contract means.

Where a court finds that the language of a contract is unclear or ambiguous and applies the parol evidence rule, it has to consider whether there is evidence outside the written agreement that is relevant to interpreting the agreement. As a result of considering this outside evidence, the courts have developed several exceptions to the parol evidence rule where outside evidence may be deemed to be relevant and admissible in interpreting a written contract. Table 7.1 summarizes these exceptions.

Ambiguous Contract Language

Where it can be shown that the language of the written agreement is unclear or ambiguous, so that the meaning of a term or provision is not certain, oral evidence or other written evidence may be used to assist in interpreting the agreement.

Example of Ambiguous Contract Language

A contract for membership in a professional organization has a term that says: "All members who are doctors and lawyers may vote at membership meetings." Fred argues that it is clear that a member must be a doctor *and* a lawyer to vote. Ginger argues that the language is ambiguous and that it could also mean that members who belong to either the medical or the legal profession may vote. Ginger, by arguing that the language is ambiguous, may introduce evidence to show that only 2 of 700 organization members are members of both professions and that, in context, Fred's interpretation is nonsensical. Ginger, having argued ambiguity, is entitled to present evidence from outside the contract to resolve the alleged ambiguity.

If the court decides that the evidence is relevant to proving that point, the evidence will be admitted to assist in interpreting the meaning of the contract notwithstanding the parol evidence rule.

Essential Collateral Agreement

A collateral agreement is a separate and independent contract with valuable consideration that could be enforced independently of the main contract or that has some impact or effect on the main contract, but is not specifically referred to in it. In this case, the court, by giving effect to the collateral contract, will modify the main contract, despite its written terms.

Example of an Essential Collateral Agreement

Alberto agrees to purchase a boat from Marina's Marina. He decides he wants a fire control system installed in the boat. The contract for the purchase of the boat is in writing and sets out a price for the boat. It also states that "a fire control system is to be added," with the price to be added to the purchase price. Alberto and Marina then agree on the fire control system to be installed by Marina. Marina presents an invoice setting out the cost of the equipment plus labour for installation. Alberto says that he is not paying for the labour. He says that the contract for the purchase of the boat included the addition of the cost of the parts for the system, not its installation. Marina argues that the cost is the cost of the parts and includes the cost of installation.

If the court finds the original purchase agreement unclear as to what "a fire control system is to be added" means, it may permit Marina to introduce evidence of the collateral agreement to provide and install the fire control system, in order to determine the meaning of the disputed term in the main contract.

TABLE 7.1 Exceptions to the Parol Evidence Rule

Ambiguous contract language	If a term is unclear or uncertain, external evidence can be used to interpret it
Essential collateral agreement	Where a contract separate from the one being considered affects how the contract being considered should be interpreted, that separate contract (called an essential collateral agreement) can be considered as evidence of meaning/construction
Essential implied term	Where a contract that by custom or convention contains a term that has been inadvertently left out, a party may produce outside evidence of custom or convention to show that a term has been omitted by mistake
Condition precedent existing outside the contract	If the parties agree that there is a condition precedent to the performance of the contract, then a party may introduce external evidence of the condition precedent, where it is not specifically referred to in the contract
Rectification	Where a term agreed to in negotiations is inadvertently omitted from the written document, a party may ask to have that term included by way of rectification or correction of the document, provided: • a mistake has been made in recording the intention of the parties • there is evidence of a common intention • there is clear and cogent evidence of the mistake

Essential Implied Term

If the parties use a form of contract that, by custom of a trade or by convention, usually contains a term that has been inadvertently left out, a party may be able to use oral and written evidence of the custom or convention to show that an implied term of the agreement has been omitted.

Example of an Essential Implied Term

Kris orders a load of grade A lumber from the building supply company to be delivered to a lot where he is building a house. The lumber is loaded on the truck but gets rained on and warps prior to delivery. Kris complains about the quality. The building supply company says, "You ordered grade A lumber, you got grade A lumber. The contract didn't say anything about the state of the goods on delivery."

If it is a custom of the building supply business to deliver supplies as ordered in good condition, Kris may be able to use oral or written evidence to show that this is an implied term of the written contract and argue that the court should "read" the implied term into the written agreement.

Condition Precedent Existing Outside Contract

condition precedent
an event (or non-event) that must occur (or not occur) before a contract can be enforced

Parties to a contract may also separately agree that the contract does not have to be performed until after a particular event, called a **condition precedent**, has occurred. If so, a party who claims that he or she is not obliged to honour the written contract because the condition precedent has not occurred may advance oral and written evidence of non-performance of the condition precedent to contradict the terms of the written agreement.

Example of a Condition Precedent

Ivan and Nan agree by written contract that Ivan will sell his car to Nan for $3,000. Nan tells Ivan before she signs that first she will have to see if she can borrow the money from the bank; if she cannot borrow the money, she says she will not be able to buy the car. Ivan orally agrees and Nan signs. Nan is unable to borrow the money, and Ivan says she is bound by the written contract.

Nan may be able to contradict the written terms of the contract by producing written or oral evidence that there was a condition precedent that makes the written sale contract unenforceable.

Rectification

Rectification is an equitable remedy available to alter the terms of a written agreement where a mistake has been made in the document. It is available in circumstances where the common law might not permit altering the written terms.

The right to this remedy arises where the parties to the contract have held long negotiations and have reached an agreement that is reduced to a written document where a mistake was made recording the terms. Consequently, the effect of the contract is quite different from what was intended by the parties. Rectification does not alter the intention of the parties. Rather, it ensures that the wording of the written agreement accurately corresponds to what the parties intended. Rectification is a powerful remedy and is used with caution, because the courts watch carefully to ensure that it is not simply a cover for trying to undo a bad bargain. The court's focus is not on interpreting the terms of the contract (as is the case when the parol evidence rule is used) but on whether the terms the parties agreed to, whatever they are or however they are interpreted, are accurately reflected in the written contract.

To successfully invoke the remedy of rectification, the party claiming rectification has to show the following with strong and clear evidence:

- *A mistake in recording the intentions of the parties:* The mistake must be clear and unambiguous. It must also be a mutual mistake—that is, both parties are mistaken, and both are mistaken in the same way.
- *Formation of a common intention:* In Canada and England, even if no prior contract has been concluded to show that a mistake has been made, if there is strong and convincing evidence that the parties achieved a position where they had a common intention, that suffices for rectification where the common intention is not reflected in the final contract document.[1]
- *Clear and cogent evidence of a mistake:* There must be clear and convincing proof of a mistake in expressing the parties' intention. The evidence may be written or oral. The standard of proof required appears to be more than the usual civil standard in contract cases of proof on a balance of probabilities. If the case turns on oral evidence, the court is likely to scrutinize this evidence with great care to ensure that a claim for rectification is not an attempt to remake a bad bargain.

Because rectification is an equitable remedy, it is subject to certain defences. Delay by the party claiming rectification may be seen as evidence of insincerity. Negative effects on third parties who are not party to the agreement but who rely on it may act as a bar to rectification. Attempts to carry out the agreement may be seen as accepting it as it stands, and rectification may then be refused. Also, if the parties cannot be restored to their original positions before making the agreement, rectification may be refused.

Example of Request for Rectification

Woodlot Canada Ltd., in Newfoundland, enters into an agreement to ship lumber to Woodhouse Ltd. in England. There have been complex negotiations involving exchanges of faxes and emails, and eventually a formal written agreement is prepared and signed by both parties. The price agreed to is £40,000, as reflected in the negotiation correspondence. When the contract is printed, the price is listed as $40,000. Woodlot immediately applies to

---

1. This is the statement of the law on this issue in the English Court of Appeal case *Joscelyne v. Nissen*, [1970] 2 Q.B. 86 (C.A.). This decision has been followed in Canada.

have the contract rectified. Woodlot argues that both parties intended the price to be in British pounds sterling (£), not dollars; that the recording of the price in the written contract as a dollar amount was a mistake in recording the terms of the contract; and that the evidence, in the form of negotiation correspondence, clearly indicates that the price should have been expressed in pounds sterling.

CASE IN POINT

Ambiguous Language Prompts Admission of Extrinsic Affidavit Evidence

From: *Certus Developments Inc. v. Strategic Equity Corp.*, [2006] A.J. No. 1104, 2006 ABQB 645.

The plaintiff, C, purchased certain lands from the defendant, S, in a commercial mall development. The transaction included a grant to the plaintiff of a right of way and easement over certain of the defendant's lands, to permit vehicles to come and go, and to permit use of parking areas by the plaintiff or its agents. At issue was whether the contract went further and permitted C to construct parking facilities for its own use on the lands granted by easement. The defendant said the contract clearly did not contemplate more than the use of existing parking areas by the plaintiff, none of which was for its exclusive use. The plaintiff said that the contract was ambiguous on that issue, and external evidence should be allowed to prove the plaintiff's position, as an exception to the parol evidence rule.

The defendant pointed to section 1 of the agreement, which granted an easement to C "to pass and re-pass over the Easement Area on foot or by vehicle as may be reasonably required for purposes incidental to or necessary for ingress to and egress from the Certus Lands," an easement "not exclusive to Certus." Rather, under section 1, the defendant, S, "retains the right . . . to pass and re-pass over the Easement Area on foot or by vehicle as may be reasonably required for purposes incidental to or necessary for ingress to and egress from the Premier Lands and for the use, without charge, of all

parking stalls located on the Easement Area." The defendant submitted that the agreement spoke for itself, that extrinsic evidence to vary or contradict the agreement was inadmissible, and that the contract did not entitle Certus to build its own private parking on the lands related to the easement.

Certus countered that the language of the agreement was ambiguous. Certus noted that while section 1 of the agreement read that S "retains the right . . . to pass and re-pass over the Easement Area on foot or by vehicle as may be reasonably required . . . for the use, without charge, of all parking stalls located on the Easement Area," section 3 read that "for the better enjoyment of the easement granted to Certus, at its own expense Certus may construct from time to time . . . improvements upon the Easement Area," such as parking facilities. Thus, Certus submitted that the extrinsic affidavit evidence filed was admissible and was sufficient to support its own interpretation of the agreement given the possible conflict of sections 1 and 3.

The court agreed with Certus, ruling that the terms of the contract were ambiguous. The court admitted affidavit evidence to clarify the terms of the contract, but found that the affidavit evidence was not credible and of no real help to the plaintiff in supporting its claim that it had a right to build its own parking facilities on the easement lands.

EXCLUSION AND PENALTY CLAUSES

Exclusion (Exemption) Clauses

Sometimes a party will insist on including in a contract an **exclusion clause**, also called an **exemption clause**, that protects that party from liability for negligence in performing contractual obligations or from failing to carry them out.

For example, most parking lot contracts include a clause that states that the lot owner is not liable for damage to your car or its contents, however the damage is caused, or for theft of the car or contents. In other contracts, the clause limits liability. For example, if you buy a roll of film that includes developing the pictures you take, the contract is likely to include a clause that says if the company loses or damages the film or fails to develop it, it is liable only for the cost of the film, even if you are a professional photographer and your pictures are worth thousands of dollars.

Generally, a party to a contract who wishes to limit liability for negligent conduct or for conduct where that party is liable though not at fault may limit liability, provided both parties agree to a limited liability clause in the contract. It is clear, however, that fraud by the party relying on an exclusion clause will not be excluded, no matter what the clause says. For example, in the parking lot example, if the company that owns the lot permits individuals to break into cars unimpeded in exchange for a "cut" of the stolen contents, the exclusion clause will not protect the company if the scheme is discovered.

Notice of an Exclusion Clause

For an exclusion clause to be effective, the party relying on it must be sure to bring the clause to the other party's attention and notice. The act of giving notice must include reasonable steps to draw the clause to the other party's attention. If, for example, the clause is buried in fine print on the back of the contract, even if the other party has accepted the contract and it is otherwise binding on him or her, that party may be able to show that the placement of the clause does not constitute reasonable steps to bring it to his or her attention.

These clauses are often inserted by the party relying on them in printed form contracts or documents that are separate from but part of the contract, such as parking lot and dry-cleaning receipts. In these cases, the courts have required that the party relying on the clause demonstrate that the offeree knew the clause was there or had ample opportunity to know it was there. For example, if a parking lot posts a large, illuminated sign that sets out the liability exclusion in plain language in large print right where you drive into the lot and pay, that may be a reasonable way of giving the necessary notice. So may printing the clause on the contract in plain language, in larger print, and in a different colour from the rest of the contract. Where the exclusion clause is referred to on the contract but posted elsewhere—for example, on a receipt—this may be insufficient to constitute proper notice of the clause.

Generally, the courts carefully examine how notice was given. Courts are reluctant to permit a party from contracting out of his or her own negligence, particu-

exclusion/exemption clause
a clause in a contract that limits the liability of the parties

larly where bargaining power is unequal, as it often is with printed form contracts, where negotiation of the terms at the time you park your car, for instance, is simply impractical.[2] However, where the contracting parties have roughly equal bargaining power, there is time to consider the terms carefully, and both parties are independently advised, the courts are more likely to let the clause stand on the ground that, with equality of bargaining power, the exclusion clause is not unilaterally imposed on one party by the other.

The courts have also made it clear that notice must be given before the contract is entered into, not afterward.[3] However, express notice need not be given in every case, particularly where both parties are relatively sophisticated and have experience with the type of contract in question or are knowledgeable about the practices and conventions in a particular trade.

For example, in one case, an owner of goods sued when the goods were damaged by the shipper. The evidence showed that the plaintiff had worked in the shipping industry and was familiar with the standard form shipping contract, which contained a standard exclusion clause. The court held that while the plaintiff was not given express notice of the clause, he certainly was aware of the existence of the clause and what it meant from his experience in the industry.[4]

PRACTICE TIP

If you are drafting an exclusion clause, use larger print, coloured ink, and/or place the clause in a text box or otherwise draw the other party's attention to it.

Strict Interpretation

If the court is satisfied that the party relying on the clause gave appropriate notice, it may still interpret the clause narrowly against that party. In particular, the **contra proferentem rule** of interpretation may be used so that the party relying on the exclusion clause must show strict compliance with the contract.

contra proferentem rule
a rule used in the interpretation of contracts when dealing with ambiguous terms according to which a court will choose the interpretation that favours the party who did not draft the contract

For example, if a parking lot contract excludes liability for theft or damage to the car by the parking company, but damage is done intentionally by an employee without the company's authorization, the clause might not operate to exclude liability. For that to happen, the clause would also have to include a phrase that excluded liability caused by the owner or by the intentional acts of employees. In other words, clauses are construed narrowly against the person who inserted them in the contract and who relies on them.

2. *Browne v. Core Rentals Ltd.* (1983), 23 B.L.R. 291 (Ont. H.C.); *Tilden Rent-A-Car Co. v. Clendenning* (1978), 83 D.L.R. (3d) 400 (Ont. C.A.).
3. *Campbell v. Image,* [1978] 2 W.W.R. 663 (B.C. Co. Ct.), *Mendelssohn v. Normand Ltd.,* [1970] 1 Q.B. 177.
4. *Captain v. Far Eastern Steamship Co.* (1978), 97 D.L.R. (3d) 250 (B.C.S.C.).

Exclusion Clauses, Fundamental Breach, and
Tercon v. British Columbia

In England, the courts developed a limitation of the application and operation of exclusion clauses in circumstances where the exempted conduct or act amounted to more than a breach of a minor term, but was a fundamental breach of the contract, where the breach went to the "root" or "heart" of the contract.

Determining whether a breach was fundamental is not always easy. If you contracted to ship goods and the shipper negligently allowed them to be destroyed, you could argue that the contract was about shipping goods and their destruction was a fundamental breach, because the subject matter of the contract had been lost. Similarly, where the goods were slightly damaged in transit, it would be hard to argue that the breach was more than minor. The problem with fundamental breach is that it is difficult to determine where the line between the two extremes lies when a breach goes from minor—where exclusion clauses apply—to major— where the breach is so significant that the exclusion clause cannot be relied on.

The courts in Canada and England have gone back and forth on the effect of fundamental breach on an exclusion clause. The impact of fundamental breach and its effect on exclusion clauses was weakened considerably as a result of the decision of the Supreme Court of Canada in *London Drugs Ltd. v. Kuehne & Nagel International Ltd.*[5] After a major review of the cases and the issue, the court was split, taking two different approaches: one approach applied the doctrine of fundamental breach and considered whether the breach undermined the entire contract so as to go to the root of the contract, in which case the exclusion clause did not apply; the other approach found fundamental breach to be an artificial doctrine that creates unnecessary complexities and uncertainty in the law. If unfairness resulted from applying an exclusion clause, it would be better to simply address the matter as an issue of unconscionability.[6] As a result of the court's split in this case, the future of fundamental breach became very uncertain.

That uncertainty came to an end with the decision of the Supreme Court of Canada in *Tercon Contractors Ltd. v. British Columbia (Transportation and Highways)*,[7] in which the Supreme Court abandoned fundamental breach altogether as a tool for determining whether a party could rely on an exclusion clause. The facts of the case are set out in the Case in Point feature below.

As an alternative to using fundamental breach as a method of determining whether an exclusion clause was enforceable, the court set out a three-part analytic scheme:

---

5. *London Drugs Ltd. v. Kuehne & Nagel International Ltd.* (1992), 97 D.L.R. (4th) 261 (S.C.C.). See, in particular, the decision of Iacobucci J. For further discussion of this case, see G.H.L. Fridman, *The Law of Contract in Canada*, 3d ed. (Scarborough, ON: Carswell, 1994), 586-88.
6. *Hunter Engineering Co. v. Syncrude Canada Ltd.* (1989), 57 D.L.R. (4th) 321 (S.C.C.).
7. *Tercon Contractors Ltd. v. British Columbia (Transportation and Highways)*, 2006 BCSC 499, rev'd 2007 BCCA 592, rev'd 2010 SCC 4, [2010] 1 S.C.R. 69.

1. *Does the exclusion clause apply to the circumstances of the case?* The court must determine whether, as a matter of interpretation, an exclusion clause applies to the circumstances established by the evidence of what the parties intended—is the breach one that is contemplated by the exclusionary clause?

2. *If the clause applies, was it unconscionable?* If the exclusion clause does apply, the second issue is whether the exclusion clause, considering all of the circumstances, was unconscionable and therefore invalid at the time the contract was made.

3. *If the exclusion clause is held to be valid at the time of contract formation and applicable to the facts of the case, the court may consider whether the clause should be enforced on the basis of public policy.* The party seeking to avoid enforcement of the exclusion clause must demonstrate an abuse of freedom of contract that outweighs the public interest in the court's enforcing contracts as made by the parties. The court noted that conduct approaching serious criminality (even though not outright criminal) or obvious fraud are examples of conduct that would override freedom of contract and render an exclusion clause inoperable.

CASE IN POINT

Exclusion Clause Not a Licence to Violate Tendering Rules

From: *Tercon Contractors Ltd. v. British Columbia (Transportation and Highways)*, 2006 BCSC 499, rev'd 2007 BCCA 592, rev'd 2010 SCC 4, [2010] 1 S.C.R. 69.

British Columbia solicited expressions of interest in the design and construction of a highway, which resulted in six teams making submissions. The province subsequently decided to design the highway itself. Tercon and Brentwood were short-listed on the tenders to construct the highway. The province chose Brentwood, but Brentwood turned out to be working in a joint venture with an unqualified bidder, so its bid technically did not meet the requirements for the province's tendering contract. The province therefore breached its own tendering contract by awarding the construction contract to an unqualified applicant. This, and related conduct by the province, constituted a breach of the implied contractual duty of fairness to bidders.

Tercon sued to recover its tendering costs, and the province defended by relying on a broad exclusion clause. At trial, the province was found to have acted in a cavalier and grossly unfair manner,

and the unfair and improper conduct by the province was not contemplated by the parties to the tendering contract. The province, deprived of any reliance on the exclusion clause, was ordered to pay Tercon's damages for breach of the tendering agreement.

The Court of Appeal set aside the decision, holding that the exclusion clause was clear and unambiguous and barred compensation for all defaults.

The Supreme Court of Canada allowed the appeal. Clear language would have been necessary to exclude liability for breach of the implied obligation, particularly in the case of public procurement. The court rejected the idea that the exclusion clause contemplated improper conduct such as that engaged in by the province, particularly where the conduct struck at the heart of the integrity of a public tendering process.

> ### Example of an Exclusion Clause
>
> JoAnn parks her car in Wanda's Parking Lot. The following is printed on the back of the parking receipt: "Wanda is not responsible for loss or damage to your car due to the negligence of Wanda or her employees." Linh, one of Wanda's employees, loses her temper and wilfully bashes in the windshield of JoAnn's car. JoAnn sues Wanda for damaging her car. Wanda says she is not liable because she is exempt as a result of the liability clause.
>
> The clause may not operate if JoAnn can show that she had no notice of it and that printing it on the back of the ticket did not constitute a reasonable step in bringing the clause to her attention before the contract was made. JoAnn may also argue that even if she had notice, the clause has to be construed narrowly—it exempts Wanda and her employees from negligence, but Linh's act was wilful and is not covered by the exclusion. JoAnn could also argue that even if Wanda is exempt, Linh is not because she was not a party to the contract and could not benefit from the exclusion. Against this, Linh might argue that if Wanda is covered Linh might also be, because Wanda could have excluded herself and, acting as Linh's agent, could have bargained an exclusion for Linh as well. Alternatively, Linh could argue that, on the basis of Iacobucci J.'s reasons in *London Drugs*, JoAnn had notice that Wanda's employees would carry out Wanda's contractual obligations and that employees such as Linh are specifically covered by the clause. This argument might fall apart, of course, because Linh's wilful conduct was, in any event, outside the exclusion clause.

Penalty Clauses

Clauses in a contract that determine in advance the manner and amount of compensation to the injured party in the event of a specific type of breach are called **penalty clauses** or compensation clauses. The courts interpret these clauses very carefully, reserving the right to ultimately decide on damages to be awarded.

Penalty clauses are used in a variety of situations and usually take one of three forms.

- A clause that provides a very low amount of compensation for a specific harm done. This may be seen as an exclusion clause rather than one providing a penalty or compensation.
- A clause that prohibits the parties from suing for breach of contract to obtain damages and allows instead substitution of other goods or repairs.
- A clause that provides for the payment of a specific sum or forfeiture of a performance bond or other security, where the sum is expressed as a pre-assessment of the parties' loss from non-performance. This is sometimes referred to as a **liquidated damages clause**, where an amount is agreed to that will presumably cover the actual loss that is likely to occur.

A penalty clause that provides for a clearly inadequate amount for a loss is really an exclusion clause and is subject to controls imposed by the courts discussed in the preceding section. A clause that limits the right to sue for damages and provides

penalty clause
a term in a contract that imposes a penalty for default or breach

liquidated damages clause
a term in a contract that attempts to reasonably estimate the damages that will be suffered if the contract is breached

alternative remedies is also subject to court scrutiny on the issue whether the clause provides adequate compensation. If a court finds that the clause provides an inadequate remedy, the injured party may be able to sue for damages despite the clause.

The type of penalty clause that has attracted much court attention is one that provides for liquidated damages on breach. Here the issue is whether the amount forfeited really is designed to compensate for damages or whether it is in the nature of a penalty. If the amount is a real pre-estimate of damages made in good faith, the court will allow the clause to stand. However, if the amount claimed is out of proportion to the damages likely to be sustained, the court may perceive it as a penalty. If the court sees it as a penalty, it is also likely to see it as a threat or form of coercion and is likely to prevent the party benefiting from the clause from relying on it.

Generally, if the court determines that a sum is a penalty, it will not enforce the clause whether the clause withholds a payment or compels one to be made. The burden of proving a penalty lies with the person who alleges that it is a fact. However, where the court finds that the sum is a penalty, it may not interfere if the clause is not unconscionable or if it is protected by statute.[8]

Where a clause has been found to require court intervention, the court may substitute a reasonable amount for the sum set out in the clause. It is not clear whether a clause that is found to be a penalty clause is simply void or not, but there are cases where the court has granted relief from forfeiture by relieving a party from having to pay the penalty, particularly where the clause has been found to be unconscionable.

> ## Example of a Penalty Clause
>
> Khan wants to have a marina showroom built by Fly By Night Construction. He is anxious to have the showroom completed and open by the Victoria Day weekend, because his most profitable season begins then. Based on past experience, he figures he will average about $10,000 a week in sales. Khan insists that Fly By Night substantially complete the building so that it can be opened by the Friday of the Victoria Day weekend. He also insists on a penalty clause in case the building is not completed on time, with Fly By Night paying $30,000 to Khan for each week after the deadline until the building is substantially completed.
>
> Fly By Night is three weeks late and objects to the clause, saying it is a penalty and not liquidated damages. The amount claimed is 200 percent more than the actual estimated damages and could be seen as a penalty, although Khan could argue that it is reasonable because actual losses are hard to estimate, and there may be other ancillary costs to Khan that cannot be anticipated. If Fly By Night is successful, the court could set an appropriate amount for damages, relieving Fly By Night of the obligation to pay a penalty.

---

8. *Dimensional Investments Ltd. v. R.*, [1968] S.C.R. 93.

CASE IN POINT

Penalty as Illegal Rate of Interest

From: *Garland v. Consumers' Gas Co.*, [1998] 3 S.C.R. 112.

Whether a penalty clause is designed to cover anticipated damages or impose a penalty is not the only issue. In this case, the issue arose as to whether a penalty clause imposed more than an unjustified penalty and also violated the *Criminal Code*'s usury provisions.[9]

Garland brought a class action against Consumers' Gas on the ground that its penalty for late payment violated the usury provisions of the *Criminal Code*. The penalty was imposed as a flat fee if payment was made after the due date. The fee was not subject to simple or compound interest and had been approved by the utility's regulatory body after extensive hearings. Evidence showed that the fee was not onerous if the gas bill was paid long after it was rendered, but if the bill was paid only a few days after it was due, the late fee could

amount to an interest rate of upward of 60 percent, contrary to the *Criminal Code*. In this case, it would also be well above the amount of any damages sustained by the gas company as a result of late payment.

The trial court dismissed Garland's action, and the Court of Appeal dismissed his appeal. However, a majority in the Supreme Court of Canada granted Garland's appeal and ordered a new trial. The *Criminal Code* defines "interest" very broadly and can include penalties for late payment, as in this case. The court noted that late payers were not encouraged to delay payments to reduce the impact of the penalty clause, and statistical evidence showed that most late payers paid up relatively quickly, resulting in the late payment charge on its face being not just a penalty but possibly usurious.

PRACTICE TIP

Some contracts use the phrase "paid as damages and not as a penalty" in a penalty clause to try to tie down the payment formula as one of damages. This approach is unlikely to work if a party challenges it: the court will look at the payment to see whether it approximates damages in the situations governed by the clause.

FRUSTRATION

A contract may become impossible to perform through no fault of either party. In some situations the court invokes the **doctrine of frustration of contract**, declaring that the contract has been frustrated and that the parties to it should be relieved of their obligations under it. The doctrine of frustration only began to develop in the 19th century. At common law, before this time, parties who made promises were expected to remain bound to carry out the terms of the agreement no matter what. The contractual promise was seen as absolute, and impossibility of performance did not excuse the obligation of performance unless the parties explicitly provided for a termination of the contract because of impossibility. For example, if Mona

doctrine of frustration of contract
a legal doctrine that permits parties to a contract to be relieved of the contractual obligations because of the occurrence of some event beyond their control that makes it impossible for them to perform the contract

---

9. *Criminal Code*, R.S.C. 1985, c. C-46.

engaged a famous portraitist, Leon, to paint her portrait, the contract might set out what would happen if Leon died before finishing the painting. In this situation, the parties might decide to terminate the contract, because Mona may not have wished to have a lesser painter do it, and Leon might not want his estate to be bound by an obligation to find someone to complete the work.[10]

However, by the 19th century, in cases where no explicit provision was made to terminate because of impossibility of performance, the courts in some circumstances began to imply terms permitting termination on the ground of impossibility. This marked the beginning of the development of the doctrine of frustration of contract, in which the courts held that in some circumstances the occurrence of certain events beyond the control of the parties made it impossible to perform the contract.

Factors Affecting Frustration of Contracts

The following are some of the situations that can lead to a finding that a contract has been frustrated:

- The impossibility arises from an act of some third party.
- The impossibility arises from some natural or external force: fire, flood, earthquake, weather, or other *force majeure*.
- The impossibility cannot be prevented by the parties and is beyond their control.
- The impossibility is not, directly or indirectly, brought about by the party who is arguing that the contract has been frustrated.
- The impossibility is caused by the death or serious physical incapacity of a party where a personal attribute of that party was required to perform the contract—for example, the party was obliged to compose a piece of music and had been chosen for his or her particular skills.
- The impossibility is caused by the subject matter of the contract's ceasing to exist—for example, a theatre is leased for a concert, burns down, and is no longer available.
- The impossibility is caused by a change in the law that is not contemplated by the parties.
- The impossibility is the result of serious delay that is not caused or contemplated by the parties.

force majeure
a major event that the parties to a contract did not foresee or anticipate that prevents performance of the contract and thus terminates it; such an event—for example, a natural disaster or war— is outside the control of the parties and cannot be avoided with due diligence

Frustration Based on Implied Term Theory

The courts used two approaches to develop the law of frustration of contract:

- the assumption of an implied term of the contract permitting termination, and
- the construction of the purpose of a contract to decide whether the contract could be terminated because its purpose could not be fulfilled.

---

10. *Paradine v. Jane* (1647), 82 E.R. 897.

In the implied term approach, the term can be seen as a condition precedent to performance of a contract. For example, if A rents a theatre from B for a performance and the theatre burns down so that it is impossible for A and B to carry out their contractual obligations, the court might see the existence of the theatre as an implied condition precedent to performance of the contract by either party, even though the parties made no explicit provision for this possibility[11] (see the Case in Point feature below for another example). In other cases, other suitable terms have been implied that deal with the frustration of a contract by the occurrence of some event neither party explicitly contemplates, but which clearly makes impossible the performance of the contract the parties agreed to.

The implied term approach rests on the idea that the contract the parties agreed to, by its nature, must have assumed or implied certain things or situations to exist in order for the contract to be performed. If the contract cannot be performed because some intervening event makes it impossible through no fault of the parties, then the contract can be seen to be frustrated because performance is no longer possible. The test for determining whether there is an implied term requiring discharge due to frustration is an objective "reasonable person" test rather than what the parties say they contemplated. If the contract has express terms for termination because of frustration, the courts will not imply a term for a situation not covered by the express term. In this situation, the courts hold that the parties, having directed their minds to include express terms, must have excluded any other basis for finding that the contract has been frustrated.

CASE IN POINT

The Vanishing Road

From: *Kerrigan v. Harrison* (1921), 62 S.C.R. 374.

The following case is a good example of the implied term approach.

Kerrigan purchased two lots on Lake Erie from Harrison. As part of the sale, Harrison promised access to the lots via Harrison Place, which ran along the lake. As a result of a storm, the shore was badly eroded; the road collapsed and disappeared into the lake. Kerrigan sued Harrison for damages and for an order requiring the repair of the road. At trial, the defendant was ordered to restore the road or replace it with a new one that served the same purpose.

On appeal to the Ontario Court of Appeal, the court held that Lake Erie was Crown property, and that as a result of erosion, the road and the land it stood on were in the lake and were therefore now Crown property, so that Harrison had no power or obligation to do anything. The Supreme Court of Canada ruled in favour of Harrison, but focused on the doctrine of frustration: the parties had contemplated only that the specific road, Harrison Place, would provide a right of way and it was an implied term that it would continue to exist; when it ceased to exist through no fault of either party in a situation not contemplated by them, Harrison's obligations to provide a right of way to Kerrigan were at an end.

---

11. *Taylor v. Caldwell* (1863), 122 E.R. 309; *Appleby v. Myers* (1867), L.R. 2 C.P. 651. These cases were followed in Canada, starting with the Supreme Court of Canada decision in *Kerrigan v. Harrison* (1921), 62 S.C.R. 374.

Frustration Based on Construction Theory

Another approach the courts took in developing the doctrine of frustration was determining that a contract had become frustrated or impossible to perform because the very basis or purpose of the contract had ceased to exist; what remained was not the contract the parties had agreed to or contemplated. In these cases, the courts subjectively tried to determine what the parties' "purpose of the adventure" or "common object of the agreement" was. Finding the common purpose of the parties involved a subjective analysis of what the parties actually said the contractual purpose was. If intervening events made fulfilling the contractual purpose impossible so that there was a radical change in the parties' obligations, then the contract could be deemed to be frustrated, and they then would be relieved of their obligations to continue.[12]

Courts in both Canada and England are now more inclined to follow the construction theory than the implied term theory[13] (see the Case in Point feature below).

Distinguishing Between Impossibility and Frustration

In some cases, the terms "impossibility" and "frustration" are used interchangeably, but they are not quite the same. "Impossibility" refers to situations where performance is physically or legally impossible. "Frustration" includes situations where performance is physically or legally possible, but the results would be very different from the purpose of the contract that the parties had contemplated. Today, cases that deal with contract frustration have gone beyond the narrower concept of impossibility to include contracts that, while technically possible to perform, are in practical and commercial terms frustrated because the original contract purpose disappeared.

Examples of Frustrated Contracts

- Farah wants to buy a load of eggplants for processing. They must be very ripe and bought late in the season. Timothy agrees to supply them. There is an express provision discharging the contract if the goods are destroyed by hail or lightning. Before they can be harvested, there is a violent earthquake that creates a fault line that swallows up and destroys all the eggplants. Farah sues for breach of contract, and Timothy's response is that the contract has been frustrated by the destruction of the eggplants. The earthquake is an act of nature not caused by either party and wholly outside their control. While there is an express term contemplating discharge from frustration, it does not contemplate earthquakes, so it could be said that the parties did not contemplate or foresee the cause of the destruction. Further, it could be said that the parties, knowing that eggplants are fragile, might have contemplated that the contract could not be carried out if the eggplants were destroyed, so an implied term permitting discharge might be

12. Fridman, *supra* note 5, at 640.
13. *Davis Contractors Ltd. v. Fareham Urban District Council*, [1956] A.C. 696 (H.L.); *Capital Quality Homes Ltd. v. Colwyn Construction Ltd.* (1975), 61 D.L.R. (3d) 385 (Ont. C.A.).

found by a court. On the other hand, because the parties did make express provisions for discharge by frustration, by not including earthquakes it could be argued that they did not intend to treat the contract as frustrated. However, if one analyzed the contract to determine what the parties intended, it could be said to be the delivery of eggplants. Where that was no longer possible, performance would be radically different from what was originally contemplated, and the contract therefore could be treated as discharged because doing what the parties intended was no longer possible.

- The Prince of Ptomania is to be crowned king. Lady Hinkle rents rooms from Professor Baloneya along the coronation route at a very high price so that she can watch the coronation procession. Unfortunately, the week before the procession there is a revolution, and Prince Ptomania is overthrown and sent into exile. Baloneya demands payment, saying, "You rented rooms for the day, Hinkle—you have to pay." Hinkle's answer is that Baloneya knew the purpose of the rental, which was why the rent was so exorbitant. Because the purpose of the contract has ceased to exist, Hinkle says she should not have to pay; the contract has been frustrated and cannot be enforced.[14]

CASE IN POINT

No Forced Land Transfer Where Right to Subdivide Is Lost

From: *Capital Quality Homes Ltd. v. Colwyn Construction Ltd.*, [1975] O.J. No. 611, 61 D.L.R. (3d) 385 (C.A.).

This case provides an example in which the court was prepared to go beyond "impossibility" to deal with frustration by constructing the contract in terms of the purposes contemplated by the parties.

The plaintiff, Capital Quality Homes, had entered into an agreement to buy a large lot from the defendant Colwyn that had been divided into 26 parcels, on which it intended to build individual homes. At the time the contract was entered into, the land was not subject to subdivision control, but just prior to the sale's closing, the *Planning Act* was amended so that the lands could no longer be subdivided into 26 lots. The defendant argued that the plaintiff had purchased a piece of land and could convey it, so that the transaction was valid; whether the land could later be subdivided was neither here nor there. Further, because the land could be conveyed, land purchases were not subject to the doctrine of frustration. The plaintiff argued that both parties understood and contemplated that the parties were conveying the land for the purpose of subdivision and,

because the legislative amendment had not been contemplated by the parties, the contract should be treated as frustrated.

The trial judge held that the contract was frustrated, and that the plaintiff was entitled to be returned to its pre-contract position with the return of the deposit. The Court of Appeal upheld this decision; it decided that the doctrine of frustration could not be fixed or limited by mechanical or arbitrary rules, so that contracts involving the sale of land could be subject to the doctrine of frustration. The court noted that the doctrine was flexible, and instead of searching for implied terms, one should look at the contract as a whole as to what the parties intended and then decide, as a result of the frustrating act, whether there was still a contract capable of fulfillment as originally contemplated by the parties. In this case, both parties knew this was a contract for the sale of land to be divided into 26 parcels; when that was no longer possible, the original purpose was gone, and the contract was properly held to be frustrated.

---

14. For a similar decision see *Krell v. Henry*, [1903] 2 K.B. 740 (C.A.).

PRACTICE TIP

In order to avoid frustration-of-contract situations—and also some of the situations that give rise to disputes about mistakes—consider including in the contract a preamble that sets out the contract's purpose, any assumptions upon which it is based, and any other background information that would assist in interpreting the contract.

Common-Law Remedies for Frustration

At common law, when a contract is terminated because performance is frustrated, the position of the parties is said to be "crystallized" or frozen. Courts generally decline to provide remedies, choosing instead to allow losses to fall as they might. For example, if one party paid a deposit, it could not be recovered. If the other party had done some work, the cost could not be recovered. In this situation there might be a setoff in which a party could apply the deposit in his or her hands to compensate for the work he or she had done. But what about contracts that required payment in advance? If one party had paid a contract price and the other party had done nothing, a windfall situation would be created for the party who was paid, while the other party would be out of pocket with nothing to show for the payment.

The unfairness of this situation was addressed by the House of Lords in *Fibrosa Spolka Akcyjna v. Fairbairn Lawson Combe Barbour Ltd.*[15] The court held that where there was a total failure of consideration owing to frustration of the contract, parties were entitled to recover moneys paid before the crystallizing event, although the court did not allow the party who made the expenditures to carry out his or her obligations to recover money for those expenditures. While some later cases seem to be more flexible, allowing recovery on the basis of what is just and reasonable whether there was total failure of consideration or not,[16] the case law does not create much order or certainty. It has been left to the legislature to do what is necessary to create clear rules for compensation when a contract is frustrated.

Example of Apportioning Losses for Frustration at Common Law

Zora wants to build a house along a clifftop for the scenic view. She hires Tariq Contractors Ltd. to design and build the house. Tariq has completed the design and bought some custom building supplies when Zora is notified by the municipality that the zoning for the property is being changed to prevent her from building any structure on the land. She has paid Tariq a deposit of about 15 percent of the value of the work done and the materials supplied by Tariq.

At common law, once the contract is frustrated, the parties' positions are crystallized, and the losses lie where they fall. Tariq could keep the deposit

15. *Fibrosa Spolka Akcyjna v. Fairbairn Lawson Combe Barbour Ltd.*, [1942] UKHL 4, [1943] A.C. 32, [1942] 2 All E.R. 122.
16. *Cahan v. Fraser* (1951), 4 D.L.R. 112 (B.C.C.A.).

but has to absorb losses for the work done and the materials supplied. Zora loses her deposit and is left with the vacant land.

Legislation Governing Frustration of Contracts

An act to deal with frustrated contracts was passed in England in 1943 and became the model statute for frustrated contracts legislation in all provinces except British Columbia and Nova Scotia. Ontario's *Frustrated Contracts Act*[17] is typical of this kind of legislation. British Columbia has a modified form of the statute that is used in the other provinces.[18] Nova Scotia still relies on the common law. Where the contract concerns the sale of **specific goods**, except in British Columbia, the subject matter may be covered by the provincial *Sale of Goods Act*[19] rather than by the common law or the provincial *Frustrated Contracts Act*.

specific goods
specific, identifiable chattels that have been singled out for contract purposes

Frustrated Contracts Act

The Act covers most but not all contracts. Among the exclusions are

- contracts governed by a specific statute that has frustration provisions, on the basis that a specific statute overrides the provisions in a general statute, such as the *Frustrated Contracts Act*;
- contracts where the parties have created express terms to deal with frustration;
- certain contracts for the carriage of goods by sea;
- insurance contracts;
- contracts for the sale of goods when the goods cease to exist before the contract is entered into without fault by either party and before risk passes to the buyer (this is likely to be a case of mistake, rather than frustration); and
- contracts where the goods cease to exist after the contract is entered into without fault by either party and before risk passes to the buyer.

The operation of the legislation is triggered when a contract governed by the law of the province where the *Frustrated Contracts Act* is in operation has become impossible to perform or has been frustrated, and the parties have been discharged from the further performance of the contract because of frustration or impossibility. The Act does not create rules for deciding *when* a contract is frustrated—that is still left to the case law. Instead, the statute regulates post-contract collapse recovery:

- Money that is paid before discharge is recoverable.
- Debts accrued but not yet paid are not to be paid.
- Total failure of consideration is not required. Even if some value was obtained, the contract can be terminated for frustration and the parties may receive compensation.

---

17. *Frustrated Contracts Act*, R.S.O. 1990, c. F.34.
18. *Frustrated Contract Act*, R.S.B.C. 1996, c. 166. Discussion in the text is based on the legislation in other provinces.
19. For example, the Ontario *Sale of Goods Act*, R.S.O. 1990, c. S.1.

- Where a party has incurred expenses to carry out the contract, the party may be allowed to keep part or all of a deposit paid by the other party or to recover some or all of the expenses.
- The court is given a reserve power to apportion losses and benefits so that if one party receives some benefit, where failure of consideration is not total, he or she will have to pay the other side a reasonable amount for that benefit.

Sale of Goods Act

Under the provincial *Sale of Goods Act*, where there is a contract for the sale of specific goods and the goods are destroyed after the contract was made but before risk passes to the buyer, either party may back out of the agreement. If the goods are not specific goods, are not destroyed, or are subject to express terms, or the risk has passed to the buyer, the parties have to look to the provincial *Frustrated Contracts Act* or to the common law for relief.

CHAPTER SUMMARY

The role of the court is to try to find and give effect to the intention of the parties to a contract when there is a dispute about its meaning or its consequences. The initial step is to classify contract statements. A representation, if factual and if it induces a party to enter into an agreement, may allow the injured party to avoid a contract if the representation is incorrect. Where there is a dispute about a term, if the term is a condition, it is deemed to be a serious provision affecting the principal purpose of the contract. If it is a warranty, it is deemed to be a subsidiary or minor provision, for which the consequences of breach are less serious.

Where a contract is in writing, the courts normally interpret the words of the agreement and will not look at oral evidence of what the parties intended. However, where the language of the agreement is ambiguous, the court may use the parol evidence rule to hear oral or written evidence about what the parties intended. Where the terms of the written agreement are clear, but are the result of a mistake, the court may invoke the equitable remedy of rectification to correct the error.

Where parties have attempted to exclude liability, the court may intervene to relieve a party from the effects of an exclusion clause where one party has exempted himself or herself from liability or imposed a clause requiring one party to pay damages to the other for failure to meet contract terms. The courts interpret exclusion clauses strictly and limit their application. Damage or penalty clauses are also closely examined to see whether the fixed damage amount bears some resemblance to the actual damage done and is not a penalty.

Sometimes a contract becomes impossible to perform through the occurrence of an event that is no fault of either party. In this situation, the courts may hold that the contract is frustrated, relieving both parties of the obligation to continue performance from the time of the frustrating event, although both sides may have to bear their own losses and benefits under the contract from the time of frustration.

KEY TERMS

condition
condition precedent
contra proferentem rule
doctrine of frustration of contract
exclusion/exemption clause
force majeure
liquidated damages clause

material representation
parol evidence rule
penalty clause
representation
specific goods
term
warranty

REVIEW QUESTIONS

True or False?

1. Stepan and Ali negotiate a contract for Ali to paint Stepan's house. Ali includes a clause that says he is not liable for damage to the property, however caused. The clause is written in small print, and Ali does not draw it to Stepan's attention. Stepan can argue that Ali should not be able to rely on the clause because it was not drawn to Stepan's attention.

2. The doctrine of *contra proferentem* is an exception to the parol evidence rule.

3. When an event or a contingency that would have been within the contemplation of reasonable parties at the time the contract was made causes the contract to be impossible to carry out, the contract is *not* frustrated.

4. Frustration and impossibility mean the same thing in the context of contracts.

5. A liquidated damages clause is never enforceable unless the amount specified closely approximates the actual damage suffered in the event of a breach.

6. Written contract terms can be either conditions or warranties.

7. At common law, if a contract is frustrated, the parties are restored to their pre-contract positions.

8. Where a party orders a delivery of a canopy tent and chairs for a Saturday afternoon retirement party and the equipment is delivered on Sunday instead, this is a breach of a warranty.

9. Where a hurricane destroys a crop that has been promised to another party under a contract before the crop can be harvested, the event may trigger the contract's *contra proferentem* clause.

10. The parol evidence rule differs from rectification in that rectification determines what the parties intended to do, while the parol evidence rule interprets what the parties have agreed to do.

Fill in the Blanks

1. A clause that determines in advance what the remedy for a breach will be is called a _____ _____.

2. A secondary term of a contract that, when breached, does not defeat the purpose of a contract is called a _____ _____.

3. The _____ _____ rule requires a court to honour the wording of a contract where that wording is clear and unambiguous.

4. Parties may seek to limit their liability under a contract by inserting an _____ clause.

5. Suliman agrees to sell his car to Arturo for $2,000. The day before the car is delivered to Arturo, it is hit by lightning and destroyed. The contract is deemed to be _____.

6. A condition _____ in a contract is a condition that must occur first in order for the contract to become enforceable.

7. Where contract terms are ambiguous, the doctrine of _____ _____ requires the court to interpret the terms in favour of the party who did not draft the contract.

8. Where one party states what is presented as a fact about the subject matter of the contract, with the intention that the other party will rely on the statement and under circumstances where the other party cannot readily verify the truth of the statement, the statement is a _____ _____.

9. Where an earthquake destroys a wedding reception hall on the day before a wedding, the event may be described as _____ _____ and will frustrate the contract.

10. A _____ is an essential term of a contract. Breach of this kind of term defeats the purpose of the contract.

Short Answer

1. Why is distinguishing among representations, conditions, and terms important?

2. What is the parol evidence rule, and what is its purpose?

3. In what circumstances can oral and other written evidence be used to interpret a written contract?

4. What is the effect of rectification on an agreement?

5. In what circumstances can a party to a contract successfully obtain the remedy of rectification?

6. Why is fundamental breach no longer the basis for barring the application of an exclusion clause? What has replaced it?

7. When might a court intervene with respect to the application of a penalty clause?

8. What sorts of events give rise to a frustrated contract? What sorts of events will not give rise to a frustrated contract?

9. Describe the theory of implied term and the theory of construction of a contract as they are used in frustration of contract cases. Which approach are courts likely to use now, and why?

10. What were the shortcomings of the common law in granting remedies in frustration cases?

EXERCISES

1. Leah owns a motorboat specially equipped for fishing. In addition to the outboard engine, it has special seats, trolling rigs, and an electronic fishfinder. She offers to sell the boat with the motor to Tranh for $20,000. They also agree that the special seats, trolling rigs, and electronic fishfinder will be included for $2,000. The written agreement refers to the sale of a boat and motor with "fishing equipment" for $22,000, with a deposit of $2,000. Before the sale is completed, Leah decides she would like to keep the fishfinder. When Tranh objects, Leah tells him they agreed to sell only what was specifically in the written agreement, and that the fishfinder is not included. Assess Tranh's chances of obtaining the fishfinder, and discuss his alternative remedies.

2. Extreme Skiing Company, a company that specializes in ski trips, offers a heli-skiing trip that involves a helicopter ride to a remote mountain slope. The price of $1,000 per person, which includes hotel, meals, and helicopter transportation, is advertised in a skiing magazine. In response to the advertisement, Allyson calls Extreme Skiing and agrees over the telephone that she and Matthias will join the trip. Extreme Skiing's representative says he will mail the enrollment forms to Allyson and Matthias. Allyson agrees that she and Matthias will meet the trip operators at the hotel the day before the trip. Two weeks before the trip date, Allyson and Matthias receive and complete the enrollment forms. They mail the forms back to Extreme Skiing along with the payment price. These are received by the company one week before the trip.

   Allyson and Matthias go to the designated hotel the day before the trip. As they and the other eight participants assemble in the hotel lobby, the trip operators hand out forms entitled "Standard Release and Waiver of Liability" and ask each participant to sign one. The form states that Extreme Skiing is not responsible for any losses or damages suffered by the participants for any reason, including negligence on the part of the company.

   Allyson and Matthias are reluctant to sign the form but are told that unless they do so they will not be allowed to go on the trip. Finally, they sign the form. The next day, all the participants are taken by helicopter to the ski slope.

During the course of the ski trip, there is an avalanche and Allyson suffers a broken leg as a result. Matthias also loses all his ski equipment. An investigation reveals that there had been an avalanche warning about the area into which the participants were flown, and that Extreme Skiing ought to have been aware of this warning.

What contract issues arise in this fact situation?

3. Cleopatra wants to buy a load of grapes to make into wine. Antony agrees to supply what is required. Cleopatra inspects one of several of Antony's vineyards in Italy and likes what she sees. She specifies that the grapes should be selected from "those located on Antony's property" and that risk will pass to the buyer on delivery to Cleopatra at her processing plant in Alexandria. Antony accepts these terms. There is express provision discharging the contract if the grapes are destroyed by hail or go down in a sinking ship. Before they can be harvested, a severe heat wave ripens them too early. The grapes are good for nothing but vinegar. Cleopatra sues for breach of contract, and Antony claims the contract is ended due to frustration. Set out arguments for and against each party's position.

4. Gangrene Ltd., located in Lower Slobovia, manufactures custom agricultural machinery. Typhus and Co. orders some custom-designed equipment from Gangrene for delivery to its location in Ptomaine. Before the equipment can be delivered, war breaks out between Slobovia and Ptomaine, and all commercial contracts between the two countries become illegal in both countries. Gangrene has spent a considerable amount of money developing and producing this custom machinery, for which there is no other market. Typhus and Co. paid a deposit worth about 10 percent of the costs incurred by Gangrene.

Advise Gangrene on its legal position with respect to contract remedies at common law and under statute. Assume that Slobovia's law is the same as the law of every province except British Columbia and Nova Scotia.

5. "The doctrine of frustration is really just another version of the law of mistake." In discussing this statement, explain how the law of mistake is both similar to and different from the doctrine of frustration.

Breach of Contract and Remedies

8

OVERVIEW

LEARNING OUTCOMES

After completing this chapter, you should be able to:

- Define breach of contract.

- Distinguish between the repudiation of a contract and an anticipatory breach.

- Explain the difference between a contract condition and a warranty and the difference between a breach of condition and a fundamental breach.

- List and explain at least four different types of remedies available in the wake of a breach of contract.

- Describe the circumstances in which a court might order the remedy of specific performance.

- Describe the remedies that courts can use to compensate a party for partial completion of contract obligations.

INTRODUCTION

breach of contract
failure, without legal excuse, to perform any promise that forms part of a contract

This chapter discusses the actions and non-actions that constitute **breach of contract** and the remedies that are available to the injured party.

Breach of contract occurs when one party to a contract fails or refuses to fulfill his or her obligations under the contract without legal excuse. However, different types of breaches have different consequences. The method of the breach must first be established, and then the nature or seriousness of the breach must be examined. Finally, the remedies available to the injured party can be determined. The injured party may be able to claim compensation for damages suffered as a result of the breach; declare that the contract has been discharged, thereby releasing the injured party from his or her obligations; compel the party in breach to perform the obligations; or apply a combination of more than one of these.

METHOD OF BREACH

repudiate
to renounce or reject an obligation

express repudiation/ express breach
the failure or refusal to perform the obligations of a contract when they become due

A party to a contract may **repudiate** the contract, thereby breaching it. The most common form of repudiation is failing or refusing to perform the obligations created by the contract when they become due. This form of repudiation is known as **express repudiation** or **express breach**. The repudiation must be clear, unambiguous, and explicit for the other party to be able to rely on it. It may take the form of an actual declaration of refusal, or simply a failure to perform.

Example of Express Repudiation or Express Breach

Samuel promises to deliver a load of gravel to Northwest Contracting Limited on a certain day. On that day he fails to deliver the gravel. In the alternative, on the day of delivery, he telephones Northwest Contracting and states that he cannot deliver the gravel as promised.

anticipatory breach
an express repudiation that occurs before the time of performance of a contract

If the repudiation occurs before the date of performance, it is an **anticipatory breach**. Again, the repudiation must be clear, unambiguous, and explicit.

Example of Anticipatory Breach

Samuel promises to deliver a load of gravel to Northwest Contracting Limited on a certain day. Before that day, he discovers that the company that supplies his gravel has increased its price, with the result that if Samuel delivers gravel to Northwest at the agreed-upon price, he will lose money. Samuel calls Northwest before the day of delivery to say that he will not be delivering the gravel.

implied repudiation
repudiation that is not express and must be implied or deduced from the circumstances

More difficult is the situation in which one party repudiates the contract by implication. **Implied repudiation** is a form of anticipatory breach, because it occurs before the performance date. The innocent party must ascertain, from the actions or statements of the other party, that he or she does not intend to perform the obligations under the contract when the time for performance arrives. The innocent party is in a difficult position. The party who appears to be repudiating by implication may still perform the contract as specified when the time comes. However, if he or she does not, the innocent party may suffer increased damages as a result of the delay in waiting to address the situation. Further, if the innocent party assumes that the other party intends to breach when that is not the case, the innocent party may take steps that result in a breach on his or her part. Because the very nature of implied repudiation relies on speculation and inference, misunderstandings may occur.

Example of Implied Repudiation

Dawn enters into a contract with Emil to paint his house. Two weeks before the day she is supposed to start work, Emil finds out that she has sold all her painting equipment to one of her competitors. Clearly, without her painting equipment, Dawn will be unable to perform her obligations under the contract. Emil might want to treat this as an implied repudiation of the contract. However, if Dawn buys new equipment before the day she is supposed to start painting, she could still perform her obligations. On the other hand, if Emil waits to find out what Dawn will do, he may not be able to find a replacement for her in time to have his house painted.

However, in some cases the nature of the implied repudiation is such that there can be no misinterpretation. This includes situations in which the implied repudiation makes performing the contractual obligations impossible.

Example of Implied Repudiation That Is Certain

Lindsey and Scott enter into a contract whereby Lindsey agrees to sell Scott her sound system. Before the date that Lindsey is supposed to deliver the sound system to Scott, he finds out that she has sold it to someone else. While this is still a case of implied repudiation, because of the certainty that Lindsey will be unable to deliver the sound system to Scott on the agreed-upon date, Scott may treat this as a breach of contract.

NATURE OF BREACH

Once it has been established that a contract has been breached, the nature or effect of the breach must be examined.

The nature of the breach is determined primarily on the basis of its seriousness. A term of a contract that is essential or goes to the root of the contract is called a condition. A minor or subsidiary term is called a warranty. The distinction between a breach of warranty and a breach of condition is important in determining what remedies are available for the breach, because a breach of a condition will wholly deprive the innocent party of the benefit he or she expected to receive under the contract, while a breach of warranty will not. This distinction is important when it comes to awarding a remedy for the breach.

It is important to examine the contract as a whole and in context to determine whether any given term is a condition or a warranty. For instance, in a contract to buy a car, the make and model of the car would be a condition, while the colour of

CASE IN POINT

Expensive Elevator Service

From: *Thyssenkrupp Elevator (Canada) Ltd. v. Grafton Developments Inc.*, 2010 NSSM 11 (CanLII).

In 1998, Nasco owned a building with an elevator. Nasco signed a five-year renewable contract with Northeast to provide general elevator maintenance, and to provide repairs when necessary. The contract specified that the cost charged for the routine maintenance could be raised once each year by a maximum increment of 3 percent.

Between 1998 and 2002, Northeast was bought out by another elevator company called Thyssenkrupp. Nasco was eventually amalgamated with another company and renamed Grafton Developments. Thyssenkrupp delivered the service promised under the Nasco/Northeast contract to Grafton (an example of contract assignment, described in Chapter 6). The contract renewed automatically for a further five years in 2003.

Around 2002, Thyssenkrupp brought the service contract into its computerized system. That system applied an annual increase of 6.9 percent to such contracts. Grafton did not notice until 2008 that the interest increases that were being applied (and had been compounding for years) were more than double what was permitted under the contract.

Upon discovering the overcharging, Grafton, which was unhappy with certain other repair charges from Thys-senkrupp, terminated the contract. This termination, which occurred in 2008, was nearly five years early based on the renewal's five-year term.

Thyssenkrupp sued for breach of contract, alleging that Grafton was in anticipatory breach. Thyssenkrupp claimed the value of its repair billings, plus lost proceeds under the contract.

Grafton argued that by charging interest increases much in excess of those permitted by the contract, Thys-senkrupp had been the party in breach.

The court held that the overcharging by Thyssenkrupp did *not* amount to a fundamental breach of the contract that would allow Grafton to repudiate (or anticipatorily breach) the contract. In support of this finding, the court noted that the overbilling was inadvertent, not intentional (had it been intentional, it would have amounted to fraud, and then likely would have been a breach). Also, the court found that overbilling is a contract problem that can easily be resolved by granting a credit, and that there was no need for Grafton to repudiate the contract entirely.

Thyssenkrupp was awarded damages for breach of contract, and the amounts it had overbilled Grafton were set off against those damages.

---

the car might be a warranty. The delivery of a car of the correct make and model, but the incorrect colour, would be a breach of warranty but not a breach of condition. However, in a contract to paint a house, the colour of the paint might be a condition, in which case painting the house the wrong colour would be a breach of condition.

fundamental breach
the failure to perform a primary obligation under a contract, which has the effect of depriving the other party of substantially the whole benefit of the contract

Fundamental breach is another category of breach. Fundamental breach is difficult to distinguish from breach of condition. Both are breaches of a major term of the contract, a term that goes to the contract's root. However, a fundamental breach is often seen as more serious than a breach of condition. A fundamental breach undermines or destroys the whole contract.

The difference between fundamental breach and breach of condition is important where the effect of an exclusion clause is being considered. *Exclusion clauses* in a contract limit the liability of one of the parties and were discussed in greater detail in Chapter 7. The law in this area is still developing, and recent developments seem to indicate that "the concept of fundamental breach is considerably more important and relevant to the determination of the rights of the parties after breach than the categorization of the term that has been breached."[1]

While there is still some ambiguity in this area, it seems that the concept of fundamental breach goes deeper than the idea of breach of condition. The court must investigate the underlying purpose and nature of the contract, the benefits that the parties intended to obtain, and the consequences of the breach to determine whether fundamental breach occurred. This can be done only by examining each individual contract and interpreting it in all the surrounding circumstances.

REMEDIES

The remedies available in the event of breach of contract include

- damages,
- specific performance,
- injunctions,
- rescission,
- restitution,
- discharge,
- *quantum meruit*, and
- substantial performance.

Damages

The most common remedy for breach of contract is the award of damages. Damages are a sum of money to compensate the injured party. The intent of the court in making such an award is, as far as possible, to put the injured party into the position that he or she would have been in had the contract been fully performed. This is a popular remedy, because with most contracts it is easy to translate the non-performance into monetary loss. Unless there is some compelling reason to award some other form of relief, the court will only award damages.

> ### Example of Monetary Loss from Non-Performance
>
> Catherine agrees to sell her lawnmower to Suzanne for $100. Suzanne takes the lawnmower and gives Catherine a cheque. However, the cheque is returned NSF. The contract has clearly been breached. The loss suffered by Catherine is the sum of $100, and an award of damages in the amount of $100 (plus, perhaps, interest on that sum) would fully compensate her.

It is important to distinguish between **liquidated damages** and **unliquidated damages**. Liquidated damages are easily ascertainable, usually by examining the terms of the contract and applying some form of mathematical calculation. If, for

liquidated damages
damages that are easily determined from a fixed or measurable standard or can be assessed by calculating the amount owing from a mathematical formula or from circumstances where no subjective assessment has to be made

unliquidated damages
damages that cannot be fixed by a mathematical or measured calculation but require information from a source outside the contract

---

1. G.H.L. Fridman, *The Law of Contract in Canada*, 3d ed. (Scarborough, ON: Carswell, 1994), 564.

consequential damages
secondary damages that do not flow from the breach of contract but from the consequences of the breach, such as loss of future profits

expectancy damages
damages that are based on a loss of expected profits

lost opportunity damages
damages that are based on a longer-term loss of business

example, the contract specified payment of the sum of $4,000 but only $1,500 was paid, applying the mathematical formula $4,000 − $1,500 = $2,500 calculates the liquidated damages. However, sometimes the damages are not so easy to calculate because the breach of a contract can have far-reaching consequences. **Consequential damages** do not flow directly from a breach of contract but from the consequences of the breach. These damages are, in a sense, one step removed from the breach itself. Consequential damages include those based on a loss of expected profits, often referred to as **expectancy damages**, and damages based on a longer-term loss of business, often referred to as **lost opportunity damages**.

Consequential damages are often unliquidated. Unliquidated damages cannot be easily calculated with a mathematical formula and usually require information that is outside the contract itself. For example, in calculating damages for loss of profit, it might be necessary to look at evidence from other, similar contracts or at the particular industry as a whole to determine the actual loss suffered. In other cases, it may be necessary to hire an appraiser, an accountant, or some other expert to assist in calculating the damages.

If the consequences of the breach were reasonably foreseeable by the parties at the time that the contract was performed, the party in breach may be liable for all the losses that flow from the breach, including consequential damages. The injured party must prove that the damages were reasonably foreseeable at the time that the contract was made. The party in breach will want to argue that the damages claimed by the injured party are too "remote" and could not reasonably have been foreseen.

Example of Reasonably Foreseeable Damages

Tents R Us Ltd. contracts to buy a load of grommets from Trusty Parts Inc. for the sum of $7,500. Trusty Parts fails to deliver the grommets, and Tents R Us is forced to buy them from another manufacturer for $8,500. Clearly, the damages immediately suffered amount to $1,000. However, Tents R Us needed the grommets to finish making a shipment of tents due to Backpacker's World Limited, for which Tents R Us expected to earn $15,000 in profits. Because of the breach by Trusty Parts, Tents R Us cannot deliver the tents on time and so loses its anticipated profits.

The consequential damages suffered include the lost profits of $15,000. In addition, the failure to deliver the tents on time to Backpacker's World, a long-time customer of Tents R Us, has damaged the relationship between the two companies. Backpacker's World will no longer do business with Tents R Us, so the long-term losses include the future loss of business from Backpacker's World. The damages might then include loss of anticipated profit over the next few years, amounting to many thousands of dollars. To claim all these damages, Tents R Us must prove that Trusty Parts knew or ought to have known that these consequences would reasonably flow from its failure to perform its obligations under the contract. The damages claim for loss of profit over the next few years is clearly unliquidated and requires some form of external evidence to support it.

CASE IN POINT

The Sick Puppy

From: *Montier v. Hall*, 2002 ABQB 70 (CanLII).

Larry and Marjorie Hall purchased a two-month-old black female Belgian sheepdog from Silvie Montier for $100.

Over the next two months, the puppy was very ill. She suffered from a recurrent bladder infection and, more seriously, from debilitating leg pain related to multiple broken bones. At four months of age, she had to be euthanized. The veterinarian conducted an autopsy and determined that the puppy had serious congenital (hereditary) osteoporosis, which was the cause of the fractures. Over the puppy's short life, the owners incurred over $800 in veterinary bills.

The owners sued Montier for the veterinary bills. They could not sue for the $100 cost of the puppy, because the contract, which included a "health guarantee," provided that if the puppy had to be euthanized before 25 months of age due to a hereditary disease, the purchasers were not entitled to a refund of their purchase money, but rather, to a puppy from the next litter born in the defendant's operation.

Montier argued that the replacement puppy was the sole remedy available under the contract. The Halls argued that they were entitled to consequential damages from the breach of contract, which, in this case, amounted to veterinary bills of more than $800. The Halls argued that if the contract provided only the remedy of a replacement puppy, then it was contrary to the *Fair Trading Act* in force in the province of Alberta.[2]

The court agreed with the Halls. Justice Lee held that the Halls were justified, as responsible pet owners, in incurring the expenses they had incurred to treat the puppy's conditions and in attempting to determine what was wrong with her. There was no legal reason for the doctrine of consequential damages not to apply to this case. The remedy of a replacement puppy was intended to compensate for the loss of the first puppy, not for consequential losses; and if it *was* intended to be the sole remedy allowed, then that provision did indeed violate the provisions of the *Fair Trading Act*.

The Halls were awarded compensation for their veterinary bills.

It is often difficult to calculate accurately the losses suffered by the injured party as a result of a breach. To address this problem, some parties include a clause in the contract that sets out the damages to be paid in the event of a breach.

If this clause is a genuine attempt to calculate in advance the loss that might be suffered, it is referred to as a liquidated damages clause. Such a clause provides incentive to the parties to comply with the terms of the contract. The courts usually uphold such a clause, even if the actual damages suffered are greater or less than the clause provides.

However, this clause must be distinguished from a penalty clause, which provides for a payment of damages far in excess of the actual damages that could be suffered or that makes no genuine attempt to correlate the damages payable with the damages suffered. (Penalty clauses were discussed in greater detail in Chapter 7.) The courts often ignore penalty clauses and instead calculate the damages award on the basis of the actual loss. Whether a clause is a liquidated damages clause or a penalty clause is often difficult to determine and is decided on the facts of each case.

---

2. *Fair Trading Act*, R.S.A. 2000, c. F-2.

Duty to Mitigate

The injured party has a duty to **mitigate** his or her losses. This means that he or she is not entitled to remain inactive in the face of the other party's breach of contract, but must take positive steps to minimize the loss suffered as a result of the breach.

While the injured party must take steps, they need not be extraordinary steps. To require that would put an inappropriate burden on the injured party. After all, the party in breach, not the injured party, was responsible for the loss.

Failing to mitigate losses may result in a court's not awarding compensation for the full loss suffered. Compensation will be limited to those damages that could not have reasonably been avoided.

> ### Example of Mitigation and Losses
>
> André contracts to sell his computer to Teresinha. Teresinha breaches the contract by refusing to complete the transaction. André can claim against Teresinha the full purchase price of the computer as the damages he suffered owing to her breach. However, if he takes no steps to mitigate his loss by trying to sell his computer to someone else, he may be denied recovery of the full amount of his loss. If he is forced to sell the computer at a lower price than the one Teresinha contracted to pay, he will be able to claim as his damages the difference between the price he would have received from Teresinha and the price he did receive from the replacement buyer. However, if he is lucky enough to sell the computer for more than the price Teresinha had contracted to buy, André will not be able to recover any damages against her because he suffered no loss. Even though Teresinha is clearly in breach, she would suffer no consequences.

A common scenario in which the issue of mitigation of loss arises is in employment law. Employees who are dismissed without good cause and without reasonable notice are generally entitled to compensation in lieu of notice (usually an amount equivalent to their pay for a few weeks or months) from the employer. However, a dismissed employee is expected to make a reasonable effort to look for a new job after he or she is dismissed. If the ex-employee makes no such effort, the compensation that would otherwise be payable by the ex-employer may be reduced to reflect this lack of mitigation.

Specific Performance

In some cases, damages cannot adequately compensate the injured party. In those cases, **equitable remedies** may be available. An example of an equitable remedy is **specific performance**, which requires the party who is in breach to perform his or her obligations under the contract. If this party refuses to comply and perform, he or she will be in contempt of court and could be subject to quasi-criminal penalties such as fines or imprisonment. Specific performance is usually available only when the contract is for the sale of unique goods or real property.

Real property is ordinarily considered unique because no two parcels of land are identical. If a buyer expects to buy land and the vendor breaches the contract by failing to complete the transaction, it is not possible for the buyer to take an award of monetary damages and replace the land that is lost. If the buyer can prove that he or she was ready, willing, and able to complete the transaction and fulfill all of his or her obligations under the contract,[3] the court can compel the vendor to complete the transaction through an order for specific performance.

If the contract is for the sale of unique goods, specific performance may be an available remedy. The goods must be so rare and unique that the disappointed buyer cannot readily find the same or similar goods from another source. Examples of rare or unique goods include antiques, works of art, and rare coins or stamps.

Specific performance is not available for contracts that involve personal services performed by an individual, such as an employment contract. In the case of a breach of an employment or a service contract, the courts are unlikely to force an individual to provide services, because this would amount to a form of servitude. Monetary damages are considered adequate compensation.

Because specific performance is an equitable remedy, certain restrictions are placed on the party asking for the remedy. Equity requires that this party come to court with "clean hands"—that is, free of any unethical behaviour. If a party does not have clean hands, he or she will be denied the equitable remedy and will be awarded monetary damages. Equitable remedies can also be denied if the injured party was partly at fault or contributed to the breach of contract in some way, or if he or she delayed for an unreasonable length of time in pursuing a remedy for the breach. These restrictions apply to all equitable remedies.

Example of Unclean Hands

Hisham, Kamal, and Salwa were business partners. Hisham leaves the partnership and then sues Kamal and Salwa. He claims that as part of the mutual agreement to dissolve the partnership, he should be allowed to take certain client contracts with him. Kamal and Salwa claim in their defence that Hisham tried to steal customers from the partnership by spreading untrue stories about the remaining partners' business practices. If the defence allegations are true, Hisham would likely be unable to claim specific performance, because his actions in defaming his former partners leave him with unclean hands. However, he might still be able to claim legal remedies such as damages (subject to any counterclaims by his former partners).

Injunctions

An **injunction** is another form of equitable remedy. Injunctions govern the behaviour of a party, either to prohibit certain actions or to compel certain actions. A **prohibitory injunction** directs a person not to do a certain thing. A **mandatory injunction** commands a person to do a certain thing. The most important considerations for the court in determining whether to grant an injunction are whether the injured party could be adequately compensated by damages instead of an injunc-

injunction
a court order that prohibits someone from doing some act or compels someone to do some act

prohibitory injunction
an injunction that directs a person not to do a certain thing

mandatory injunction
an injunction that commands a person to do a certain thing

---

3. Proving one is ready and willing is sometimes called "tendering" performance. Tendering was discussed in Chapter 6.

tion, and whether it is fair and just to grant the request for the injunction. The court will not grant an injunction if the injured party could be adequately compensated by an award of damages, or if it would be unfair to, or cause irreparable harm to, the party in breach.

The courts most often grant a prohibitory injunction when the contract contains an express provision that is a promise by one party that it will not do a certain thing. This is also known as a **negative covenant**. If the party goes on to commit the prohibited act, the injured party can then apply to the court for an injunction to stop it.

negative covenant
a promise in a contract to refrain from doing a certain thing

Example of Negative Covenant

Chem-Products Ltd. rents land from Pristine Properties Inc. The rental agreement contains a negative covenant that Chem-Products will not use the land to store certain chemicals. If Chem-Products then uses the land to store these chemicals, one of the options available to Pristine Properties is to ask the court for an injunction prohibiting Chem-Products from doing so.

While it is helpful to have a negative covenant in the contract, it is not necessary to have such a covenant before the court will grant a prohibitory injunction. A contract may include an implied promise that could be used as the basis for a prohibitory injunction.

Example of Implied Promise

Assume that in the above example, Pristine Properties carries on business on the property adjacent to Chem-Products. Chem-Products dumps garbage on the property and emits loud sounds at all hours of the night and day that adversely affect the business next door. Pristine Properties can make a request for a prohibitory injunction. Although there may not be a specific negative covenant in the contract prohibiting garbage dumping and noise, the court may recognize an implied promise not to interfere with Pristine Properties' business. This would be true even if there was no statutory remedy available to Pristine Properties (for example, municipal noise bylaws).

A mandatory injunction, while not the same as specific performance, can often have the same effect. Courts are less willing to grant mandatory injunctions in circumstances where they would not grant specific performance, as in contracts involving personal services performed by an individual. However, the courts have granted mandatory injunctions in cases "to prevent the breach of an agreement under which the plaintiff obtained from the defendant exclusive rights to the manufacture and distribution in two provinces of certain patent and proprietary remedies, [and] to prevent the improper termination of an automobile franchise agreement."[4]

Injunctions can be a very powerful remedy but, because the litigation process can be long and time-consuming, a lawsuit in which a party seeks an injunction may take years to come to trial. By then, the behaviour that the injured party sought

---

4. Fridman, *supra* note 1, at 798.

to prohibit may have done irreparable damage. In such a case, a party may seek an **interlocutory injunction**, also called an **interim injunction** or a temporary injunction. This kind of injunction is awarded by the court on an "emergency" basis, and sometimes even in the absence from court of the party who is the target of the injunction. An interlocutory injunction allows the injured party to prevent ongoing damage from occurring while awaiting the trial and final determination of the matters in dispute. At trial, the injured party will usually ask for the injunction to be made permanent.

Rescission

Rescission is both a common-law remedy and an equitable remedy, although the term is used most commonly to refer to the equitable remedy. The purpose of rescission is to put the parties in the position they would have been in had the contract never been made. This approach contrasts with the purpose of damages, which is to put the parties in the position they would have been in if the contractual obligations had been performed.

Common-law rescission may be available to a party if the contract is **void** or **voidable** at his or her option. This would be an option with a void contract, such as a contract in which one party is a minor, or with a voidable contract, where the terms of the contract allow one party to avoid it as of right or upon the occurrence of some event. In these cases, that party has the right to rescind the contract without having to resort to the court for a remedy. The right to rescind a contract is different from the right to terminate or discharge a contract. A contract that is discharged is terminated or ended. A contract that is rescinded never existed.

Equitable rescission can be granted by a court only as a remedy for a breach of contract by the other party. The intent is to restore the parties to their original positions. There is some similarity between common-law and equitable rescission, but equitable rescission is broader and is available in more circumstances. However, those circumstances must be exceptional. Again, the courts will not award an equitable remedy, including the remedy of rescission, where damages adequately compensate the injured party. In restoring the parties to their original positions, the courts will order that moneys and property that had been exchanged be returned and that both parties be relieved of their obligations under the contract.

Rescission is awarded most often in cases that involve fraud, misrepresentation, or duress. Rescission can also be granted in cases that involve mistake, which was discussed in more detail in Chapter 5.

> ### Example of Rescission
>
> Lina buys a refrigerator from Arnold's Appliances for $750. When the refrigerator is delivered and installed, Lina discovers that the freezer section of the refrigerator does not work. She wants to return the refrigerator and get her $750 back. She is asking for rescission. Arnold's Appliances offers to refund half the purchase price to compensate her for the non-functioning freezer. Arnold's Appliances is offering damages. In such a case, the court would likely award the remedy of rescission because a refrigerator with a non-functional

interlocutory/interim injunction
a temporary injunction granted by a court before the final determination of a lawsuit for the purpose of preventing irreparable injury

rescission
the cancellation, nullification, or revocation of a contract; the "unmaking" of a contract

void contract
a contract that does not exist at law because one or more essential elements of the contract are lacking; an unenforceable contract

voidable contract
a contract that may be avoided or declared void at the option of one party to the contract; once it is declared invalid no further rights can be obtained under it, but benefits obtained before the declaration are not forfeit

freezer section is of little value to Lina, and she could not be adequately compensated by an award of damages.

There are some restrictions on granting rescission in addition to the usual restrictions on equitable remedies. First, rescission cannot apply to part of a contract. If rescission is granted, the whole contract is rescinded. Second, it must be possible to restore the parties to their original positions (for example, the property that was the subject matter of the contract has not been destroyed or has not diminished substantially in value through use). Third, the rescission cannot prejudice any innocent third party (for example, a third party who has purchased the property that is the subject matter of the contract).

Restitution

restitution
a remedy in which one seeks to rescind a contract; if granted, restitution restores the party, as far as possible, to a pre-contract position

Restitution is an equitable remedy, the purpose of which is to restore the parties, as much as possible, to the position in which they would have been had no contract ever been made.

Often, restitution can be accomplished by the remedy of rescission, discussed above. In some cases, however, simply rescinding the contract might not restore the parties to their pre-contract positions, because it could allow the party in breach to retain the benefits obtained under the contract, such as earned profits.

In such cases, some form of compensation or recovery is necessary. Restitutionary recovery is based on the idea that the party in breach must disgorge to the injured party any benefits he or she gained under the contract before its rescission, where it would be unjust for him or her to retain such benefits. This approach must be distinguished from that of damages. The measure of damages is the amount of the loss of the injured party. The measure of restitutionary recovery is the amount by which the party in breach was unjustly enriched under the contract. Under the **unjust enrichment doctrine**, a party who breaches a contract at the expense of another should not be permitted to benefit from his or her wrongdoing. Therefore, a person who has been unjustly enriched at the expense of another can be required to make restitution in the form of payment of money.

unjust enrichment doctrine
the principle that a person should not be permitted to inequitably gain a profit or benefit at the expense of another

Discharge

discharged
released, extinguished; a discharge of a contract occurs when the parties have complied with their obligations or other events have occurred that release one or both parties from performing their obligations

In some circumstances, an injured party may choose to treat a contract as having been **discharged** as a result of breach by the other party. This is most common in cases where the injured party has not yet completed performance of his or her obligations under the contract.

If this common-law remedy is available, the injured party no longer has any obligations under the contract and may treat it as being at an end. The injured party may then claim damages for breach of contract. The party in breach cannot compel the injured party to perform his or her obligations under the contract and cannot claim damages for non-performance by the injured party. However, an injured party who chooses to treat a contract as having been discharged may not claim remedies that are incompatible with this remedy, such as specific performance or rescission. In addition, an injured party who continues to accept the benefits of a contract after becoming aware of the breach may later be prohibited from claiming that the contract had been discharged by the breach and may be restricted to claiming damages only.

Quantum Meruit

The doctrine of **quantum meruit** is most commonly relied on in two situations: first, where the contract is silent as to the consideration for the goods or services, and second, where the contract has been partially performed and the value of the performance must be determined.

If one party requests goods or services from another whose occupation it is to provide such goods or services, payment is understood and expected. That person may deliver such goods or services without a price being discussed. Nevertheless, this is not a situation of a gratuitous promise; payment is expected by both parties, and only the amount of the consideration has not been specified.

Even though the consideration is not specifically mentioned in the request, an agreement of this type will not fail for lack of consideration. The law will imply a promise to pay in a request for goods or services.

Where there is no mention of price, the implied promise is for payment of what the services are reasonably worth, or payment for *quantum meruit*. However, parties who have negotiated a contract that contains a term as to the price to be paid for the goods or services cannot later rely on the doctrine of *quantum meruit* to get a better price. *Quantum meruit* can be relied on only where the contract is silent as to the amount (quantum) of the consideration.

In determining what goods or services are reasonably worth, the courts look to the prices charged by similar suppliers and fix the contract price accordingly.

The remedy of *quantum meruit* is also available when the injured party has partly performed his or her obligations under the contract at the time of the repudiation by the other party. *Quantum meruit* is considered a quasi-contractual remedy. The injured party is entitled to compensation for the work performed even if it was not completed. The terms of a contract usually do not include a valuation of partially completed work. The doctrine of *quantum meruit* allows the injured party to obtain a valuation of, and compensation for, the work performed. The injured party must show that it was in fact the other party who repudiated the contract or made the completion of the contract impossible. This remedy is not available when the injured party has completed his or her obligations under the contract, in which case the appropriate remedy is damages.

> **quantum meruit**
> an equitable doctrine that states that no one should unjustly benefit from the labour and materials of another; under those circumstances, the law implies a promise to pay a reasonable amount, even in the absence of a contractual term for price; loosely translated as "as much as is deserved"

Example of Quantum Meruit

Cameron hires Deborah to renovate his kitchen for the sum of $5,000. Deborah has completed approximately 75 percent of the job when Cameron decides that he no longer wants the renovations and refuses to pay her or to let her finish. Deborah must prove that Cameron repudiated the contract, and because she did not complete it, she must claim the remedy of *quantum meruit* for compensation for the work done. Because she completed 75 percent of the contract, she is entitled to claim 75 percent of the contract price, or $3,750.

Substantial Performance

substantial performance
performance of contractual
obligations that does not
entirely meet the terms of
the contract but nevertheless
confers a benefit on a party

Quantum meruit is normally not available to the party who repudiates a contract. However, the doctrine of **substantial performance** may be available. This doctrine recognizes that performing contractual obligations that do not entirely meet the terms of the contract but nevertheless confer a benefit on a party is of value and must be taken into consideration in determining the damages recoverable by the party claiming injury for non-performance and by the party claiming compensation for the partial performance.

Example of Substantial Performance

Tony agrees to build a cottage for Marijke for $40,000. Tony builds the cottage but fails to complete the porch according to Marijke's design. Marijke claims that Tony has breached the contract and refuses to pay him the $40,000. Tony can argue the doctrine of substantial performance because he has substantially complied with the terms of the contract. A court would likely award Marijke damages to compensate her for the porch and deduct these damages from the amount of money it would order Marijke to pay Tony. If, for instance, it would cost Marijke $4,000 to have someone else complete the porch according to her design, she would be ordered to pay Tony the remaining $36,000.

CHOICE OF REMEDIES

The remedies available to an injured party depend in part on the method of breach and the nature of the breach. In the case of *anticipatory breach*, the injured party has the option of waiting for the date on which the performance is due. If the other party fails to perform on that date, the anticipatory breach becomes an *express breach* or *express repudiation*, and the injured party may proceed according to the nature of the breach. However, the injured party also has the option of claiming a remedy as soon as he or she learns of the anticipatory breach.

If the nature of the breach is a breach of *warranty*, or a minor term of the contract, the injured party may not choose to treat the contract as having been discharged or to rescind the contract. In breach of warranty, the court will usually award damages to compensate the injured party. This means that the injured party must still comply with his or her obligations under the contract. However, if the breach is a breach of *condition*, or a major term of the contract, the injured party may choose to treat the contract as having been discharged or may rescind the contract. The injured party also has the choice of treating a breach of condition as a breach of warranty and accepting the lesser remedy of damages. However, the injured party does not have the option of treating a breach of warranty as a breach of condition.

If the contract contains an exclusion clause, the injured party may have no remedies available for breach of warranty or breach of condition. However, if the breach is a *fundamental breach*, the injured party may be able to argue that the exclusion clause should not apply. If successful, the injured party would be able to claim damages, discharge, rescission, or other equitable remedies where appropriate.

The availability of equitable remedies to the injured party depends on the facts of each case. While the courts will look at the nature of the breach in determining whether to grant an equitable remedy, the primary considerations are still whether common-law remedies will adequately compensate the injured party and whether the injured party has come to court with "clean hands."

CHAPTER SUMMARY

A party may breach a contract through an express or implied repudiation by failing to perform the contract obligations. A party may also commit an anticipatory breach by communicating his or her intention to repudiate the contract before the time or date set for performance.

A party may commit a breach of condition, which is a breach of a term that goes to the root of the contract, or a breach of warranty, which is a breach of a minor term of the contract. A party may also commit a fundamental breach, which is a breach of the foundation upon which the contract is based. Fundamental breach is usually considered in contracts where there is an exclusion clause that purports to relieve one party of liability in the event of a breach. Remedies available for the breach often depend on whether the breach was a fundamental breach, a breach of a condition, or a breach of warranty.

In the event of a breach of contract, the injured party is most commonly entitled to an award of damages to compensate for the loss flowing from and consequential to the breach. Damages are intended to put the injured party in the position that he or she would have been in had the contract not been breached. An injured party may also claim the equitable remedies of specific performance, injunction, rescission, restitution, or the quasi-contractual remedy of *quantum meruit*.

In the event of a breach of condition, the injured party is ordinarily entitled to claim rescission, discharge, or damages. However, in the event of a breach of warranty, the injured party is usually restricted to an award of damages.

KEY TERMS

anticipatory breach

breach of contract

consequential damages

discharged

equitable remedies

expectancy damages

express repudiation/express breach

fundamental breach

implied repudiation

injunction

interlocutory/interim injunction

liquidated damages

lost opportunity damages

mandatory injunction

mitigate

negative covenant

prohibitory injunction

quantum meruit

repudiate

rescission

restitution

specific performance

substantial performance

unjust enrichment doctrine

unliquidated damages

void contract

voidable contract

REVIEW QUESTIONS

True or False?

1. Loss of profits flowing from a breach of contract are a form of liquidated damages.
2. Implied repudiation of a contract can occur after the performance date.
3. The breach of a condition in a contract will wholly deprive the innocent party of the benefit expected under the contract.
4. The party injured by a breach of contract has no obligation to take positive steps to minimize the loss suffered as a result of the breach.
5. In a standard form contract, the exclusion clause favours the party who drafted the contract.
6. The purpose of restitution, as a remedy for breach of contract, is to put the parties so far as possible in the position they would have been in if all contractual obligations had been met.
7. The remedy of rescission cannot apply to part of a contract.
8. A party who has abandoned a contract can claim compensation for the work he completed before the abandonment.
9. Specific performance is always available as a remedy for breach of contracts for the sale of real property.
10. Where a party commits a breach of a warranty, not of a condition, no damages will be awarded.

Fill in the Blanks

1. Failing or refusing to perform the obligations created by the contract when they become due is known as express _____ or express _____.
2. Consequential damages based on a long-term loss of business are often referred to as _____ _____ damages.
3. When damages cannot adequately compensate the party injured by a breach of contract, _____ remedies may be available.
4. If a contract contains an exclusion clause, the injured party may have no remedies available for breach of warranty or breach of condition, unless the breach is a _____ one.
5. The doctrine of _____ _____ allows the injured party to obtain a valuation of, and compensation for, the work he or she has performed.
6. The issue of mitigation of loss commonly arises in the context of _____ law.
7. Under the _____ _____ doctrine, a party who breaches a contract at the expense of another should not be permitted to benefit from his or her wrongdoing.

8. A term of a contract that is essential or goes to the root of the contract is called a _____.

9. A _____ injunction directs a person not to do a certain thing, whereas a _____ injunction commands a person to do a certain thing.

Short Answer

1. What is the most common form of repudiation of a contract?
2. What options are available to the innocent party in the event of anticipatory breach?
3. Explain the difference between breach of a condition and breach of a warranty.
4. Explain the difference between breach of a condition and fundamental breach.
5. What is the purpose of damages?
6. Compare a clause that provides for liquidated damages and one that is a penalty clause. How do they differ?
7. What is the test for determining the remoteness of consequential damages?
8. What is the purpose of rescission?
9. With what conditions must a party comply to claim an equitable remedy?
10. What conditions must be present for the courts to enforce a claim for *quantum meruit*?

EXERCISES

1. Cheryl contracts to sell her moped to Jean for $900. However, a few days before Jean is supposed to pick up the moped, Cheryl phones to tell her that she has changed her mind and no longer wants to sell it. Jean is concerned, because to buy the same or similar moped elsewhere would cost at least $1,200. How would you characterize the breach committed by Cheryl? What remedies are available to Jean? If she claims damages, how would she calculate such damages? Would such damages be liquidated or unliquidated?

2. Sylvie, a scientist, enters into a contract with Central Hospital to perform research for them exclusively for a period of two years. However, during that time, Central Hospital discovers that Sylvie is also working on a research project for another hospital. What remedies are available to Central Hospital? What factors would the court take into consideration in determining what remedies to grant to Central Hospital?

3. Nicholas, a carpenter, contracts with Alexandra to build an addition to her house for $15,000. When he has completed all the work except the installation of two windows, he refuses to complete the contract. Can Alexandra discharge the contract? Can she rescind the contract? Is Nicholas entitled to be paid anything for his work? Why or why not? What remedies are available to Alexandra?

4. Gilbert bought a vacuum cleaner from Sullivan Cleaning Machines one month ago. During that time, the vacuum cleaner has broken down eight times, and Gilbert has been able to use it only once. Gilbert wants to return the vacuum cleaner and get his money back. Sullivan Cleaning Machines says that the vacuum cleaner can be repaired and has offered to repair it at no cost. However, Gilbert says that he has returned the vacuum cleaner twice for repairs but the problem has not been solved. The contract also states that Sullivan Cleaning Machines is not liable for any defects in the vacuum cleaner and that it makes no warranties as to the condition or fitness for purpose of the vacuum cleaner. The company further states that the customer shall be entirely responsible for the cost of any repairs. What remedies are available to Gilbert? What remedy would he prefer? What arguments would Sullivan Cleaning Machines make? What remedy would a court be likely to award?

5. Elite Manufacturers Ltd. has prepared a contract bid for a lucrative contract with Bijou Theatres Inc. to construct its new multiplex theatre. Elite Manufacturers is told by an inside source at Bijou Theatres that it has a very good chance of getting the contract because none of the other bidders has much experience in building theatres. The bid must be submitted by noon on January 15. Elite Manufacturers contracts with Express Courier Co. to deliver the bid package. Express Courier advises that it can deliver the package by 10:00 a.m. on January 15. The courier slip, which is filled out and signed by an employee of Elite Manufacturers, states in very fine print on the back, "Carrier's liability for loss, damage, destruction, or injury to a shipment shall not exceed the lesser of $1.50 per pound or $50." Unfortunately for Elite Manufacturers, the bid is not delivered on time and the company does not win the contract. Discuss the issues that arise in this case with respect to breach of contract, and render a decision.

PART II

TORT LAW

Introduction to Torts

9

OVERVIEW

LEARNING OUTCOMES

After completing this chapter, you should be able to:

- Describe the four basic elements of a tort.

- Understand what is meant by duty of care and standard of care.

- Explain the general classification system for torts.

- Explain the concept of intent as it relates to torts.

- List and distinguish the different levels of intent (guilty mentality) recognized in tort law.

- Understand which level of intent is required for each of the general classes of tort.

INTRODUCTION

When something goes wrong between parties who have a contract with each other, the wronged party can easily establish that the other party had assumed certain responsibilities within the relationship: those responsibilities are often explicitly expressed in the contract itself.

Many wrongs, however, occur between parties who do not share a contractual relationship and who may never even have met. Where there is no contract to act as evidence of the parties' duties toward each other, the hurt party, if he or she hopes to recover, must successfully prove that the other party owed some kind of **extra-contractual** (outside of contract) duty of care, and that that duty was not carried out, or at least not to an acceptable standard.

Lawsuits that require proof of a duty of care and of failure to meet that duty are argued using the **doctrine** of torts. A tort, as noted in Chapter 1, is a wrong that occurs between two or more parties. The doctrine of torts applies not only to harm to people, but also to damage to property and to harm to intangibles such as personal or business reputation, contractual relations, or business goodwill. The word "tort" comes from the French language, in which it simply means "wrong." As you will learn below, tort law addresses a wide variety of wrongs and a wide range of damages (categories of harm) that flow from those wrongs. Before exploring that range, however, you should understand the fundamental elements of a **cause of action** in tort. Each of these elements is discussed in fuller detail in later chapters, but the following sections provide a basic outline.

extra-contractual
outside of contract

doctrine
journal articles, treatises, and other writing of legal scholars on any legal subject, used by lawyers and judges as an aid to interpreting or developing the law

cause of action
a set of factual elements that entitle a plaintiff to sue

THE FOUR ELEMENTS: DUTY, BREACH, CAUSATION, AND HARM

Duty

Inevitably, the actions of every human being on the planet have the potential to influence the conditions of the planet for every other human. Consider, for example, the issue of fossil fuel depletion. There is, presumably, only so much crude oil under the Earth's surface. Every time an individual uses a drop of gasoline (made from crude oil), the total is depleted—and the rest of humanity deprived—of that one drop forever. By choosing to use a car, therefore, and burning a few litres of the world's gasoline, an individual affects the access of the rest of the world to that resource. It could be said that by driving, this person has reduced others' resource-consumption prospects—an action that could be interpreted as *harm* to their interests.

However, it is highly unlikely that the rest of us could successfully sue this driver for his or her actions, because society (environmental morality aside) does not recognize a clear, enforceable legal obligation on drivers not to use up everyone else's oil. In other words, we do not attribute a duty of care (with respect to resource consumption) to the individual driver. In the absence of a duty of care to act in a certain way in the interests of others, a person's actions are morally neutral—neither right nor wrong. It is only when we attribute a duty of care to a person that we bring ourselves into a position to analyze his or her actions and, potentially, to find those actions wanting.

The concept of duty of care is fundamental to the doctrine of torts. If there is no duty, there is no tort. We will return to the concept of duty of care—a much more complicated idea than it first appears—in our coverage of negligence in Chapter 12. For now, it is enough to understand that four basic elements are required to establish a tort, and duty is the first one.

Breach

The second element of tort is breach. The idea of breach is now familiar: in contract, breach occurs when one party fails to properly or fully carry out his or her obligations as described in the terms of the contract.

Breach in the tort context is somewhat analogous to contract, except that instead of falling short of adherence to his or her contract duties, the **tortfeasor** (the person who commits a tort) falls short in discharging (carrying out, living up to) his or her duty of care.

tortfeasor
the person who commits a tort

In the context of contracts, establishing breach requires the plaintiff to compare the defendant's service, product, result, and so on with what was promised under the contract. If, for example, the defendant promised to build six townhouses and built only four, then that defendant would be found to be in breach.

In the context of torts, there are no contract terms to refer to. The relationship between the plaintiff and defendant—which is based on (implied) duty—is rarely explicitly defined and exists only in the minds of the parties in the form of individual expectations. How, then, can the defendant's compliance with his or her duty of care be measured? How can breach of an unelaborated duty be proven?

The answer is by comparing the defendant's actions to an acceptable **standard of care**. Defining the content of that standard is an exercise that occupies the bulk of the arguments made in many tort cases.

standard of care
legal criteria against which a defendant's conduct is measured to determine whether he or she has been negligent

To summarize, breach is the defendant's failure to discharge his or her duty of care to an acceptable standard of care.

Causation

It is possible, of course, to have a duty of care, fail to discharge it, yet not trigger any negative consequences. Consider, for example, a commercial deep-sea fishing operator that is required to have one personal flotation device (PFD) for every passenger on board the boat, but has none. While on their fishing cruise, a party of fishers drink too much, and one man climbs up to stand on the deck railing as a stunt. He falls back onto the boat deck, cutting his head on the outside corner of the cabin. Had he fallen overboard, the lack of PFDs might have led to his drowning, but instead he fell in the opposite direction.

In this scenario, three of the four elements of tort—duty, breach, and harm—are present: the fishing operator had a duty of care (to provide PFDs to passengers); he was in breach of that duty by failing to provide those PFDs; and someone got hurt. However, the breach of duty was not the cause of the harm (the head injury) that occurred. Without causation—a causal link between the breach and the harm—there can be no tort.

Harm

The final element of tort is harm. Usually (but not always, as we will learn in the next chapter in the context of intentional torts), a plaintiff who brings a lawsuit in tort must allege that the wrongful actions of the defendant caused him or her some kind of harm compensable by money—personal injury, damage to property, or certain other kinds of harm, such as damage to business reputation.

Not all forms of harm are capable of supporting a tort lawsuit. For example, it is not currently possible to sue in tort for a "broken heart," disappointment, or other emotional upsets that fall short of psychiatric illness. An overview of the kinds of tort damages recognized by law (and capable of supporting a cause of action in tort) is provided in Chapter 12.

CLASSIFICATION OF TORTS

Tortfeasor's Intent

The most common, and probably most logical, model for the classification of individual torts organizes those torts according to the nature or level of intent possessed by the tortfeasor when carrying out the tort.

LAW IN PRACTICE
What's the Difference Between "Intent" and "Intention"?

In reading about intent in criminal law and tort law, you may find the words "intent" and "intention" used interchangeably. A review of dictionaries does not help much in distinguishing between the two words, which are very close in meaning. "Intention" is more common in general use, while "intent" is somewhat characteristic of a legal or formal context. "Intention" may also be used to signal a general state of mind, while "intent" is sometimes chosen to signal greater specificity.

In reading about torts in case law or in other texts, you should know that there is no important difference between the use of "tortious intent" and "tortious intention," or other similar expressions.

Because most tortfeasors brought before the court resist admitting harmful intent, plaintiffs support their allegations about intent through inferences drawn from the facts. For example, if a defendant who is the plaintiff's business competitor can be proven to be knowledgeable about the market for a product and about the market share possessed by the plaintiff, and, having this knowledge, develops her own product packaging that is confusingly similar to that of the plaintiff's, the plaintiff may ask the court to draw the inference that the similar packaging design was an intentional attempt by the defendant to pass her product off as the plaintiff's (this is the basic foundation of the tort of **passing-off**). Passing-off is a tort based on what is known as **direct intent** (something done with conscious purpose).

passing-off
a defendant's false representation of its goods or services, made with the intent of confusing consumers that they are the goods or services of the plaintiff

direct intent
done with conscious purpose

In other cases, the plaintiff may be less able to establish direct intent on the part of the defendant, but may still be able to prove a case in tort. The reason for this is that a *spectrum* of levels of intent is capable of supporting tort liability, ranging from direct intent at one extreme to the complete lack of either intent or carelessness (in other words, moral innocence) at the other. The area of liability at the most "innocent" end of the spectrum is known as absolute liability and is so inconsistent with the general theory of tort as to not really be tort law at all. Absolute liability is commonly taught and learned along with torts simply because it shares certain other qualities (liability outside contract; compensable harm to people, property, or intangibles). Figure 9.1 illustrates the spectrum of levels of intent in tort.

The Major Categories

Keeping the spectrum of intention in mind, read the following sections, which outline the major categories of torts. Each category will be examined in detail in subsequent chapters.

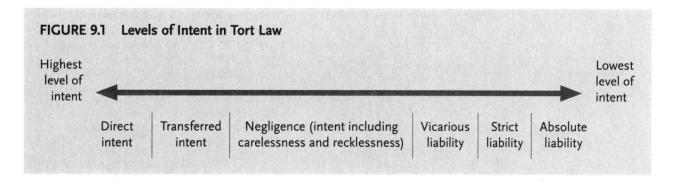

FIGURE 9.1   Levels of Intent in Tort Law

LAW IN PRACTICE
Mind Maps

Figure 9.2 is an example of a mind map. A mind map is a visual tool, perhaps less familiar than the more common flow charts or graphs. Some people find mind maps a useful way to brainstorm, to make study notes, or to organize thoughts about a central idea, where the concepts involved are not hierarchical. (Hierarchical concepts can be readily represented using a flow chart or concept map.) Mind maps do not impose a strict left-to-right or up-to-down reading pattern, which can be limiting; this is one of the reasons they can be effective for brainstorming.

In general, a mind map is organized according to branches: the major ideas are represented by longer or thicker branches with subordinate ideas radiating from them. Some mind maps allow the designer to connect ideas informally without suggesting a direct or hierarchical connection (for example, see the connections drawn on the map of torts between nuisance and intentional torts, between nuisance and negligence, and between nuisance and strict liability, with the reason for each connection described on the connecting branch).

If you like the idea of mind mapping, you may want to try it out when organizing your study notes. Mind mapping can also be used in legal practice, to help break down a client's problem into specific issues and to analyze those issues individually without losing sight of the bigger picture.

Mind maps can be drawn by hand or using computer software. This one was hand-drawn by the author and then adapted into electronic form using a software program.

FIGURE 9.2 Torts Mind Map

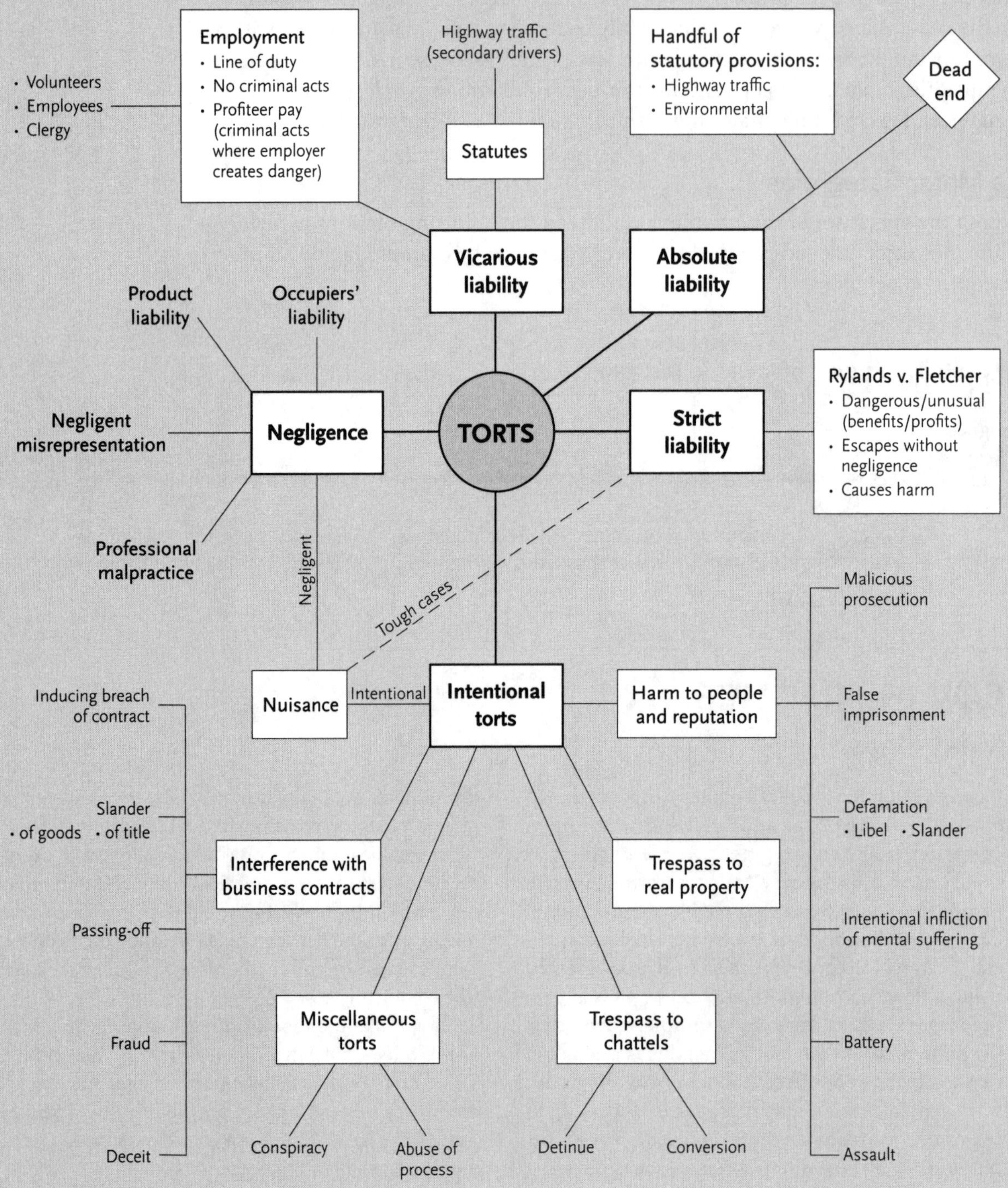

Intentional Torts

Intentional torts are just that—wrongs undertaken with the intent to do the thing done, which turns out to be harmful. Because they are done with intention, torts in this category are more likely than other torts to be capable of forming the basis of a criminal charge as well as a civil lawsuit. Not every tortious intent, however, is sufficiently morally culpable to amount to criminal *mens rea*, because an intentional tort is based on an intentional act, not necessarily an intent to do harm.

What's the difference? Consider, for example, a situation in which a woman belongs to a culture in which it is inappropriate for men to touch unmarried women. A man who is not from this culture and is unaware of this religious rule grasps the woman's arm without warning to assist her in descending from a bus. The man intended to touch the woman, but did not intend to cause harm (in this case, an injury to her dignity). The woman may choose to sue the man in tort for battery and may succeed, because battery is a tort based on any unwanted touching. However, the woman would be unlikely to succeed in having the man prosecuted for the crime of assault, because the man, not knowing his action was unwelcome, did not have the necessary *mens rea* for an assault conviction.

Intentional torts can include actions that cause harm (including nominal harm; more on this in the next chapter) to people, physical property, or intangible property (such as reputation). Intentional torts will be examined in greater detail in Chapters 10 and 11.

Transferred Intent

The concept of torts of **transferred intent** was developed to address situations in which the defendant's intentional act was directed at one party or that party's property, but harmed a different party or that party's property. For example, consider the situation in which an employee is fired and, in a rage, slashes the tires of what he or she believes to be his or her employer's car, but which turns out to be a rental. The intent was to damage the employer's car, not the rental company's property. Does the fact that the employee had no wrongful intent toward the rental company negate the tort? To allow this result would seem illogical and unfair. For that reason, where a defendant intended to commit an act, it is sufficient, to support a tort, that the act was done. It is not necessary that the identity of the victim correspond with the defendant's specific expectations.

transferred intent
intent to harm another party that results in harm to a third party

Negligence

Next on the spectrum of levels of intent is negligence. Negligence is a complex, layered concept that will be addressed in Chapter 12. For the purpose of this overview, the important message is that negligence covers not just a single point on the intent spectrum, but rather a range. Levels of intent that can constitute negligence run from *wilful blindness*—closing the conscious (but not always the unconscious) mind to the likely harmful consequences of one's actions—through *recklessness* (acting without thinking about consequences), *carelessness* (acting without sufficient care or thought), and *accident* (making a fairly honest error that, in hindsight, may have been within one's power to prevent).

One's Own Intentional Act and Failure to Report a Colleague's Similar Act: Separate Torts, Rules Ontario Court

From: *Sommerfield v. Lombard Insurance Group*, 2005 CanLII 8718 (Ont. S.C.).

Liability insurance is insurance purchased by an individual or a corporation against the potential cost of having to pay a legal settlement or judgment based on the insured's own legal default (often, the insured's torts). For example, a community centre may purchase liability insurance in case of claims based on slip-and-fall accidents in its parking lot.

It is common for liability insurance policies to *exclude* coverage for (decline to cover) claims based on the insured's intentional wrongful acts.

In January 2004, a former student of Toronto's Upper Canada College launched a $15 million lawsuit against the college and four former teachers, alleging that all four teachers had sexually assaulted him between 1986 and 1990, and that none of the four, who did not act in concert but who allegedly knew of one another's acts, had reported the wrongful acts of the others.

The teachers requested that the insurance company that had provided liability insurance to the college and its staff defend the action. The insurance company refused to do so, citing a provision excluding its liability for intentional wrongful acts.

The teachers argued that while the alleged assaults might fall within the category of acts for which liability was excluded, negligence was *not* excluded. The teachers suggested that the statement of claim filed against them by the student charged two separate classes of harm: intentional harm (the sexual assaults) and also negligence. The negligence claim was based on each teacher's alleged failure to report the wrongful acts of his fellow teachers, a behaviour that, the teachers argued, was a separate wrong, and not merely derivative from the alleged assaults themselves.

The Ontario Superior Court of Justice agreed with this analysis and ruled that intentional sexual assault and the failure to report a colleague's sexual assault on the same victim are two separate harms with two different legal bases (one in intentional tort and one in negligence). Because the insurance policy excluded liability only for intentional harm, the insurer had a duty to defend the teachers against the portion of the claim that related to negligence.

Negligence is at the heart of tort. The core principles that make up the law of tort—duty of care and breach through failure to meet a standard of care—are best demonstrated in the context of negligence. Practically speaking, the bulk of modern personal-injury or property damage cases are based on this doctrine.

Vicarious Liability, Strict Liability, and Absolute Liability

Moving along the intent spectrum toward moral innocence, there comes a point where the preventability of certain accidents becomes debatable. Consider, for example, a case where a property owner has bought property that, unbeknownst to him, has toxic contaminants from some long-past industrial use (a tannery, for example) buried deep underground. A record-breaking wet spring season causes these long-undisturbed contaminants to leach into an underground spring, which then contaminates a river. The current landowner is clearly without moral guilt for the contamination, but who will pay for the cleanup?

What about an employer bank that employs someone who seems to be a competent and pleasant employee with no discipline record and strong references? After an investigation triggered by a customer's complaint, it comes to light that the employee has been skimming thousands of dollars out of customers' accounts over a period of several years. Is the employer liable to pay?

Scenarios like these are difficult to "squeeze" into the traditional tort analysis, because it is difficult for the plaintiff to prove that the defendant (the property owner in the first case, the bank in the second) had the *capacity* to do a better job than he actually did in carrying out his duty of care, because he had no knowledge of any risk of harm. Nevertheless, these scenarios can lead to substantial harm. Leaving the plaintiff without remedy seems unfair.

The doctrines of **vicarious liability**, **strict liability**, and **absolute liability** have evolved to provide a tort-style remedy in a narrow range of cases in which there are public policy reasons for requiring a morally innocent (or near-innocent) party to pay for unexpected harm. The most important public policy reason cited for these rules is that the defendants, in these cases, have often benefited economically— either directly or indirectly—from the activities that led to the harm (the property owner, from owning the toxic land; the bank, from the employee's services). In other words, the general legal principle of "(s)he who profits must pay" underlies liability in these unusual cases. Vicarious liability, strict liability, and absolute liability will be covered in greater detail in Chapter 14.

Nuisance

One important area of tort that is not easily situated on the intent spectrum is nuisance. Nuisance is a tort based on conditions prevailing or activities carried out on land. A plaintiff occupier of land who seeks to base a lawsuit on nuisance must prove that conditions prevailing or activities carried out on the defendant's land affect the plaintiff's use (includes business and personal use) or enjoyment (usually non-business enjoyment) of his or her land. Nuisance lawsuits generally arise between neighbours broadly defined (that is, they need not be truly contiguous neighbours, but are usually within a few kilometres, at most, of each other).

The reason that nuisance does not have a specific place on the intent spectrum is that it can be either intentional (for example, a neighbour who plays very loud music at night with the intent to disturb those around him) or negligent (for example, a neighbour who cannot afford to maintain her roof, such that shingles blow off in high winds, damaging neighbouring homes).

Nuisance will be discussed in greater detail in Chapter 10 in the context of intentional torts affecting land, but it is worthwhile remembering that some nuisance conditions or actions are not intentional.

Other Classification Criteria

Within the general categories of tort based on level of intent, there are subcategories, as a review of Figure 9.2 (page 188) reveals.

The general class of intentional torts can be subdivided into five categories:

vicarious liability
the liability of a principal (an employer) for the negligent or tortious acts of the principal's agent (an employee) done within the scope of the agent's authority or employment

strict liability
liability that is imposed even though no negligence or intentional tort occurred

absolute liability
liability that is imposed automatically (usually under a statute) when certain conditions are met, without reference to negligence or intent

1. torts based on injury to the person, or to reputation: for example, battery and defamation;
2. torts based on harm to chattels: for example, conversion and detinue;
3. torts based on interference with land: for example, trespass and some forms of nuisance;
4. torts based on interference with rights or the legal process: for example, false imprisonment, malicious prosecution, and abuse of process; and
5. torts based on harm to business interests: for example, passing-off or inducing breach of contract.

These individual torts (and their related definitions) are discussed in Chapter 10.

There are also subcategories within the law of negligence—for example, negligence on the part of providers of professional services is often called "professional malpractice" and is characterized by specific rules. When a person gives advice outside the bounds of a contract governing that advice, there can sometimes be negligence liability based on a narrow doctrine known as *negligent misrepresentation*. Finally, where an owner of land is held liable for injury to visitors because of conditions present on that land, the liability is imposed under legislation generally described as occupiers' liability law. These subcategories of negligence (and their related definitions) are discussed in Chapter 14.

CHAPTER SUMMARY

The objects of this chapter were twofold: first, to familiarize the reader with the four essential elements of tort liability; and second, to describe the system for classifying torts.

The four elements of tort liability are (1) the existence of a duty of care on the defendant's part, (2) breach of that duty of care (which occurs when the defendant's actions fall short of a standard of care), (3) causation, and (4) harm. Depending on the specific kind of tort that is being alleged, these elements will be easier—or more difficult—to prove. In a few cases, for example, in the context of intentional torts like battery, there is no need to prove the element of harm.

The concept of duty of care is one of the most complex in tort law and is a fairly recent innovation. Also layered and challenging is the concept of standard of care, which requires the court to compare the actual behaviour of the tortfeasor with the projected behaviour of an imagined "reasonable person."

The most logical model for classifying torts is that based on the role of intent. Torts can be classified on an intent spectrum that runs from direct (conscious) intent at one extreme to complete lack of intent (moral innocence) at the other. The major categories of tort, in the order that they fall on this spectrum, are intentional tort, negligence, vicarious liability, strict liability, and absolute liability. Vicarious, strict, and absolute liability deviate considerably from the normal formula for torts described at the beginning of this chapter. Another important area of tort—nuisance—is difficult to place on the spectrum because it can occur either intentionally or negligently.

Finally, within the major categories of tort, there are subcategories. In the context of intentional torts, the subdivisions are based on the type of harm: to the person, to chattels, to land, to legal rights, or to business interests. In the context of negligence, the subcategories are distinguished on the basis of the nature of the activity that gives rise to the harm—for example, the delivery of professional services (under contract), the giving of extra-contractual advice under limited circumstances, or the conditions present on land when people visit.

KEY TERMS

absolute liability
cause of action
direct intent
doctrine
extra-contractual
passing-off

standard of care
strict liability
tortfeasor
transferred intent
vicarious liability

REVIEW QUESTIONS

True or False?

1. All intentional torts are also capable of being charged as crimes.
2. If there is no duty of care between parties, there can be no tort.
3. If a defendant throws a rock over a fence with the intention of hitting one person, but the rock hits a different person, the defendant will be liable in tort to the person actually hit.
4. A nuisance claim can never be based on an intentional act.
5. Determining the duty of care requires the court to compare the actual behaviour of the tortfeasor to the projected behaviour of an imagined "reasonable person."
6. Liability in tort always requires an intent on the alleged tortfeasor's part to cause harm to the plaintiff.
7. Tort liability can be based on harm to intangible assets, like business reputation.
8. Certain relationships between people—for example, the relationship between lawyer and client—trigger a higher than normal standard of care (higher than the general standard).
9. In order to obtain damages in tort, the plaintiff must *always* demonstrate measurable harm.
10. An action that constitutes an intentional tort need *not* include an intent to cause harm.

Fill in the Blanks

1. _____ intent describes the element of intent in a tort in which the tortfeasor intends to cause harm to one party, but harms a different party instead.

2. Where the law holds that a party is liable for damage he or she caused in the complete absence of any intent or negligence, the tort is one of _____ liability.

3. Acme Co. designs its product and packaging to closely match the product and packaging of a well-respected competitor in the hope that consumers will mistake Acme's product for the competitor's. These facts may form the basis for the tort of _____ _____.

4. The crime of assault, when prosecuted as a tort, is known as _____.

5. Wilful _____ is a form of negligence.

6. A party commits _____ when she allows toxic runoff from her factory to pollute the property of a neighbour.

7. An _____-contractual duty of care is a duty of care that arises outside the terms of a contract.

8. Tort intention ranges on a _____ from complete moral innocence to direct intent.

9. Professional malpractice is a subcategory of _____.

10. The four main elements of tort are duty, breach, _____, and harm.

Short Answer

1. Place the following levels of intent in order on the spectrum, from highest to lowest:
   - recklessness
   - vicarious liability
   - transferred intent

2. How does a court determine whether a defendant is in breach of his or her duty of care?

3. List at least one form of harm that is not compensable under the law of tort.

4. If a person owes a duty of care to another and breaches that duty of care, but no harm actually results, can he or she be sued for the breach?

5. Can a defendant owe a duty of care to someone she has never met? How?

6. Define what constitutes a "breach" in the context of tort law.

7. Explain the difference between direct intent and transferred intent.

8. Explain how the concept of "he who profits must pay" underlies most forms of vicarious, strict, and or/ absolute liability in modern tort law.

9. Is nuisance an intentional tort or a form of negligence? Explain.

10. What is a mind map and how is it used?

EXERCISE

Read the following scenario and suggest at least two kinds of torts that might be alleged in the plaintiff's statement of claim:

In the 1970s, the plaintiff Laura Norberg was plagued by recurring headaches of unknown origin. Her sister offered her some tablets of an addictive painkiller called Fiorinal, which helped with the pain. Eventually, the cause of the headaches was determined and treated; but by this time, Ms. Norberg was addicted to the painkillers.

Over the next couple of years, Ms. Norberg sought out different doctors in an effort to obtain continued access to Fiorinal. In 1982, she became the patient of a Dr. Wynrib. Complaining of an ankle injury, Ms. Norberg convinced Dr. Wynrib to prescribe her Fiorinal. Eventually, he began refusing on the grounds that her pain should have subsided and that the drug was addictive. Ms. Norberg persisted in her requests and confessed to the doctor that she was addicted. Dr. Wynrib wrote her a new prescription, but only after she agreed to certain sexual favours, which she began providing. After going along with the doctor's requests on several occasions in exchange for pills, Ms. Norberg eventually brought a lawsuit against him.

Intentional Torts

10

OVERVIEW

LEARNING OUTCOMES

After completing this chapter, you should be able to:

- Define "intentional tort."

- Describe four general categories of intentional torts.

- Explain the basic elements of several intentional torts.

- Understand the specific defences to the tort of defamation.

- Explain the doctrine of nuisance and what must be proven to succeed in a lawsuit based on nuisance.

- Understand the role of tort doctrine as a remedy for business wrongs, including intellectual property infringement and intentional interference with business interests.

INTRODUCTION

This chapter provides a general overview of intentional torts. At least 17 different intentional torts are recognized under Canadian law, each with its own separate history, doctrine, and individual rules. With that in mind, you will quickly realize that detailed coverage of these torts is not possible within the context of this brief text, and so the aim of the chapter is simply to familiarize you with the general principles that apply to intentional torts as a class and briefly introduce the specific torts themselves. Defences to intentional torts are covered in Chapter 11, with the exception of certain specialized defences that apply only to the tort of defamation. For clarity, it makes sense to introduce them as part of the coverage of defamation, and so they will be explained here.

BASICS OF INTENTIONAL TORTS

The Role of Intention

intentional tort
a tort that, once proved, is presumed to have been deliberately committed

Intentional torts are distinguished from the broader context of tort because, in committing one, the tortfeasor is presumed, based on the facts, to have acted intentionally. Although this presumption can be rebutted (challenged or disproved), it is not a common strategy for three reasons: first, because a tort lawsuit is a civil action, not a criminal prosecution, the plaintiff need only prove his or her allegations on a balance of probabilities. Second, even if the defendant could successfully disprove his or her intention to commit the tort, he or she would likely simply be found liable in negligence for the same act. Finally, history has shown that a defendant's efforts are generally better focused on proving a defence: for example, the plaintiff consented to the act complained of.

Duty of Care and Standard of Care

The presumption that a tort was committed intentionally constitutes a powerful legal "shortcut" for the plaintiff. The issues of duty and standard of care that must be carefully proven in the context of a negligence action are more or less a formality in intentional tort. As you will learn in the chapters about negligence, a defendant's duty of care is dependent largely on foreseeability: whether the defendant was (or should have been) aware of the consequences of his or her actions before taking them. In an intentional tort case, the presumption that the defendant consciously intended his or her actions (and usually, their consequences) makes it nearly impossible to argue that he or she could not foresee at least some of the implications of acting. The law makes it clear, as you will learn, that for the plaintiff to recover, the defendant need not have foreseen every detail of the resulting harm, its extent, or even, in some cases, the identity of the plaintiff.

In addition, the duty of care issue is further simplified, in intentional tort, by the existence of legislation prohibiting many acts that form the basis of torts. If striking another person, taking property without permission, or using a competitor's trademark without licence are all illegal acts, the defendant, who has a duty to obey the law, automatically breaches his or her duty of care in doing any of these things. Because the legal standard of care, with respect to these actions or any other illegal actions, is not to commit them at all, doing them automatically falls short of the required standard of care.

Intentional Torts as Formulas

The ease with which many of the elements of intentional torts are established makes them attractive as causes of action on which plaintiffs will frame their cases. To argue an intentional tort successfully, however, a plaintiff must establish that the facts that led to the alleged harm fall within certain strict parameters. These parameters can be understood as the basis for tort "formulas." If the facts fit the formula, the plaintiff may have a case in intentional tort. If the facts deviate, or a required element is missing, the plaintiff may, instead, have to rely on the doctrine of negligence, which imposes a more rigorous analysis of such issues as duty and standard of care.

As an example of a (fairly restrictive) formula, consider the tort of intimidation. To prove the tort of intimidation, the plaintiff must establish each of the following elements:

- the defendant had the intention to make the plaintiff obey his or her wishes or to cause harm to the plaintiff by threat;
- the defendant made a threat (to the plaintiff) that the plaintiff's non-compliance would result in the defendant's committing an illegal act (whether against the plaintiff or a third party);
- the plaintiff complied with the defendant's wishes to avoid the threat being carried out; and
- the threat, the plaintiff's compliance with the defendant's wishes, or both caused the plaintiff actual harm.

When the elements of this tort are considered, it quickly becomes clear that a fact scenario satisfying all the elements would be extremely rare. Indeed, very few Canadian cases have been argued on the basis of this tort since it was recognized in 1964[1]—and, quite possibly, not a single one was successful.

Although many other intentional torts are less exotic, this example highlights the importance of intentional tort "formulas" as a tool for narrowing causes of action.

Intentional Torts and Proof of Harm

Another feature of some intentional torts that tends to favour plaintiffs is the presumption of harm.

As you learned in the previous chapter, one of the four essential elements of negligence is harm: even if a plaintiff can prove that the defendant owed him or her

---

1. The tort was introduced in *Rookes v. Barnard*, [1964] A.C. 1129 (U.K.H.L.).

a duty of care, breached the duty, and caused some kind of consequence, if that consequence cannot be framed in terms of damages recognized by the law, the plaintiff will not be able to recover compensation.

There is an exception to this rule, however, when it comes to many intentional torts. Unless the elements of an intentional tort include the establishment of actual harm or loss (that is, proof of harm is part of the formula), if the tort can be proven, there is presumed to be harm—in other words, the tort *is* the harm. Where the damage is trifling or cannot be measured, a court may order **nominal damages** (a low amount of token damages) to acknowledge the wrong done to the plaintiff. Nominal damages typically range from $1 to $1,000.

nominal damages
a low amount of token damages awarded to acknowledge the wrong done to the plaintiff

The policy reason behind the presumption of damages is that a defendant who intentionally does something to harm another should not be permitted to escape liability on the ground of low damages, because if judges allowed this to happen, the law would not be seen to be brought to bear against those who do wrong. An additional reason sometimes stated for awarding nominal damages is "as a peg on which to hang costs"[2]—for example, in a jurisdiction in which the rules of civil procedure preclude costs (the defendant's reimbursement of some of the plaintiff's legal fees) where there is no damage award.

Nominal damages are awarded most commonly in cases involving harm to the person or reputation—for example, assault or defamation, or in trespass cases where no damage to property is done.

INTERPERSONAL TORTS

Assault

assault
the intentional creation of the apprehension of imminent harmful or offensive contact

The trickiest aspect of the tort of **assault** is that it is quite different from the much better-known *crime* of assault. Whereas the crime of assault usually requires the application of force to another (or at least the attempt to apply force), "assault" in tort law is much closer to what would be considered "threatening" in common usage.

The classic Canadian definition of tort assault is provided in *Canadian Tort Law*, now in its 9th edition,[3] as follows: "The intentional creation of the apprehension of imminent harmful or offensive contact." This definition makes it clear that a pleading based on assault must include evidence that:

- the defendant *intended* to create apprehension—that is, one cannot accidentally startle someone and thereby commit assault;
- the plaintiff's fear or expectation was that physical contact—and not, for example, a verbal scolding—was going to occur; and

---

2. The most commonly cited authority for the "peg on which to hang costs" principle is *Beaumont v. Greathead* (1846), 2 C.B. 494 at 499, 135 E.R. 1039.
3. Allen M. Linden & Bruce Feldthusen, *Canadian Tort Law*, 9th ed. (Markham, ON: LexisNexis Canada, 2011).

- the contact feared must have been capable of being carried out imminently, not later: for example, one cannot assault someone by sending them a threatening email or text from a different location.

The law of assault has also clarified what is not essential to this tort. A successful allegation of assault is *not* dependent on any of the following:

- an actual threat (there need only be the plaintiff's reasonable apprehension caused by the defendant's action),
- any follow-through on the threat, or
- harm.

Harm based on assault is presumed, and is normally compensated through nominal damages unless, for instance, the assault caused actual harm (for example, causing the plaintiff to crash his or her car during an assault by someone in the passenger seat). Although assault alone can form the basis of a cause of action, it is often argued together with other torts, such as battery, intentional infliction of mental suffering, or trespass.

Battery

Battery, which was once also called "trespass to the person," is any non-consensual physical contact or touching by the defendant to the plaintiff's physical person.

Over the years, many cases have been argued on the basis of what constitutes touching or how the defendant's physical person is defined. It is now settled law that touching can:

- be sexual or non-sexual;
- involve any part of the defendant's body;
- include an unwanted kiss or hug or spitting on someone;
- occur with or without a weapon;
- involve the use of any other kind of instrument, including a plant, an animal, or a liquid;
- include any thrown object; and even
- go unnoticed by the plaintiff at the time it occurs (for example, gently sticking a "kick me" sign on the plaintiff's back that the plaintiff does not notice until he or she undresses).

The plaintiff's physical person is defined as any part of the plaintiff's body including hair, clothes, and shoes, even if he or she cannot feel the contact (for example, lifting a person's skirt with a yardstick is battery).

Now that we have settled all the technicalities of battery, the key issues in these cases tend to relate to defences, especially consent or self-defence. Defences to intentional torts will be discussed in the next chapter.

Finally, battery is the traditional basis for lawsuits arising from medical procedures performed with no consent or completely invalid consent. The general rule is that free (uncoerced), full, and informed consent is required from the patient

battery
any non-consensual physical contact or touching by the defendant to the plaintiff's physical person

before a medical practitioner can deliver treatment, unless the emergent nature of the situation makes obtaining consent impossible or life-threateningly time-consuming. In the absence of an emergency, failing to obtain any consent at all is battery; obtaining consent so uninformed that the patient is not aware of even the most basic nature of the treatment is battery; and obtaining flawed consent (for example, after giving a confusing or incomplete description of the treatment and its risks) is negligence. The relationship between consent and negligence will be discussed again in the context of professional malpractice in Chapter 14.

Intentional Infliction of Mental Suffering

In a 1938 journal article,[4] University of Minnesota law professor William L. Prosser, who would later become dean of the College of Law at the University of California, Berkeley and a renowned expert on torts, made the following pronouncement:

> It is time to recognize that the courts have created a new tort. It appears, in one disguise or another, in more than a hundred decisions, the greater number of them within the last two decades. . . . It consists of the intentional, outrageous infliction of mental suffering in extreme form.

Prosser went on to explain that until the turn of the 20th century, courts had been very reluctant to "accept the interest in peace of mind as entitled to independent legal protection." With the stealthy introduction of the tort he coined **"intentional infliction of mental suffering,"** he noted some softening in that reluctance, observed that law was in a period of growth, and noted that "the ultimate limits" of that growth were "as yet only a matter of conjecture."

Three-quarters of a century have passed since that conjecture. Professor Prosser would likely, if he were alive today, approve of the restraint that judges have employed in expanding the limits of recovery for disruption of "peace of mind." Successful recovery of compensation for "intentional infliction of mental suffering" has been restricted to cases in which the plaintiff can prove "[t]he performance of an act, or the making of a statement (probably false) that is calculated to cause mental anguish and, in fact, causes such mental anguish."[5]

Cases decided in this area have added further stipulations:

- the act or statement cannot be accidental or innocent but must be intentional;
- in general (but it has not been required in every single case), if the tort is based on a statement, the statement must be a lie or at least calculated to mislead; and
- the plaintiff's reaction must be more than just a temporary upset: it must amount to a disturbance in health capable of being diagnosed or confirmed by a physician, though it need not be a recognized psychiatric disorder.

intentional infliction of mental suffering
an act or (false or misleading) statement that is calculated to cause mental anguish, results in a disturbance in the plaintiff's health, and is capable of being diagnosed or confirmed by a physician

---

4. William L. Prosser, "Intentional Infliction of Mental Suffering: A New Tort" (1938-1939) 37 Mich. L. Rev. 874.

5. Margaret Kerr, JoAnn Kurtz & Laurence M. Olivo, *Canadian Tort Law in a Nutshell*, 3d ed. (Toronto: Carswell, 2009) at 23.

High-Handed Firing Leads to Claim for Intentional Infliction of Mental Suffering

From: *Prinzo v. Baycrest Centre for Geriatric Care*, 2002 CanLII 45005 (Ont. C.A.).

Iole Prinzo worked in the beauty salon of the Baycrest Centre for Geriatric Care for more than 17 years as an administrator and hairstylist. Up until a management change in 1996, she was described as a "model employee." The new management that came into power in 1996, however, viewed the beauty salon services as a target for downsizing and recommended that Prinzo be terminated in January 1997. The board accepted the recommendation in October 1997, but no action was immediately taken.

On November 20, Ms. Prinzo slipped and fell in the parking lot, injuring her arm. She came back to work for a few days, but the injury worsened. On November 27, she received a letter advising her that she would be laid off, but no effective date for the layoff was given. On November 28, her doctor advised that she was unfit for any kind of work due to her injury, and she was off work until February 9, 1998.

Between December 4, 1997 and her return to work, the employer began a series of calls to Prinzo asking when she would be fit to return to work. The court found that these calls were harassing, especially in the light that the caller suggested that Prinzo was malingering (faking hurt), despite the fact that she had submitted her doctor's report that she was unfit to work. On December 23, the employer sent a letter to Prinzo alleging that her doctor had cleared her to work (he had not), and that her failure to return would be deemed a "refusal to work," with consequences flowing from that. The court found that the employer's motivation to get Prinzo back to work was based on a policy at the workplace that prohibited the layoff of a person who was away on disability.

The calls to Prinzo continued into the spring. Prinzo hired a lawyer who requested, on January 15, that the harassing calls be stopped. They continued.

On the day Prinzo returned to work on February 9, a meeting was immediately arranged with human resources. Prinzo asked to have a support person accompany her to the meeting; the request was denied. The meeting took two hours; in attendance were Prinzo and four representatives of the employer. At the meeting, the employer made negative comments about Prinzo's performance, including a comment about being concerned for the safety of residents around her. Ms. Prinzo found this comment extremely upsetting.

On March 11, she received a formal termination letter.

In the wake of the termination, Prinzo suffered documented physical symptoms including weight gain, blood pressure problems, complication of her diabetes, and a disabling loss of self-esteem.

Prinzo sued her former employer, alleging intentional infliction of emotional suffering. The trial court found that the conduct of the employer when terminating Prinzo was a "separate actionable wrong" (that is, separate from her allegations with respect to the contract and statute-based termination issues), and that the following three conditions were met:

1. flagrant or outrageous conduct;
2. calculated to produce harm; and
3. resulting in a visible and provable illness.

The appeal court upheld both these findings and the trial court's award of $15,000 in damages for intentional infliction of mental suffering.

False Imprisonment

The tort of **false imprisonment** is based on the confinement within a fixed boundary of a person against that person's will. The case law has identified the following essential elements of the tort:

- The confinement must be intentional.
- The person confined must not have consented.
- The person confined must believe that serious consequences would follow an attempt to escape (usually, the plaintiff must fear one of three things: application of force to himself or herself or to a third party; serious bodily harm—for example, as a result of jumping out of a window; or a criminal charge resulting from escape).
- The confinement must occur without lawful authority (for example, if the person is arrested, the arrest can be deemed false imprisonment only if (1) there is no arrest warrant, or (2) the arresting officers lack reasonable and probable grounds for making an arrest). Also, certain forms of brief detention without warrant or reasonable grounds (for example, a random driver stop under the RIDE program) are tolerated under the criminal law.

Other factors have been found *not* to be fundamental to the tort. First, confinement using barriers is not necessary, only control of movement. For example, a suspected shoplifter can be falsely imprisoned by being instructed (for example, by a store clerk) to "wait right here for the police" on the sidewalk outside a store. If the person feels compelled to comply to avoid danger (for example, that of being tackled to the ground by a security guard if he or she leaves), the person is imprisoned, regardless of the fact that he or she is not confined. This kind of barrier-free confinement is sometimes called **psychological confinement**.

Second, perhaps oddly, it is possible that the plaintiff need not have known that he or she was confined at the time the confinement occurred.[6] (This detail comes from an Irish case that has not been extensively cited in Canada, although it was followed by the Alberta Queen's Bench in 2008.[7] In the Irish case, the plaintiff was "confined" for a time before knowing she was actually under arrest.) In such a case, there is likely limited potential for the expansion of the circumstances in which a plaintiff will be able to recover damages for a false imprisonment of which he or she was unaware.

Finally, it is widely accepted law that the plaintiff need not be able to prove measurable harm. Like assault and trespass, false imprisonment is an intentional tort of presumed harm: the imprisonment itself is the harm and is automatically compensable, if the elements are proven, by nominal damages if there are no other damages.

In practice, the circumstances most likely to give rise to a tort lawsuit based on this tort involve the investigative detention of suspects, either by store security guards or police. There have also been cases in the United States about the experi-

---

6. *Murray v. Ministry of Defence*, [1988] 2 All E.R. 521 (U.K.H.L.).
7. *C.H.S. v. Alberta (Director of Child Welfare)*, 2008 ABQB 513.

ence of being confined in an aircraft that has landed, but where the passengers have not been allowed to exit the plane, for example, because an arrival gate is not yet available. The aircraft plaintiffs have generally not been successful in their suits because the airline can usually rely on the defence of legal authority.

Malicious Prosecution

Malicious prosecution is a fairly narrowly defined tort. To succeed in proving it, the plaintiff must show that:

- the defendant initiated a criminal proceeding against the plaintiff;
- in so doing, the defendant was motivated by "malice or a primary purpose other than that of carrying the law into effect";
- there was no reasonable or probable cause for bringing the proceeding; and
- the proceedings were ultimately terminated in the plaintiff's favour.

malicious prosecution initiation of a criminal proceeding with malicious intent for no reasonable or probable cause

A defendant may decide to initiate a criminal proceeding because he or she is wholeheartedly, but mistakenly, convinced of the plaintiff's guilt. Even if the defendant is very aggressive in pursuing a conviction, he or she will not be liable in tort if the reason for the aggressive prosecution is a sincere but mistaken belief. The defendant will be liable only if he or she was motivated by malice or an improper purpose.

In early cases concerning malicious prosecution, the motivation requirement was often simply expressed as "malice" (hence the name of the tort). However, some important Canadian cases and academics have noted that a more accurate description of the kind of motivation that is needed in these cases is "malice or a primary purpose other than that of carrying the law into effect."[8]

Malicious prosecution can be argued only in relation to criminal proceedings, not civil litigation. The case law has clarified that to "initiate a criminal proceeding" can include a range of acts—for example, a victim's or witness's request that the police lay a charge, police actions in laying a charge and investigating a crime, or the Crown's actions in prosecuting a crime.

One of the reasons that this tort is fairly rare is that one individual is not single-handedly capable, on his or her own, of causing the trial of a criminal charge. The witnesses must provide evidence sufficient to support a charge; the police must lay a charge; the Crown must choose to prosecute the charge; and the judge must allow the charge to go ahead (for example, at the conclusion of a preliminary hearing); all without successful opposition on the part of defence counsel. This tort requires that the prosecution be unreasonable from the beginning, which means that in proven cases, despite the efforts of defence counsel to persuade them, none of the parties who assist the party motivated by an improper purpose will have taken steps to drop or dismiss the unreasonable charge—a circumstance that, one would hope, would be a rare failure of the justice system.

8. See, for example, *Miazga v. Kvello Estate*, 2009 SCC 51, [2009] 3 S.C.R. 339; *Lamb v. Benoit et al.*, [1959] S.C.R. 321; and *Oniel v. Marks et al.*, 2001 CanLII 24168, 195 D.L.R. (4th) 59 (Ont. C.A.).

Despite this hurdle, malicious prosecution is alleged fairly often. The success rate is low, with most plaintiffs failing to establish either an improper purpose on the part of the defendant (because zeal for justice does not equal improper purpose) or unreasonableness, or both.

A few cases have been argued on the basis of what is meant by the proceedings being terminated "in the plaintiff's favour." It is now settled law that an acquittal is not the only ending that is in the plaintiff's favour—a stay of proceedings (where the prosecution is terminated by the judge before there is a ruling on guilt or innocence) also counts as an ending in the plaintiff's favour.[9]

Finally, there is some support in Canadian law for the principle that "presumed harm," as described above in relation to battery and false imprisonment, is *not* a part of the law of malicious prosecution. Instead, a plaintiff alleging this tort must establish independent, quantifiable harm in order to recover damages.[10]

Defamation

defamation
intentional harm to a person's reputation in the community

Whereas the tort of battery usually involves an intentional harm to the physical person, **defamation** is about intentional harm to a person's reputation in the community.

Distinguishing Defamation from Privacy Violations and "Identity Theft"

In the years since the introduction of the Internet, the topic of harm to personal privacy and identity—like defamation, a harm to non-physical aspects of personhood—has attracted a great deal of attention. While defamation has some connections to the issue of privacy, the Canadian common law did not until recently recognize an intentional tort of invasion of privacy.

Four jurisdictions—British Columbia, Manitoba, Saskatchewan, and Newfoundland and Labrador—have introduced a tort-style action based on invasion of privacy through a provision in the provincial privacy act in force in those provinces.[11] In Quebec, the Civil Code provides for the compensation of invasion of privacy with an award of damages. In Ontario, there is no pure invasion of privacy tort, but the recognition of a common-law tort of "intrusion upon seclusion" came with the January 2012 decision in *Jones v. Tsige*[12] (see Case in Point, below).

In light of the inconsistency in Canadian law with respect to the intentional tort of invasion of privacy, it is useful to know that privacy and identity violations in our society are sometimes addressed by the law of negligence and, more recently, under a range of privacy statutes (see Table 10.1).

---

9. *Romegialli v. Marceau*, [1964] 1 O.R. 407 (1963), 42 D.L.R. (2d) 481 (C.A.).

10. See, for example, *Teskey v. Toronto Transit Commission*, 2003 CanLII 12871 (Ont. S.C.).

11. For a summary of those provisions, see "Compendium of Canadian Legislation Respecting the Protection of Personal Information in Health Research," online: Canadian Institutes of Health Research <http://www.cihr-irsc.gc.ca/e/31444.html>.

12. *Jones v. Tsige*, 2012 ONCA 32 (CanLII).

TABLE 10.1 Privacy Legislation in Canada

Federal Statutes	Examples of Provincial Statutes
Privacy Act	Alberta *Freedom of Information and Protection of Privacy Act*
	British Columbia *E-Health (Personal Health Information Access and Protection of Privacy) Act*
Personal Information Protection and Electronic Documents Act	Nova Scotia *Personal Information International Disclosure Protection Act*
	Ontario *Municipal Freedom of Information and Protection of Privacy Act*

CASE IN POINT

No Pure Invasion of Privacy Tort in Ontario, but Damages Available for "Intrusion upon Seclusion"

From: *Jones v. Tsige*, 2011 ONSC 1475 (CanLII), 2012 ONCA 32 (CanLII).

The issue whether a tort of invasion of privacy exists in Ontario has been highly contentious, especially in the past 30 years. In the early 1980s, judges deciding cases like *Capan v. Capan*[13] and *Saccone v. Orr*[14] boldly noted and then ignored the suggestion that no such tort existed and ordered damages anyway. These cases were followed by the 1991 decision in *Roth v. Roth*,[15] in which Mandel J., in awarding damages, explained:

> In my view, whether the invasion of privacy of an individual will be actionable depends on the circumstances of the particular case and the conflicting rights involved. In such a manner the rights of the individual, as well as society as a whole, are served.

In 2006, when faced with a defendant's motion to strike out a plaintiff's claim based on the non-existence of the "tort of invasion of privacy," Stinson J. of the Ontario Superior Court of Justice reviewed the conflicting cases on the subject and refused to strike out the pleading. He noted that protection of privacy is a Charter value, and that although the Charter does not apply to lawsuits between private individuals, the decision in *M. (A.) v. Ryan*,[16] among others, makes it clear that Canadian courts are expected to develop the common law in a manner consistent with Charter values. He concluded that:

> With advancements in technology, an individual's personal data can now be collected, accessed (properly and improperly), and disseminated more easily than ever before. There is a resulting increased concern in our society about the risk of unauthorized access to an individual's personal information. The traditional torts such as nuisance, trespass, and harassment may not provide adequate protection against infringement of an individual's privacy interests. Protection of those privacy interests by providing a common law remedy for their violation would be consistent with *Charter* values and an "incremental revision" and logical extension of the existing jurisprudence.

In 2011, however, the same court (Ontario Superior Court of Justice) issued a contrary judgment in *Jones v. Tsige*.[17] That case involved a lawsuit based on the "tort of invasion of privacy" brought by a plaintiff named Sandra Jones. According to the facts before the court, Ms. Jones was an employee of the Bank of Montreal, as was the defendant, Winnie Tsige. Ms. Jones and Ms. Tsige worked at different branches. Over the course of four years and on

---

13. *Capan v. Capan*, [1980] O.J. No. 1361 (H.C.J.).
14. *Saccone v. Orr* (1981), 34 O.R. (2d) 317 (Co. Ct.).
15. *Roth v. Roth* (1991), 4 O.R. (3d) 740 (Gen. Div.).
16. *M. (A.) v. Ryan*, [1997] 1 S.C.R. 157, 1997 CanLII 403.
17. *Jones v. Tsige*, 2011 ONSC 1475 (CanLII).

174 separate occasions, Ms. Tsige accessed and reviewed Ms. Jones's private personal banking information without legal authority.

In considering whether Ms. Jones was entitled to succeed in an action based on a tort of invasion of privacy, Whitaker J., writing for the court, reviewed the same cases that Stinson J. had reviewed five years before, with the addition of one other: the 2005 Ontario Court of Appeal decision in *Euteneier v. Lee.*[18] In deciding *Euteneier,* the Court of Appeal noted that:

> [Plaintiff] Euteneier properly conceded in oral argument before this court that there is no "free-standing" right to dignity or privacy under the *Charter* or at common law.

On the basis of this single sentence—written by the Court of Appeal, which ranks higher, under the common-law system of precedent, than does the Ontario Superior Court of Justice—Whitaker J. felt bound to decide that despite the carefully reasoned decision in *Somwar,* there is still no such thing in Canadian common law as a tort of invasion of privacy.

Sandra Jones appealed the decision, and the appeal decision was rendered in January 2012.

In allowing Ms. Jones's appeal, the Court of Appeal considered both the Canadian cases about a tort of invasion of privacy and the US doctrine of "intrusion upon seclusion" (looking into private aspects of a person's life without permission where such looking would be highly offensive to a reasonable person), which has been formally accepted as part of the tort law of the United States.

The court found that the facts in the case fell squarely within the description of intrusion upon seclusion, and held:

> The explicit recognition of a right to privacy as underlying specific *Charter* rights and freedoms, and the principle that the common law should be developed in a manner consistent with *Charter* values, supports the recognition of a civil action for damages for intrusion upon the plaintiff's seclusion.

After recognizing this new cause of action, the court summarized the elements that would need to be present to establish that the tort has been committed:

> [F]irst, that the defendant's conduct must be intentional, within which I would include reckless; second that the defendant must have invaded, without lawful justification, the plaintiff's private affairs or concerns; and third, that a reasonable person would regard the invasion as highly offensive causing distress, humiliation or anguish.[19]

The court ordered Tsige to pay Jones damages in the amount of $10,000, and reversed the trial court's order of costs against Jones at the trial level.

Two Forms of Defamation

Returning to the subject of defamation, defamation in general is the making of a false statement about a party that "tends to lower [that] person in the estimation of right-thinking members of society."[20] There are two subcategories of the tort: libel and slander.

libel
making a defamatory statement by publishing or broadcasting it

slander
making an oral defamatory statement

Libel is the making of a defamatory statement by publishing or broadcasting it; **slander** is the making of an oral defamatory statement.

There have been a number of cases that have turned on determining precisely the kinds of activities that amount to "publication or broadcast." The reason plaintiffs have argued these cases—and have made an effort to distinguish between libel and slander—relates to damages: where a plaintiff can prove libel, damages are considered to be "at large" (automatic; they need not be specifically proven). How-

18. *Euteneier v. Lee,* (2005), 77 O.R. (3d) 621 at para. 63, 260 D.L.R. (4th) 145 (C.A.).
19. *Jones v. Tsige, supra* note 12, at para. 71.
20. *Botiuk v. Toronto Free Press Publications Ltd.,* [1995] 3 S.C.R. 3 (1995), 126 D.L.R. (4th) 609.

ever, damages for slander are "at large" only if the slanderous statements fall into one of four prescribed categories:

1. statements that discredit the plaintiff's pursuit of his or her business or profession;
2. statements that suggest (falsely) that the plaintiff has committed a criminal offence;
3. statements that suggest that the plaintiff has a "loathsome or contagious disease" (for example, leprosy or an STI); or
4. statements that suggest that a woman is "unchaste."

As you can likely tell from the wording of these categories, these archaic-sounding principles come from the common law. The common-law recovery principles themselves have been, to some extent, replaced by legislation in most jurisdictions—for example, the Ontario *Libel and Slander Act*[21] (counterparts exist in other provinces and territories). Nevertheless, the basic rule remains: damages for libel are automatic, but damages for slander are automatic only under a limited range of circumstances.

For this reason, the content of "publication or broadcast" remains significant. In general, publication is *any* print writing; it need not actually be commercially released by a publisher. It is settled law that postings on a website (for example, on a blog, on Facebook, and so on) or communications via email qualify as "published" libel. As for what is encompassed by "broadcast," in the 2005 decision in *Romano v. D'Onofrio*,[22] the Court of Appeal sent a case back to trial to consider the issue whether comments made over a microphone at a banquet were "broadcast." The case was decided with reference to the Ontario *Libel and Slander Act*, which defines "broadcasting" and "broadcast" as follows (at s. 1(1)):

> "broadcasting" means the dissemination of writing, signs, signals, pictures and sounds of all kinds, intended to be received by the public either directly or through the medium of relay stations, by means of,
>
>> (a) any form of wireless radioelectric communication utilizing Hertzian waves, including radiotelegraph and radiotelephone, or
>>
>> (b) cables, wires, fibre-optic linkages or laser beams,
>
> and "broadcast" has a corresponding meaning.

No new trial decision in the *Romano* case about microphone communications has been released, which suggests that the case settled, leaving the microphone question a live issue, and demonstrating that the courts seem to take a very generous view about what falls into the categories of publication or broadcast.

---

21. *Libel and Slander Act*, R.S.O. 1990, c. L.12.
22. *Romano v. D'Onofrio*, (2005), 77 O.R. (3d) 583, 2005 CanLII 43288 (C.A.).

Proving Defamation

To prove either slander or libel, a plaintiff must prove three key elements. The first relates to the recipient of the message. If the message is allegedly a slanderous statement, it must be established that the statement was made to a third party, because an insult spoken to the plaintiff himself or herself is not slander. Similarly, in the case of libel, a defendant cannot libel a party by, for example, sending that party an email. The broadcast or published statement must be intended to reach, and actually reach, at least one other party.

Second, the allegedly slanderous statement or libellous communication must be specific enough that the third party can reasonably infer that it referred to the plaintiff specifically. For example, a tirade, in a blog, about "dishonest politicians" is not libel of any particular politician, unless sufficient particulars are given so that a specific target can be reasonably inferred. For example, it is not libel to spread untrue rumours about dishonest politicians, but a comment about "dishonest city councillors from the west end who oppose expansion of the downtown subway system and drive a giant black 2011 Cadillac Escalade" could be libel if a particular councillor fits this description.

Finally, the statement that is alleged to be slander or libel must meet the common-law test in that it (1) is untrue or false and (2) tends to lower the person in the estimation of right-thinking members of society.

Defences to Defamation

There are a number of general defences to intentional torts, which will be introduced in Chapter 11. However, there are four specific defences to defamation that are best understood if introduced here, in the proper context: truth, absolute privilege, qualified privilege, and fair comment.

TRUTH

Stated simply, a true statement cannot be defamation.

ABSOLUTE PRIVILEGE

absolute privilege
a defence against defamation for statements made in a court or parliament, or between spouses

Absolute privilege is a narrow protection that applies to otherwise defamatory statements made in certain specific contexts. In Canada, absolute privilege applies to:

- statements made in court (though this privilege does not negate a potential charge of perjury);
- statements made in a parliament or legislature (there is an exception: the defence does *not* extend to statements suggesting that a member of parliament is a liar, or is lying—these words are considered to be "unparliamentary language"); and
- statements made between spouses (about third parties).

Where the defence applies, it protects a defendant against allegations of defamation even where the defendant's statement was untrue or was made with malice.

QUALIFIED PRIVILEGE

Qualified privilege is a defence designed to protect those who have a duty to make statements that would otherwise be considered defamation.

qualified privilege
a defence against defamation for statements made while fulfilling a duty

For example, s. 23 of the Nova Scotia *Children and Family Services Act*[23] imposes a duty on *any* person who suspects that a child is in need of protection (for example, because of suspected child abuse) to report that suspicion to a designated agency. (Similar legislation exists in other Canadian jurisdictions, sometimes with penalties attached for non-compliance.) This duty exists regardless of the fact that a person's suspicions may turn out to be unfounded, and reporting them would otherwise potentially be slander (reporting that a person is a child abuser when it is untrue). Another example is in the context of job references—for example, a person's former employer may be asked by a potential new employer to comment on the candidate's performance. The former employer may feel a duty to say that part of the reason for terminating the employee was the belief that the employee was sexually harassing others, but no one came forward with a formal complaint. This sort of comment also has the potential to form the basis of a slander lawsuit.

Because there are good public policy reasons to protect the kinds of communications described above, the defence of qualified privilege can be used in these circumstances, but it is narrowly defined and requires that:

- the defendant has a duty to give the impugned information,
- the giving of the information is done *without malice*, and
- the giving of the information takes place with proper discretion so as to minimize the potential to harm the reputation of the plaintiff (for example, a negative job reference should be given in the course of a private conversation, not left as a message in a voice mail box accessible by others).

FAIR COMMENT

Fair comment is a defence to defamation used by individuals and organizations whose mandate is the dissemination of information to the public—for example, members of the media.

fair comment
a defence against defamation used by individuals and organizations whose mandate is the dissemination of information to the public

In general, the media strive to report truthful information (as noted above, truth is a complete defence to defamation). However, where sources are resistant and good information is limited, the media may deem it necessary to report conclusions drawn from the available information that ultimately turn out to be false. (These conclusions often fall under the realm of "opinion.") Ordinarily, these reports would expose their authors to liability for defamation. The defence of fair comment exists to protect the honest and well-meaning reporters of "unfounded" opinions based on true facts, in the absence of malice.

The necessary elements of the defence of fair comment are as follows:

- the report must be on a matter of public interest—for example, trivial matters reported to titillate the public (for example, unfounded reports that a celebrity marriage is failing) will not meet the test;

---

23. *Children and Family Services Act*, S.N.S. 1990, c. 5.

- the comment must be based on fact (for example, if the comment is an opinion, it must flow from true facts);
- the comment must be expressed as an opinion, or otherwise reasonably interpreted as an opinion (it must not be disguised as fact);
- the comment must pass the following test: on the basis of the true facts, could any person *reasonably* come to the opinion reflected in the comment?; and
- the defendant must not, in making the comment, have been motivated by malice.

See Figure 10.1.

Anti-Defamation Legislation

In some jurisdictions, legislation that prohibits defamation is now in place. For example, in Ontario, the *Libel and Slander Act* prohibits libel and slander, defines the term "broadcasting," extends privilege (protection from allegations of libel) to certain kinds of communications, restricts access to nominal damages under certain circumstances, prescribes limitation periods, and establishes rules relating to evidence and to costs. Similar statutes exist in other Canadian jurisdictions.

INTERFERENCE WITH POSSESSIONS

The next category of torts involves harm to, or interference with, possessions other than land. These torts traditionally describe interference with physical objects, which in law are sometimes called **chattels**. In some US states, the principles have been extended to apply to intangible possessions—for example, an Internet domain name or data contained in a computer (apart from the computer itself).[24] The 2007 decision of the English House of Lords in *OBG Ltd. v. Allan*,[25] however, made it clear that an intangible asset cannot be the subject of this type of lawsuit under English law. Canadian courts have considered few cases about the application of these torts to intangibles; however, the 2000 Ontario Superior Court decision in *Brant Avenue Manor Limited Partnership v. Transamerica Life Insurance Co. of Canada*,[26] a case about conversion of business goodwill, offers some support for the application of these torts to intangibles.

The general name for this category of tort is "trespass to chattels," distinguishing it from "trespass to the person" (battery) and "trespass to land"—the category that most people think of when they hear the word "trespass."

The two forms of trespass to chattels or interference with possessions are **detinue** and **conversion**. Some lawmakers recognize a minor distinction between these two and the general category of trespass to chattels: in the case of detinue and conversion, the defendant must take possession of the chattel and, in doing so, deprive

chattels
possessions other than land

detinue
wrongful possession of a chattel that belongs to another

conversion
wrongful possession that includes exercise of rights of ownership, preventing the actual owner from exercising such rights

24. *Kremen v. Cohen*, 325 F.3d 1035 (9th Cir. 2003); *Louis E. Thyroff v. Nationwide Mutual Insurance Company, et al.*, 2007 NY Int. 29.
25. *OBG Ltd. v. Allan*, [2007] UKHL 21.
26. *Brant Avenue Manor Limited Partnership v. Transamerica Life Insurance Co. of Canada* (2000), 48 O.R. (3d) 363, 2000 CanLII 22368 (S.C.).

FIGURE 10.1   Defamation Defences Flowchart

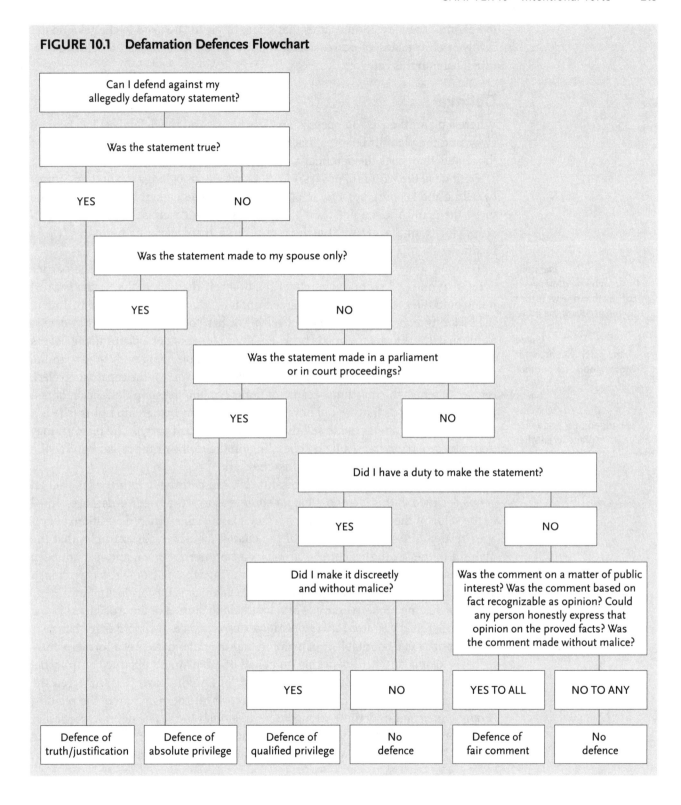

the plaintiff of its use. Some cases that refer simply to "trespass to chattels" do not involve a clear taking of possession. Cyber-trespass cases, discussed below, sometimes fall into this category.

Detinue

Where a plaintiff once had possession of a chattel, and the defendant has taken it away, and the plaintiff believes that he or she has a greater right to possession of the chattel than does the defendant, the plaintiff may choose to sue in detinue.

Detinue is the wrongful possession of a chattel that belongs to another. Simply by taking and keeping possession of the chattel, the defendant has committed the tort—the plaintiff need not show that the defendant "exercised rights of ownership," for example, by selling the chattel to a third party or by using it in a business.

bailment
an agreement between parties that one will store the goods of the other

bailee
the party who holds or stores goods for another

bailor
the party who has handed over goods for storage to another

Detinue sometimes arises in **bailment** situations—that is, where the parties agree that one will store the goods of the other. If the **bailee** (the holder/storer) holds onto the goods beyond the agreed-upon termination date for the bailment, the **bailor** (the one who has handed over his or her goods for storage) may decide to sue in detinue to get the goods back. For example, consider a plaintiff who leaves a sewing machine at a repair shop for repair and, upon being presented with the bill, refuses to pay because the machine still does not work. If the repair shop clerk refuses to return the machine because of non-payment, the shop clerk has retained possession of goods that are not hers without exercising ownership rights (she has not, for example, attempted to sell the machine to a third party). The plaintiff may under these circumstances (and depending on the terms of the repair contract he signed) have a claim in detinue against the clerk.

The preferred remedy for a successful claim in detinue is return of the actual goods detained. If this is impossible for some reason, the remedy is damages equal to the value of the goods. In addition, if the plaintiff has suffered additional damages related to loss of possession of the chattel (consider, for example, that the plaintiff in the sewing machine example is a commercial tailor, and has not been able to earn money as a tailor for the period during which he or she was without a sewing machine), the plaintiff may be awarded damages for this loss as well.

An interesting modern example of reliance on the tort of detinue occurred in the 2011 case of *South Simcoe Railway Heritage Corporation v. Wakeford*.[27] In that case, the plaintiff was a charitable organization and the defendant was a former volunteer. The defendant, while working on behalf of the plaintiff, obtained an Internet domain name for the plaintiff organization, but, upon leaving, transferred the domain name to himself. In an attempt to recover the domain name, the plaintiff brought an action in detinue, along with three other torts. The detinue portion of the action was, unfortunately, dismissed because the relevant limitation period had expired, leaving open the question whether detinue applies to a case like this.

---

27. *South Simcoe Railway Heritage Corporation v. Wakeford*, 2011 ONSC 1234.

LAW IN PRACTICE
Tort Protections for "Cyber-Property"

An emerging area in the common law is the treatment of cyber-property. "Cyber-property" is a word sometimes used to describe individuals' interests in intangible features of the Internet, such as domain names.

This area of law is complicated for two reasons. First, it straddles two legal disciplines: property law and tort law. Second, as yet, no strong consensus about the legal status of cyber-property exists.

Property law is concerned with identifying and guarding a range of ownership rights with respect to property. Some of those rights flow from physical possession of property (an idea that does not translate very well to intangibles), and others flow from legal processes such as registered transfer of title.

Torts like trespass to chattels, detinue, and conversion are enforceable by the plaintiff only if the plaintiff can bring the item interfered with within the definition of "property." Some Internet intangibles seem capable of being treated in this way; for example, a domain name is something that one must pay for, and with payment comes exclusive use. This sounds much like other forms of personal property. But what about bandwidth or processing power? Can a party have a property interest in those forms of personal property?

Lawyers and judges in several jurisdictions—including Canada and multiple US states—have grappled with cyber-property issues on an *ad hoc* case-by-case basis, and the decisions have sometimes been inconsistent. In the United States, there seems to be a clear movement in the direction of recognizing websites, domain names, and bandwidth as property, and of allowing plaintiffs to use tort doctrine (for example, the tort of conversion) to police infringement. Canadian courts have so far been more hesitant.

In his award-winning 2006 article, "Electronic Trespass in Canada: The Protection of Private Property on the Internet,"[28] author James MacDonald examines the US jurisprudence and the work of other scholars and explains that the tort of trespass to electronic chattels (sometimes called "electronic trespass") has been successfully argued in the United States in cases about issues such as spam control, web robots that engage in "screen scraping" for data, and the use of spyware. MacDonald notes that this trend is not universally welcome; for example, he reproduces the following quotation from one of the cases (*Ticketmaster Corp. v. Tickets.com, Inc.*[29]):

> [W]hat is being attempted [in the cases allowing recovery based on "electronic trespass"] is to apply a medieval common law concept in an entirely new situation which should be disposed of by modern law designed to protect intellectual property interests.

28. James MacDonald, "Electronic Trespass in Canada: The Protection of Private Property on the Internet" (2006) vol. 5, no. 3 C.J.L.T., online: Canadian Journal of Law and Technology <http://cjlt.dal.ca/vol5_no3/index.html>.
29. *Ticketmaster Corp. v. Tickets.com, Inc.*, 2000 U.S. Dist. LEXIS 12987 (C.D. Cal. 2001) [*Ticketmaster*], aff'd 2001 U.S. App. LEXIS 1454 (9th Cir. 2001), 2003 U.S. Dist. LEXIS 6483 (C.D. Cal. 2003) [*Ticketmaster II*].

MacDonald cautions, however, that there are many forms of harm that occur on the Internet that have nothing to do with intellectual property interests (like copyright), and so counting on the creation of new intellectual property solutions will not fully address the problem. He also examines, and then rejects, the doctrine of nuisance as a viable method for controlling harm to cyber-property.

Returning to the emerging doctrine of electronic trespass, MacDonald points out that in the physical world, consent received from a property owner is a full defence to trespass: it is not possible to commit trespass if one has permission to enter. MacDonald suggests that consent is an appropriate mechanism for controlling intrusion on cyber-property. He reviews many practical methods by which consent can be extended, limited, and withdrawn by cyber-property owners and concludes:

> By allowing the content of consent to be decided on a case-by-case basis, courts can develop a flexible notion of implied consent informed by notions of netiquette and common practices, and identify situations when the implied consent has been restricted. This will allow electronic trespass to be used to curtail less desirable activities, and support the use of technological means to prevent unwanted access without unduly limiting the socially useful aspects of the Internet.[30]

Conversion

Conversion begins the same way as detinue—with the defendant taking possession of a chattel in which the plaintiff asserts greater ownership rights. However, to "convert" the property (and fall within the scope of this tort), the defendant must then exercise rights of ownership in respect of the chattel and prevent the plaintiff from exercising his or her own rights of ownership.

Rights of ownership include:

- using the chattel as if it were one's own (for example, finding a bike in a park and riding away on it);
- making changes to the chattel (for example, stealing a neighbour's wooden patio chair and burning it for firewood);
- using the chattel to earn income (for example, stealing a taxicab and charging people to ride in it); and
- taking the plaintiff's chattel and selling it to a third party.

The common thread in these situations is that the defendant has done something with the chattel that is inconsistent with the plaintiff's ownership rights.

Conversion overlaps partially, but not completely, with the crime of theft. Not all thefts are conversions (where there are no rights of ownership exercised, a theft could be more akin to detinue), and not all conversions are thefts (because it is possible to convert a chattel that one has found or otherwise acquired innocently).

---

30. MacDonald, *supra* note 28, at 173.

The remedy for conversion depends on whether the chattel is recoverable. If possible, the chattel will be ordered returned to the plaintiff, with damages for its conversion and for any reduction in value caused by the conversion (for example, if the chattel is damaged through the defendant's use). If the chattel is not recoverable, damages will be equal to the chattel's value, plus an amount of damages (sometimes nominal) to compensate for the act of conversion.

Where deprivation of the chattel has caused losses to the plaintiff (for example, the converted chattel was a piece of business equipment, and the plaintiff's business was affected), damages for this loss of use will be added to the total.

In a 1988 case about a breach in the confidentiality of employment records, the Supreme Court of Canada considered the issue whether taking unauthorized access to confidential records was conversion. The court found that it was not conversion, because the defendant's exercise of rights of ownership over the records did not oust the plaintiff's own exercise of ownership rights. In other words, what the defendant took away was the privacy of the records, not the records themselves.[31]

INTERFERENCE WITH REAL PROPERTY

"Real property" or "real estate" simply means land and/or permanent structures built on the land. There are two main—and very distinct—forms of interference, with real property recognized under the law of torts: trespass and nuisance.

Trespass

The tort of trespass to real property has been replaced by statutory provisions in all Canadian jurisdictions. The *Criminal Code*[32] regulates what was once "trespass" by means of provisions relating to, for example, breaking and entering. There are also provincial statutes regulating trespass—for example, Ontario's *Trespass to Property Act*.[33] Conviction on such an offence generally results in a fine.

Despite the existence of these statutory protections, the occasional plaintiff still brings a tort suit in trespass. Like battery and false imprisonment, trespass, if proven, is automatically compensable; however, where there is no damage to property, the nominal damages are low enough to discourage most plaintiffs from incurring the necessary legal fees.

Related to trespass is the issue of occupiers' liability. If a trespasser is injured while on someone else's property, the trespasser may actually have a cause of action against the occupier. Occupiers' liability will be discussed in Chapter 14.

Nuisance

As noted in Chapter 9, the tort of nuisance is somewhat of an anomaly in that it can be, but *need not be*, an intentional tort.

31. *R. v. Stewart*, [1988] 1 S.C.R. 963.
32. *Criminal Code*, R.S.C. 1985, c. C-46.
33. *Trespass to Property Act*, R.S.O. 1990, c. T.21.

Nuisance is the cause of action of choice where the conditions prevailing on land, or activities being carried out on land, negatively affect another land occupier's use and enjoyment of his or her own land.

A wide range of behaviours have been found in law that constitute a nuisance. Classic examples involve:

- noise;
- excessive shade (for example, where one neighbour erects a tall shed that shades another neighbour's garden) or excessive light (for example, bright outdoor lighting—like baseball field lights—left on late that disturb residential neighbours);
- odours and air pollution;
- polluting waterways that flow into others' lands; and
- projectiles (golf balls, baseballs, and so on) that stray from one property onto another.

In general, an occasional or minor annoyance (one loud summer barbecue, for example) will be insufficient to found a case in nuisance. Also, the defendant will generally need to show harm more substantial than simple aggravation. Some kind of concrete consequence must flow from the nuisance for it to be actionable (also, if the harm is trivial, so will the damages be).

For example, if one neighbour has an apple tree, fails to collect the fallen apples, the apples rot, and for a two- or three-week period, there is a natural increase in the number of wasps in the vicinity, a neighbour who dislikes the wasps will generally not have a case in nuisance. However, if instead of an untended apple tree, the defendant has a stagnant swimming pool half-filled with three years' worth of undrained gunk, and the pool becomes a breeding ground for so many mosquitoes that a neighbour is forced to avoid going into his own backyard, the court may well assess damages in nuisance.

In considering the two above examples, you may notice a distinction based on reasonableness. Apples fall from trees all over the world, and failing to collect them is not a highly unreasonable use of one's land. However, in the light of media campaigns about cleaning up standing water and bylaws creating offences about the same issue, refusing to drain a pool that has become a swamp likely *is* unreasonable in an urban setting. This distinction—between reasonable and unreasonable uses of one's land, and reasonable and unreasonable measures to control nuisance—is woven throughout the nuisance jurisprudence, if not always explicitly stated.

There are exceptions, however: in the 2009 case of *Suzuki v. Munroe*,[34] Suzuki successfully sued Munroe in nuisance by alleging (and to some extent proving) post-traumatic stress disorder caused by the commonplace noise coming from the ordinary, properly functioning air conditioning unit installed at Munroe's house, which was next to, and audible from, Suzuki's house.

---

34. *Suzuki v. Munroe*, 2009 BCSC 1403 (CanLII).

As is the case with many other torts, some aspects of nuisance law have been eclipsed by statute; in this case, environmental law statutes. When you consider that environmental harm can be characterized as the deleterious effects of one party's actions on other people's land, the connection becomes clear. There is also a connection between nuisance law and a narrow doctrine called strict liability, which will be discussed in Chapter 14.

INTERFERENCE WITH BUSINESS OR CONTRACTS

The next batch of torts involves the wrongful interference with contracts, **intellectual property**, or other business interests.

Like the other intentional torts introduced in this chapter, these torts are formulaic and therefore limited in application. It is important for you to understand that this handful of "business torts" does not represent the full scope of situations in which businesses or business people can recover for harm done; in fact, the majority of lawsuits involving alleged harm to business interests are argued under the general doctrine of negligence. Where the elements exist to support a claim, it is, however, almost always expedient for plaintiffs to frame a claim in intentional tort, because of the evidentiary "shortcuts" introduced earlier in this chapter.

intellectual property
legal rights that result from intellectual activity in the industrial, scientific, literary, and artistic fields

Fraud (Deceit) and Fraudulent Misrepresentation

Fraud, also known as *deceit*, is a tort with a well-known counterpart in criminal law. Since a criminal prosecution does not provide financial compensation to the victim of a fraud, this is an area in which parallel criminal and civil proceedings are common.

A defendant commits fraud when he or she

1. intentionally (or even just recklessly)
2. makes a representation (oral, written, or some other way)
3. knowing that it is false or misleading
4. under circumstances where he or she knows the plaintiff is likely to act on that statement and suffer damages (usually economic loss) and
5. the plaintiff does act and does suffer damages.

A defendant who commits fraud often does so by making a false statement to influence a plaintiff to enter into a contract that the plaintiff would not otherwise have accepted. For this reason, many of the cases that consider the tort of fraud also deal with contract issues, which can lead to much confusion with respect to issues such as limitation periods, remedies contemplated within the contract versus remedies outside the contract, and so on. In general, if the alleged fraud relates to a contract, a plaintiff should frame its statement of claim in both contract and tort.

Fraudulent misrepresentation is a specific, as well as the most commonly argued, subcategory of the tort of fraud. In fact, some judges use fraud/deceit and fraudulent misrepresentation interchangeably (see, for example, *Rosenich v. Welke*).[35]

fraud
intentional misrepresentation that causes another to suffer damages; also called deceit

fraudulent misrepresentation
intentional fraud that causes another to enter into a contract

---

35. *Rosenich v. Welke*, 2003 ABQB 876 (CanLII).

Fraudulent misrepresentation, however, seems almost exclusively reserved to cases where deception leads to the plaintiff's making a contract, whereas the slightly more general "plain fraud" is pleaded in certain non-contract situations (for instance, situations involving consent to sex obtained through lies or blackmail; see, for example, *Saint-Laurent c. Hétu*[36]).

Fraudulent misrepresentation (an intentional tort) is distinguishable from negligent misrepresentation (a subcategory of negligence) on the basis of the level of intent that the defendant is alleged to have possessed. Where the plaintiff is unsure about the defendant's intent, it is recommended that the plaintiff plead both causes of action.

fraudulent concealment
deliberate hiding, non-disclosure, or suppression of a fact or circumstance with intent to deceive or defraud in a contractual arrangement

Another subcategory of fraud is **fraudulent concealment**. A common scenario in which fraudulent concealment is relied upon is that in which a plaintiff seeks to bring a claim outside the normal limitation period, alleging that the defendant has, by fraud, concealed certain facts that would have made the plaintiff aware, in time to sue, that he had a cause of action.

Finally, because of the moral overtones associated with accusations of fraud, there is some support in the common law for awards of "double costs" payable to the defendant where the plaintiff pleads a case in fraud and then fails to prove it: see, for example, *Rosenich v. Welke*.

Intimidation

Intimidation, unlike many of the other torts in this section, is not strictly a business tort, because it need not involve interference with business interests. However, it often does, because the basis of the tort is the defendant's use of threats to obtain the plaintiff's compliance with the defendant's wishes, and the defendant's wishes often have something to do with money or financial advantage. It would not be incorrect, however, to classify this tort as an interpersonal tort, at least in some instances.

As noted above, the formula for the rarely pleaded tort of intimidation requires that (1) the defendant had the intention to make the plaintiff obey his or her wishes or to cause harm to the plaintiff by threat; (2) the defendant made a threat (to the plaintiff) such that the plaintiff's non-compliance would result in the defendant's committing an illegal act (whether against the plaintiff or a third party); (3) the plaintiff complied with the defendant's wishes to avoid the threat being carried out; and (4) the threat, the plaintiff's compliance with the defendant's wishes, or both caused the plaintiff actual harm.

Inducing Breach of Contract

inducing breach of contract
intentional incitement to terminate a contract prematurely

Although the tort of fraudulent misrepresentation is usually committed in a bid to influence a plaintiff to enter into a contract, the tort of **inducing breach of contract** has as its object the premature termination of a contract.

The defendant in these cases is usually *not* a party to the contract. The plaintiff is the contract party who incurs a loss due to the breach. For example, consider a

---

36.   *Saint-Laurent c. Hétu*, 1993 CanLII 4380 (Que. C.A.).

case of two employers competing for the same employee. The plaintiff is the first employer, who has just received a signed contract of employment from the employee (who is neither plaintiff nor defendant). The defendant, who is the second employer, offers the employee double the salary promised by the plaintiff in a bid to get the employee to breach his or her contract with the first employer and sign on with the second.

To succeed in a suit based on inducing breach of contract, the plaintiff must show that the defendant's actions were without legal justification. This does not mean that the actions must be illegal. The case law suggests that any interference with contractual relations will generally be improper, and serving one's own business interests is not "legal justification." The kinds of justification that have been successfully pleaded as a defence to this tort generally relate to a legislated duty. For example, if a police officer arrested a drug dealer before the dealer could deliver prepaid drugs to a client, the police officer would have legal justification for inducing the drug dealer's breach of contract.

Slander of Goods and Slander of Title

Slander in the context of the tort of defamation is described as the making of false statements to harm a person's reputation. **Slander of goods** and **slander of title** are twin torts based on the same action, but with different subjects: in the first case, goods (usually commercial goods) and in the second case, real estate ("title" to land). Sometimes the term "malicious falsehood" is used to describe false statements made with the intent to injure.

Slander of goods and slander of title are commercial torts, which are generally committed by a defendant who is a business competitor of the plaintiff in an effort to reduce the plaintiff's market share.

To understand slander of goods, consider the example of two competing manufacturers of toiletries designed to control acne. One manufacturer, in a bid to increase its own market share, uses social marketing applications like Facebook or Twitter to disseminate false rumours that the other manufacturer's products cause some undesirable side effect (hair loss, for example), and sales of that manufacturer's products decrease. This tactic may constitute slander of goods.

Slander of title is usually committed to discourage third parties from entering into a transaction with the plaintiff. The motivation of defendants who commit this tort may vary. For example, where a plaintiff lists a property for sale and the defendant wishes to buy it at a reduced price, the defendant might make a false statement about environmental contamination on the property to drive the price down.

The basic formula for slander of goods or title is:

- the defendant makes a statement it knows to be false;
- the statement is made for an improper purpose (usually, with intent to reduce the public opinion of the plaintiff's goods or title); and
- the plaintiff suffers a financial loss as a result, generally because the reputation of the plaintiff's goods or title is thereby affected, and third parties decline to deal with the plaintiff.

slander of goods
false or misleading statements intended to decrease a competitor's market share

slander of title
false or misleading statements intended to deter another from entering into a transaction

In contrast to slander of a person, slander of goods or title is not restricted to oral statements, but also includes written/published or broadcast statements. In other words, in this case, "slander" means the same thing as slander and libel combined mean in the defamation context.

Under the common law, slander of goods or title is not a tort of presumed harm. There is no entitlement to nominal damages if the tort is proved; instead, the plaintiff must demonstrate actual financial losses to receive an award of damages. This common-law rule has, however, been altered by statutes in some jurisdictions. For example, s. 17 of the Ontario *Libel and Slander Act* waives the requirement that a plaintiff prove actual damages (here called "special damages"):

> 17. In an action for slander of title, slander of goods or other malicious falsehood, it is not necessary to allege or prove special damage,
>
> > (a) if the words upon which the action is founded are calculated to cause pecuniary damage to the plaintiff and are published in writing or other permanent form; or
> >
> > (b) if the words upon which the action is founded are calculated to cause pecuniary damage to the plaintiff in respect of any office, profession, calling, trade or business held or carried on by the plaintiff at the time of the publication,
>
> and the plaintiff may recover damages without averment or proof of special damage.

Passing-Off

Whereas slander of goods involves the defendant's finding fault with the plaintiff's goods, the tort of passing-off is the highest form of flattery.

Passing-off occurs when a defendant attempts to benefit from the plaintiff's business by bringing to market goods of its own that are confusingly similar to those of the plaintiff. The specific act that constitutes the tort is the defendant's making a "false representation" that its own goods are the plaintiff's goods.

This false representation need not be an oral statement; it can instead involve the use of a trademark similar to the plaintiff's trademark, or a logo, design, or packaging identical to or confusingly similar to the plaintiff's. Goods sold in this manner are commonly referred to as "knock-offs."

Not every plaintiff will be capable of proving passing-off. For a plaintiff to succeed, its goods must be distinctive in some way, and a certain amount of business goodwill must be associated with that distinction. A good example is the distinctive patterned fabric used to make classic Louis Vuitton purses and luggage. This luggage is unusually expensive in relation to other luggage, and so other designers have often sought to imitate the distinctive pattern in a bid to ask a higher price for their own goods.

Not every imitation constitutes passing-off. In many cases, the imitation is not especially close, and the goods are sold in circumstances where the average consumer would not be fooled into thinking the merchandise is a luxury product (for example, patterned wallets using the same brown-and-beige colours as the Louis Vuitton pattern but in a quite different design and sold in a discount department store). Whether or not goods are being passed off is a question of fact for the court to decide. In some cases, the court has found that the defendant was merely attempting to capitalize on a general trend and had no intention of misleading the public.

Issues involving the unauthorized use of another party's intellectual property (trademarks, patents, copyright) are regulated under a number of statutes; however, the tort of passing-off is still used in cases that do not fit comfortably within the limits of regulation (for example, the fake trademark is quite different from the copied mark).

MISCELLANEOUS TORTS

Two more intentional torts that do not fall into any of the categories already discussed are worth mentioning: conspiracy and abuse of process.

Conspiracy

Conspiracy is a tort designed to extend liability for a second tort to defendants who may have been involved in the planning stages of the second tort, but not in carrying it out.

conspiracy
an agreement between or among parties to deceive, mislead, or defraud others of their legal rights, or to gain an unfair advantage

For example, consider a situation in which a group of five friends plans a prank that involves attaching chains to a person's expensive car and lifting it up into the branches of a tree using a winch while the "victim" is inside a restaurant. All five friends are involved in the planning: friend one arranges to have dinner with the victim to distract him; friend two provides the chains and winch system but is not available to be there on the day of the actual prank; friend three brings a video camera to record the victim's reaction; and friends four and five do the actual work of lifting the car into the tree.

Unfortunately, the victim's reaction is much angrier and less gracious than the friends had hoped. Worse, the winch jams, and the car cannot be taken down that evening, leaving the victim forced to take a cab 50 kilometres to work the following day. Finally, during the course of the following day, the car slips out of the chains and falls to the pavement, sustaining serious damage.

The plaintiff sues in detinue, claiming damages not only for the detinue, but for the damage to the vehicle and for the cab fare. For good measure, he adds a claim for intentional infliction of mental suffering (not likely to succeed, but he figures he might as well). The problem is, friends four and five, who actually raised the car, have just graduated from college and are not yet employed, so it will be impossible to enforce a judgment against them.

Luckily for this plaintiff, there is the tort of conspiracy, which, in this case, allows him to add friends one, two, and three to his claim.

The elements of the tort of conspiracy are:

1. an agreement
2. made between two or more people
3. to commit a lawful or unlawful act by lawful or unlawful means
4. that was directed at the plaintiff or has, as a predominant purpose, harmed the plaintiff or his or her property.

Note that actual harm to the plaintiff or his or her property need *not* be proven to establish this tort; nor does the plan actually need to be carried out (though at least one concrete step—in this case, for example, a call to the owner of the winch equipment—needs to have been taken). Nominal damages are available to punish the *making of the agreement* to carry out the tort.

Abuse of Process

The last tort on the list is **abuse of process**. It is essential at the outset to make a distinction between the *tort* of abuse of process—which is rarely successfully proved—and the *general doctrine* of abuse of process, which can be alleged by one party against the other at various stages of litigation or administrative proceedings.

General accusations under the doctrine of abuse of process are brought by a party who feels that the other party is corrupting, complicating, manipulating, or confounding court or tribunal processes for some improper purpose, such as to create delay or escalate costs (a common allegation, for example, is that one party is "motioning to death" the other party). If the judge or arbitrator finds that there has in fact been abuse of process, he or she may order a remedy: for example, an order declining to hear any further motions, an order directing a party to comply with a rule (for example, providing proper disclosure) within a time limit, or an order of increased costs at the end of the matter. The availability of remedies for abuse of process is a common-law rule of civil procedure, not a cause of action in its own right.

The tort of abuse of process, by contrast, *is* a stand-alone cause of action. It is made out where the defendant uses the court process for an improper purpose. This tort is distinguishable from malicious prosecution in three important ways:

1. it can relate to *either* criminal or civil proceedings;
2. the plaintiff need not demonstrate that there was a lack of reasonable grounds on which to base the proceedings; and
3. the plaintiff need not establish that the proceedings ended in his or her favour.

The key element that must be proved is that the defendant, in bringing the proceedings, was motivated not by any of the "normal" reasons for bringing litigation (for example, recovering damages, getting "revenge" for a harm, intimidating or antagonizing the defendant, inducing settlement, silencing a libel, and so on), but rather, by some other, improper purpose. When one considers that revenge, intimidation, antagonism, and impoverishment do *not* qualify as improper purposes, it becomes clear that proving an improper purpose is a challenge, and that a successful claim based on abuse of process is rare. See the Case in Point feature, below, for an example of a successful claim.

Gang-Up on Vulnerable Lawyer Leads to Damages for Malicious Prosecution, Abuse of Process, and Intentional Infliction of Mental Suffering

From: *Neff v. Patry*, 2008 BCSC 163 (CanLII).

At the beginning of the story that led to this claim against defendants Linda Patry and Terry Anderson, Barrie Neff was a lawyer with a history of depression working as in-house counsel for a credit union.

Neff met the plaintiff Terry Anderson in 1986 when he assisted her and some of her fellow trailer park residents in a landlord and tenant matter. After Anderson and her husband separated in 1988, the pair began dating.

The romance was described as a "love–hate" relationship—volatile and characterized by heavy drinking, depression on the part of both parties, arguments, and ardent love letters from Anderson to Neff. Anderson accused Neff of breaking up her first marriage and refusing to marry her. After the two broke up, she made additional accusations: that Neff had threatened her father, had abused her children, had sexually abused his own daughter, and had been violent toward her. The court found Anderson's evidence to be unreliable and found her to be mentally unstable. She was a survivor of childhood sexual abuse and a head injury in the course of a bank robbery that had left her with post-traumatic stress disorder.

After Neff broke up with Anderson, he moved to another town, where he worked as an arbitrator of landlord and tenant disputes. In the course of this work, he ran afoul of another woman, Ms. Linda Patry. Patry, a medical doctor, was the defendant landlord in one of his arbitrations. Neff made some findings of misconduct on her part in making his arbitral decision. Patry became offended. She complained about Neff to his superiors at the Residential Tenancy Branch. In part due to these complaints, Neff's contract at the Branch was not renewed.

Patry next brought a judicial review proceeding to challenge the result in the arbitral decision Neff had made that had gone against her. The judicial review proceeding included dozens of pages of allegations, by Patry, that Neff was biased and unprofessional, exceeded his authority, bullied witnesses, intimidated Patry, and surreptitiously taped the proceedings without authority (in fact, the cassette recorder was on a desk for all to see and was used routinely in these proceedings).

Terry Anderson, Neff's former girlfriend, attended at the initial hearing days for the judicial review proceeding (initially in support of Neff) and listened to all this evidence from Patry. Anderson contacted Patry and, united in their anger against Neff, became friends and began conspiring to bring down Neff. Anderson swore an affidavit against Neff that was never filed in the proceedings.

While awaiting the conclusion of the judicial review, Patry contacted the police, asking them to charge Neff with allegedly tampering with the audio tapes of the arbitration. She gave them Anderson's affidavit, which contained allegations of violence against her and others.

Patry also lodged a complaint against Neff with the Law Society of British Columbia, urging the Law Society to take disciplinary action against him. She attached the judicial review documents, including her own affidavit and Anderson's. The Law Society, however, declined to pursue the complaint.

Somewhere along the line, Anderson regretted her false affidavit and, with the help of her psychologist, wrote a long statement "correcting" her original affidavit. She never signed it, however; instead, she went into a rage and, with the psychologist present, swung a briefcase at the plaintiff and broke his arm.

Meanwhile, the defendant Patry continued communicating with the police. She swore statements alleging that Neff was violent, a bully, manipulative, and "a narcissistic sociopath capable of anything criminal."

The police arrested Neff on a charge of criminal harassment. His arrest led to an indefinite adjournment of the judicial review proceedings. (Patry, apparently, had figured out that criminal charges unfold faster than civil litigation!)

Patry also swore statements against Anderson's psychologist, Neff's judicial review lawyer, and five other lawyers, alleging "a cover-up and suspicion of organized crime and corruption."

Patry and Anderson continued their attempts to get the Law Society to discipline Neff, filing dozens of pages of additional "documentation."

The judicial review judge dismissed what he characterized as an "ill-conceived" application.

The Law Society again declined to discipline Neff or any of the other lawyers who had been implicated.

All criminal charges against Neff were eventually stayed.

Undeterred, Anderson made a statement to police a few years later that Neff was responsible for the death of a young woman whose remains had been found in a remote area. When asked by police on what grounds she had him called in for questioning, she testified that "she had no particular basis to accuse him of the murder, other than she believed it and that he was capable of murder."

As the allegations against him mounted, Neff began to unravel. He neglected and eventually gave up his legal practice. He gained a massive amount of weight. He lost his house and his office, and he lived in his car for awhile. He went on welfare. He made multiple suicide attempts.

Finally, in his late 50s, he moved to the Alberta oil sands to work as a pipe-fitter and high-rigger. He filed a claim against Patry and Anderson based on malicious prosecution, abuse of process, intentional infliction of mental suffering, and negligence. He won on all grounds except negligence. The court awarded him a mere $50,000 in damages, finding that some aspects of his "downward spiral" could be attributed to his own problems with depression. The court did, however, add a punitive damage award of $10,000 against the defendant Patry only, noting that because of Anderson's post-traumatic stress disorder and troubled past, she was not fully responsible for her actions.

CHAPTER SUMMARY

Intentional tort, once proved, is presumed to have been intentionally committed. This presumption creates an evidentiary "shortcut" in that the plaintiff need not call evidence to prove to the court that the defendant had a duty of care toward the plaintiff and breached it. Because intentionally harming another is automatically wrong, the response to these two prefatory issues is automatically "yes."

Besides offering ease of proof, some intentional torts also attract automatic (though sometimes nominal) damages once proven. This means that the plaintiff need *not* lead evidence describing and quantifying the harm he or she has suffered in order to recover; instead, the fact that the tort has occurred at all counts as harm. By proving actual damages, the plaintiff can request a damage award greater than the nominal amount.

Because intentional torts offer evidentiary shortcuts and sometimes nominal damages, their application is fairly restricted. Intentional torts can generally be described in terms of a formula of elements, all of which must be satisfied for the tort to be proved.

This chapter introduced five different subcategories of intentional torts: interpersonal torts, torts of interference with possessions, torts of interference with real property, torts of interference with business or contracts, and two "miscellaneous" torts that do not fit readily into any of the foregoing categories.

The interpersonal torts introduced are assault, battery, intentional infliction of mental suffering, false imprisonment, malicious prosecution, and defamation. Unlike criminal assault, tort assault does not require physical contact between the plaintiff and defendant but instead is comparable to "threatening"—that is, creating an apprehension of imminent physical contact. Battery is any non-consensual physical contact between the defendant and the plaintiff. It need not be direct contact (the contacting object can, for example, be thrown), violent, or body part on body part: the defendant could touch the plaintiff's dress sleeve with an umbrella, for example. The key issue is lack of consent.

To prove intentional infliction of mental suffering, the plaintiff must usually prove that the defendant performed an act or made a statement (usually false) that was intended to cause the plaintiff mental anguish, and did. The mental anguish must be more than just transient or trivial and must generally amount to a physical or psychological condition diagnosable by a physician.

False imprisonment occurs any time the defendant confines the plaintiff within set limits without the plaintiff's consent and under circumstances where it would be difficult, dangerous, or legally unadvisable for the plaintiff to escape. Malicious prosecution occurs when the defendant, motivated by malice, initiates a criminal prosecution against the plaintiff without reasonable grounds, and the proceeding ends in the plaintiff's favour.

Defamation has two forms: libel and slander. Slander is defamation through an oral statement; libel requires broadcast or "publication," which is loosely defined. In both cases, to count as defamation, the statement must be untrue and likely to lower the plaintiff in the estimation of right-thinking members of society. There are a number of defences to defamation available: truth, qualified privilege, absolute privilege, and fair comment.

The intentional torts of interference with possessions are detinue and conversion. Both require that the defendant take possession of a chattel of the plaintiff and deprive the plaintiff of its use. Conversion goes a step further, and requires that the defendant do something inconsistent with the plaintiff's ownership interests—for example, reselling the chattel. "Trespass to chattels" is a general term that encompasses both conversion and detinue. The doctrine of trespass to chattels has been extended in some jurisdictions to interference with Internet-related properties, such as domain names or bandwidth. The availability of an action in Canada based on trespass to chattels to protect cyber-property is not yet clearly established.

Two very different torts involve interference with real property (land and buildings). The first—trespass—has been codified into statute form in most jurisdictions; however, the occasional plaintiff still sues in common-law trespass when he or she wants to pursue damages (rather than simply allowing the authorities to fine the trespasser). The second tort of interference with property is nuisance. Nuisance is really a distinct area of the law in its own right, not just one of many intentional torts and, in fact, it need not always be intentional. A party commits nuisance when he or she allows conditions on his or her land, or an activity carried out on the land, to affect another party's (often a neighbour's) use and enjoyment of his or her land. Nuisance can be the result of noise, excessive light or shade, odours, or any other intrusion on neighbouring land. Normal or natural uses of one's land—or fleeting excesses of noise, light, and so on—do not constitute nuisance. Nuisance is the basis of many lawsuits every year.

Intentional torts that arise mainly in the context of business include fraud (deceit) and fraudulent misrepresentation, intimidation, inducing breach of contract, slander of goods and slander of title, and passing-off. Common-law fraud, unlike criminal fraud, often allows successful plaintiffs to recover some of the economic losses that resulted from the fraud. Fraudulent misrepresentations are often made to induce a plaintiff to enter into an unwise contract.

Intimidation is an unusual tort that requires that the defendant provoke the plaintiff into carrying out the defendant's wishes by means of threat that the defendant will do an unlawful act. Inducing breach of contract is a tort alleged by a contract party against a third party in circumstances where the third party has caused the other contract party to breach the contract.

Slander of goods, slander of title, and passing-off are torts designed to compensate plaintiffs who have interfered with commercial interests. A defendant usually "slanders" the plaintiff's goods because the defendant is a competing merchant attempting to gain market share. Slander of title involves statements designed to discourage potential buyers or lessors from contracting to buy or lease the plaintiff's real estate. Passing-off is committed by a defendant who attempts to take advantage of the plaintiff's good business reputation (or the reputation of the goods) by convincing the public that its own goods (sometimes called "knock-offs") are those of the plaintiff.

The final two intentional torts discussed in this chapter fit into none of the above categories. The first—conspiracy—is designed to cast a net of liability broad enough to catch defendants who, while they did not participate in carrying out some other tort (for example, conversion), were involved in the planning of the tort and took some step toward its completion. They will be liable for conspiring even if the tort was never actually carried out.

The final tort discussed in this chapter was abuse of process. It is important to distinguish the tort of abuse of process from the general doctrine of abuse of process as a problem that arises during the course of litigation. A defendant commits the tort of abuse of process when he or she uses a legal process (whether criminal or civil) for an improper purpose, while motivated by malice or the intent to harm the plaintiff. Whether the process ends in the plaintiff's favour is irrelevant to establishing this tort. The range of purposes for litigation (or for initiating criminal charges) deemed *not* to be improper is wide, and so a plaintiff only rarely succeeds in a case based on the tort of abuse of process.

KEY TERMS

absolute privilege	fraudulent concealment
abuse of process	fraudulent misrepresentation
assault	inducing breach of contract
bailee	intellectual property
bailment	intentional infliction of mental
bailor	suffering
battery	intentional tort
chattels	libel
conspiracy	malicious prosecution
conversion	nominal damages
defamation	psychological confinement
detinue	qualified privilege
fair comment	slander
false imprisonment	slander of goods
fraud	slander of title

REVIEW QUESTIONS

True or False?

1. The defendant need not have made physical contact with the plaintiff to have committed the tort of assault.
2. To be libel, a published or broadcast statement must be untrue.
3. Nuisance must be intentional to be actionable.
4. If a plaintiff cannot prove one or more elements of an intentional tort, she may still succeed in getting a judgment, but her damages will be reduced.
5. To prove assault, the plaintiff must show that he had a reasonable apprehension of harm to his person, reputation, or property.
6. Intentional infliction of mental suffering can be committed simply by telling a lie.
7. Fraud can be the basis for a criminal charge *and* a tort lawsuit.
8. Nominal damages without proof of actual financial loss are available as a remedy for the tort of intimidation.
9. The maker of a statement that would otherwise constitute slander will not be liable in defamation if the statement is made to the plaintiff alone.
10. The maker of a statement that would otherwise constitute slander will not be liable for defamation if he has a duty to make the statement, and makes it discreetly and without being motivated by malice.

Fill in the Blanks

1. Any non-consensual physical contact or touching by the defendant to the plaintiff's physical person qualifies as the tort of _____.
2. When the tort of false imprisonment involves no physical barriers, it is sometimes called _____ _____.
3. Publishing or broadcasting a defamatory statement is _____, whereas making an oral defamatory statement is _____.
4. The wrongful possession of a physical object that belongs to another person is the tort of _____.
5. Taking a person's bike and selling it to a third party would qualify as the tort of _____.
6. The tort of _____ – _____ occurs when the defendant attempts to benefit by trying to market goods that are confusingly similar to the plaintiff's.
7. When the manufacturer of a product disseminates false rumours about the competing product of another manufacturer, the tort of _____ ____ _____ has occurred.
8. The law of torts recognizes two forms of interference with real property: _____ and _____.
9. _____ is a tort designed to extend liability for a second tort to defendants who were involved in the second tort's planning stages but not in carrying it out.
10. Malicious prosecution can be argued only in relation to _____ proceedings.

Short Answer

1. a. Is there a tort of invasion of privacy in Canada? Explain.
   b. If you answered "no" to question (a), how might a Canadian plaintiff obtain legal redress for an alleged invasion of privacy?
2. a. What is meant by the suggestion that courts have been conservative in applying the doctrine of intentional infliction of mental suffering?
   b. What is the rationale for restricting the availability of recovery on the basis of intentional infliction of mental suffering?
3. Compare and contrast the torts of slander of goods and passing-off.
4. If the facts of a scenario may support *either* slander or libel, why might a plaintiff choose to frame his claim in libel?
5. Explain why there is a presumption of damages in the case of intentional torts, even where the harm done to the plaintiff is trifling or cannot be measured.
6. What evidence must be included in a pleading based on the tort of assault?
7. Why is the tort of malicious prosecution a rare one?

8. Define the tort of nuisance, and identify some of the criteria that must be met for a nuisance to be actionable.

9. Identify the two forms of trespass to chattels and explain the difference between them.

EXERCISES

Below are three fact scenarios. Each notes a suggested (tort) cause of action. Each scenario, however, is missing one or more of the required elements to support the tort. Read each scenario and identify the missing element.

1. *Malicious prosecution:* Hussain is angry at his neighbour Andy over a dispute about who should pay for a fence between their two properties. Hussain is aware that Andy is a heavy drinker and often drives his car while impaired. One evening, after watching Andy lurch unsteadily out of his house and down the steps, get in his car, and drive away, Hussain phones the local police station and reports that he suspects that a driver with licence plate XXX XXX (Andy's) is driving under the influence. Police arrest Andy six blocks from his home. However, owing to a break in the chain of custody of the breathalyzer results (which clearly showed Andy was impaired), the charges against Andy are dropped.

2. *Intentional infliction of mental suffering:* Joanna is due to get married one week from now. Helena did not get asked to be a bridesmaid and her feelings were hurt. While out clubbing, Helena sees Joanna's fiancé Ben making out with another woman in a booth. Helena looks closer, and the "other woman" is Paulette, one of the bridesmaids. Helena is delighted. She takes a picture of Ben and Paulette *in flagrante delicto* (in the act) on her cellphone camera, and immediately forwards it to Joanna. Joanna breaks off the wedding. In the ensuing weeks, she falls into a depression and loses 20 pounds.

3. *Passing-off:* Inigo is a trend-spotter. He prides himself on picking up on trends early and capitalizing on them. While visiting a fashion show in Milan in 2011, he notices that popular designer Herve Michel (fictional) is showing all his models for fall in fringed suede Inuit-style boots. Inigo contacts an Inuit craft collective in Nunavut and orders a shipment of similar boots. He creates posters from the photos he took of the Herve Michel collection in Milan. He rents a table at a local flea market, puts up his Herve Michel photos as a backdrop, and displays his suede boots for sale.

Defences to Intentional Torts

11

OVERVIEW

LEARNING OUTCOMES

After completing this chapter, you should be able to:

- Understand what is meant by a true defence.

- Understand what is meant by a "partial" defence or mitigating factor.

- List the main defences available against intentional torts.

- Explain the elements of each defence.

- Understand how a plaintiff's consent is shaped by the range of contact considered "normal" in the context of the activities in which the plaintiff participates.

- Explain the discoverability rule and how it determines the application of limitation periods.

INTRODUCTION

In Chapter 10, you read about a number of defences available to a defamation claim. Those defences were discussed in that context because they were specific to that tort.

In this chapter, you will learn about a number of defences of more general application: in other words, defences that can be asserted against more than one kind of intentional tort.

defence
the collected facts and method adopted by a defendant to protect against and counter a plaintiff's action

First, however, you should understand what is meant by a **defence** and how it is used. You have learned that an intentional tort is a formula, made up of a number of set elements, that is recognized in the case law as an appropriate basis upon which to found a claim (a "cause of action"). A defence is also a formula with required elements; except in the case of a defence, successful proof of all the elements either prevents the plaintiff from proving the defendant's liability or reduces that liability. A defence that completely eliminates the defendant's liability is sometimes called a "complete" defence or a "true" defence; a defence that reduces damages but does not affect liability is sometimes called a partial defence.

Table 11.1 summarizes the defences to intentional torts. Each is discussed in detail in the sections that follow.

TABLE 11.1   Defences to Intentional Torts

Defence	Defeats tort (true defence)	Does not defeat tort (partial defence)	No damages available	Reduces all damages	Eliminates "nominal" damages but not compensatory damages
Consent	✓		✓		
Self-defence or defence of others using only reasonable force	✓		✓		
Self-defence or defence of others using unreasonable force					
Provocation using reasonable force		✓		✓	
Provocation using unreasonable force		✓ (arguable)		✓ (arguable)	
Necessity	✓				✓
Legal authority	✓		✓		

When a plaintiff brings a lawsuit based on tort, the cause of action and the facts that support it are described in a document called a statement of claim. The elements of and facts supporting any defence that will be relied upon by the defendant are set out in the statement of defence that is filed in response to the statement of claim.

We now turn to the defences most often relied upon against intentional tort claims.

CONSENT

A plaintiff cannot succeed in recovering damages for any intentional tort based on an action of the defendant's to which the plaintiff consented. Consent is a complete defence.

The burden of proving that the plaintiff consented falls on the defendant—that is, the defendant must bring evidence to show that the plaintiff consented, because the general presumption is that a person would not normally consent to another person's tortious conduct.

Express or Implied Consent

A plaintiff can consent either expressly or impliedly. Express consent is a consent made either orally or in writing, usually in response to the defendant's request or statement concerning the action about to be taken.

Implied consent is a consent that must be established by drawing inferences from the plaintiff's behaviour. For example, the plaintiff and defendant meet in a bar and head back to the plaintiff's apartment. Once inside, the plaintiff drags the defendant into a bedroom, kisses the defendant, and enthusiastically removes his clothes. The two then proceed to have intercourse. If the plaintiff brings a battery lawsuit based on non-violent sexual contact, the defendant may have a defence based on implied consent.

As you might imagine, proving implied consent can be fairly challenging. Proving express oral consent, in the absence of witnesses, can also be challenging.

Waivers: Express Written Consent

From the defendant's perspective, the simplest form of consent to prove is express written consent. The most common example of express written consent is a **waiver**: a contract through which the defendant offers some sort of opportunity to the plaintiff (for example, a chance to ride on a zip-line) in exchange for the plaintiff's payment and the plaintiff's signature on a document that "holds the defendant harmless" in the event that something goes wrong.

waiver
a form of express written consent

A valid waiver generally provides considerable detail about the typical risks associated with the activity offered, so that the plaintiff is well informed. It is an established legal principle that uninformed consent is no consent at all; in other words, if a plaintiff is not aware of the risks he or she faces, or is not aware that he or she is giving up the right to sue in tort, consent is not valid.

Litigation involving the interpretation of waivers is much more common in the context of negligence, discussed in Chapter 12, than in the context of intentional tort. This is so because there are only a few circumstances in which a plaintiff of sound mind would consent to conduct that would otherwise constitute an intentional tort. One example, however, is violent sports. A plaintiff who signs up to compete in a boxing match, or even in a full-contact hockey league, will likely sign a waiver that includes consent to contact that would otherwise constitute battery.

Consent: Sex, Brawls, and Other Contact Sports

The most common tort allegation to attract a consent defence is battery. Human beings come into physical contact all the time, and it is not the norm, in our society, to ask first and touch later; therefore, unwanted physical contact happens every day and creates the potential for an allegation of battery.

Trivial or Normal Contact

Whether we are likely to be touched by others depends on the circumstances. Some situations are low-contact: if we go for a job interview, we will expect to shake hands and to have no other physical contact with anyone. But if we get into a subway car during rush hour, we generally do so with the understanding that we may be jostled, pressed into other bodies, or even grabbed by someone who has lost his or her balance. If we decide to travel to a foreign country by aircraft, we realize that there is some possibility that we will be patted down by security agents. If we sign up to play football, we know we may be violently tackled in the 10 seconds after the quarterback says "hut."

The law of tort provides that when a plaintiff engages voluntarily in an activity in which contact is normal (like riding the subway at rush hour), the plaintiff has given his or her implied consent to that normal contact. The plaintiff has not, however, consented to any unwanted contact that is *not* normal for the activity. For example, a rush-hour subway rider impliedly consents to pushing, jostling, or being crowded or pressed, being coughed on, being accidentally bumped by briefcases, but *not* to having his or her buttock intentionally squeezed by a passenger who takes advantage of the crowding for this purpose. All of the normal contact would *not* be battery, but the buttock squeeze would be.

Contact Beyond the Limits of Normal

The same analysis—normal or typical contact versus unusual contact—is applied when analyzing contact in two specific contexts: sexuality and contact sports.

Sorting out consent to sexual touching is a very challenging exercise for two reasons: first, human beings do not normally communicate the precise limits of their consent in specific terms before engaging in sexual contact; and second, sexual contact generally happens in private, without witnesses. For this reason, courts are forced to make assessments of the credibility of the plaintiff and the defendant and to apply certain general social norms ("most people do not like to suffer/inflict pain during sex"; "sexual contact between people with a wide age difference is abnormal") that may not actually apply to the parties before the court.

Determining the limits of consent in contact sports is easier, for a number of reasons. First, participants may have signed a waiver that explicitly describes the "normal" contact associated with the sport. Second, sports have rules prohibiting certain kinds of contact—for example, the rules against "horse collar" tackles in football, against eye-gouging in mixed martial arts, against cleats-first slide tackles in baseball, and against "boarding" in hockey. Knowing the kinds of actions that lead to penalties in sport, however, does not make these actions battery. What it does is inform prospective players that while these actions will normally result in a penalty or sanction against the offending player, *they have been addressed by the rules because they regularly occur*. Therefore, these rules, in effect, take the actions that lead to recognized sanctions *out of* the realm of battery.

For these reasons, the battery cases that come out of contact sports tend to relate to contact for which there is no standard penalty: contact that is either unusual or committed with unusual violence. An example of unusual contact would be the incident in which boxer Mike Tyson bit off a portion of opponent Evander Holyfield's earlobe in a boxing match in 1997. An example of unusually violent contact would be the head-butt to the chest delivered by Zinedine Zidane to Marco Materazzi in the 2006 soccer World Cup. The Case in Point feature below discusses an incident in a hockey game that led to both a criminal charge and a civil suit for battery.

CASE IN POINT

Hockey Punch with Intent to Injure Leads to Criminal Charge and Tort Suit

From: *R. v. Bertuzzi*, 2004 BCPC 472 (CanLII).

In February 2004, the Vancouver Canucks and the Colorado Avalanche, National Hockey League (NHL) division rivals, were fairly close in the pre-playoff standings. In a game on the evening of February 16, 2004, Colorado player Steve Moore checked Canucks captain Markus Naslund, leaving him with a concussion and some other injuries.

The check was not penalized, to the dismay of many of the Canucks players.

In the days following the incident, Canucks players made some comments, reported in the media, suggesting that they would be seeking revenge against Steve Moore. However, when the players met in another game on March 3, although there was some taunting between the players in an effort to provoke Moore into a fight, no revenge seems to have been taken.

Five days later, the teams met again, this time before Vancouver's home crowd. During this game, a fight broke out between Vancouver player Matt Cooke and Steve Moore, but this fight ended in a draw. Later in the game, Vancouver player Todd Bertuzzi mounted a persistent

campaign of goading and baiting, trying to get Moore to fight. Finally, when Moore had skated away for at least the third time, Bertuzzi grabbed Moore's sweater, punched him forcefully from behind, making contact with the side of his head, and fell to the ice on top of Moore. Other teammates piled onto the two fallen players. When the dogpile was finally cleared, Moore did not get up.

Moore suffered soft tissue injuries to his head, lacerations to his face, a concussion, and two separate fractures to his neck.

In the wake of the incident, the following consequences unfolded: the league suspended Bertuzzi for the remainder of the season and the playoffs; Bertuzzi was charged in British Columbia with assault causing bodily harm; and plaintiffs, including Steve Moore, sued Bertuzzi in battery.

Bertuzzi was eventually allowed to return to hockey, although not until 17 months after the incident. He was convicted of assault causing bodily harm, and the sentence he received was a conditional discharge. A convict who has been given a conditional discharge is required to comply with certain conditions: in Bertuzzi's case, a one-year probation order was imposed, during which he was required to "keep the peace," to report to a probation officer, to do 80 hours of community service, and not to play hockey against Steve Moore (Steve Moore, in fact, never returned to NHL play after the attack). Convicts who comply with the terms of the conditions imposed are entitled, at the end of the term, to be deemed never to have been convicted of the offence. As Bertuzzi did comply, the proceeding did not result in a criminal record for him.

Seven years later, the civil lawsuit against Bertuzzi (the Canucks and their ownership are also defendants) has not yet been settled and is expected to go to trial in 2012.

Consent to Medical Treatment

Problems with consent to medical treatment can go in two legal directions: to a claim based in battery or to a claim in negligence. We will revisit negligence-based medical treatment claims in Chapters 12 and 14.

In deciding whether to pursue a consent-to-treatment claim in battery or in negligence, there are two central issues: the first is the nature of the consent, if any, that the plaintiff gave for whatever medical treatment he or she received. The second consideration is whether the treatment was competent (but unwanted) or incompetent or negligent.

Turning first to the issue of consent, a claim in battery (called "medical battery" in these cases) can succeed only if there was *no* consent to the medical treatment. No consent means one of three things:

1. The plaintiff's consent was never asked for (see emergency exception, below).
2. The plaintiff was not competent to consent (due to incapacity; capacity in this context is the same as capacity for any kind of contract).
3. The plaintiff consented without having even a basic understanding of the nature of the treatment that was being done.

With regard to the first situation, there is an exception in emergencies. If the plaintiff requires treatment on an emergency basis to save his or her life or prevent serious harm and is unable to consent, and there is no guardian or relative able to consent for him or her, a medical practitioner who provides emergency treatment will be protected from a claim in battery.

The second situation is self-explanatory and is familiar from the context of contracts.

The third situation is the one most likely to be contentious. In order for consent to medical treatment to be valid, it must be two things: full and informed. "Full consent" means consent to the entirety of the treatment—for example, the plaintiff's consent to being administered an anesthetic is not consent to the operation that follows. "Informed consent" is consent that is granted after having received information about the nature of the treatment, the likely effectiveness of the treatment, the foreseeable side effects, and any other details that might be relevant sufficient to permit the plaintiff to make a fully reasoned decision about consent.

If the plaintiff lacks substantial information about what he or she is consenting to, consent is invalid (null), and he or she can sue for medical battery. If the plaintiff has *some* information about the treatment, but the information is insufficient, consent is flawed but possibly not invalid, and he or she should sue in negligence.

As noted in the Case in Point feature below, there is a second consideration for plaintiffs choosing between a battery and a negligence suit. That consideration relates to the quality or outcome of the treatment. In most litigation about medical treatment, the real issue is the plaintiff's dissatisfaction with the results of the treatment given, not whether or not there was treatment at all. Where a plaintiff has been treated and feels the treatment was ill-chosen or incompetently delivered,

CASE IN POINT

Physician's Patient Information "System" Establishes Consent

From: *Taylor v. Hogan* (1994), 119 Nfld. & P.E.I.R. 37, 1994 CanLII 9740 (Nfld. C.A.).

After suffering what seemed to be symptoms of a worsening case of endometriosis (a disease of the lining of the uterus), Lynn Taylor checked into hospital for a diagnostic procedure called a laparoscopy. She awoke to find she had been given a colostomy (bowel surgery requiring the external collection of bodily wastes). After another surgery three weeks later to reverse the colostomy, she suffered a stroke that left her with no ability to speak, no sensation in her right hand, and persistent neurological problems.

A laparoscopy—the procedure Taylor was first admitted for—is a primarily diagnostic procedure that involves the making of two small incisions in the abdomen and the insertion of a special light and camera into the abdomen to observe problems, for example, a spreading of endometrial tissue. In some cases, including Taylor's, the physician attempts to "unstick" adhesions (scarring) caused by earlier operations as part of the procedure.

While exploring Taylor's abdomen, the defendant, Dr. Hogan, accidentally punctured her bowel. He immediately called in a general surgeon (one experienced with bowel-repair surgery) to repair the tear. That surgeon was forced to perform a temporary colostomy (redirecting the exit from the bowel to outside the body to allow the bowel to heal).

Taylor sued Hogan in negligence and in medical battery. While much of the case turned on issues of negligence relating to the puncture accident, and a possible connection between the colostomy reversal surgery and the stroke Taylor suffered, Taylor based her medical battery claim on the allegation that she did not know even the basic nature of the laparoscopy: she assumed that the light and camera would be inserted vaginally, not through surgical incisions.

At trial, Hogan confessed that he could not recall the specific consent conversation he had had with Taylor (a common feature of medical malpractice cases, especially where a medical specialist does dozens of similar procedures every year). He testified that he dealt with all laparoscopy patients in the same way, including explaining the nature of the procedure and inviting questions. The court was not convinced that he had fully informed Taylor, and after reviewing the written materials given to her, found that it was *not* made clear that a laparoscopy is a surgical procedure. The trial court ordered damages based on medical battery.

The court also found that Dr. Hogan was negligent in proceeding with the laparoscopy (which the court found was contraindicated) and in puncturing the bowel. However, the court did not find a causal connection between the surgery and the stroke.

On appeal, the Court of Appeal of Newfoundland upheld the trial court's finding of negligence but overturned the ruling that the first surgery was a battery. In doing so, the court held that Hogan's "evidence respecting his standard preoperative practice of explaining to all his patients the nature and scope of a laparoscopy was admissible and should have carried great weight." Failing to take into account this evidence was a significant error in law. The Court of Appeal held that on the basis of the doctor's evidence about his "system" or standard practice when dealing with patients, Taylor had received sufficient information to know that the laparoscopy was a surgical procedure and that there were surgical risks associated with it, including the risk of bowel injury. Taylor's consent was not null, and without a null consent, there could be no battery.

or that the results were poor, a claim based in negligence is a much better fit. The reason for this is that the analysis of the issue will likely involve discussion of the standard of care that was owed to the plaintiff, and whether the defendant medical practitioner deviated from that standard of care.

As discussed in Chapter 10, standard of care is essentially "skipped over" in intentional tort cases. If a defendant is alleged to have committed an intentional tort, he or she is assumed to have failed to meet the standard of care, which was "no touching." Where the real issue in the case is the quality of care given, a negligence suit is more appropriate. Claims based purely on battery tend to be reserved for cases in which the treatment was completely unjustified (for example, a plaintiff scheduled for an appendectomy is instead given a tubal ligation) or the treatment went against the plaintiff's religion.

SELF-DEFENCE

self-defence
justifiable self-protection when a person reasonably perceives a threat and responds in a reasonable manner

Self-defence is a familiar defence, at least in the context of criminal law. Self-defence, like consent, is a complete defence to tort.

When pleading self-defence, a defendant must be careful to distinguish the defence from the defence of provocation, which will be discussed below.

Purpose of Self-Defence

A defendant who is arguing self-defence is generally claiming that the action he or she took that led to the plaintiff's claim in tort (most often, a claim in battery) was taken in an attempt to protect himself or herself from the plaintiff. Where the action goes beyond this purpose—for example, it becomes retaliation—the court will generally not permit the plaintiff to rely on self-defence.

The narrow purpose of self-defensive action is to deter the plaintiff from continued or future aggression. A defendant cannot rely on self-defence to prevent non-aggressive types of harm—for example, a defendant cannot attack a plaintiff who is selling knock-offs of the defendant's wares at a flea market.

In some jurisdictions, and especially under the criminal law, defendants have successfully avoided liability in battery after taking defensive action to protect not themselves, but others; however, very few cases of this nature have been considered under Canadian tort law.

A self-defence situation that *has* been considered in Canada is "defence of property." It is not legal, under Canadian criminal law, to use wounding force to protect one's chattels. The law[1] does, however, permit the use of reasonable force (usually very minor force) to remove a trespasser from one's real property (land or buildings) as long as the trespasser has first been asked to leave on his or her own power and has been given reasonable opportunity to do so. "Defence of property" has been relied upon, for example, in cases involving the ejection of rowdy patrons from nightclubs by bouncers.

---

1. Provisions permitting the use of reasonable force to eject trespassers can be found in provincial anti-trespass statutes such as the *Trespass to Property Act*, R.S.O. 1990, c. T.21.

Reasonable Force

Even where the defendant is justified in acting in self-defence, the defendant is not entitled to use more force than is reasonably necessary under the circumstances to repel the plaintiff's own use of force. If the defendant uses excessive force, the defence will fail, and the plaintiff will succeed in his or her action in battery.

What constitutes excessive force is a factual issue that requires careful consideration in each individual case. In general, the defendant's force must not be much greater than the plaintiff's, and the defendant is required to avoid actually injuring the plaintiff if possible.

Two areas in which the use of force has been controversial are defence of property and citizen's arrest. As noted above, a property occupier is entitled to use reasonable force to remove a trespasser who refuses to leave on his or her own. The limits of this force have, however, been fairly closely curtailed, and most property owners would do best to make one low-force attempt and, if that fails, to call police.

The question of force in support of citizen's arrest was considered by the Ontario Court of Appeal in *R. v. Asante-Mensah*.[2] In that case, a taxi driver had been persistent in violating rules about picking up passengers that had been established by Pearson International Airport in Toronto. The driver had been given a written warning, but continued to violate the rules. Ultimately, an airport inspector (not a peace officer) arrested him under the power of citizen's arrest. The driver and the inspector struggled, and the driver was charged with assault for the purpose of resisting arrest. At his criminal trial, he relied on the defence of self-defence and argued that the power of citizen's arrest does not include the right to use force. The Crown argued that because it is not practically possible to make an arrest without a certain amount of force, the use of force is implicit in citizen's arrest.

The Court of Appeal reviewed the jurisprudence and agreed with the Crown. In holding that there is a right to use reasonable force inherent in the statutory power of citizen's arrest, the court found that common-law rules with respect to use of force are relevant to the analysis of statutory powers, and that there is a well-established common-law right to use reasonable force incident to arrest.

Defendant's Honest Belief

Defendants have successfully relied on self-defence even in circumstances where the plaintiff was not actually about to use aggression toward the defendant, but the defendant *believed* that the plaintiff did have this intent.

It is not enough that the defendant believe that the plaintiff is likely to become aggressive; the defendant must also believe that the plaintiff's aggressive action is imminent (about to happen). For this reason, a defendant will not be allowed to assert a defence of self-defence where, for example, the defendant has driven to the plaintiff's home and attacked him or her in response to the plaintiff's threat made by telephone.

---

2. *R. v. Asante-Mensah*, 2001 CanLII 7279 (Ont. C.A.).

PROVOCATION

The defence of **provocation** often arises out of the same kinds of facts that might support a defence of self-defence or defence of others; and so it is not uncommon to see both defences (provocation and self-defence) pleaded together or alternatively in a statement of defence.

Unlike consent and self-defence, provocation is not a true defence. Even if successfully established through evidence, it does not defeat the plaintiff's tort claim in battery, but rather acts as a **mitigating factor** with respect to damages. This means that where the court accepts that the defendant was provoked into committing the tort alleged by the plaintiff, the court will still find the defendant liable, but may reduce the damages payable to reflect the plaintiff's own share of fault.

Because provocation involves an acknowledgment of the plaintiff's own partial responsibility for the harm, it is similar in some respects to contributory negligence—a defence to negligence—which will be discussed in Chapter 13.

To establish provocation, the defendant must prove (1) objectionable conduct by the plaintiff that (2) affected the defendant's self-control, (3) occurred immediately prior to the defendant's wrongful act, and (4) provoked the defendant's wrongful act.

An aspect of provocation that can be contentious at trial is the third ingredient listed above: immediacy. Whether the alleged tort occurred sufficiently soon after the provocative act depends on the facts in the case.

CASE IN POINT

"Defence of Others" Fails, but Provocation Succeeds

From: *Defosse v. Wilde*, 1998 CanLII 13485 (S.K.Q.B.).

This case provides a good illustration of the difference between self-defence (here, defence of others) and provocation.

As in many other cases involving these particular defences, the litigation arose out of a bar fight. The plaintiff, who had a history of alcoholism, went to a bar, got drunk, and argued with his father and sister, who had accompanied him. The plaintiff left the bar and his sister followed.

The defendant, who knew the parties, also followed.

Once outside, the plaintiff and his sister continued to argue, and the plaintiff pushed the sister. The defendant rushed in to defend the sister, pushed the plaintiff to the ground, and punched him repeatedly until other patrons made him stop.

The plaintiff suffered wounds to the face, a serious but non-permanent eye injury, a neck strain, and a concussion.

The plaintiff sued the defendant for battery. The defendant raised the defences of defence of others and provocation.

At trial, the court found that the defence of defence of others could not succeed, because the defendant had used excessive and unreasonable force. Therefore, the defendant was convicted of battery. However, the defence of provocation (not a true defence; rather, a mitigating factor) *did* succeed, with the judge concluding that the plaintiff "undoubtedly provoked [the defendant] by punching him, tearing off his shirt, and using foul language." The damages awarded to the plaintiff were reduced as a result.

The defence of provocation is more readily accepted in civil law (as a defence against a tort claim) than it is in criminal law. Under the criminal law, provocation is accepted as a defence only against murder, and only to reduce the charge to the lesser charge of manslaughter. Under the criminal law, the question of immediacy has come under scrutiny in the context of "battered wife syndrome," a specialized defence based on provocation, because in some of those cases, a battered spouse was on trial for murdering her spouse at a time *not* closely related to the provoking acts. Battered wife syndrome is, in that sense, an exception to the basic defence of provocation in that it requires less immediacy than is normally needed to prove the defence.

Other provocation questions—such as whether a sexual assault victim provoked her attacker by wearing revealing clothing—have long since been resolved by the criminal courts; however, this particular issue was revived in Ontario in 2010 when a police speaker suggested to a group of university students that they would be less likely to be sexually assaulted if they refrained from dressing like "sluts." This comment caused a political uproar that led to a demonstration dubbed the "Slut Walk," in which women dressed provocatively and marched to raise awareness of sexual assault of women.

A final issue with respect to provocation is exactly how it reduces damages. Because provocation makes the defendant's actions less intentional (reduces what would be called, under the criminal law, *mens rea* or guilty mind), courts are fairly consistent in holding that provocation reduces, or even precludes, punitive damages. However, judges have not always agreed about the impact of provocation on compensatory damages: damages that compensate the plaintiff for actual losses (for example, medical bills and lost wages) or for pain and suffering. This question was considered by the Saskatchewan Court of Queen's Bench in *Defosse v. Wilde* (discussed in the Case in Point feature, above). That court considered both lines of cases before holding that provocation can, in fact, reduce all damages, including compensatory damages.

NECESSITY

Necessity is a rarely used defence in tort, simply because circumstances that meet the formula for this defence rarely arise. To succeed in a necessity defence, the defendant must establish (1) that he or she committed what would otherwise be a tort against the plaintiff (2) in an effort to avoid a much more serious harm.

The "more serious harm" is usually something that threatens either the defendant or a third party. The plaintiff need not even be present at the time of the harm.

Examples of situations in which this defence has been used successfully in a tort action are very rare. In a 1947 Alberta case, *Dwyer v. Staunton,*[3] a court found a defendant not liable in trespass after the defendant drove over the plaintiff's land because the road was blocked with snow. Examples of the use of the necessity

---

3.   *Dwyer v. Staunton*, [1947] 4 D.L.R. 393 (Alta. Dist. Ct.).

defence are much more common in the context of criminal law. For example, in *R. v. Trencs*,[4] a man was acquitted of driving while his licence was suspended when he drove his elderly father to hospital from a mall in the father's car when the father suddenly became ill and was unable to drive. The defence, however, is not the same in the criminal law as it is in tort law, because under the criminal law, the defendant who is alleging necessity has not necessarily harmed another person out of necessity—he may simply have, as in *Trencs*, committed a victimless crime.

Hypothetical examples of situations that might give rise to a necessity defence include a stranded hiker who breaks into a cabin to avoid freezing to death while lost in the woods, or an onlooker who tries to save someone from drowning by taking a surfboard that doesn't belong to him to paddle out to the victim. Perhaps the reasonableness of acts such as these is the real reason why it is rare to see lawsuits that could be defeated using a necessity defence.

Even where the defendant successfully meets the test for necessity, he or she may still be liable to compensate the plaintiff. In a US case from 1910, a ship's crew was forced to dock a ship at someone else's dock instead of setting out to sea in a violent storm. The ship smashed into and destroyed the dock. While the court found that the ship's crew was entitled to rely on "private necessity privilege" when it docked the ship, the owner of the ship was still held liable to pay compensation for the damage.[5]

DURESS

The defence of duress may or may not exist in tort law. Some commentators consider duress—the state of feeling compelled to do something as a result of external pressures—to be a subcategory of necessity; others consider duress to be a factor that negates consent; and yet others recognize it as a separate defence in tort.

Duress has long been recognized as a defence or a mitigating factor (or both) in criminal law. The utility of the concept of duress is clearer under the criminal law, because it is easy to understand the impact that duress has on a defendant's *mens rea*. Consider, for example, a situation in which an older brother forces a younger brother to assist in a drug trafficking activity by threatening the younger brother with violence should he not comply. Clearly, under this circumstance, the younger brother's intent, with respect to the trafficking activity, is less direct than it would be if his participation were voluntary and free of threat.

Because the specific degree of *mens rea* is not as central an issue in tort as it is under the criminal law, the application of duress in tort law is less clear. Where duress is raised as an issue in tort cases, it is generally put forward as an argument against consent (see, for example, *British Columbia (Attorney General) v. Malik*[6]).

The decision in *Taber v. Paris Boutique and Bridal Inc.*[7] seems to stand for the principle that there is currently no separate, free-standing tort of "undue influence"

---

4. *R. v. Trencs*, 2011 ONSC 450 (CanLII).
5. *Vincent v. Lake Erie Transp. Co.*, 109 Minn. 456, 124 N.W. 221 (1910).
6. *British Columbia (Attorney General) v. Malik*, 2009 BCSC 595 (CanLII).
7. *Taber v. Paris Boutique and Bridal Inc.*, 2009 CanLII 48500 (Ont. S.C.).

or duress under Canadian law. As you learned in Chapter 5, undue influence and duress are recognized as defects that can affect contracts. Situations in which a defendant alleges duress outside the context of contract are likely to be sufficiently rare as not to warrant the development of a separate tort doctrine of duress.

LEGAL AUTHORITY

In some cases, a tort defendant will argue that while his or her actions may have inconvenienced or even harmed the plaintiff, the defendant acted on the basis of a legal duty, or at least within the bounds of legal authority.

The defendant's proving that the alleged tortious conduct was permitted or even required by legal authority is a full defence to the tort.

The most common context in which this defence is raised is in relation to acts by law enforcement—for example, the plaintiff has been detained or arrested and is suing police, customs officers, or other law enforcement personnel for battery or false imprisonment. In these cases, the defendant officer will often raise the defence of legal authority to establish that the circumstances of the case made the law enforcement action legal such that the actions were not battery or false imprisonment.

The status of a defendant as a law enforcement officer is not, in itself, sufficient to establish the defence. Law enforcement personnel are required to act within the bounds of the statutes that apply to their duties (for example, the *Criminal Code* or the Charter), as well as the common-law principles that support those statutes.

Police do not have legal authority to search a person in the absence of a search warrant or of reasonable and probable grounds about some particular issue—for example, the person has a weapon that might harm police when the person is detained or the person may destroy evidence concealed on his or her body (for example, shoplifted clothing). In other words, there is no general authority for police to search individuals on a hunch in the hope of discovering evidence. Where a police officer did so, he or she would not likely succeed in raising the defence of legal authority.

LIMITATION PERIOD

The final defence discussed here is not a defence in the true sense of the word; it is simply a barrier to a claim. However, because the issue comes up very frequently in the context of tort law, it makes sense to include it in a discussion of defences.

A **limitation period** is a period defined by statute (for example, the Manitoba *Limitation of Actions Act*,[8] which has counterparts in all Canadian jurisdictions) within which a plaintiff must commence his or her claim. Where the plaintiff fails to commence a claim before the end of the legislated period, the claim is said to be "statute-barred" and cannot proceed.

limitation period
a period defined by statute within which a plaintiff must commence his or her claim

The most common statutory limitation period is two years; however, there are both longer and shorter periods imposed in certain circumstances.

8. *Limitation of Actions Act*, C.C.S.M., c. L150.

Short Limitation Periods

The classic context in which plaintiffs can lose the right to sue due to short limitation periods is with respect to lawsuits against municipalities.

Municipalities are frequent targets of lawsuits for two reasons. First, they are responsible for the construction and maintenance of a great number of public facilities (roads, rinks, pools, recreation centres, city halls, libraries, and so on), and it is not uncommon for individuals to get hurt while using these facilities (for example, people trip while stepping off curbs, damage their cars by driving over potholes, or hit their heads in falls on rinks). Second, individuals tend to believe that municipalities are "deep-pocket defendants" in that they are usually capable of paying damage claims, because they have access to public funds and carry good insurance.

If lawsuits against municipalities were without limits, municipalities would lose the financial capacity to provide the services we expect from them. In an effort to limit the volume of lawsuits, many municipalities impose (through legislation) unusually stringent limitation periods for suits brought against them. For example, it is not uncommon for a slip-and-fall lawsuit against a municipality to be barred where the would-be plaintiff has failed to notify the municipality of his or her intention to sue within 10 days of the accident.

Although rules like this may seem unreasonably strict, you should realize that in many cases, plaintiffs successfully get around very short limitation periods by relying on the discoverability rule, discussed below.

Long Limitation Periods

In some circumstances, unusually long limitation periods are in place for certain kinds of lawsuits. An example of a long limitation period is the one that applies to suits based on childhood sexual assault or assaults against people who lacked capacity to sue for other reasons (for example, cognitive deficit). The Ontario *Limitations Act*[9] provides as follows with respect to assaults against vulnerable victims:

Assaults and sexual assaults

10(1) The limitation period . . . does not run in respect of a claim based on assault or sexual assault during any time in which the person with the claim is incapable of commencing the proceeding because of his or her physical, mental or psychological condition.

Presumption

(2) Unless the contrary is proved, a person with a claim based on an assault shall be presumed to have been incapable of commencing the proceeding earlier than it was commenced if at the time of the assault one of the parties to the assault had an intimate relationship with the person or was someone on whom the person was dependent, whether financially or otherwise.

Same

(3) Unless the contrary is proved, a person with a claim based on a sexual assault shall be presumed to have been incapable of commencing the proceeding earlier than it was commenced.

---

9. *Limitations Act, 2002*, S.O. 2002, c. 24, Sched. B.

In effect, these provisions suspend the limitation period indefinitely for certain classes of victims. Similar provisions exist in other Canadian jurisdictions.

The Discoverability Rule

Although statutory limitation periods impose some controls on overdue lawsuits, there are many circumstances in which the plaintiff's delay in pursuing a claim is justifiable when the facts of the claim are considered.

Particularly in cases involving physical injury or illness, the full extent of the injury or illness may not be obvious until long after the incident or condition that caused the harm. For example, health experts now know that there is a very strong causative link between exposure to certain kinds of materials (for example, asbestos) and specific illnesses (for example, mesothelioma—a type of cancer); however, the symptoms of the illness may not appear for years or even decades after the exposure that likely caused it. If limitation periods were always enforced strictly, victims of slow-developing illnesses and injuries would be denied compensation not because of procrastination on their part, but rather, simply because of the nature of their disease.

To ensure fairness to victims in this position, courts have long recognized a rule called the **discoverability rule**, which allows plaintiffs to sue outside the "normal" limitation period where the necessary information that would have supported a lawsuit was unavailable within that period. The discoverability rule has been codified into statute in many jurisdictions—for example, in the Ontario *Limitations Act* mentioned above, it is expressed in these terms:

discoverability rule
a rule that allows plaintiffs to sue outside the limitation period where the information needed to support a suit was unavailable within that period

Discovery

5(1) A claim is discovered on the earlier of,

    (a) the day on which the person with the claim first knew,

        (i) that the injury, loss or damage had occurred,

        (ii) that the injury, loss or damage was caused by or contributed to by an act or omission,

        (iii) that the act or omission was that of the person against whom the claim is made, and

        (iv) that, having regard to the nature of the injury, loss or damage, a proceeding would be an appropriate means to seek to remedy it; and

    (b) the day on which a reasonable person with the abilities and in the circumstances of the person with the claim first ought to have known of the matters referred to in clause (a).

Presumption

(2) A person with a claim shall be presumed to have known of the matters referred to in clause (1)(a) on the day the act or omission on which the claim is based took place, unless the contrary is proved.

As noted in this section—and as reflected in the common law related to the discoverability rule—the onus of proving that the claim was not known or knowable before the expiry of the limitation period is on the plaintiff who is seeking to overcome the effect of missing the limitation date. The common law also makes it clear that a claim is known or knowable on the date that the *material facts* (the essential and relevant facts) that support the claim are known or knowable.

CHAPTER SUMMARY

This chapter introduced the most commonly used defences to intentional tort. In a civil lawsuit, the plaintiff bears the burden of proving, on a balance of probabilities, that the defendant committed an act that is recognized as wrong and compensable (in this case, an intentional tort). A defendant may seek to shift the balance of probabilities in his favour by introducing evidence of his own establishing a defence. Chapter 10 introduced a set of defences that are particular to the tort of defamation; this chapter dealt with defences that have general application (that apply to more than one kind of intentional tort).

A defence, like an intentional tort, is typically expressed as a formula with required elements—except that in the case of a defence, successful proof of all the elements either prevents the plaintiff from proving the defendant's liability or reduces that liability. A defence that completely eliminates the defendant's liability is sometimes called a "complete" defence or a "true" defence; a defence that reduces damages but does not affect liability is sometimes called a partial defence or a mitigating factor (because it mitigates—reduces—the defendant's liability for damages). Table 11.1 summarizes these defences to intentional torts.

Consent by the plaintiff to the actions of the defendant is the most common defence asserted in torts. Consent can be either express (expressed through words or writing) or implied through the plaintiff's actions. For example, a plaintiff who participates in a prizefight, even if he or she signs no waiver and never mentions the issue of consent, would be considered to have consented to the normal or typical risks of prizefighting.

Express consent is the easiest kind to prove. Witnesses can testify in support of verbal consent and, where consent is made in writing (through a waiver, for example), the document will be evidence in court. Implied consent is harder to prove.

Issues relating to consent in particular contexts (sports, sexual activity, crowded spaces, medical treatment) were discussed in this chapter. The general rule is that a plaintiff who engages in an activity, unless he or she clearly specifies otherwise, will be deemed to have consented to the contact that is a normal part of that activity (including the contact that is the subject of recognized penalties in sports), but not to highly unusual or especially violent contact. In the medical context, a plaintiff's consent is closely tied to the information that has been provided to him or her about the treatment; a plaintiff must be informed in order for consent to be effective.

Self-defence and defence of others are true defences—that is, they eliminate the defendant's liability—but only where the force used to defend oneself or another is reasonable and proportional to the threat. There are other requirements as well—for example, the threat must be of physical harm, and the harm feared must be imminent.

Defence of property is a defence of narrow application in Canada, but it has been recognized in certain traditional contexts (for example, where a security person uses a reasonable amount of force to eject a trespasser after sufficient warning is given).

Provocation is *not* a true defence. Where a defendant can prove that he or she was provoked into committing the tort, damages may be reduced to reflect the plaintiff's role in the harm that came to him or her—an effect similar to what you will see in the context of contributory negligence, discussed in Chapter 13.

Necessity is a rarely used defence. A defendant who pleads necessity may do so in an attempt to avoid nominal damages (for example, damages for trespassing without causing damage) where he or she has committed a tort in the course of trying to prevent a serious and greater harm. There are few examples of reliance on the necessity defence in Canada. It is possible that a court could accept the defence of necessity (and refuse to order nominal damages), yet still hold the defendant liable to compensate the plaintiff for physical damage to property or harm to the person. Duress is sometimes mentioned as a subcategory of necessity, but as a defence, it is most commonly raised in the context of contracts, as you learned in Chapter 5.

The defence of legal authority is asserted most commonly by police and other law enforcement defendants. Where a defendant had authority (or a duty) based on law (whether statute law or common law) to do the act complained of, this authority is a full defence to the alleged tort; however, if the defendant exceeds the confines of his or her authority (for example, using excessive force or violating a plaintiff's Charter rights), this defence will be lost.

Finally, this chapter discussed limitation periods. Limitation periods are not a defence per se, but are probably the most commonly raised argument in opposition to a tort lawsuit. Statutes in every jurisdiction in Canada establish deadlines by which certain types of legal action must be commenced in order to be eligible for hearing by the courts. The most common limitation period is two years; however, much shorter and much longer ones are in effect in certain circumstances. According to the discoverability rule, which exists at common law and has been incorporated into many statutes, the "clock" upon which a limitation period begins to run begins at the moment at which the plaintiff was aware of, or ought to have been aware of (based on the standard of a reasonable person), the material facts (for example, the diagnosis of an illness) upon which a claim could be based.

KEY TERMS

defence
discoverability rule
limitation period
mitigating factor

provocation
self-defence
waiver

REVIEW QUESTIONS

True or False?

1. Where a plaintiff uses excessive force, the defence of provocation will never be available to him or her.
2. A plaintiff can, under the law of tort, consent to being battered by the defendant.
3. Signing up to play contact hockey implies consent to being cross-checked even without a waiver that includes a discussion of cross-checking.
4. The defence of legal authority makes it impossible to sue a police officer for assault under any circumstance.
5. A valid waiver need only provide a general account of the risks involved in the activity offered.
6. Judges in Canada unanimously agree that provocation should reduce the compensatory damages awarded to a plaintiff.
7. The most common statutory limitation period is two years.
8. A tort defendant's proving that the alleged tortious conduct was permitted by legal authority is a full defence to the tort.
9. Tort defendants who merely believed that the plaintiff was about to use aggression toward them—even where the plaintiff actually had no such intention—have successfully relied on self-defence.
10. In a case where a plaintiff is suing outside the "normal" limitation period, the onus of proving that the claim was known or knowable before the expiry of the limitation period is on the defendant.

Fill in the Blanks

1. The most common tort allegation to attract a consent defence is _____.
2. The _____ rule allows plaintiffs to sue outside the "normal" limitation period in cases where the information needed to support a lawsuit was unavailable during that period.
3. The classic context in which plaintiffs can lose the right to sue due to short limitation periods is that of lawsuits against _____.
4. A defence that completely eliminates the defendant's liability is sometimes called a _____ defence; a defence that reduces damages but does not affect liability is sometimes called a _____ defence.
5. The most common example of express written consent is a _____.
6. If the plaintiff in a case of medical mistreatment lacks substantial information about what he or she is consenting to, consent is invalid (null), and he or she can sue for _____ _____.

7. The defence of provocation, even if successfully established through evidence, does not defeat the plaintiff's tort claim in battery, but rather acts as a _____ _____ with respect to damages.

8. The period defined by statute within which a plaintiff must commence his or her claim is known as a _____ period.

9. _____ consent must be established by drawing inferences from the defendant's behaviour.

10. Being grabbed by someone on the subway who has lost his balance is an example of _____ contact and does not constitute _____.

Short Answer

1. Why is litigation involving the interpretation of waivers not very common in the context of intentional torts?

2. What is the formula for the defence of necessity, and why is it a rarely used defence in tort?

3. Why is sorting out consent to sexual touching a difficult task?

4. Under what conditions does the law permit a person to use force in removing a trespasser from his or her real property, and what is an example of a situation where "defence of property" might be used as a defence?

5. What must a defendant prove to establish provocation, and what aspect of provocation can be contentious at trial?

6. Explain why the kinds of actions that typically lead to penalties in sport (fighting in hockey, for example) do not give rise to charges of battery, though these actions are tortious in other contexts.

7. Under what circumstances is consent not required for medical treatment and a claim in medical battery not available to a victim of medical mistreatment?

8. Why are the limitation periods for suing municipalities particularly short?

9. What is the rationale for not strictly enforcing statutory limitation periods in cases involving physical injury or illness?

EXERCISES

1. An argument breaks out in a high school hallway between Tatiana and Crystal. Tatiana has accused Crystal of stealing her new headphones, and is facing Crystal in the hallway, screaming at her. A circle of students has formed around the two girls. Suddenly, Crystal's twin sister Loni bursts through the group and violently tackles Tatiana to the ground, exclaiming that she was at the mall with her sister the previous day when Crystal

purchased the headphones that Tatiana is claiming were hers. Tatiana breaks her wrist in the fall. Tatiana sues Loni in battery.

a. Can Loni rely on the defence of self-defence? Why or why not? If you answered "yes," is this a full defence to the allegation?

b. Can Loni rely on the defence of "defence of others"? If you answered "yes," is this a full defence to the allegation?

c. Can Loni rely on the defence of provocation? If you answered "yes," is this a full defence to the allegation?

2. From 1979 to March 11, 1987, Harold worked in an ammunition factory. Beginning in 1991, Harold began suffering insomnia, abdominal pain, and tingling in his hands and feet. However, he attributed these symptoms to the aging process and to diabetes, a disease he had been diagnosed with five years earlier. In 1993, however, while aged only 52, Harold began suffering severe memory loss, daily headaches, and disorientation. On July 19, 1993, his family physician suggested that he might be suffering from lead poisoning. Harold removed everything he could think of from his home that might be contaminated with lead—painted items, and so on. However, his symptoms failed to improve. On March 2, 1994, while watching television, Harold learned that workers can be exposed to high levels of lead while working in ammunition manufacturing. Harold immediately called a lawyer to commence a lawsuit against his former employer.

a. On what date would the limitation period that applies to this lawsuit begin? Support your answer.

b. Assuming that the typical limitation period applies to this lawsuit, what is the last date on which Harold can commence his action?

3. Read the decision in *Battrum v. British Columbia* (2009 BCSC 1276 (CanLII)) and answer the following questions:

a. The *Battrum* case is an example of an effort by a court to limit suits in battery based on the delivery of medical services. Do you believe that courts go too far in protecting medical personnel from such claims? Why or why not?

b. The medical battery claims most likely to be successful involve plaintiffs who are unconscious at the time of treatment, whether due to accidents or due to the administration of an anesthetic. Where a plaintiff is conscious and capable of consenting, should he or she *ever* be able to base a claim in battery?

c. What steps might paramedics/EMS staff take to limit their exposure to suits based on medical battery?

Negligence: The Basics

12

OVERVIEW

LEARNING OUTCOMES

After completing this chapter, you should be able to:

- Explain the three pillars of liability in negligence: wrongful conduct, causation, and harm.

- Understand the concept of duty of care and list factors that establish a duty of care.

- Describe the concept of standard of care, including the "reasonable person" test.

- Explain cause in fact and distinguish it from cause in law.

- Describe how courts determine and assign liability for harm with multiple causes.

- List categories of compensable harm.

INTRODUCTION

negligence
a tort based on careless conduct or conduct that creates a reasonably foreseeable risk of harm

As you learned in Chapter 9, a defendant cannot be found liable in **negligence** for harm done to a plaintiff until three elements are established: (1) wrongful conduct on the part of the defendant, (2) a causal connection between the defendant's wrongful conduct and the harm to the plaintiff, and (3) measurable harm to the plaintiff.

In Chapter 9, the first element—wrongful conduct—was broken down into two parts: (1) the existence or recognition of a duty of care owed by the defendant to the plaintiff and (2) breach of that duty of care. Both facets of wrongful conduct will be explored in this chapter.

In the discussion of intentional torts in Chapters 10 and 11, we noted that the proof of intentional torts permits certain evidentiary "shortcuts"; for example, where a defendant intentionally harms a plaintiff, there is no need to prove a duty of care, because it is illegal in our society to intentionally harm another. Also, proving several intentional torts (for example, battery and false imprisonment) is sufficient to establish the plaintiff's right to damages without further proof of quantifiable harm. Neither of these shortcuts is available in negligence. Because of the more thorough analysis required in a negligence suit, plaintiffs often attempt, where possible, to frame their claims in intentional tort. However, many major claims—and most claims involving novel fact scenarios—are too complex to permit this.

This chapter will introduce the principles that underlie the three key elements of tort and the many legal tests that have been developed to assist in applying those principles. Chapter 13 will go on to explain the mechanics of proving negligence, the remedies available in negligence claims, and the defences available against negligence. Chapter 14 will introduce certain specialized areas of tort law that have developed as extensions from the basic principles.

THE FIRST ELEMENT: WRONGFUL CONDUCT

What Makes Conduct Wrong?

The notion of wrongful conduct is at the heart of tort law (as you might recall, the term "tort" is French for "wrong"). As in criminal law, a finding of liability in tort flows from a legal determination that the defendant is "in the wrong." However, a tort defendant need not be quite as wrong as a criminal defendant and, in some cases, need not be *morally* culpable, only *factually* culpable, because whereas criminal responsibility depends on a finding of intention (*mens rea*), responsibility in negligence can flow from actions that are simply careless or even close to accidental. As you learned in Chapter 9, there is a continuum of intention in tort law, and negligence falls toward the middle of the continuum between intentional tort and strict or absolute liability. In a nutshell, a finding that a person was negligent requires a finding that he or she was required to take at least some degree of care in his or her actions, but did not.

Duty of Care

The requirement to take care in one's actions is called a **duty of care** and is an essential legal principle. Under the law of tort, unless the defendant owed the plaintiff a duty of care, there can be no finding that the defendant was negligent.

To establish a duty of care, the plaintiff must prove two factors:

1. That it was reasonably foreseeable that the defendant's actions (or omissions) could cause harm to a person or property.
2. That, at the time of the impugned action (or omission), a person or property was sufficiently proximate (nearby or otherwise connected) to the defendant to suffer harm.

The first factor is called "foreseeability"; the second, "proximity."

With respect to foreseeability, it is not necessary that the plaintiff prove that the defendant actually foresaw the harm complained of; only that a reasonable person in the position of the defendant would have reasonably foreseen the harm.

duty of care
the legal obligation to exercise care in favour of a plaintiff and his or her interests

The Donoghue Case

This notion of foreseeability provides the key for establishing a duty of care where no formal legal relationship exists between the parties. The concept of negligence—the imposition of liability for behaviour outside of the bounds of contract—is a relatively recent development in the common law. While sanctions for bad behaviour have existed since ancient times, the theoretical basis on which we ground the modern analysis of negligence was not fully established until the British House of Lords rendered a decision in 1932, in the case of *Donoghue v. Stevenson*.[1]

In the *Donoghue* case, the plaintiff was a woman who went to a café with a friend. The friend bought her a bottle of ginger beer (ginger ale), and when she was partway finished drinking it, she discovered a decomposing snail in the bottle and became sick. She sued, primarily for "nervous shock."

While her cause of action seems obvious by today's standards, it was not at the time. In 1932, the concept of consumer protection was just emerging, and while it was accepted that the plaintiff could have sued under the law of contract for having been sold a defective product, she was not the purchaser of the product (her friend was), and so there was no privity of contract. The court was forced to rule on the issue whether, even in the absence of a contract between the parties, the maker of the ginger beer (Stevenson) could be held liable for harm to a consumer.

The court found that he was indeed liable. In deciding in Donoghue's favour, the court explained that a maker of a food product can reasonably expect that people other than the immediate purchaser will consume the product, and there is no logical reason why liability for harm flowing from the poor quality of the product should be restricted to the purchaser alone. Or, in other words, if the manufacturer

---

1. *Donoghue v. Stevenson*, [1932] All E.R. Rep. 1, [1932] A.C. 562 (U.K.H.L.).

could foresee harm to a person other than the purchaser, the manufacturer could be liable to that harm based on having foreseen it.

The concept of proximity is less controversial than the concept of foreseeability: sometimes, although one can foresee theoretical victims of one's action, if there are no actual victims, there is no liability. For example, consider a driver who, through failure to keep her eyes on the road, swerves into the lanes reserved for oncoming traffic. If there is an actual driver coming toward her and she hits him, she will be liable in negligence, because harm from taking her eyes off the road was foreseeable, and the oncoming driver was proximate (nearby). However, if she swerves into the wrong lane at a time when there is no oncoming traffic, she will not be liable in negligence; not only because no one will bother to sue her, but also because no one was proximate to her when the careless act occurred.

It is not uncommon for judges and legal scholars to collapse the basic duty of care test into one analysis, asking, for example, was there a "sufficient relationship of proximity based upon foreseeability" between the plaintiff and the defendant?

That combined foreseeability-and-proximity wording comes from *Anns v. Merton London Borough Council*.[2] The *Anns* case is an important case in that it expanded the duty of care test to include a public policy analysis.

The Anns Test

The *Anns* case concerned a block of townhouses that collapsed because of a structural deficiency (foundations dug too shallowly). During construction, the town council had the power to inspect the foundations (and was given notice of their construction), but was not under a statutory duty to do so, and did not do so.

When the foundations failed, the town council was named as a defendant. In considering whether the council was capable of owing a duty of care to the tenants, the court—which in this case was the British House of Lords (per Lord Wilberforce)—expressed its reasoning in the form of a two-part test. In order for a duty of care to arise,

1. there must be a sufficient relationship of proximity based upon foreseeability between plaintiff and defendant; and
2. there must not be "any considerations which ought to negative, or to reduce or limit the scope of the duty or the class of person to whom it is owed or the damages to which a breach of it may give rise."

The court found that while harm to tenants from failing to inspect construction was foreseeable and proximate, it would be contrary to public policy to hold the council liable for the harm. To do so would force council to change its policy so that it had to inspect every single project, and to uncover all potential defects—something that was beyond the council's capacity, both financially and with respect to expertise.

Also relevant was the issue of who should bear the risk of liability associated with the building project. The builder stood to profit from the construction, because it

---

2. *Anns v. Merton London Borough Council*, [1978] A.C. 728.

was building the units for resale; the council, however, stood to earn nothing and would be spending taxpayer dollars to conduct the inspection. To hold the council liable to bear a risk with no corresponding hope of reward or reimbursement ran counter to the equitable principle that holds that "he or she who profits should pay."

Interestingly enough, the *Anns* test was eventually overruled in England; however, it continues, in a modified form, to influence Canadian law and the law of some other countries, in the form of a proviso that where public policy reasons demand otherwise, a duty of care will *not* apply, even when the usual elements for one are met.

A more recent application of a public policy analysis to the issue of duty of care came up in a case about host liability for the actions of drunk guests. In that case, *Childs v. Desormeaux*,[3] the host held a "BYOB" party. One guest at the party had a history of drinking too much. The hosts served no alcohol other than a very small amount of champagne at midnight for a New Year's toast; however, guests brought and drank their own alcohol. Sometime after midnight, the guest with the drinking problem decided to leave the party. When questioned about his fitness to drive, he claimed he was all right, and he drove off. He was involved in an accident that led to the lawsuit.

In deciding that the hosts were not liable for the plaintiff hurt in the crash, the court found that there was no proof that the hosts knew that the guest was impaired when he left. The court also held that the amount of alcohol one chooses to consume and the decision to drive drunk are inherently personal decisions, and that it would be contrary to public policy to hold private hosts responsible for monitoring or controlling guests' drunk driving behaviour.

It is interesting to compare the *Childs* case with the cases that involve the liability of *commercial* hosts (for example, bars) for the actions of drunk patrons who leave the bar. It is well-settled law, in Canada, that a commercial host will indeed be responsible for the foreseeable actions of a patron who has been over-served. The difference? Public policy: bars stand to profit from serving alcohol, and so, based on the principle of "he or she who profits should pay," it is in line with public policy to hold them liable for the consequences of over-serving.

The Edwards Test

The *Anns* test, through repeated application in Canada, has been refined and elaborated upon. The case *Edwards v. Law Society of Upper Canada*[4] has taken the *Anns* test one step further, to include a preliminary "threshold" step, as follows:

1. Does the relationship between plaintiff and defendant fall within one of the recognized categories of duty of care? If not:
2. Are the parties sufficiently proximate that the harm would be foreseeable?
3. Are there public policy reasons *not* to impose a duty of care in this novel situation?

---

3. *Childs v. Desormeaux*, 2006 SCC 18.
4. *Edwards v. Law Society of Upper Canada*, 2001 SCC 80 (CanLII).

This test—known as the *Edwards* test—requires that the court first consider whether an "automatic" duty of care arises between the parties because of the special relationship between them.

Certain classes of plaintiff-and-defendant pairs have come before the courts enough times, in negligence cases, that the courts automatically deem the defendant to owe the plaintiff a duty of care. The kinds of plaintiff–defendant pairs that give rise to an automatic duty of care include:

- driver and fellow drivers;
- parent and child;
- employer and employee;
- professional and client (for example, doctor and patient); and
- neighbour and neighbour.

The *Edwards* test takes into account four separate issues:

1. relationships between the plaintiff and the defendant;
2. foreseeability;
3. proximity; and
4. public policy.

The *Edwards* test is now the most current test for duty of care under Canadian law.

Breach of a Duty of Care

As noted above, wrongful conduct has two elements: the existence of a duty of care and breach of that duty.

Once the plaintiff has proven that the defendant owed him or her a duty of care, the plaintiff must go on to prove that the defendant breached that duty of care. To do so, the plaintiff must show that the defendant fell short of the standard of care that applied under the circumstances.

Standard of Care

Introduction

standard of care
how well, how carefully, or how thoroughly a person carried out the duty of care owed to another

Standard of care is an expression that describes how well (or badly), how carefully (or carelessly), or how thoroughly (or neglectfully) a person discharged (carried out) the duty of care that he or she owed to another. In general, a person will be found to have met the relevant standard of care if he or she took all the steps that were reasonable, under the circumstances, to avoid doing harm to the plaintiff.

In some cases, a plaintiff who owes a duty of care may take some steps to discharge it, but may not go far enough, and by falling short, may harm the plaintiff. For example, a parent may ask her sister to babysit the parent's toddler for a day. The sister may feed the toddler and change his or her diapers (thus providing some care), but may leave a basement door open so that the toddler falls down an unguarded set of stairs and breaks an arm. The plaintiff toddler (through his litigation guardian—usually the parent) will likely be able to sue his or her aunt under the doctrine of negligence, because by undertaking to care for the child, the aunt

Do Physicians Owe a Duty of Care to the Potential Unborn Babies of Women for Whom They Prescribe Drugs?

From: *Paxton v. Ramji*, 2008 ONCA 697 (CanLII).

The Ontario Court of Appeal was asked to consider what duty of care, if any, a physician who prescribes teratogenic drugs (drugs that can cause birth defects) owes to patients' not-yet-conceived children.

According to the facts of the case, Jaime Paxton was born with very serious birth defects because her mother took the acne drug Accutane while pregnant.

There is a recognized medical protocol (known as PPP, for "pregnancy protection program") that doctors are expected to follow when prescribing Accutane, a known teratogenic drug to women of childbearing age. The doctor in this case followed the protocol imperfectly, and relied on the fact that the father had had a vasectomy, which had been effective in preventing conception for 4.5 years prior to the mother's taking Accutane.

The vasectomy failed, baby Jaime was conceived, and she was born with serious health problems. She (through her litigation guardian) sued the doctor.

At trial, the court found that the doctor owed a duty of care to the baby, but that he had met the standard of care by following the PPP criteria to some extent.

Jaime Paxton appealed the trial court decision on the basis that the doctor failed to meet the standard of care. Dr. Ramji cross-appealed, on the basis that the trial judge was wrong in finding that he owed a duty of care to the unborn baby in the first place.

The law with respect to duties of care owed to unborn babies is exceptionally complicated, not just in Canada, but around the world. The Ontario Court of Appeal, in this case, found in favour of the doctor, holding that a physician prescribing treatment to a mother does *not* owe a duty of care to the fetus. This is despite the fact that negligent drivers who kill babies in utero *do* owe a duty of care to those babies.

In coming to this conclusion, the court applied the first branch of the *Anns* test and found that the relationship between the doctor and the baby is not suf-

ficiently proximate to give rise to a duty of care. The court's reasoning was as follows:

1. A doctor does owe a duty of care to a mother (or potential mother) to advise her about what treatment to take, and the risks of that treatment, including to unborn children.

However:

2. Courts have long held that it is contrary to public policy to hold mothers legally responsible for the impact of their health decisions on unborn babies; and doctors can advise mothers, but are not in a position to *enforce* their advice.

This approach leads to two barriers to imposing a duty of care to the unborn on doctors: (1) the doctor does not have the power to exercise the care required by the duty, and (2) the doctor's duty of care to the mother might sometimes conflict with a duty to the baby, if such a duty existed—for example, epilepsy drugs that are necessary to the mother but dangerous to the fetus.

The court in *Paxton* found that these two barriers interfered with the proximity of the relationship between the doctor and the unborn child, because the doctor could not carry out a duty to the child without, in some cases, breaching his duty to the mother.

Therefore, the *Paxton* fact scenario failed the first part of the *Anns* test on the ground of non-proximity. The court also mentioned that there were good public policy reasons for not imposing a duty of care toward unborn babies on doctors (for example, the potential to cause conflicts of interest).

Jaime Paxton sought leave to appeal the case to the Supreme Court of Canada. The Supreme Court denied her leave to appeal, which is generally considered a signal that the court agrees in principle with the decision of the court below.

assumed a duty of care yet failed to take reasonable steps to protect the child's safety, thus failing to meet the standard of care. (If the daycare, in this example, were provided not by a relative but by a hired daycare provider, the parent would likely also be able to sue for breach of contract.)

In an example like this, however, some readers may think to themselves, "What if the sister had no children of her own, had little experience with the behaviour of toddlers, and simply didn't consider the possibility of the toddler falling down the stairs?" These readers would question whether it is fair to impose liability on the sister under these circumstances. The fact that this question arises demonstrates that the precise limits and contents of the standard of care in any particular case are always subjective: in other words, if you asked 10 people to describe the precise standard of care that applies to an aunt's babysitting her sister's toddler, you might get 10 different answers.

Judges understand this issue of subjectivity with respect to standard of care, but they must find a way to make decisions anyway, because people need resolution of their legal disputes. The method that the law prescribes for determining whether a defendant met the applicable standard of care involves comparing the defendant's behaviour with that of another person in the defendant's position.

Who is that other person? He or she is an imaginary "reasonable person in the same situation" who exists only in the mind of the judge.

Who Is the Reasonable Person?

To be able to compare the defendant's behaviour with that of the reasonable person, a judge must first concoct and describe the reasonable person and his or her behaviour. To do so, the judge must listen to the evidence provided by the plaintiff's and defendant's lawyers. The lawyers are expected to suggest how a reasonable person in the defendant's position would or should have acted.

The defendant's lawyer, of course, will generally suggest that the defendant himself or herself *did* behave reasonably, and that the "reasonable person" and the defendant are exactly alike. The defence, then, will attempt to call witnesses to say that if they had been in the position of the defendant, they would have done exactly the same things as the defendant did.

The plaintiff's lawyer will suggest the opposite: that a reasonable person would have done better, or done more, than the defendant did. He or she will call witnesses to describe what they have done or would do in similar circumstances, and will suggest that this evidence represents what is "reasonable."

The judge will weigh both sides' evidence and will make findings with respect to the content of reasonable behaviour based on the evidence available.

The case law suggests that, in general, the court will describe the reasonable person as someone who:

- has reasonable skill in what he or she does;
- has ordinary intelligence;
- acts with reasonable prudence; but
- is not perfect.

"Perfect" performance is not expected from a reasonable person or from the defendant, because to do so would be unfair. While the risk that materialized and became the subject of the plaintiff's claim may seem, at trial, like something any defendant should have considered and avoided, it is important to remember the expression "hindsight is 20/20." The judge (and jury), in hearing the facts of the case, will have had a much clearer understanding of the risks than would have been available to even a careful defendant at the time.

The specific content of what is reasonable or unreasonable behaviour has been found to depend on what the defendant is doing, where he or she is doing it, and who he or she is doing it for.

Assume a defendant is performing an activity that requires skills shared by most people (for example, washing a car in his own driveway). The defendant will be expected to demonstrate ordinary skills—for example, he or she should not leave a bucket on the sidewalk for people to trip over or fail to clean up car wax spilled on the pavement.

When a defendant is doing an activity on his or her own private property, he or she may be held to a lower standard of care than if he or she were performing it in a public place—for example, a person might be reasonable in not looking around before opening an umbrella on his or her own front porch; but if the same umbrella is opened while the person is seated in a baseball stadium, he or she must look around to ensure that he or she will not poke someone in the eye.

Finally, where a person is doing something for, or around, other adults of normal intelligence, he or she is entitled to rely on those adults to take steps to protect their own safety. For example, a person with no toddlers in the house can reasonably leave the basement door open. However, the same action, as we noted above, can be a breach of standard of care when taken in a house with a toddler afoot.

These examples describe ordinary, safe, non-skilled activities; the standard of care changes, however, when the activities taken are more dangerous, or where the person undertaking the activity has special skill.

Standard of Care for Dangerous Activities

Where the defendant's activity is unusually dangerous, the courts apply a modified "reasonable person" test.

An activity is usually identified as unusually dangerous for one of three different reasons:

- there is a high potential that something will go wrong;
- there are a large number of people, or especially vulnerable people, who would be affected if something went wrong; or
- even if the risk of something going wrong is low, the consequences, if that risk materialized, would be extremely negative.

An example of the first factor is motocross racing. The rate of accidents and crashes in motocross events is so high that collisions and accidents are considered part of the sport. Participants are aware of these risks and generally waive them in writing, but the designers of courses are expected to take special precautions to make the course—and spectators—as safe as possible, given the near-certainty that accidents will occur.

An example of the second factor—number or type of potential victims—might be welding repairs undertaken in a nursing home. Welding comes with a risk of fire, and a fire in a nursing home is more serious than a fire in other buildings because there is often a high density of residents with mobility problems, making evacuation a challenge.

An example of the third factor—unusual but catastrophic risks—might be air travel. As most readers know, airplane crashes are hundreds of times less likely than automobile crashes, but the consequences of an airplane crash (especially in a populated area) are often fatal to large numbers of people. For this reason, a great deal of money and time is devoted to improving the safety of air travel.

Where a defendant undertakes a dangerous activity, he or she is expected to take special precautions to address the elevated risks associated with the activity. "Reasonableness" in carrying out dangerous operations means taking extreme care, even if there are high costs associated with those precautions. If the costs associated with protecting others are low, and a defendant still does not take precautions, the court will be more likely to find that the defendant did not meet the required standard of care.

Standard of Care for Experts

Sometimes, an activity is better characterized as difficult than dangerous. For example, there are hundreds of appendectomies performed in Canada every year, and the majority of patients recover well with no ongoing damage to health. However, a very small percentage of Canadians know how to perform a safe appendectomy. This means that we consider those people who do know how to do it to be "experts."

There are experts in all kinds of different fields—not just in formal professions like medicine or accounting. Anyone who has ever had a terrible home haircut in childhood knows that there are experts—and non-experts—in hairdressing. There are experts in dog training, drywall installation, teaching English as a second language, and a host of other areas.

When it comes to standard of care, experts who are asked to complete work in their area of expertise are not held to the same "reasonable person" standard that would apply to a non-expert doing the same work. Rather, they are held to the standard of a "reasonable expert."

A reasonable expert is a person who is reasonably competent (compared with his or her peers) in the work about which he or she professes expertise.

So how does a judge (who is not likely an expert in the same area as the defendant) assess the expert defendant's expertise? He or she does so by considering the evidence of other experts, who testify about their normal practices and procedures.

For example, imagine that the defendant is a home renovator. While conducting renovations, he knocked down a wall without determining what kind of wiring was within the wall, and caused extensive electrical damage that the plaintiff had to pay another contractor to fix. When asked what steps he or she took to determine whether there was wiring in the wall, the defendant said, "I checked to see if there were any outlets on that wall, and since there weren't, I figured it was safe to knock it down."

In trying to establish that this conduct fell short of the standard of care, the plaintiff would likely call other contractors to testify about how *they* determine whether it is safe to demolish a wall. Those other contractors would likely say things like, "Before I knock down any walls, I make sure to review the electrical plans from the original construction," or, "I use a special testing device to locate electrical wires in the wall."

The defendant would then try to find witnesses who say that *their* standard practice is just to look for outlets on the wall.

After considering the evidence of all witnesses, the judge must then decide who to believe. More precisely, the judge will synthesize the witnesses' evidence and express the content of the standard of care as it should be defined in a case like this. For example, the judge might say, "On the basis of the evidence before me, a reasonable person would either review the electrical plans or use a device to locate wires before making a decision to demolish a wall."

In some cases, the court will have additional aids at its disposal (besides witness testimony) to assist in determining whether an expert is competent. These include:

- regulations that apply to the expert's industry (for example, regulations made under the *Technical Standards and Safety Act*[5]);
- standards of practice created by a body that regulates the profession (for example, the *Rules of Professional Conduct* created by the Law Society of Upper Canada, the body that regulates lawyers);
- standards that an expert is expected to meet in order to be licensed by an association that confers credentials or a licence on the expert (for example, the requirements for obtaining an aircraft inspector's licence); and
- "best practices" and tips published by member organizations to which the expert belongs.

Finally, when it comes to the requirement of competence for experts, the extent of an expert's experience is irrelevant. The court will not hold a "new" expert (for example, a newly graduated lawyer) to a lower standard of competence than would be applied to a lawyer with 25 years of experience. If both the new lawyer and the experienced lawyer represent themselves as competent to, for example, do the legal work for a real estate transaction, they will both be held to the standard of a reasonably competent real estate practitioner. The reason for this is that a member of the general public, in hiring an expert, is in no position to analyze the expert's level of expertise (or else the member of the public could just do the job himself or herself!). We need to be able to trust that when we hire a plumber, or a lawyer, or a veterinarian, that person can competently do the work we associate with those roles, without our having to ask to see diplomas or to contact references.

5. *Technical Standards and Safety Act*, S.O. 2000, c. 16.

Standard of Care for Minors or People with Impairments

Finally, where the defendant is a child, a teenager, or a person with a physical disability or a cognitive impairment, the court may hold that the "reasonable person" standard does not apply, because the defendant is not capable of performing to that standard. Instead, the defendant's behaviour may be compared with that of a reasonable child, teen, or person with the same impairment.

THE SECOND ELEMENT: CAUSATION

Introduction

In the context of the intentional torts discussed in the preceding chapters, proving causation is relatively simple, because given that the defendant *intended* some kind of harm, it is difficult for the defendant to argue that his or her actions did not *cause* the harm.

Negligent acts, by definition, are not intentional. Where there is no intention to cause harm, drawing a direct line between the acts of the defendant and the harm to the plaintiff can sometimes be difficult. For this reason, establishing causation occupies a considerable portion of the court's time in many negligence cases.

Two Kinds of Causation

For the purpose of imposing liability in negligence, the court considers two different kinds of causation: (1) cause in fact and (2) cause in law. Both kinds of causation must be proven, on a balance of probabilities, before the defendant will be found liable in negligence.

cause in fact
the factual link between one person's actions and another person's harm

As might be expected from the name, determining **cause in fact** requires a practical analysis of the details of the incident or condition that led to the harm, as well as any other factors that contributed to the harm. The cause-in-law analysis is a remoteness analysis: the court considers how closely connected the defendant's actions were to the harm and whether a more indirect connection was reasonably foreseeable to the defendant. The doctrine of **cause in law** allows the court to interject public policy into the analysis and permits the court to relieve against liability where it would be unfair to hold the defendant responsible for harm he or she could not easily anticipate.

cause in law
the proximity or remoteness of one person's actions in causing another person's harm

Cause in Fact: The "But For" Test

The cause-in-fact analysis requires the court to ask the obvious question: Did the actions (or omissions) of the defendant cause the harm that the plaintiff is complaining of?

For cause in fact to be proven, the defendant's actions need not be the *sole* cause—there can be other contributing factors. For example, where a plaintiff passenger is injured in a car accident, there may have been more than one factor:

- the defendant driver may have been driving too fast;
- the road may have been icy; and/or
- the plaintiff may have failed to wear his or her seat belt.

However, the defendant's actions do need to have been an *essential* factor contributing to the harm. In the car accident scenario, the mere fact of icy roads or non-wearing of a seat belt would not have led to an injury *unless* the defendant contributed the essential element—driving too fast.

To determine whether a defendant's actions were an essential factor in the harm to the plaintiff, the court applies the "but for" test: "*But for* (if not for) the actions of the defendant, would the harm have been caused to the plaintiff?"

An example of a case that turned on the but for test is *Saccone v. Fandrakis*.[6] In that case, Saccone was about to leave a movie theatre when he heard a noise outside. He looked out the window and saw that his van had been pushed into a snowbank. He also saw a white Mustang backing away from his van.

Saccone believed that the white Mustang had hit his van and that it was about to leave the scene of the accident. He ran outside, ran across the road, and jumped off a 2- to 3-foot ledge to reach his van. He badly injured his knee when jumping. As it turned out, the other driver, Fandrakis, was not, in fact, leaving the scene; he was just moving out of the road.

Saccone sued Fandrakis in negligence, alleging that Fandrakis's collision with his car was the cause of his knee injury. The "rescuer" doctrine in negligence provides that when you cause an emergency, you are liable for the injuries to rescuers. Saccone tried to rely on this doctrine.

The court, however, found Fandrakis not liable. In hitting the parked van, Fandrakis had not caused an emergency. In running to stop Fandrakis from leaving the scene, Saccone was not acting as a rescuer. The court found that Fandrakis's collision with the van was not the cause in fact of Saccone's knee injury.

Cause in Law: The Remoteness/Public Policy Test

The second type of cause that must be proved in order to establish negligence is cause in law.

There are usually few public policy reasons to avoid finding people at fault when they commit harm intentionally. However, the situation is different in the case of negligence. Where a person causes harm unintentionally, it can sometimes seem unfair to impose liability on him or her where the risk of harm, from his or her actions, was too remote to have been readily foreseen.

The doctrine of cause in law allows the court to limit liability in negligence where public policy reasons—and fairness—demand it.

If a defendant's action was an essential factor in a plaintiff's harm, cause in fact is established. Remember—we owe a duty of care any time we can foresee harm, even in a general sense, to another; we need not to have foreseen the exact type of harm. However, sometimes we can do harm in circumstances where we could not have reasonably foreseen the harm. Sometimes, a constellation of unlikely factors comes into play in a manner that causes an accident or injury that no one would ever have expected.

---

6. *Saccone v. Fandrakis*, 2002 BCSC 73 (CanLII).

A scenario like this occurred in a famous US case, *Palsgraf v. Long Island Railroad Co.*[7] In that case, the plaintiff was standing near railroad tracks next to a large and heavy set of commercial weigh scales (this was 1928!). Many yards farther down the platform, a railway guard boosted a passenger roughly onto a departing train. The passenger, when jostled, dropped a package containing explosives, which exploded on contact with the track. The explosion caused the weigh scales several metres away to fall on the plaintiff, causing injury.

The plaintiff sued the railway employee for boosting the passenger the way he did. The court held that while the railway guard's actions were the cause in fact of the plaintiff's injuries (they passed the "but for" test), they were *not* the cause in law, because the consequences of the railway guard's actions were not foreseeable to him (nor to anyone else). For this reason, it would not be fair for the court to hold him liable in negligence.

Cases with Complex Causes

Introduction

The goal of the "but for" test discussed above is to determine whether or not the behaviour of the defendant was an essential factor in the event or chain of events that caused harm to the plaintiff. What if that behaviour was an essential, but *minor* factor? Should the defendant be found liable for all of the harm, simply because he or she is the one the plaintiff has chosen to sue? Or should an attempt be made, by the court, to distribute liability fairly among those who "deserve" it?

CASE IN POINT

Defendant Not Responsible for Far-Fetched and Serious Consequences of Minor Driving Lapse

From: *Falkenham v. Zwicker* (1978), 93 D.L.R. (3d) 289 (N.S.T.D.).

After reading the facts in *Palsgraf*, above, you may conclude that there will never again be a case with consequences quite so unpredictable. The decision in *Falkenham v. Zwicker*, however, reminds us that truth *is* sometimes stranger than fiction. Yet, a completely unpredictable chain of events will not lead to a defendant's liability.

In *Falkenham*, the defendant was speeding while driving out in the country in winter conditions when a cat ran into the road. The driver braked suddenly to avoid the cat, swerved, and hit a fencepost instead, destroying a section of fence.

The farmer repaired his fence; but in the springtime, after the snow melted and the cattle were put out to pasture, some cows found and ate fencing staples that had fallen to the ground as a result of the crash. The cows suffered serious harm, and the farmer sued the driver.

The court held that the defendant driver's speeding was indeed the cause in fact of the harm to the cows (but for her speeding, they would not have been harmed), but because the chain of events was so unpredictable, it was not the cause in law. She was liable for the harm to the fence, but not the harm to the cattle.

7. *Palsgraf v. Long Island Railroad Co.*, 162 N.E. 99 (N.Y. Ct. App. 1928).

The answer is that the courts *do* try to share liability among defendants where there is more than one defendant. Because of this, a defendant who receives a statement of claim from a plaintiff will usually seek to "join" any other unnamed potential defendants into the litigation. From the plaintiff's point of view, the fact that the court will try to spread liability is a reason for ensuring that all potential defendants—and especially those who can be expected to pay (for example, governments, large corporations, and insurance companies)—are included as defendants.

Once all the defendants are identified, how does the court assess their relative liability? First, the case is identified as a case with complex causes.

What Is Complex Causation?

By **complex causation**, the courts generally mean:

- cases involving multiple causative factors (for example, the actions of multiple individuals acting separately but contributing to a single outcome, weather conditions that aggravate harm, and problems with products as well as with their users);
- cases involving contributory negligence on the part of the plaintiff; and
- cases involving medical conditions not caused by plaintiff or defendant (for example, where a plaintiff develops psychosomatic pain after the underlying cause of the pain has resolved).

complex causation
multiple causative factors, including possible contributory negligence on the part of the plaintiff and/ or conditions not caused by plaintiff or defendant

How Are These Factors Addressed?

To address the interplay of a wide range of factors, it is best to follow a system. The Supreme Court of Canada, in deciding the 1996 case *Athey v. Leonati*,[8] created a system of steps for analyzing complex cases. The *Athey* steps are applied to each defendant in turn, and go like this:

1. *First, to establish basic cause in fact, apply the "but for" test.*
2. *Address multiple causes:*
   a. to attract liability, a defendant's actions need not be the *only* cause;
   b. where another cause was not a tort (for example, weather was a factor), the defendant bears the full responsibility (that is, there is no "deduction" for weather or natural causes);
   c. where another defendant contributed to the harm, liability should be divided between the defendants;
   d. where the plaintiff's actions are one of the causes, apply the principles of contributory negligence (discussed in the next chapter).
3. *Each defendant is liable only for the injuries caused by that defendant.* (For example, if the plaintiff suffers a concussion in a car accident, then goes to a walk-in clinic to have the concussion checked out and slips and falls on a puddle on the clinic floor, the driver of the car who hit him is not responsible for the slip-and-fall injury.)

8. *Athey v. Leonati* (1996), 140 D.L.R. (4th) 235.

4. *Apply the "thin skull" rule* (discussed below).
5. *The defendant is liable only for the injuries and losses that the plaintiff suffered as a result of the defendant's negligence.* (In some cases, the plaintiff will have other, compounding problems that would have arisen anyway and that cannot be attributed to the defendant.)

The decision in *Dushynski v. Rumsey*[9] illustrates step number 5. In that case, an unfortunate plaintiff suffered car accidents in 1985, 1988, 1991, and 1993. After the fourth accident, she found herself seriously disabled and afflicted with chronic pain syndrome that was likely the cumulative result of all of the accidents. She sued Rumsey, the defendant in the fourth accident, and attempted to have the court impose liability on Rumsey for the chronic pain syndrome.

However, the Court of Appeal held that, in compensating her, Rumsey should be required to compensate her only for the difference between her state of health after the third accident and after the fourth; in other words, Rumsey was not expected to compensate her as though she had been absolutely fine before the fourth accident.

As you can see from the facts in *Dushynski v. Rumsey*, there are two kinds of complex causation cases—the kind where the harm happened all at once (and where all the defendants could conceivably be before the court at once), and the kind where the harm was the result from causes building up over time. Unfortunately for plaintiffs in the second category of cases, it may not be possible to get full compensation for cumulative harm, because as time goes on, it can be more and more difficult to locate past tortfeasors.

THE THIRD ELEMENT: HARM

The third and final element that must be proven before a plaintiff can succeed in negligence is that the wrongful act of the defendant caused harm to the plaintiff.

While "harm" is a broad term in general parlance, the kinds of harm that satisfy the test for negligence are narrower than the full range of imaginable harm in a number of ways.

First, harm that supports a claim in negligence must not fall too far outside the categories of harm that have already been recognized under this doctrine. To be compensable, harm must be actual harm to a legally recognized interest.

Actual Harm to a Legally Recognized Interest

Over the years, courts have been asked to compensate plaintiffs for a very wide range of types of harm. At the moment, recovery of damages under the law of tort is restricted to cases in which the plaintiff can prove one of the following categories of harm:

- damage to goods or real property that can be seen/measured/proved;
- devaluation of real property that can be proved (for example, as a result of environmental contamination due to negligence);

9. *Dushynski v. Rumsey*, 2003 ABCA 164 (CanLII).

- pain and suffering, even if it has eased;
- lasting or permanent injuries;
- loss of income or opportunity related to an injury;
- future economic losses related to an injury;
- psychological harm that is provable (recognized by the medical community and diagnosed; for example, post-traumatic stress disorder);
- "nervous shock" (more or less an archaic description of the previous category); and/or
- provable damage to reputation or business interests.

The following categories of harm do *not*, at present, attract compensation under Canadian law:

- mental anguish, grief, stress, hurt feelings, embarrassment, and so on, that is *not* diagnosed as a recognized psychiatric illness;
- pure economic loss—that is, losing money in a way that is unrelated to the devaluation of your own property, reputation, or business interests; and/or
- losing certain "rights," like the right not to be born, the right to compete in a competition, and so on.

The decision in *Clifford Morris et al. v. Johnson Controls Ltd.*[10] is an example of a case that was unsuccessful because the plaintiffs could not prove actual harm to a legally recognized interest. In this case—a type of case called a **class action**—the defendant company was hired to work on boilers on a military base. During the course of the work, the defendant caused some asbestos insulation to dislodge. The plaintiffs, residents of the base, were exposed to asbestos fibre "snow." Asbestos has long been recognized as posing a risk to human health.

class action
a lawsuit brought by one party who represents many persons with similar claims

At the time the class-action lawsuit was commenced, none of the plaintiffs were suffering from any asbestos-related symptoms; however, they were afraid of the potential risks to which they had been exposed, most notably, the risk of cancer. They brought a claim in negligence.

The defendant brought a motion to have the plaintiffs' claim struck out for failure to disclose a cause of action. The basis of the defendants' objection to the plaintiffs' claim was that the claim did not allege any harm—that is, it did not allege any facts that the plaintiffs would be able to prove to meet the test for the third element of negligence (harm). The plaintiffs did not have cancer; they were just afraid they might get cancer later.

Unless it is part of a recognized, diagnosable psychiatric condition, fear is not harm, according to negligence law.

Nevertheless, the court declined to grant the motion to dismiss the cause of action. Even though the plaintiffs' claim never mentioned the doctrine of nervous shock, the court held that it was at least *possible* that a court hearing the case could rule that fear of a future illness amounts to nervous shock.

---

10. *Clifford Morris et al. v. Johnson Controls Ltd.*, 2002 MBQB 313 (CanLII).

The court held that only in very rare cases should a court deny a plaintiff the opportunity to argue for a novel cause of action, and that this was not one of those rare cases:

> A motion for failure to disclose a reasonable cause of action is a partial vacuum missing the essential pressure and evidence of the trial process. It is only against such an evidentiary background that the Plaintiffs' case can be properly tested.

Proving Harm

Besides falling within—or being analogous to—one of the existing recognized categories of harm, harm that supports a claim in negligence must be capable of being proven objectively through evidence.

How do you prove harm? Nearly always, through witness evidence.

In some cases, the witnesses who testify on behalf of an injured plaintiff will be the people who were familiar with the plaintiff's condition and capabilities before the accident, and who have had a chance to observe his or her condition and capabilities after the accident. Falling into this category of witnesses would be:

- family members and close relatives of the plaintiff;
- the plaintiff's employer (supervisors, and so on); and
- individuals who have observed the plaintiff taking part in activities and hobbies (for example, teammates from the plaintiff's recreational hockey league, members of the plaintiff's book club, church members, and neighbours).

The other category of witnesses that may be called upon to describe harm to a plaintiff is experts. An "expert," in the context of litigation, is any person who possesses special skill or knowledge (greater than ordinary skill or knowledge) in an area of specialization.

When attempting to prove damages in a negligence case, the types of experts called to testify will depend on the nature of the harm alleged. Some categories of experts that might be useful include:

- contractors, architects, construction tradespeople, building inspectors;
- auto mechanics, engineers of all kinds;
- physicians and medical specialists of all kinds;
- mental health experts, including therapists and social workers; and
- actuaries (statisticians), who can quantify the future impact (for example, on life expectancy or earning potential) of present injuries.

When seeking to describe harm, the plaintiff's counsel will encourage experts to focus on "before and after." The goal of damages is to put a plaintiff, to the degree possible, back into the same position he or she was in *before* the wrongful act. Therefore, the plaintiff's witnesses must be able to "paint a picture" of (and prove) two states:

1. what the plaintiff (or his property) was like before the defendant's wrongful act, and
2. what the plaintiff (or his property) is like after the defendant's wrongful act.

The plaintiff, his or her counsel, and the experts must then seek to place a dollar value on the "gap" between these two states. That dollar value represents the compensation (damages) that the plaintiff is seeking from the defendant.

Remoteness of Harm and the "Thin Skull" Rule

Introduction

In the section on cause in law, above, we considered the question of remoteness as it relates to causation: If the defendant's actions caused the plaintiff's harm, but the consequences were so surprising or unlikely as to be unforeseeable, should the defendant be liable to compensate the plaintiff for those consequences?

The answer, in the context of causation, was "no." A defendant should not be held liable for very unexpected consequences.

The causation analysis focuses on *manner* of harm: the connection between the defendant's actions and the consequences to the plaintiff.

There is another context in which the issue of remoteness comes into play, and that is with respect to *nature* of harm. This version of the remoteness analysis asks us to consider the question: What if the defendant could foresee doing *some* harm to the plaintiff, but the harm that actually occurs is different from the harm that the defendant anticipated? Is the defendant liable?

The general answer to this question is "yes."

There are two ways in which actual harm can confound the defendant's expectations: by being different in nature from the harm anticipated or by being much worse than the harm anticipated.

Different-from-Expected Harm

Where the defendant could foresee *any* kind of harm flowing from his or her actions, he or she will be liable for other kinds of harm, even if they were unexpected.

Consider this fictional example: there is one spot left on the high school cheerleading team, and twin sisters—Tracy and Macy—are vying for it. Hoping to secure her spot, Tracy plots to "accidentally" trip Macy at the top of a flight of stairs, hoping she will fall and break a leg. Macy does fall, but instead of breaking a leg, she breaks her brand-new $1,200 watch. Is Tracy liable to replace the watch, even though her intention was to harm Macy's body, not her possessions? Of course.

As long as some harm was foreseeable to the defendant, the defendant will be liable for *any* harm that occurs.

Worse-Than-Expected Harm, and the "Thin Skull" Rule

As a general rule, the defendant is liable for whatever degree of harm his or her actions cause the plaintiff, whether or not he or she could foresee the degree of harm. For example, if the defendant ties the sleeping plaintiff's shoelaces together as a prank, expecting the plaintiff to awaken, trip, and maybe sprain a wrist, but instead the plaintiff hits his or her head on the corner of a coffee table, sustaining permanent brain damage, the defendant is liable for the brain damage. This seems intuitively fair; when we do negligent or dangerous things, we should not be permitted to deny liability when our actions go further wrong than we had intended.

But what about situations when we do only slightly negligent things, and the consequences are catastrophic—not because of any fault of our own, but because of a hidden vulnerability of the plaintiff's?

Cases like this are rare, but there is a special rule designed to deal with them: the "thin skull" rule.

The quaintly named "thin skull" rule simply holds that, as long as the defendant could foresee causing some kind of harm to a plaintiff's health, the defendant is liable for *whatever* harm happens, even if the extent of that harm was not foreseeable.

In classic "thin skull" cases, the plaintiff has an underlying condition that, at the time of the defendant's wrongful act, has no symptoms and is completely unknown not only to the defendant, but also to the plaintiff. However, when the defendant's wrongful act occurs, the underlying condition causes the plaintiff to suffer much more serious harm than either party could have expected. Courts have held that when this happens, the defendant is liable to compensate the plaintiff for the harm, even though the harm was completely unforeseeable.

The case that established the "thin skull" rule was *Smith v. Leech Brain & Co.*,[11] which, despite the name, has nothing to do with either leeches or brains.

In *Smith v. Leech Brain*, the plaintiff suffered a burn on his lip while working for the defendant. Three years later, the plaintiff died of cancer. The cancer had been triggered by the burn, because the plaintiff had an underlying susceptibility to cancer.

The court found the defendant liable to the plaintiff's widow for the loss of her husband, because in allowing the plaintiff to be hurt at work, the defendant had to "take his victim as he finds him." This is the essence of the "thin skull" rule.

It is useful at this point to think back to the facts in *Dushynski v. Rumsey*, the case of the woman who had been in four separate car accidents. As you may recall, the court found that Rumsey, the defendant in the fourth accident, was not liable for the chronic pain condition that Dushynski had developed as a result of the cumulative effect of all of those accidents. You might wonder why the "thin skull" rule did not apply in that case.

The reason is simple: Ms. Dushynski *knew* that she had been in three other accidents before the Rumsey accident happened. For a defendant to be liable for unexpected catastrophic harm, neither the defendant nor the plaintiff must be aware of the underlying vulnerability of the plaintiff. *Dushynski v. Rumsey* is an example of what has been dubbed a *"crumbling* skull" case. Defendants are not liable for the unexpected harm in crumbling skull cases.

---

11. *Smith v. Leech Brain & Co.*, [1961] 3 All E.R. 1159 (Q.B.).

PROVING NEGLIGENCE: A REVIEW

As has already been discussed, the burden of proof, in negligence, is on the plaintiff. This means that the plaintiff is responsible for calling evidence to prove the three elements (wrongful conduct, causation, harm) that make up negligence.

While technically the defendant needs to serve a statement of defence, the defendant is not obligated to call any evidence to counter the plaintiff's case; he or she can just wait and hope that the plaintiff will not meet the standard of proof. In practice, however, nearly all defendants who go to trial do choose to call evidence.

At trial, the plaintiff and defendant have different goals in presenting their evidence.

The plaintiff's proof objectives are to prove three elements:

1. a wrongful act (duty of care + breach),
2. causation, and
3. harm.

The defendant's proof objectives fall into two categories:

1. to refute the plaintiff's evidence by calling evidence that tends to show that the plaintiff cannot establish the three elements (called proving a general defence), or
2. to prove a specific defence.

We will cover these objectives in the next chapter.

The evidence provided by the plaintiff and the defendant must, to be effective, meet the civil standard of proof, which is "on a balance of probabilities": that it is at least 51 percent likely that the version of the facts put forward is true.

CHAPTER SUMMARY

In order to establish a successful claim in negligence, a plaintiff must prove three elements: wrongful conduct on the part of the defendant, a causal connection between the defendant's wrongful conduct and the harm to the plaintiff, and measurable harm to the plaintiff.

The first element, wrongful conduct, has two component parts: first, the plaintiff must have owed the defendant a duty of care; second, the plaintiff must have breached that duty of care.

Certain set relationships—for example, doctor–patient or neighbour–neighbour—are automatically considered to involve a duty of care. However, where the connection between plaintiff and defendant does not fall within one of these recognized categories, the court must apply legal tests to determine whether a duty of care exists. The *Edwards* test requires a four-part analysis: (1) Did plaintiff and defendant fall into a recognized category? If not: (2) In doing the act complained of, should the defendant have reasonably foreseen a potential for harm? (3) Was there a potential victim sufficiently proximate to the defendant's actions to warrant the imposition of liability? (4) Are there any public policy reasons that would make it inappropriate to impose a duty of care under the circumstances?

Once a duty of care is established, the court will consider whether it was breached by determining whether the defendant, in taking action, met the required standard of care. This analysis is completed by comparing the defendant's actions with the actions of a "reasonable person" in the same circumstances as the defendant. This imaginary reasonable person is reasonably competent and reasonably careful, but not perfect. Where the defendant, in doing the action complained of, was acting in his or her capacity as an expert, the reasonable person test will become the "reasonable expert" test.

If the defendant is found not to have met the required standard of care, the court will then turn to the issue of causation. The court will apply the "but for" test to determine cause in fact—that is, whether the defendant's behaviour was an essential cause of the harm to the plaintiff. The court will also apply a remoteness analysis to determine whether the defendant's actions were the cause in law of the plaintiff's harm, or whether the manner in which the harm occurred was too remote to attract liability.

Some cases have complex causes: they involve the separate actions of multiple individuals; they involve negligence on the part of the plaintiff; or they occur partly as a result of causes outside human control—for example, weather or underlying vulnerabilities of the plaintiff. The decision in *Athey v. Leonati* established a framework for considering the interplay of these factors and for sorting out the extent of liability of multiple individuals.

Once causation is established, the court will move on to the final steps in determining liability: assessing whether the plaintiff suffered harm that is compensable in law (actual harm to a recognized legal interest); and whether the defendant is liable for the full extent of the harm, even if the seriousness of the harm was unforeseeable to the defendant at the time of the tort.

KEY TERMS

cause in fact

cause in law

class action

complex causation

duty of care

negligence

standard of care

REVIEW QUESTIONS

True or False?

1. For a plaintiff to be able to recover full damages under the "thin skull" rule, the plaintiff must not have been aware of his or her latent health condition before the defendant committed the wrongful act.

2. If a plaintiff can prove that the defendant is an expert, the plaintiff need *not* prove breach of a standard of care, because liability is automatic.

3. If a plaintiff cannot prove that the defendant's act was the cause in fact of his injury, he can still recover damages if he proves that it was the cause in law.

4. When nature, weather, or some other non-tort cause contributes to a successful plaintiff's injury, the damages awarded to the plaintiff are reduced by a percentage to reflect the non-tort cause.

5. To support a claim in negligence, the defendant's actions must be the sole cause of the harm to the plaintiff.

6. Unless it is part of a recognized, diagnosable psychiatric condition, fear is not harm, according to negligence law.

7. Where the defendant in a negligence case could foresee any kind of harm flowing from her actions, she will be liable for unexpected harm that her actions cause.

8. A defendant in a tort case will be found to have met the relevant standard of care if he or she took all the steps that were reasonable, under the circumstances, to avoid doing harm to the plaintiff.

9. Proving that the plaintiff has suffered harm sufficient to support a claim in negligence is nearly always done through witness evidence.

10. The *Donoghue* test continues to influence Canadian law in the form of a proviso that a duty of care will not apply where public policy reasons demand otherwise, even where the usual criteria for a duty of care are met.

Fill in the Blanks

1. To determine whether a defendant's actions were an essential factor to the harm to the plaintiff, the court applies the _____ _____ test.

2. The _____ _____ rule holds that, as long as the defendant could foresee causing some kind of harm to a plaintiff's health, the defendant is liable for whatever harm happens, even if the extent of that harm was not foreseeable.

3. Under the law of tort, unless the defendant owed the plaintiff a duty of care, there can be no finding that the defendant was _____.

4. For the purpose of imposing liability in negligence, the court considers two different kinds of causation: cause in _____ and cause in _____.

5. To establish a duty of care, the plaintiff must prove two factors: _____ and _____.

6. The _____ test is now the most current test for duty of care under Canadian law.

7. The method the law prescribes for determining whether a defendant meets the applicable standard of care involves comparing the defendant's behaviour with that of a "_____ person in the same situation."

8. A defendant cannot be found liable in negligence for harm done to a plaintiff until three elements are established: (1) wrongful conduct on the defendant's part, (2) a _____ connection between the defendant's wrongful conduct and the harm done to the plaintiff, and (3) measurable _____ done to the plaintiff.

9. Cases involving multiple causative factors, contributory negligence on the plaintiff's part, and medical conditions not caused by plaintiff or defendant are identified by the courts as having _____ causation.

10. When trying to establish the relevant standard of care in a negligence case involving a defendant who is an expert, courts aim to ascertain the standard of a "reasonable _____."

Short Answer

1. a. The cause-in-law test makes it clear that where the chain of events that led to harm to a plaintiff is completely unforeseeable, the defendant will not be liable for the harm that ensues. What is the reasoning behind this?

   b. Why do you think that remoteness works differently when it comes to extent of harm—that is, why are defendants found liable for harm that is more serious than they could have imagined?

2. What three questions compose the *Edwards* test for determining whether the defendant in a negligence case owed the plaintiff a duty of care?

3. How does a judge, when trying to determine whether to hold the defendant in a negligence case to the standard of a "reasonable expert," assess the defendant's expertise?

4. What is the usual way of proving objectively, through evidence, that a harm will support a claim in negligence?

5. List four classes of relationships in which, according to the courts, the defendant automatically owes the plaintiff a duty of care.

6. How do courts, as they try to determine whether the defendant in a negligence case met the applicable standard of care, define the hypothetical "reasonable person" by whose standard they measure the defendant's performance?

7. Explain why the "thin skull" rule did not apply to the case of *Dushynski v. Rumsey*—that is, the case where the plaintiff developed chronic pain syndrome after four separate car accidents, then sued the defendant in the fourth accident and tried to have the court impose liability on him for her medical condition.

8. Sum up the difference between criminal responsibility and tort responsibility.

9. Why is a bar or tavern in Canada much more likely than a private host to be held responsible for the foreseeable actions of a guest who has been over-served alcohol?

EXERCISES

1. A fire breaks out in a two-storey department store, and the fire alarm triggers a shutdown of power to the elevators and escalators. There is thick smoke in the lingerie department on the second floor. Cindy runs toward the top of the escalator, where she sees a stranger in a wheelchair waiting, unable to get down the inoperable escalator. No other people are in sight, and the fire department has not yet arrived. Cindy runs down the escalator steps without doing anything to help the stranger, who suffers severe smoke inhalation before she is rescued by the fire department.

   a. Did Cindy owe a duty of care to the stranger, and if so, did she breach it? Research this question and explain your answer.

   b. Comment on the answer, and consider whether you agree or disagree with it, taking into account public policy considerations.

2. Teresa Smart, a single mother, has just been fired from her job. She claims that her termination is the fault of a daycare centre called "PA Play" where her sons Eddy and Ashton were enrolled nearly three years ago.

   In June 2008, her children Eddy (then aged nine) and Ashton (then seven) participated in a PA Play daycare program that included out-trips to local attractions on PA days. The younger boy, Ashton, has severe behavioural problems that have still not been fully diagnosed. He tended to have violent, confrontational tantrums when he felt overwhelmed by new situations or new people. The staff at PA Play had mentioned to Teresa on two separate occasions that caring for Ashton, especially on out-trips, was a challenge for staff, and occasionally raised safety concerns. Teresa's response was that the staff needed to be prepared to deal with *all* children, not just easy children. She also said that the best way to deal with Ashton, when he was being difficult, was to allow him to be in Eddy's group, even though he did not meet the age requirements.

   On June 11, PA Play took the children, including the two Smart brothers, on an out-trip to Centre Island near Toronto. Sometime near the end of the outing, Ashton Smart began acting up. His counsellor, Jamie Perkins, struggled to control him, and Ashton threw a full-blown tantrum. In the midst of the tantrum, and while he was trying to deal with the other eight kids under his care, Jamie Perkins believed he saw Tanya Symmonds with her group of kids, approximately 50 yards away, having a snack in the shade. Eddy Smart was part of Tanya's group. At his wits' end, and remembering Teresa Smart's advice, Jamie told the child: "Go see Eddy, over there under the trees. Tell Tanya that I said it was okay if you go home with their group."

   Ashton Smart headed off at a run.

   Upon returning by ferry to the Toronto Island docks, Jamie Perkins encountered Tanya Symmonds, inquired about Ashton, and learned that Tanya had never seen Ashton. Jamie had been mistaken about the group under the tree; they were kids from a different daycare altogether. Ashton Smart was nowhere to be found, and the counsellors realized he had been left on the island.

By the time the mistake was discovered, a ferry back to the island was boarded, a counsellor travelled to the island, and Ashton was located. The seven-year-old boy had been alone for more than three hours and was hysterical. Teresa Smart was also hysterical when she learned about the situation, through a phone call from the daycare centre at 4:45 p.m.— before Ashton was found.

Teresa Smart never sent either child back to PA Play. As a gesture of support, her employer allowed her to stay home with the boys on PA days. But she began to have nightmares about the incident, and she was also having panic attacks during the day, at work. On several occasions, she became so distressed that she had to leave early.

In May 2010, Teresa's work situation changed, and she was transferred to a new office. Her new boss did not permit Teresa to take all PA days off. Teresa's anxiety escalated and her panic attacks occurred almost daily. She began leaving work without permission, her productivity dropped, and eventually—in January 2011—she was dismissed for cause.

Teresa is now suing PA Play and Jamie Perkins in negligence. She is claiming damages for a mental illness (anxiety disorder) and for lost income due to her job loss. She has a physician's report that supports her claim; however, another physician who will be a witness for PA Play is expected to testify that it is common for parents—especially single parents—of children with severe behavioural problems to suffer from depression, anxiety, and panic attacks.

a. Did PA Play owe Ashton a duty of care? Did Jamie Perkins? Did the defendants owe Teresa a duty of care? Discuss your answer with reference to at least two elements of the duty of care.

b. What was the standard of care owed by the daycare and the counsellor to the plaintiffs?

c. Were the actions of PA Play and Jamie Perkins the cause in fact of Teresa Smart's job loss?

d. Were the actions of PA Play and Jamie Perkins the cause in law of Teresa Smart's job-loss damages?

Defences, Limits on Liability, and Remedies

13

OVERVIEW

LEARNING OUTCOMES

After completing this chapter, you should be able to:

- List at least three defences to negligence.

- Explain the effect of the plaintiff's own negligence on the defendant's liability.

- Explain how damages are apportioned when parties not before the court are partially responsible for harm to a plaintiff.

- Describe the purposes for which courts order tort remedies.

- Distinguish between general damages and special damages.

- Distinguish between aggravated and punitive damages and understand the circumstances under which either will be awarded.

- Discuss some of the challenges of calculating damages in cases involving permanent or catastrophic injury.

INTRODUCTION

As you learned in the previous chapter, in a negligence case, the plaintiff bears the burden of proving that the defendant had a duty of care and breached it, causing compensable harm to the plaintiff. If the plaintiff can prove all these elements on a balance of probabilities, he or she will generally be entitled to a remedy.

In the great majority of negligence cases, a defendant seeking to avoid liability will do so by trying to prevent the plaintiff from proving at least one of the three elements of negligence (wrongful conduct, causation, and harm). In a few cases, however, the facts permit the defendant to attempt to prove a specific defence.

The concept of specific defences has already been introduced in this book: a specific defence is a set of circumstances that, when proven, has been recognized in previous court decisions as a bar to liability. As you learned in Chapter 11, true defences are those that, when proven, completely eliminate the liability of the defendant. Partial defences serve only to reduce the defendant's liability in damages.

In this chapter, you will learn about the defences that can be argued in response to a plaintiff's allegations of negligence. These defences are few and, in recent years, courts and legislatures have taken steps to limit their application to very narrow circumstances; as a result, they are often argued in addition to a general defence based on trying to refute the plaintiff's proof of the elements of negligence.

You will also learn about the remedies that courts award to successful plaintiffs, and the purposes behind those remedies. You will learn the difference between the two most common forms of damages: general damages and special damages; and between two rarer categories of damages: aggravated damages and punitive damages. We will also briefly introduce some of the challenges faced by plaintiffs who must calculate damages for a permanent or catastrophic injury.

DEFENCES TO NEGLIGENCE

Limitation Periods

As you learned in the context of intentional torts, "limitation period" is not actually a defence. However, a claim that is filed beyond the applicable statutory limitation period is considered to be "statute-barred" unless the plaintiff can prove that the material facts that support the claim were not discoverable (known or capable of being known) until after the limitation period had expired.

The same principles—limitation period applies unless the discoverability rule requires otherwise—apply in negligence cases.

Voluntary Assumption of Risk

volenti non fit injuria
(Latin) "no harm is done to someone who is willing"; a true defence that negates the defendant's liability based on the plaintiff's understanding and acceptance of the risks

A long-standing defence in negligence law is voluntary assumption of risk, or **volenti non fit injuria**. This defence, sometimes called simply *volenti*, translates literally as "no harm is done to someone who is willing." *Volenti* is a true defence, which means that when it is proven, it completely negates the defendant's liability in negligence.

In order to successfully argue *volenti*, the defendant must prove two things:

1. that the plaintiff *understood and accepted*, either *expressly* or *impliedly*, the virtually certain risk of injury that was involved in the activity; and

2. that *both* plaintiff and defendant understood that the *defendant assumed no responsibility to take due care* for the safety of the plaintiff, and the *plaintiff did not expect the defendant to assume that responsibility.*

An express acceptance of risk could be shown through the plaintiff's signature on a waiver exempting the defendant from liability.

Implied acceptance of risk is harder to prove than express acceptance, but is more often seen in these cases. Implied acceptance of risk is generally proved by asking the judge to draw inferences from the plaintiff's conduct—for example, a sober plaintiff knowingly accepts a ride from a very drunk driver.

In recent times, and especially since the decision in *Joe v. Paradis*[1] (see the Case in Point feature below), courts have added an important third element to the *volenti* defence:

3. The plaintiff must have accepted not only the physical risks of the activity, but also the legal risks. In other words, *in undertaking the activity, the plaintiff must have communicated that he or she was giving up a legal right to sue in negligence, or there must have been an understanding between the parties to that effect.*

Volenti is not exactly the same as consent, because the plaintiff is not consenting to a specific act of the defendant's (for example, consenting to allow the defendant to kick him during a martial arts demonstration), but rather, is expressing a willingness to engage in risky conduct without the protection that would normally flow from the defendant's duty of care.

Apart from the context of sober people riding in cars driven by drunk people, the *volenti* defence is almost never argued any more. It has been almost completely eclipsed by cases about waivers, which by their nature, are contract-based.

Illegality

The defence of illegality, like voluntary assumption of risk, has a fancy Latin name: ***ex turpi causa non oritur actio***, often shortened to *ex turpi causa*. The literal translation is "an action does not arise out of a shameful cause." This defence, like *volenti*, is a true defence that eliminates the defendant's liability.

Originally, the defence of illegality worked this way: if the plaintiff suffered harm through the negligence of the defendant while the plaintiff was committing an unlawful act, the plaintiff could not recover damages.

However, this defence has been altered and narrowed over the years by the case law. The modern expression of the defence of illegality, at least in Canadian law, can be found in *Hall v. Hebert*,[2] which stands for the principle that a plaintiff will not be permitted to profit from an illegal act or to be reimbursed for the payment of a criminal penalty.

ex turpi causa non oritur actio
(Latin) "an action does not arise out of a shameful cause"; a true defence that eliminates the defendant's liability based on the action's illegality

---

1. *Joe v. Paradis*, 2008 BCCA 57 (CanLII).
2. *Hall v. Hebert*, [1993] 2 S.C.R. 159.

Volenti Defence Requires Understanding of Risks and Agreement to Waive Rights

From: *Joe v. Paradis*, 2008 BCCA 57 (CanLII).

Several important Canadian cases (including *Lehnert v. Stein*[3] and *Hall v. Hebert*) have examined the *volenti* defence against the backdrop of the general evolution of the law of negligence. The judges in these cases have sought to limit the way the defence operates in two important ways. First, the courts have held that the *volenti* defence is not available unless there is an understanding or agreement between the parties that the plaintiff is waiving his or her right to sue the defendant in negligence; and second, for that understanding to be possible, the plaintiff must actually have turned his or her mind to, and understood, the risks involved in the activity.

In *Joe v. Paradis*, neither of these two tests were met. *Joe v. Paradis* was about an accident involving a pickup truck driven by a drunk driver that resulted in a lawsuit by an even drunker passenger. Since neither the driver nor the passenger had any clear recollection of events immediately before, during, and after the crash (the facts had to be provided by a slightly more sober passenger), the court found that "there was no evidence that the parties ever considered the question of legal liability in the event of an accident, let alone tacitly agreed to waive liability for negligent driving in that event." The court held that to free the defendant from all liability under these circumstances would be to "[manipulate] the *volenti* doctrine to avoid the comparative fault regime of the *Negligence Act*."

According to the authors of a well-respected British legal text,[4] this narrowing of the defence of *volenti* is warranted because *volenti* is a complete defence (that is, it eliminates the liability of the defendant if proven) and therefore, the way it operates is inconsistent with the modern theory of contribution in negligence—that is, all the parties who shared in causing harm should share in compensating for it.

The reasoning in *Joe v. Paradis* was followed by the Ontario Court of Appeal in *Jelco Construction Limited v. Vasco (Euca Welding)*,[5] placing this new narrow view of *volenti* well on its way to becoming solid Canadian law.

The court in *Hall v. Hebert* also said of the defence:

> It will be available wherever the conduct of the plaintiff giving rise to the claim is so tainted with criminality or culpable immorality that as a matter of public policy the court will not assist him to recover.

This new emphasis on profit and reimbursement means that the defence is not used much anymore in personal injury cases. One example of its use, however, is the decision in *Baird v. R.*[6]

The facts in *Baird* were very interesting. Baird (the plaintiff) and his girlfriend were travelling by car and checked into a British Columbia motel late one night.

---

3. *Lehnert v. Stein*, [1963] S.C.R. 38 at 44, 36 D.L.R. (2d) 159.
4. Anthony Dugdale & Michael A. Jones, eds., *Clerk & Lindsell on Torts*, 20th ed. (London: Sweet & Maxwell, 2010).
5. *Jelco Construction Limited v. Vasco (Euca Welding)*, 2010 ONCA 444 (CanLII).
6. *Baird v. R.*, 1992 CanLII 937 (B.C.C.A.).

While checking in, they were loud and boisterous and were flourishing a considerable amount of cash. They ultimately requested that the clerk keep several thousand dollars in cash in the motel's main safe overnight.

The motel clerk became suspicious and called police. The police attended at the motel in the morning and arrested Baird. They also seized the money from the safe. The previous day, there had been a big heist on a Loomis armoured car on the Gardiner Expressway in Toronto. The police somehow connected Baird (who was now in British Columbia) with this heist.

While in police custody, Baird partially confessed to the robbery, but then refused to give a detailed statement without his lawyer present. Surprisingly, a couple of days later, the police released him, and he was never charged in connection with the heist.

Baird later sued the government for his cash back (the cash the police took from the safe). The government argued *ex turpi causa* (illegality). The court allowed the argument and refused to grant Baird his money back, even though Baird was never charged or convicted in connection with the theft. The court ruled that Baird's semi-confession was enough evidence of his wrongdoing to allow the government to succeed in relying on the illegality defence.

Contributory Negligence

By far the most commonly argued defence in negligence cases is **contributory negligence**. Unlike *volenti* and illegality, contributory negligence is not a true defence: if successfully proven, it reduces, but does not normally eliminate, the damages payable by the defendant.

contributory negligence
a partial defence that reduces the defendant's liability on the basis of the plaintiff's own negligence

Historically, if a defendant could prove that the plaintiff was contributorily negligent, the defendant was completely absolved from liability. That rule was eventually changed to better reflect the parties' shared responsibility. Provincial legislation (in Ontario, the *Negligence Act*;[7] counterparts exist in other jurisdictions) now makes it clear that where there is contributory negligence, the damages will be **apportioned** among all negligent parties, whether they are defendants or plaintiffs.

apportionment
the practice of awarding damages based on the contribution of each negligent party

To succeed in proving contributory negligence, the defendant must prove that the plaintiff's own actions (usually in themselves negligent) contributed to the harm that the plaintiff suffered. The principle of contributory negligence is based on the notion that plaintiffs have a duty to take precautions for their *own* safety, and cannot simply count on the defendant to protect them.

The classic contributory negligence scenario involves a plaintiff being in a car crash that was the defendant's fault and suffering injuries. If the evidence suggests that the plaintiff was not wearing a seat belt, and that his injuries resulted in part from not wearing a seat belt, the plaintiff will be held to be contributorily negligent, and will recover only the share of his losses that did *not* relate to not wearing a seat belt.

---

7. *Negligence Act*, R.S.O. 1990, c. N.1.

Post-Operative Smoking Against Doctor's Orders Leads to Contributory Negligence Finding

From: *Dumais v. Hamilton*, 1998 ABCA 218 (CanLII).

A patient visited a surgeon to get a "tummy tuck" operation. In this patient's case, the operation was elective—it was not a medically necessary procedure, but rather done for cosmetic reasons (to make the plaintiff look slimmer).

In taking the plaintiff's medical history, the surgeon learned that she was a smoker. He advised her that she would need to cut back on smoking in the weeks leading up to the surgery, and that she had to refrain from smoking at all for at least a week after surgery. The surgeon did not provide a reason for these instructions.

The patient had the surgery on March 9. On March 11, while still in the hospital, she told the surgeon she had smoked. He repeated his instructions not to smoke, and wrote on her chart "No smoking!"

The patient did not smoke in the hospital anymore, but resumed smoking after she was discharged on March 13, four days after her surgery. Her incision healed badly. She required readmission to hospital on March 24, but by April 5, when she had to be readmitted again, large amounts of skin on her stomach had died, leaving her permanently disfigured. Skin necrosis is a known but rare complication of this type of surgery. Smoking makes it more likely to occur.

She sued the surgeon.

At her trial, the court considered whether the patient should be considered contributorily negligent for the harm that occurred to her because she smoked against doctor's orders. The court held that she was *not* negligent, because the doctor failed to tell her *why* she should not smoke.

The surgeon appealed. The Court of Appeal did find the patient contributorily negligent, explaining that she had been given clear and repeated warnings not to smoke, and that she knowingly ignored those warnings. While it would have been preferable for the doctor to have explained the reasons for avoiding smoking, warning the patient repeatedly was enough. Liability was apportioned 50/50 between the patient and the doctor.

Apportioning Liability Among Multiple Tortfeasors

The concept of contributory negligence was created to ensure that where the plaintiff had a share in causing the harm to himself or herself, he or she would be responsible for bearing the burden of a share of the loss. But what about situations in which multiple individuals *other* than the plaintiff have contributed to the harm?

Courts also recognize that multiple defendants may share in responsibility for harm and may not share that responsibility equally. Fairness to defendants requires that the court attempt to apportion liability among them.

In coming to a decision about liability (who owed a duty of care to the plaintiff, and who breached it, causing harm), courts dealing with multiple tortfeasors typically attempt to express the sharing of liability in the form of a percentage—for example, the court may find that Defendant A was responsible for 60 percent of the harm, Defendant B was responsible for 25 percent, and the plaintiff was responsible for the remaining 15 percent. This apportionment is provided for under statute in all Canadian jurisdictions (the statutes are typically called *Negligence Act*, *Contributory Negligence Act*, or *Tortfeasors Act*).

However, the court retains a strong interest in ensuring that the plaintiff is properly compensated for his or her injuries, whether or not all of the defendants who were responsible for the harm are before the court or can afford to pay. For this reason, the attribution of liability as between defendants is not always completely fair.

As a general rule, under Canadian common law, defendants who cause harm to a plaintiff have **joint and several liability** for that harm. This means that where only one or some of the tortfeasors are before the court, the court can require that tortfeasor (or tortfeasors) to pay compensation for *all* of the harm done to the plaintiff, even if that tortfeasor was responsible for causing only a portion of it.

Where the court requires a tortfeasor to pay compensation for a greater share of the harm to the plaintiff than that for which the tortfeasor was responsible, the overpaying tortfeasor has a right to sue other tortfeasors for reimbursement.

Because having to sue other tortfeasors requires bearing the costs of a whole separate proceeding, most defendants, when served with a statement of claim, attempt to have all other potential defendants added to the litigation or add cross-claims or third-party claims in an attempt to restrict their own liability.

In an interesting twist on the right to obtain a contribution from a defendant not before the court, in some cases, a defendant is successful in recovering from a co-tortfeasor in this way even if there was no court judgment—just a settlement entered into between the litigation parties: see, for example, *A.R. (Al) Smith Ltd. v. Turner.*[8]

joint and several liability
the principle that all tortfeasors are collectively and individually liable for the plaintiff's loss

REMEDIES

Purposes of Tort Remedies

From the plaintiff's perspective, the main purpose in bringing a lawsuit in tort is to obtain a remedy from the court. A remedy is any order designed to rectify the harm done by the defendant to the plaintiff.

By far, the most common purpose for ordering a remedy in a tort case is compensation. Because litigation is expensive, it is very unusual for a plaintiff to pursue it under circumstances where there was little actual harm, simply to "teach the defendant a lesson." Compensatory remedies are designed to "repay" the plaintiff, in money, for losses suffered (even if those losses were not money losses, but rather, losses of another type, for example, loss of quality of life).

Compensation is not the only possible purpose of a tort remedy. Other possible purposes or goals that a court may keep in mind when ordering a remedy include:

- **denunciation** of the defendant's wrongful act;
- **deterrence** (giving a reason for this defendant, and for other potential defendants, to avoid doing the same kind of harm in future); and
- punishment.

denunciation
the formal or public expression of disapproval (often on moral grounds and often on behalf of civil society) of an act or omission

deterrence
a sanction imposed by the court upon a defendant designed to reduce the likelihood of reoffence

---

8. *A.R. (Al) Smith Ltd. v. Turner*, [1985] 2 W.W.R. 424 (B.C. Co. Ct.).

Because civil litigation is private justice (government does not take responsibility for it) and because of the cost, denunciation, deterrence, and punishment are far less common purposes for remedies in tort than they are in the criminal law. As we have noted throughout this book, some of the actions that can give rise to an action in tort (especially intentional torts) could also support a criminal charge; and so some defendants are required to pay a compensatory remedy in a civil tort suit, but may also be subject to a punitive remedy in a criminal prosecution.

Compensatory Remedies

Damages are the usual compensatory remedy.

Damages are calculated by reference to the nature and seriousness of the harm, and also take into account actual out-of-pocket financial losses.

There are two categories of compensatory damages awarded in tort cases: general damages and special damages. These labels are unfortunately not very helpful when trying to remember which is which.

Special Damages

special damages
damages that are known and described at the time of trial

Despite the name, **special damages** are the more commonplace category of damages, and those best understood by the general public.

Falling into the category of special damages are those damages that are precisely known and described (and often supported with receipts) by the time of trial. For example, special damages include:

- money actually spent to repair something (for example, a dock that was damaged when a boat was driven into it);
- medical bills for treatment received; and
- lost income caused by an injury, in cases where the plaintiff's income was regular (for example, where the plaintiff received a set hourly, weekly, or daily wage and missed a set amount of work).

Special damages are not usually controversial, but may be challenged where, for example, repair costs are inordinately high or far higher than the market average, or where the plaintiff has sought an expensive unconventional treatment unsupported by medical evidence or clinical trials.

General Damages

general damages
estimated damages unsupported by evidence of value

General damages are damages not capable of being supported by receipts or other evidence of value. Instead, they are estimated and subjective.

General damages are designed to compensate for past, present, or future losses that are not easily quantified at the time of trial and that, in the case of future losses, may not be fully predictable. The classic example of a category of general damages is "pain and suffering."

As you might imagine, the quantum of general damages is often vigorously opposed by the defence, and often requires determination by a court. General damages are generally the "negotiable" part of a plaintiff's damages claim—the part that the plaintiff may "estimate high" to encourage an acceptable settlement.

General damages have been awarded for:

- *past* pain and suffering;
- *future* pain and suffering;
- *past* or *future* loss of quality of life (for example, losing the ability to play a favourite sport because of an injury);
- *past* or *future* loss of income, where income cannot be precisely calculated;
- loss of life expectancy;
- the *future* cost of medical care, physiotherapy, and so on; and
- loss of business reputation.

Compared with special damages, general damages require much more effort to prove in court. They are typically proved by the testimony of witnesses, including expert witnesses. As explained in Chapter 12, a plaintiff typically seeks to prove general damages by quantifying in monetary terms the gap between his or her condition before the defendant's wrongful act and afterward. In doing so, the plaintiff may call individuals who know him or her personally and who can testify to the change in his or her condition, as well as experts who can testify about the typical long-term prognosis of a particular kind of injury or illness.

Punitive Damages

Special damages and general damages are awarded in a wide range of tort cases. The third category of damages—**punitive damages**—is awarded much less often. Punitive damages are reserved for rare cases in which the court believes that damages should serve not only a compensatory function, but also other functions such as denunciation and deterrence.

punitive damages
a remedy awarded by the court for purposes beyond compensation, such as denunciation or deterrence

Punitive damages, sometimes called "exemplary damages," do not relate directly to the harm done. Instead, they are awarded by the court in exceptional circumstances to punish or deter the defendant or other potential defendants.

Punitive damages are typically awarded where the defendant's conduct was unusually malicious, callous, outrageous, or flagrant, or where the defendant profited financially from the tort. Because these factors suggest a *mens rea* element, punitive damages are most commonly—but not exclusively—awarded in intentional tort cases, where it is clear that the defendant had the opportunity to avoid the intentional act, but did it anyway. However, punitive damages have been awarded in negligence scenarios as well, for example, in product liability cases (which are discussed in the next chapter) where the defendant realized that its product was unsafe, yet did not act quickly to take it off the market.

Although US punitive damages awards can be very high, in Canada, these awards tend to be more modest (for example, an extra $10,000 may be awarded). An exception is cases in which the defendant's tort would have been easily prevented but was not and harmed a large number of people—for example, a serious preventable workplace accident.

Aggravated Damages

Though often confused with punitive damages, **aggravated damages** are *not* the same.

Aggravated damages fall somewhere between general and punitive damages in their nature and are awarded in situations where, due to the defendant's outrageous conduct, the harm is more severe than it would have otherwise been.

For example, consider a situation in which a plaintiff underwent surgery provided by a person who posed as a plastic surgeon, but who was not qualified as such. The surgeon performed a liposuction procedure on the plaintiff without bothering to sterilize the equipment, and the resulting infection that the plaintiff developed made the bad liposuction job look even worse because of the extreme swelling and severe scarring. In a case like this, the defendant was not only negligent, but flagrantly so, because he or she misled the plaintiff about his or her credentials and knowingly skipped an essential step (sterilizing the equipment). In such a case, the plaintiff would likely succeed in obtaining an award of aggravated damages.

Major Personal Injury Claims

Although the same general principles of damages apply to all tort cases, a particular subset of cases—major personal injury claims—are especially complex from a damages standpoint.

These claims are those in which there is an extreme and enduring difference in the condition of the plaintiff before the accident (or illness) and afterward. In these cases, the defendant may be required to pay a massive damages award designed to compensate the plaintiff for losses that extend well into the future, sometimes for the rest of the plaintiff's life.

For example, if a normal four-year-old boy is hit by a car and suffers a massive brain injury that does not reduce his life expectancy, but *does* eliminate his earning capacity, the plaintiff has to project damages based on questions such as the following:

- What kind of career would the plaintiff have chosen?
- Suppose the court decides he would have been a contractor, like his father. What will a contractor be earning in the year 2070?
- At what age would the plaintiff have retired, had he been able to work?
- If the plaintiff needs 24-hour nursing care, what will nursing care cost in the year 2095?

These are daunting questions and require that the plaintiff hire actuaries to estimate the damages.

To complicate things further, the award is adjusted so that interest earned on a present-day investment of the damages will actually provide for the damages, which are paid out in installments over time. For example, the actuaries may decide that in order to replace his income and pay for his future nursing care, the lifetime cost for the plaintiff who is now four years old is $6 million in 2012 dollars. But the amount needs to be adjusted to reflect inflation, so perhaps it is really $11 million; but then again, investing the money for the next 80 years and paying it out bit by bit will generate considerable interest, presuming the markets perform in the future in similar ways as they have performed in the past. As you can see, any amount of damages that is calculated taking all these factors into account will be highly speculative; however, it is the task of the plaintiff (and his experts) to convince the court of the reasonableness of all aspects of the speculation.

LAW IN PRACTICE
"Hot-Tubbing" Experts?

An evidence trend that began in Australia in the 1970s has attracted some recent attention here in Canada. The practice, called "hot-tubbing," involves the presentation of expert evidence for both sides of the dispute through a single panel presentation.

Certain kinds of cases—including complex personal injury litigation—require the presentation of a great deal of expert evidence, some of it contradictory. When this evidence is presented using the traditional rules of court, all of the prosecution's witnesses go first (including experts, regardless of the topic they are discussing). The defence experts who will be refuting the evidence of these prosecution experts may not testify until several days later, and the time lag between the sets of conflicting testimony can be confusing for the trier of fact.

The "hot-tubbing" method overcomes some of these problems by bringing together all the expert witnesses on a particular topic (say, the prognosis for the plaintiff's recovery and expectations about his or her future capabilities) from both sides. The members of the panel of witnesses typically take turns summarizing their information, then discuss the discrepancies in that information, then respond to questions from the bench, and then are cross-examined by the opposing counsel. The result is that all the expert evidence on a particular issue is presented at once, making it easier for the judge and/or jury to sort it out.

Expert hot-tubbing is not common in general civil litigation in Canada (it can be compelled only in certain federal courts at the moment), but it is more widely used and seems to be growing in popularity in certain administrative tribunal decisions—for example, those of the Ontario Municipal Board.

Not all lawyers support hot-tubbing: those who are opposed sometimes suggest that the practice makes it difficult for counsel to control the delivery of evidence (your own side's expert may say certain things that are not completely supportive of your case, and about which you would have avoided questioning that witness). However, it offers undeniable advantages to the trier of fact in a complex case, and it remains to be seen whether the practice will eventually be embraced here.

Fatal Accidents

In some cases, a defendant's wrongful act leads to the death of the plaintiff.

At first blush, it would seem that, because damages are a compensatory remedy and the plaintiff is deceased, there is no one to compensate. Also, a dead plaintiff, compared with a severely disabled one, has far less future loss when items such as nursing care are considered. Is it possible that a defendant is "off the hook" for damages when he or she actually kills the plaintiff instead of wounding him?

The answer is, generally not. While the plaintiff may have little in the way of future loss, the plaintiff may have dependants—for example, children or elderly parents—who will be placed in a precarious economic position by his or her death. Even certain individuals who were not financially dependent on the plaintiff (for example, a wife who has always earned her own money) may suffer other forms of loss (such as the loss of care and companionship) upon his death.

When an individual is killed as the result of a tort, his or her estate becomes the plaintiff in a lawsuit against the defendant. There are statutes in most jurisdictions (in Ontario, the *Trustee Act*[9]) that establish rules for such lawsuits.

Other rights against a defendant exist under provincial family law statutes, which often provide for claims for "pecuniary benefits" (support) for dependants.

Preventive Remedies

In some tort or quasi-tort cases, the plaintiff seeks not damages for actual harm, but prevention of potential future harm. In these cases, the court may be persuaded to act before the harm occurs to prevent the tort from happening in the first place. To do so, the court will order a preventive remedy.

Injunctions

injunction
a court order intended to prevent future harm, enjoining a defendant to cease an activity or not do it at all

A common remedy sought to prevent future harm is an **injunction**.

Courts have the power to enjoin defendants (order an injunction against them) who are in the midst of some kind of action (for example, clear-cutting a tract of land) or who are about to do something (for example, use a trademark without authorization on a product). The effect of the order is to make the defendant subject to a penalty should the defendant continue or proceed.

For example, where a defendant is widely advertising that he or she will be putting on a Woodstock-style concert in his or her field, a neighbouring landowner may pursue an injunction to prevent the defendant from going through with it; or, where one neighbour is pumping large quantities of water out of a stream that runs through several properties, the other property owners may seek an injunction to stop the pumping to prevent the stream from drying up.

In order to obtain an injunction, a plaintiff generally needs to establish that if the defendant were to do or complete the act, the plaintiff would be entitled to damages from the defendant. A court is more likely to order an injunction in circumstances where the act that the defendant is about to undertake is irreversible, or where stopping the act at this point will greatly reduce the damages that the defendant would owe to the plaintiff.

---

9. *Trustee Act*, R.S.O. 1990, c. T.23.

Declaratory Orders

A declaratory order is an order "declaring," with the force of law, a certain fact. In general, a declaratory order states that a certain person has a certain legal right, which may be important in a case where a defendant or potential defendant seems to be about to violate that right.

For example, where one neighbour has drawn up plans to chop down a particular stand of trees, and another neighbour claims that a portion of the treed land belongs to him or her or to the municipality, the second neighbour may, instead of asking for an injunction, ask the court to make an order declaring that the disputed land does not belong to the person who wants to cut down the trees.

Ex Parte Orders

Because of their urgent nature, the court will sometimes grant injunctions or declaratory orders on an *ex parte* basis, which means, without having the defendant before the court. The court generally prefers, in the interests of fairness, to have both parties participate in any hearing that might affect them; however, where the situation is an emergency, the court may determine that the harm that would result from a delay to await the participation of the other party would outweigh the loss of fairness. This is especially true if the order is for an injunction that simply prevents the defendant from proceeding, because if it turns out that the order was unwarranted, the defendant could simply have it overturned on appeal.

CHAPTER SUMMARY

The most common defence to a negligence action is what is known as a general defence, meaning the defendant simply tries to refute the plaintiff's proof of at least one of the elements of negligence. Another common general defence is the "defence" of limitation period—in other words, an argument by the defendant that the plaintiff's action is statute-barred. Just as you saw in intentional tort cases, unless the plaintiff can use the discoverability rule to its advantage, an action brought outside the limitation period will not succeed.

Because these are general defences to negligence, there are a few specific defences—the kind that require that the defendant prove certain elements of his or her own. The first of those is the defence of *volenti non fit injuria* ("*volenti*"), also known as voluntary assumption of risk.

A defendant who is attempting to rely on the defence of *volenti* must prove that the plaintiff knew that there was an almost certain risk of injury associated with an activity involving the defendant, and knew the defendant would not take any steps to protect the plaintiff, and yet expressly or impliedly agreed to participate in the activity anyway. In modern *volenti* cases, it is also sometimes necessary for the plaintiff to understand that by participating in the activity, he or she is giving up a right to any legal remedy against the defendant should an injury occur. In many modern cases, *volenti* is established through the use of waivers, which introduces an element of contract law into the traditional tort analysis.

The second specific defence to negligence is *ex turpi causa non oritur actio* ("*ex turpi causa*"), also known as the defence of illegality. When it was first developed, this defence provided that if the plaintiff suffered harm through the negligence of the defendant while the plaintiff was committing an unlawful act, the plaintiff could not recover damages. Modern case decisions have narrowed the scope of this defence, so that now a plaintiff who has committed an unlawful act cannot seek reimbursement of a fine or penalty or the return of money or goods obtained illegally (for example, a drug dealer cannot sue a customer for conversion if the customer stole drugs and failed to pay).

The most commonly argued specific defence to negligence is contributory negligence. To succeed in proving contributory negligence, the defendant must prove that the plaintiff's own actions (usually in themselves negligent) contributed to the harm that the plaintiff suffered. The principle of contributory negligence is based on the notion that plaintiffs have a duty to take precautions for their *own* safety, and cannot simply count on the defendant to protect them.

Besides requiring the plaintiff to bear some of the responsibility for a loss, a defendant can also seek to have the loss shared by other defendants who contributed to the harm. Under Canadian common law, defendants who cause harm to a plaintiff have joint and several liability for compensating the plaintiff. This means that a court can require any single tortfeasor to pay compensation for *all* of the harm done to the plaintiff, even if that tortfeasor was responsible for causing only a portion of it. The court will then permit tortfeasors who have borne more than their fair share of damages to sue other tortfeasors for reimbursement.

Remedies are also covered in this chapter. The most common purpose for the awards made to successful plaintiffs is compensation (not punishment or deterrence, as seen in the criminal context). Compensation takes the form of damages (a money payment).

Damages fall into four principal categories: special damages, general damages, punitive damages, and aggravated damages. Special damages are defined as out-of-pocket costs (for example, medical bills, a repair bill, loss of past income) that can be quantified before the trial begins.

General damages are a more subjective category of damages designed to compensate the plaintiff for non-financial losses, such as pain and suffering or loss of quality of life. Also included in general damages are amounts designed to compensate the plaintiff for future losses (for example, loss of earning capacity or life expectancy) that cannot be accurately quantified at the time of trial.

Punitive damages are a rare category of damages that have a punitive or deterrent (rather than compensatory) purpose and are designed to send a message that the defendant's behaviour has been flagrant, callous, malicious, or otherwise worthy of punishment. Finally, aggravated damages are a category of damages awarded where some aspect of the defendant's behaviour unnecessarily increased the harm to the plaintiff flowing from the defendant's activity.

While most tort plaintiffs seek damages as their remedy, in a few cases, the plaintiff seeks instead to *prevent* harm by requesting a preventive remedy. The two main types of preventive remedies are injunctions (an order that the defendant cease an activity, or not do it at all) or declaratory orders (usually, an order clarifying one party's legal rights). In emergency circumstances, a preventive order can sometimes be obtained on an *ex parte* basis, meaning without the defendant present in court.

KEY TERMS

aggravated damages
apportionment
contributory negligence
denunciation
deterrence
ex turpi causa non oritur actio

general damages
injunction
joint and several liability
punitive damages
special damages
volenti non fit injuria

REVIEW QUESTIONS

True or False?

1. For a defendant to succeed in proving the defence of *volenti*, he must establish that the plaintiff both understood and turned her mind to the risks associated with the activity that led to injury.
2. Punitive damages may be available in a tort case based on negligence.
3. A plaintiff can sue for either special damages or general damages, but not both.
4. The "defence" of limitation period can be raised only in intentional tort cases, not in negligence cases.
5. An injunction is available only if the action the plaintiff seeks to enjoin (prevent) has not yet begun.
6. Where the court finds that a person who is not part of the litigation was partially responsible for the plaintiff's injuries, the court can require the defendants who *are* part of the litigation to pay that person's share of the damages.
7. Compensation is the only possible purpose of a tort remedy.
8. Damages for "pain and suffering" are an example of special damages.
9. A common defence to a negligence claim is that the applicable statutory limitation period has expired.
10. Illegality is a true defence to negligence.

Fill in the Blanks

1. A common remedy sought to prevent future harm is
    an _____.

2. A long-standing defence in negligence law
    is _____ _____ of risk, or *volenti non fit
    injuria.*

3. By far the most commonly argued defence in negligence cases
    is _____ _____.

4. Because of their urgent nature, the court will sometimes grant injunctions
    or declaratory orders on an ____ _____ basis, which means without
    having the defendant before the court.

5. By far the most common purpose for ordering a remedy in tort
    is _____.

6. Where there is contributory negligence, the damages will
    be _____ among all negligent parties, whether they are
    defendants or plaintiffs.

7. Lost income caused by injury, money spent to repair something, medical
    bills for treatment received: these are examples
    of _____ _____, which are the most
    commonplace category of damages.

8. An evidence trend known as "_____," which
    began in Australia in the 1970s, involves presenting expert evidence for
    both sides of the dispute through a single panel presentation.

9. Under Canadian common law, defendants who cause harm to a plaintiff
    have _____ and _____ liability, which means that
    where only one or some of the tortfeasors are before the court, the court
    can require that tortfeasor (or tortfeasors) to pay compensation for all of the
    harm done to the plaintiff, even if that tortfeasor was responsible for only
    some of the harm.

10. _____ _____ are damages not capable
    of being supported by receipts or other evidence of value.

Short Answer

1. Explain the difference between punitive damages and aggravated damages.

2. Why are some lawyers not supportive of the evidence trend known as
    "hot-tubbing"?

3. In what contexts is the *volenti* defence used nowadays, and why is it not
    more widely used?

4. How does a defendant prove contributory negligence, and what principle is
    it based on?

5. Why is the attribution of liability between defendants not always completely fair?

6. What is the difference between *volenti* and consent, as a defence to negligence?

7. What are special damages, and under what circumstances are they controversial?

8. Why is the quantum of general damages often vigorously opposed by the defence?

9. Why are major personal injury claims especially complex from a damages standpoint?

EXERCISES

1. Twelve-year-old George was hit by a snowplow. Both his legs were badly broken, requiring three separate surgeries, a one-month hospital stay, and six months of physiotherapy. George's right arm was severed just below the elbow, a devastating injury for him, considering that he was a nationally ranked hockey player in his age category and had planned, if he did not make the NHL, to take over his father's plumbing business. The accident occurred because the snowplow driver was "doing doughnuts" in the driveway of a hockey arena as a youth hockey team was exiting the building.

   a. Which categories of damages should George claim in his statement of claim?

   b. If you suggested George should claim general damages, give at least two examples of the types of harm he should claim for.

   c. If you suggested George should claim special damages, give at least four examples of the types of harm he should claim for.

2. Tammy was a heroin addict. Charles was her dealer. Tammy owed Charles $4,000 and had been successfully avoiding him for weeks, until one night around 3 a.m., while out driving, she realized he was following her in his car. After trying unsuccessfully to lose him for several blocks, Tammy pulled over, took a crowbar from the floor of her car, and approached Charles's car, which had also pulled over. Tammy stood in front of Charles's car and held up the crowbar, prepared to smash Charles's windshield if he got out of his car. Charles rolled down his window to talk to Tammy. The conversation became heated. Inadvertently, Charles's foot slipped off the brake and the car hit Tammy, running her over and pinning her under the car. She was permanently disabled in the accident.

   Do you believe that Tammy would be barred from recovering damages under the doctrine of illegality? In the alternative, do you believe that Charles will be found not liable for Tammy's injuries based on the defence of *volenti*? Discuss.

3. Go online and find three different waivers—the kind used by providers of high-risk activities (for example, extreme sports) in an attempt to avoid liability in negligence. Read the waivers and compare them. Based on your understanding of negligence law, tort law generally, and defences to torts, which waiver do you think will be most effective? Explain your choice.

Special Classes
of Liability

14

OVERVIEW

LEARNING OUTCOMES

After completing this chapter, you should be able to:

- Understand the concept of occupiers' liability and know what duty an occupier owes to various entrants to a property.

- Explain product liability and how it permits some manufacturers and others to be held liable even in the absence of a contract.

- Describe the special standard of care that applies to professionals and how professional liability is assessed.

- Define "negligent misrepresentation" and describe the elements required to establish liability for it.

- Understand the circumstances under which one party can be held liable for the wrongful acts of another.

- List exceptional situations in which a party who is not morally culpable or even careless might be held liable under the doctrines of strict or absolute liability.

INTRODUCTION

As the law of negligence evolved, certain distinct branches in the doctrine began to develop. The concepts of negligence were found by many plaintiffs to be particularly well-suited to certain kinds of fact situations—for example, one person hurt himself or herself on another person's land, or a professional provided substandard service to a client.

These groups of cases with similar facts gave rise to subdoctrines with their own—often complex—sets of rules. In many of these cases, to assist in organizing the doctrines or in managing their details, legislatures have passed statutes that codify the law.

In this chapter, you will be introduced to the most important subdoctrines of negligence law: occupiers' liability, product liability, professional malpractice or negligence, negligent misrepresentation, strict liability, and vicarious liability.

OCCUPIERS' LIABILITY

occupiers' liability
the duty of care that those who occupy real property (through ownership or lease) owe to people who visit or trespass

Occupiers' liability is (or, in some jurisdictions, including Ontario, *was*) a subclass of negligence that developed as a self-contained category. Many provinces have replaced the common law of occupiers' liability with an occupiers' liability statute. In Ontario (though not in every province), the statute completely replaces the common-law doctrine of occupiers' liability.

The codification of occupiers' liability was motivated by at least two separate developments: first, the common law of occupiers' liability had become very complicated and needed to be simplified; and second, our society's beliefs about the rights of entrants to land was evolving more quickly than the common law.

Evolving Views About Entrants' Rights

Over the last century and a half, our views about private property have changed fairly dramatically. There has been a shift in our perception of the value of personal rights compared with property rights.

The early Canadian view of property was closer to that which prevails today in some of the US states: "a man's home is his castle." That saying reflects the right of individuals to do just about anything to protect their property, and the view that those who enter on someone else's property enter at their own risk.

The modern Canadian approach, by distinction, reflects a much greater emphasis on human rights and safety, and holds that our rights to protect our property are subordinate to our duty to promote safety.

As this general view of property shifted, the law of occupiers' liability did not quite keep up. Because the evolution of the common law requires private parties to bring cases on individual facts, it sometimes happens that instead of growing systematically according to a rational plan, the law in a certain area becomes a jumble of exceptions. In the case of occupiers' liability law, the rules concerning an occupier's duty of care varied depending on the "category" of entrant; however, these rules were difficult to apply in practice, because individuals' purposes, upon entering land, are not always completely ascertainable and are not always readily categorized. The result was a complex web of rules that was confusing to both land occupiers and entrants onto their land.

The Old System

As you learned above, occupiers' liability is now governed by statute in most jurisdictions. To understand the doctrine, however, it helps to learn a little about the "old" system and about how it has been simplified to suit modern times.

The common law of occupiers' liability focused on:

1. defining "occupier,"
2. classifying "entrants," and
3. imposing varying duties of care based on the kind of entrant a plaintiff was.

In the process, the analysis moved further and further away from the general, tried-and-true negligence analysis that you learned about in the previous chapter. Most modern occupiers' liability statutes include some of the common-law concepts—such as the concept of "occupier"—but dispense with much of the scheme of classifying entrants.

Under that scheme, there were four general categories of entrants to land: trespassers, licensees, invitees, and contractual entrants. Occupiers owed a different duty of care to each class, as follows:

*   *Trespassers:* This category included, for example, burglars, as well as 10-year-old boy scouts lost in the woods. The duty of care owed to trespassers was extremely low—the occupier had no duty to protect them, but could not set traps on purpose to harm them or catch them.

*   *Licensees:* This category included individuals who had very limited "colour of right" to come onto the occupier's land. Some examples would be snowmobilers in areas where crossing other people's land on a snowmobile is usual, lost children (unless they were counted as trespassers), or political candidates from the party the occupier does *not* like who may come to the door to canvass.[1] This was a very vague category. An occupier might or might not, under the old common law, owe a very low duty of care toward these people. That duty possibly required the occupier to post signs about *unusual* risks on his or her property—for example, "Caution: Volcano" or "Beware of Tiger."

*   *Invitees:* This category included party guests, neighbours who come to a real estate open house, one's children's friends, anybody who wants to put anything in one's mailbox, and so on. The common law required an occupier to protect these entrants from certain known risks; for example, the occupier might be expected not to allow giant icicles to fall onto the heads of these visitors at the front door, or if the porch was falling off, the occupier might

---

1. Some cases have suggested that anyone who walks up the front walk to one's door is an invitee, not a licensee.

be required to cordon it off. Dangerous dogs would need to be locked up; slippery spills would need to be mopped up.

• *Contractual entrants:* These are customers who come in to buy something (until they buy, they may be only invitees). This category also includes service people, for example, a plumber coming onto the property to complete repairs. An occupier would need to take significant measures to protect these entrants, including shovelling the walk for them and regularly inspecting the premises to identify and remedy possible risks.

As you can see, the categories were not very well defined, making it hard for the average person to know what to do to avoid liability. It was also confusing to have to think about what a "trap" might be, or what an "unusual" danger is, or what precautions would be sufficient for which kind of visitor, or at which precise moment an invitee became a contractual entrant, and so on. This generalized confusion led to inconsistent decisions and, ultimately, to the decision to replace the common law with statutes.

Occupiers' Liability Statutes

In Ontario, the statute that governs occupiers' liability is the *Occupiers' Liability Act*.[2] Similar statutes exist in other Canadian jurisdictions.

An essential element of these statutes is a definition of "occupier." The definition provided in s. 1 of the Ontario statute is as follows:

"occupier" includes,

(a) a person who is in physical possession of premises, or

(b) a person who has responsibility for and control over the condition of premises or the activities there carried on, or control over persons allowed to enter the premises,

despite the fact that there is more than one occupier of the same premises.

As was the case under the common law, the "occupier" need not be the holder of title to the property; and in fact, the legal owner may, in some cases, *not* be an occupier, especially if the owner does not often come onto the premises. The reason for this is that the key factor that makes a person an occupier is having control over the condition of the premises.

Control is a logical choice for establishing occupancy because the person who has physical control over the property can affect conditions on the property by:

• creating risks,
• identifying risks,
• warning about risks,
• protecting visitors from risks, or
• fixing or eliminating risks.

---

2. *Occupiers' Liability Act*, R.S.O. 1990, c. O.2.

Just as the statutes define "occupier," they also define "premises." The Ontario definition (in s. 1) is as follows:

"premises" means lands and structures, or either of them, and includes,

(a) water,

(b) ships and vessels,

(c) trailers and portable structures designed or used for residence, business or shelter,

(d) trains, railway cars, vehicles and aircraft, except while in operation.

Occupier's Duty of Care to Entrants

Whereas under the common law there were four separate levels of duty of care to be considered, depending on the classification of an entrant, under most occupiers' liability statutes there are just two: a general duty of care and an exception for wrongdoers.

General Duty of Care

The Ontario statute describes the general duty of care as follows:

3(1) An occupier of premises owes a duty to take *such care as in all the circumstances of the case is reasonable* to see that persons entering on the premises, and the property brought on the premises by those persons *are reasonably safe* while on the premises. [Emphasis added.]

Note also that the duty requires the occupier to take care not only for people, but also for their property.

This duty is very similar to the general duty of care of an ordinary person toward another person, but there are a couple of extra wrinkles: s. 3(2) explains that the duty exists "whether the danger is caused by the condition of the premises or by an activity carried on on the premises."

For example, if a farmer allows the public to come onto his or her property to buy apples at a fruit stand, and allows the area around the stand to become excessively muddy, the farmer will be liable for slip-and-fall injuries due to the condition of the property. If the same farmer instead hosts a tractor-pull event on the property, and a spectator runs out in front of a tractor and is run over, the farmer will be liable because of an activity carried out on the property.

Right to Limit Liability

Because it is important to allow occupiers to occasionally have dangerous conditions existing on their land (for example, during construction), an occupier is permitted, under most statutes, to "restrict, modify, or exclude" his or her duty. To do so, the occupier must generally take clear steps to communicate this exclusion to entrants—for example, by warning them of the risk, by posting signs (including, ideally, signs limiting liability), and, where possible, by physically restricting access to the risky area.

Where an occupier conducts a dangerous activity on his or her land, and occupants visit for the purpose of participating (consider, for example, a rural occupier who has built a dirt-bike course on private property), the best way to "restrict, modify, or exclude" liability is to require the entrants to sign a waiver before participating.

Besides allowing occupiers to restrict their liability for accidents, most occupiers' liability statutes allow entrants to waive their rights to be protected by the occupier's duty of care.

Exception for Wrongdoers

The same provision that, in the Ontario statute, allows entrants to waive their rights to engage in risky activities also allows wrongdoing entrants (trespassers, burglars, and so on) to "waive" their rights to be safe on property:

> 4(1) The duty of care provided for in subsection 3(1) *does not apply in respect of risks willingly assumed by the person who enters on the premises,* but in that case the occupier owes a duty to the person to not create a danger with the deliberate intent of doing harm or damage to the person or his or her property and to not act with reckless disregard of the presence of the person or his or her property.
>
> (2) *A person who is on premises with the intention of committing, or in the commission of, a criminal act shall be deemed to have willingly assumed all risks* and is subject to the duty of care set out in subsection (1). [Emphasis added.]

You may have noticed that this section clearly reflects the history of the common-law development of this area of law; the wording about creating dangers and acting with reckless disregard hearkens back to the common-law rules about not setting traps.

Hard-to-Monitor Property and Benign Trespassers

Sections 4(1) and 4(2) of the *Occupiers' Liability Act,* if they stood alone, would have the potential to apply harshly against accidental trespassers who wander onto land. This is especially true where the land is such that the occupier cannot easily monitor all of it on a regular basis.

Sections 4(3) and 4(4) provide that "benign" trespassers (that is, not criminals, but people who do not have permission to enter and who trespass onto certain kinds of land where it is challenging to monitor the conditions and risks) are subject to the same standard of care as applies to burglars. In other words, the occupier cannot intentionally put benign trespassers at risk or be reckless regarding their safety.

In creating this standard of care, the legislation provides examples of the kinds of properties where it is difficult to monitor or control risks (from s. 4(4)):

> (a) a rural premises that is,
>> (i) used for agricultural purposes, including land under cultivation, orchards, pastures, woodlots and farm ponds,
>> (ii) vacant or undeveloped premises,
>> (iii) forested or wilderness premises;

    (b) golf courses when not open for playing;

    (c) utility rights-of-way and corridors, excluding structures located thereon;

    (d) unopened road allowances;

    (e) private roads reasonably marked by notice as such; and

    (f) recreational trails reasonably marked by notice as such.

Although the very low "don't create risks and don't be reckless" standard for occupiers applies to trespassers on hard-to-monitor land, some cases have suggested that an occupier's standard of care toward trespassers is higher where the property is easier to monitor. Many readers may have heard of cases where, for example, a homeowner has been held liable in negligence for injuries to someone who has been hurt while sneaking into the homeowner's pool uninvited.

As you learned above, if these individuals entered with a criminal purpose, the low standard of care in ss. 4(1) and 4(2) applies. Where an *adult* intentionally trespasses to swim in a pool, he or she likely does have criminal intent—break-and-enter intent, or at least trespassing. But where a *child* does the same thing, the child may *not* be deemed to have criminal intent, because children may not understand that trespassing is illegal. For this reason, property owners with risks on their property—pools, dangerous dogs, uncovered dug foundations—are well-advised to take steps to prevent entry by children. There is a traditional negligence concept, developed through the common law, called the **attractive nuisance** rule that provides that an occupier who creates an attractive nuisance (a big pile of fresh snow, a pond with a swing-out rope over it, a sand pile, etc.) and who does not effectively prevent access to it and/or shield it from view will be liable if children are attracted to it and are hurt.

attractive nuisance
a dangerous condition of property that may arouse the interest of children

PRODUCT LIABILITY

Introduction

As you learned in Part I, where goods purchased under contract fail to live up to the seller's promises or are otherwise defective, the purchaser can usually sue for damages or, in certain cases, rescind the contract altogether. Because the purchaser's options in the event of dissatisfaction are often set out right in the contract itself, pursuing a contract remedy is often fairly straightforward and will, in many cases, satisfy the purchaser.

However, in a few cases, a product may be so defective that it actually causes harm to the purchaser, to his or her property, or both. Especially where the harm is serious, getting one's purchase money back is not a sufficient remedy. Consider, for example, a case where a person purchases hair dye. The dye runs into his or her eyes during rinsing and renders the purchaser permanently blind. Receiving a refund of the $12.95 that was spent on the hair dye is a patently insufficient remedy.

The second important reason that contract law may be inadequate to protect the users of dangerous goods is that those users are not always the purchaser. Consider, for example, a poorly designed commercial trampoline sold to schools and gymnastics clubs. If the trampoline collapses unexpectedly under certain conditions, it will hurt child users at the schools and the clubs, none of whom will have been the purchaser of the trampoline. The same problem arises where dinner party guests are poisoned by food purchased and served by their host, or where a person finds a discarded (and defective) skateboard under a park bench and the wheels fall off the first time he or she drops off a curb.

Individuals may also be harmed by products they receive as gifts, inherit, borrow, buy second-hand, win, or steal. In all of these situations, there is no contract between the manufacturer, distributor, or retailer of the product and the end user. The injured end user has no cause of action in contract.

The doctrine of product liability, which is based on negligence, serves two key purposes: it provides a back-up cause of action where there is no contract between the parties; and it allows the plaintiff to recover damages for losses that contract law does not cover, for example, pain and suffering and damage to other property due to the malfunction of a product.

The rationale for extending liability for harm to end users who have no contract with a manufacturer or distributor is clear: negligence law is based on the concept of a duty of care to a foreseeable victim. It would be difficult for manufacturers or distributors to argue that only the immediate purchaser of a product is a foreseeable victim of its malfunction.

Defining Product Liability: Sources

Product liability might be defined as is tort liability that arises out of negligence on the part of a producer, manufacturer, distributor, or retailer of a product. The negligence that gives rise to liability can arise at one (or more) of three distinct stages in the life cycle of a product:

1. the manufacture of the product,
2. the distribution of the product, or
3. the design of the product.

Negligent Manufacture

We will explain negligent manufacture first because it is the simplest scenario to understand, and the simplest for a plaintiff to prove.

A product will be found, by a court, to have been negligently manufactured where the finished product is found to have deviated from the intended design *and*, as a result, to have harmed the plaintiff.

A negligently manufactured product will generally have been properly designed and, had it been made to the designer's specifications, would have been safe. In these cases, however, somewhere in the manufacturing process, something has gone wrong, and the end product comes off the assembly line, or out of the mould, in a defective state, and then makes its way into the hands of the consumer, who is hurt as a result of the defect.

For example, consider a case in which a manufacturer of seatbelt webbing (the smooth, flat ribbon of nylon that is used for seat belts) has not properly maintained the looms on which the belts are woven. This lack of maintenance causes the loom to malfunction, resulting in lumps and snags in the seatbelt webbing. The lumps are not noticed, the seat belts are installed, and the car is purchased. When the consumer is involved in a collision, a lump in the webbing prevents the seat belt from tightening, and the driver is badly injured as a result. This driver would likely be able to sue the seatbelt manufacturer, basing his case on the doctrine of product liability due to negligent manufacture.

From the defendant's perspective, negligent manufacture presents a lower total risk, from a liability perspective, than does negligent design, because it tends to affect only certain batches of a product, and not the entire inventory.

Negligent Distribution

Negligent distribution is the rarest of the three product liability scenarios.

A product is said to be negligently distributed when there is nothing inherently wrong with the product's design or manufacture, but something goes wrong in the distribution process and harm results.

The most common way a product's distribution can do harm relates to the nature of the end user. Some products—notably drugs, but also personal safety devices and even clothing—are intended for users with a particular profile: for example, someone who has a particular health condition (and not others) or is a particular size, age, or gender. The product may be designed to be safe for this person but *not* for other people (consider, for example, a women's blouse with buttons that is sold instead as a baby's christening gown, and leads to the baby choking on a button when left unattended).

Products that are safe for certain users and not others (especially drugs) often have restrictions on how they are to be distributed; for example, a drug may require a physician's prescription, and physicians may get detailed instructions from the drug manufacturer about who should, and should not, receive the drug.

If these restrictions are not followed, or if the distributor or retailer disregards instructions about a product (consider a sporting goods store employee who tells a 160-kilogram man that a child's personal flotation device "will do fine" for him), the distributor could be sued under the doctrine of product liability on the basis of negligent distribution.

The Internet-based sale of prescription drugs is a modern context in which there is a high potential for problems with distribution. Many drugs have the potential to have harmful effects on individuals who do not fit the recommended patient profile. Some drugs interact dangerously with other drugs; some should not be used by patients with certain health conditions; and still others react differently depending on the patient's age, or even gender.

Negligent Design

Negligent design is the product liability scenario with the highest potential risk exposure for defendants (because it affects the entire inventory) and the scenario that is hardest to prove. Proving negligent design will be addressed below, in the discussion of standard of care.

A product is said to be negligently designed when something about the way it is conceived or designed makes it dangerous to the end user, *and* the designer knew or ought to have known that this danger existed, or else failed to sufficiently research the product's safety before bringing it to market.

Where a product is negligently designed, every single individual product has the potential to harm a plaintiff, even though in actuality, only a few plaintiffs may be harmed. For this reason, this area of negligence poses a significant liability risk to defendants. When a problem with design safety is communicated to a defendant, the defendant generally has the duty to act quickly to communicate the problem to end users to prevent harm. Product "recalls" are often a result of the manufacturer's attempt to meet this duty (though product recalls can also be seen in cases of negligent manufacture, for example, where a vegetable packager detects *Listeria* or *E. coli* bacteria on a particular batch).

Standard of Care and Proving Product Liability

Standard of care is a very thorny issue in product liability cases.

There are good public policy reasons for encouraging producers to invent new products, and there is public demand for these products. When a new product is invented, or a product is manufactured in a new way, there are limits on the inventor's or manufacturer's ability to predict all the possible things that could go wrong with it.

To some extent, testing can help make these predictions. However, testing is expensive and adds to the ultimate cost of the product. There are competing pressures on producers, both to make safe products and to offer products at affordable cost. For this reason, the standard of care in product liability often involves an attempt to balance these competing pressures.

Standard of Care in Negligent Design Cases

Some of the "tools" used by the courts in attempting to determine the standard of care of producers are:

1. *Industry codes:* Does the product meet pre-established safety ratings recognized in the industry? If testing is usual in this industry, did the producer comply with testing requirements?

2. *Statutory regulation:* Do the product and its manufacture comply with all applicable statutes?

Some recent cases have used what has been described as a "risk-utility" approach to analyzing product performance, risks, and producer efforts to design a safe product (see, for example, the decision in *Ragoonanan Estate v. Imperial Tobacco Canada Ltd.*[3]). The following factors are considered when conducting a risk-utility analysis of the defendant's design:

---

3. *Ragoonanan Estate v. Imperial Tobacco Canada Ltd.*, 2000 CanLII 22719 (Ont. S.C.).

- the utility of the product to the plaintiff and the general public;
- the ability of the plaintiff to avoid injury through careful or reasonable use of the product;
- the ability of the plaintiff to discover the risks prior to injury;
- the possibility of reasonably foreseeable harm;
- the existence of a safer design than the one used; and
- the possibility of the producer spreading the cost of a safer product design.

In the *Ragoonanan* case, the product at issue was a type of cigarette that apparently lacked a self-extinguishing design (having to do with the way the tobacco is packed). This self-extinguishing design is apparently common to many cigarette brands.

In *Ragoonanan*, a 16-year-old smoker probably (it could not be proved) dropped a cigarette on a couch when he fell asleep. The resulting fire killed him and two other children. The children's family sued under the doctrine of product liability based on negligent design, arguing that the cigarette manufacturer could have designed its product to incorporate the self-extinguishing design well known in the industry, but chose not to, instead choosing to produce a less safe cigarette.

The cigarette manufacturer applied to the court to strike out the victims' pleading on the ground that it disclosed no reasonable cause of action. The cigarette maker's position was that the deaths were entirely the result of negligence on the part of the young smoker.

The court refused to strike the pleadings, holding that even if the smoker's case failed the risk-utility test (utility of the product, ability of plaintiff to avoid risks, and so on), the other two children who died were *not* contributorily negligent, and the risk-utility analysis would apply differently to them. The case was eventually settled out of court.

Standard of Care in Negligent Manufacturing Cases and Negligent Distribution Cases

Proving a failure to meet the standard of care is much easier in cases based on negligent manufacturing or negligent distribution, because the behaviour of the defendant, in these cases, is simply measured against what happens when things *do not* go wrong.

For example, in the case of manufacturing problems, when an individual product, or a single batch of a product, is found to be defective, the plaintiff has the non-defective products or batches to compare it against. In these cases, the non-defective ones act as a sort of ready-made standard of care.

In the negligent distribution context, the plaintiff will generally compare what actually happened when the product was distributed against guidelines (for example, the prescribing guidelines prepared by a drug manufacturer) or industry standards that are followed by the majority of distributors.

Punitive Damages Available in Product Liability Cases

From: *Vlchek v. Koshel*, 1988 CanLII 3116 (B.C.S.C.).

In this case, the plaintiff was seriously injured when the Honda all-terrain vehicle (ATV) she was riding as a passenger crashed and flipped over.

At trial, the plaintiff argued that the ATV was made for use by the general public, but could not be safely operated by the general public, especially over rough terrain, and that the manufacturer failed to warn the public of the risks associated with the vehicle and failed to recall it.

In addition to general and specific damages, the plaintiff included a claim for both aggravated and punitive damages.

In a separate hearing to consider whether punitive damages (also referred to, in this case, as "exemplary damages") are even available in a product liability case, the court considered a long line of decisions that stood for the general principle that punitive damages are not available in a product liability case. The reasoning expressed in these authorities was that a designer or manufacturer of a product cannot have the intent (*mens rea*) necessary to support a punitive damages case because in designing or producing its product (even if negligently), the defendant cannot be said to have any malice toward, or flagrant disregard for, the safety of a particular end user.

Indeed, in nearly all previous cases about punitive damages, the defendant knew the plaintiff and intentionally disregarded his or her well-being or safety.

However, after an analysis of these cases, the court found that the defendant's conscious direction of wrongdoing against a specific plaintiff was not an *essential* part of the law of punitive damages, but rather, one of a number of factors that supported the imposition of these damages. The essential purpose of punitive damages, the court held, is to correct or punish "socially reprehensible" behaviour that may or may not be directed at a particular individual.

PROFESSIONAL LIABILITY AND MALPRACTICE

Professional liability is not unlike product liability, in that the plaintiff counts on the defendant to supply something, and the thing supplied is defective and causes harm. In product liability, what is supplied is a product; in professional liability, what is supplied is expertise.

Professionals, for the purpose of this area of negligence, are those who claim a specialized knowledge or skill with respect to their services, and who invite the public to rely on that claim.

A Claim in Contract or in Tort?

In general, a professional's services are offered under a contract. This means that when things go wrong, the customer has a remedy in contract. The doctrine of professional liability, however, establishes that the customer also has a remedy in tort. While the customer cannot claim the same (duplicate) compensation under both doctrines, the customer has a *choice* about whether to sue in contract or under the doctrine of professional liability (a tort).

As you learned in Part I, a claim in contract is generally easier to prove than one in tort, because in a contracts case, the contract itself is evidence of the expectations of the parties. Why would a person who has received what he or she believes to be poor-quality professional services choose to sue in tort, if a contract claim is easier to prove?

Usually, the reason is that damages in tort can sometimes be greater than those available in contract—especially if the plaintiff is pursuing exemplary or punitive damages.

Note, however, that the cases in this area establish that where a contract imposes limits on liability, the plaintiff will not be able to get around this by suing in tort instead. For example, consider a plaintiff who agrees to undergo free medical treatment with an experimental drug (to allow the manufacturer to test the drug). The plaintiff is asked to sign a contract waiving his or her right to sue for harmful side effects in exchange for free access to the drug. If the plaintiff is harmed through his or her participation in the study, the courts will not allow this plaintiff to disregard the waiver contract and bring a lawsuit based on professional liability.

The Standard of Care for Professionals

As you have already learned, a professional, instead of being held to the standard of care of a reasonable person, is held to the standard of care of "a reasonably careful and competent practitioner practising in similar circumstances."

What this means, precisely, varies from profession to profession.

An important indicator of the standard of care within a profession is "general practice" or "accepted practice." Each profession has a myriad of conventions, procedures, and practices that members of the profession are expected to incorporate into their work habits.

A lawyer is expected to keep his or her own business accounts and funds (such as business revenues and expenses) separate from the funds held in trust on behalf of clients (for example, money that a client has given the lawyer to be used as a down payment on a mortgage that the lawyer is arranging). In the medical field, a well-known surgical best practice involves counting the instruments that will be used for an operation before and after the surgery.

Where a plaintiff alleges professional negligence, and the evidence suggests that the professional failed to observe a principle of accepted practice, the plaintiff may be able to assert that the professional fell short of the standard of care.

Other tools for establishing the standard of care for a professional include:

- professional codes of conduct,
- practice guidelines established by a regulatory body (like a law society or a college of pharmacists), and
- legislation and regulations that apply to the profession.

In some professions, there is a distinction between generalists and specialists; for example, the Law Society of Upper Canada, which regulates Ontario lawyers, allows practitioners who meet certain criteria to promote themselves as "specialists in family law" (or in other areas). Where a person is designated as a specialist—and what constitutes a specialist, within the profession, can be objectively defined—the standard of care may be elevated to the standard of "a reasonably competent specialist in X."

Conversely, there is no separate category for novices or beginners: beginner practitioners of a profession are not subject to a lower standard of care; instead, they are expected, while they are developing their expertise, to restrict their practice to those cases/patients/problems that they are competent to manage.

Medical Negligence

Medical care leads to a proportionately high percentage of professional negligence claims compared with other professional services, not because physicians and other health-care professionals are less competent than other professionals, but because unsuccessful medical treatment (or negligence in medical treatment) has direct and sometimes serious implications for human health and quality of life.

Successful medical malpractice or negligence suits can lead to large damages awards. Surgeons are more likely to be sued than other classes of medical care providers, and obstetric, pediatric, and neonatal care generate an especially high proportion of claims in many jurisdictions.

Negligence Versus Battery

Battery, an intentional tort, was discussed in Chapter 10. As you learned in the context of intentional torts, when a physician administers treatment to a patient without the patient's consent, whether or not the treatment is competent, the patient can sue in battery. When a patient *does* consent to the treatment, but the treatment is given incompetently, the patient can sue in negligence.

Informed Versus Uninformed Consent

informed consent
a legally capable patient's consent to a specific medical treatment, in which the patient is informed by the practitioner of the nature and purpose of the treatment, its risks and benefits, and the risks of not proceeding with it

Where a patient gives consent that does not constitute **informed consent**, and the results of the treatment do not meet the patient's expectations, the patient may have a claim in negligence even where the treatment was competent and consistent with accepted practice.

Consent is not considered to be informed consent if the risks of the treatment, and the likely results of the treatment, are not properly explained to the patient.

At the very least, the patient must know what the basic nature of the treatment is. For example, if the patient knows he or she is about to have "an operation of some sort," but does not know that the operation is a colectomy that will result in his or her having to wear an ostomy bag, the patient's consent to the "operation of some sort" will likely be void, and he or she will be able to sue in battery.

By contrast, if the patient does understand the basic nature of the treatment, but important risks have not been explained to him or her, the plaintiff's consent will be non-informed consent, and he or she will be able to sue in negligence.

When a plaintiff claims, after the fact, that had he or she known all the risks he or she would not have gone ahead with the surgery—even if avoiding the surgery would likely have caused *worse* harm—must the court accept that assertion? Not necessarily. The court will apply what has been called a "modified objective test" to determine what a reasonable patient, informed of all the risks before treatment, would have chosen. The modified objective test is usually expressed as follows: On the basis of a full description of the risks, what would a reasonable person with some of the key attributes of this plaintiff (for example, age, sex, family status, occupation) have decided to do?

If the court deems that a reasonable person in the same position as the plaintiff would have agreed to have the treatment, the plaintiff will usually not be able to succeed at trial in a suit based on rare but known risks.

CASE IN POINT

Was Disclosure of Medical Risks Sufficient? Depends on the Patient

From: *Reibl v. Hughes*, [1980] 2 S.C.R. 880.

The Supreme Court of Canada's 1980 decision in *Reibl v. Hughes* was a landmark decision in the area of medical negligence. The court's reasoning has often been praised for its practicality and clarity, and the principles for which the decision stands continue to be applied today.

Before *Reibl v. Hughes*, plaintiffs who underwent medical treatment that they later regretted sometimes tried to "squeeze" the facts of their cases under the heading of battery, arguing that incomplete disclosure of the risks of a treatment was the same as no disclosure at all. Where there was no disclosure, there was no consent, and hence the treatment constituted battery.

Mr. Reibl, the plaintiff in this case, followed that trend when he argued that the risks of an operation were not fully disclosed to him before the surgery, and that that failure of disclosure made the operation a battery.

At the age of 44, Reibl was diagnosed with a blockage in an artery. This blockage threatened his cardiac health; however, reversing the blockage was not deemed essential to keeping him alive—it was simply recommended as a way of somewhat reducing his risk of a stroke or heart attack.

The surgery typically performed at that time (1970) to clear blocked arteries was fairly well established, but was still major surgery with significant risks. One of the risks was that Reibl would suffer a stroke during the surgery or in the post-operative period. However, not performing the surgery and leaving the blockage in Reibl's artery also carried a risk of stroke. When the surgery was explained to him, the surgeon did not discuss the stroke risk in detail except to say that *not* having the surgery carried a greater risk of stroke than having it.

At 44 years old, Reibl was still working and was just a year and a half away from having his pension vest.

Though the surgery was competently performed and was successful, during or immediately after it, Reibl had a stroke that left him paralyzed on one side of his body and impotent. He sued in battery, alleging that he was not fully informed of the risks and so did not give informed consent.

At trial, the judge agreed, finding the doctor liable in battery. The Court of Appeal allowed the doctor's appeal and ordered a new trial, *ruling out* liability in battery. Reibl appealed to the Supreme Court of Canada.

The Supreme Court found that, in light of the decade that had elapsed between the surgery and its decision, it was not fair to put Reibl through a new trial, and that the trial record was good enough to support a determinative appeal decision.

On the issue of battery, the Supreme Court noted that attempting to equate flawed disclosure with no disclosure to support a finding of battery was not an appropriate way to address these kinds of cases:

> The popularization of the term "informed consent" for what is, in essence, a duty of disclosure of certain risks of surgery or therapy appears to have had some influence in the retention of battery as a ground of liability, even in cases where there was express consent to such treatment and the surgeon or therapist did not go beyond that to which consent was given. It would be better to abandon the term when it tends to confuse battery and negligence.

Instead of carrying on with the semantic gymnastics required to distinguish informed consent from no consent at all (while ignoring the possibility of ill-informed consent), the court found that it made more sense to apply a full negligence analysis to these cases.

In performing that analysis, determining whether the communication of risks to the patient was adequate required a review of each case on its facts, considering a range of factors:

The materiality of non-disclosure of certain risks to an informed decision is a matter for the trier of fact, a matter on which there would, in all likelihood, be medical evidence but also other evidence, including evidence from the patient or from members of his family.

Applying that kind of analysis to this case, the court held that while, as a general rule, a patient might decide to have a surgery after being told that the risk of (eventual) stroke from not having it outweighed the risk of (im-mediate) stroke from having it, Reibl's situation was unique: he was young and only 18 months away from having his pension vest. In his particular case, waiting to have the surgery may well have been reasonable, and he may well have chosen to wait had he been given a fuller explanation of risks.

The doctor was found liable in negligence for failing to fully disclose the risks in light of the particular circumstances of his patient.

Defence of Therapeutic Privilege

Just as an emergency scenario (unconscious patient, surgery needed to save his life) sometimes provides a defence to battery, certain conditions—for example, a patient who cannot understand the description of the risks, or who cannot emotionally cope with the need to decide about consent—may support a defence called the defence of therapeutic privilege.

A medical practitioner who relies on this defence generally does so on the basis that the patient was not in a position to communicate his or her best interests, but the physician made a decision about what those best interests were and proceeded.

For example, a physician may, upon examining a patient, realize that the patient has the serious infection commonly described as "flesh-eating disease," and that the patient, who is refusing to allow the physician to remove the affected tissue, is also delirious from fever. Knowing that the patient's life is at imminent risk, the physician may sedate the patient (where possible, this will be done with the consent of a relative of the patient's) and remove the affected tissue to prevent the potentially fatal spread of the infection.

Legal Malpractice

Lawyers are also sometimes subject to lawsuits based on negligence, though to a lesser extent than are physicians.

The issue most likely to complicate a lawsuit in negligence against a lawyer is that the plaintiff, in order to succeed, must show harm.

If, because of a lawyer's alleged negligence, the plaintiff loses his or her case, what is the harm he or she suffered? The simple answer is that the damages he or she *would* have won, had the case been won, are his or her harm.

However, there are problems with this approach. First, and most important, it is impossible to know whether, had the plaintiff been successful, the court would have awarded all the damages that were asked for (bear in mind that plaintiffs often "inflate" damages claimed so that they have bargaining room to negotiate settlements).

Had the trial actually happened, or happened competently, the plaintiff would have had to have proven his or her damages. When this has not taken place—for example, the judge threw out the pleadings because the lawyer drafted them incompetently—the damages will *not* have been proven.

Second, just the mere fact of having a competent lawyer does not mean that a plaintiff will *succeed* at trial.

Because of these two big problems, a lawsuit to determine damages against a lawyer for negligence involves two tough challenges:

- reconstructing what the original court would have accepted as proven damages, and
- determining what the chance is that the plaintiff would have won.

The most common way to handle damages in a lawsuit in negligence against a lawyer is to determine, on a balance of probabilities, whether or not the case would have been won had the lawyer been competent. If the plaintiff can prove that it is at least 51 percent likely that he or she would have won, the plaintiff will be awarded, against the lawyer, the damages he or she should have had from the defendant.

In some cases, though, the plaintiff is awarded those damages multiplied by the odds of winning. For example: $40,000 in damages proven × 70 percent chance of winning = $28,000.

Even this approach, however, can be somewhat unfair, because it does not reflect what would have been the plaintiff's chances of actually recovering the damages from the defendant. Many defendants are impecunious (broke) and cannot pay judgments ordered against them; but all Canadian lawyers are required to carry malpractice insurance, and so they tend to be easy to collect from.

NEGLIGENT MISREPRESENTATION

Like professional liability, **negligent misrepresentation** is also an area in which a plaintiff seeks to impose liability on a defendant on the basis of the defendant's (bad) advice.

negligent misrepresentation
a careless representation made by a defendant while having no reasonable basis to believe it to be true

Although professional liability flows from contractual relationships between clients and their professional advisers, negligent misrepresentation cases need *not* flow from contractual relationships.

There does, however—like in all negligence cases—have to be a duty of care owed by the defendant to the plaintiff.

The basic elements of the tort doctrine of negligent misrepresentation were set out in *Queen v. Cognos Inc.*[4] Those elements are:

- there must have been a duty of care based on a special relationship between the parties;
- the advice given must have been untrue, misleading, or inaccurate;
- the adviser must have been negligent in giving the advice;
- the advisee must reasonably have relied on the advice; and
- the advice must have resulted in a financial loss for the advisee.

---

4. *Queen v. Cognos Inc.*, [1993] 1 S.C.R. 87.

One of the harder elements to prove is the existence of a "special relationship." Some of the factors that might support a special relationship are:

- the person who gives the advice is an expert in that area;
- the advice is given in a business setting, not a social setting;
- the person who receives the advice asked for the advice, and it is foreseeable that he or she would rely on it; or
- the advice was intended to be actionable advice—not merely opinion.

A major turning point in the doctrine about negligent misrepresentation was the 1963 decision in *Hedley Byrne & Co. Ltd. v. Heller & Partners Ltd.*,[5] which established that a defendant could be held liable for a negligent misrepresentation that led to **pure economic loss** on the plaintiff's part.

pure economic loss
the loss of money unrelated to injuries or to damage to goods or real property

Pure economic loss is the loss of money that is unrelated to injuries or to damage to goods or real property.

STRICT LIABILITY

strict liability
liability that is imposed even though no negligence or intentional tort occurred

The application of **strict liability**, under the common law, is both rare and narrowly defined.

Strict liability is tort liability that is imposed *even though there was no negligence, nor any intentional tort.* This kind of liability is imposed in certain narrow circumstances in which there was *no* intention at all (no wrongdoing, no moral guilt, no recklessness).

The Rule in Rylands v. Fletcher

Strict liability was formally recognized through the decision in a 19th-century case, *Rylands v. Fletcher.*[6] This case arose out of activities carried out on lands that belonged to the Earl of Wiltshire. The earl had a large property, with various forms of industry being carried out upon it by commercial tenants (such as they were, back in the mid-1800s). These included a textile mill and a coal mine.

The operators of the textile mill decided they needed a reservoir to hold the water necessary to run the mill. They asked the earl for permission to build a reservoir, got permission, and planned and carried out the construction properly, employing qualified engineers. Part of the reservoir was constructed above the existing coal mine.

There was no evidence that the reservoir was constructed negligently. However, water escaped from it through a mine shaft and flooded the mine, causing damage.

Despite the lack of evidence of negligence, the court found the defendant reservoir builders liable. At the first level of court, the judge based liability on the notion that if someone brings something inherently dangerous (in this case, a lot of water)

---

5. *Hedley Byrne & Co. Ltd. v. Heller & Partners Ltd.*, [1964] A.C. 465 (U.K.H.L.).
6. *Rylands v. Fletcher* (1866), L.R. 1 Ex. 265 (Ex. Ct.); aff'd (1868), L.R. 3 H.L. 330.

onto land, and that dangerous thing escapes onto a neighbour's land and causes harm, then the person who brought it onto the land is liable for the damage. The House of Lords (appeal court), in affirming the decision, articulated the issue slightly differently, holding that if a person makes an unnatural use of land, and that use causes harm to another (despite there being no negligence), then liability will follow.

Modern Application

This notion of liability without negligence has come to be known as "strict liability," or the "doctrine in *Rylands v. Fletcher*."

Despite the different expressions of the rule, the *Rylands* case has tended to be relied on as an authority for imposing liability in cases where neither nuisance law nor negligence law really fit, but it seems fair to hold the defendant liable.

In most of the cases that have succeeded, three things have had to be shown:

1. the defendant brought something capable of causing harm onto his or her land;
2. the defendant made use of the thing for his or her own profit or benefit; and
3. the use of the thing, in addition to being dangerous, was unusual or non-natural.

The final ingredient in a strict liability case is escape: the thing usually needs to have, through unnatural and hazardous use, escaped onto neighbouring land. For example, in the Canadian case of *Schenck v. Ontario*,[7] road salt applied by road crews became a salt spray that damaged the plaintiff's orchard.

The doctrine is very problematic because it is difficult to determine what constitutes a hazardous thing, or a hazardous or unusual or unnatural use of a thing, or an "escape." It is also hard to determine where strict liability starts and where negligence begins. In the original *Rylands* case, the water escaped completely unintentionally; however, in some other cases, the escape involved some level of carelessness, which, arguably, is closer to negligence.

Defences to Strict Liability

Consent is a defence to strict liability. Where the plaintiff is likely to benefit, or has benefited, from the actions of the defendant (or the presence of the dangerous thing on the defendant's land), then the plaintiff may be considered to have consented to the activity. Where the plaintiff has consented to the activity, the defendant cannot be liable in strict liability.

Another defence to strict liability is based on the plaintiff's own actions. Where the plaintiff does something to cause the escape of the dangerous thing, the plaintiff cannot succeed in strict liability. For example, if one plaintiff entices the defendant neighbour's pet tiger to jump the fence by waving a steak at it, the plaintiff

---

7. *Schenck v. Ontario* (1981), 131 D.L.R. (3d) 310 (Ont. H.C.); additional reasons 142 D.L.R. (3d) 261.

cannot sue in strict liability. This is different from negligence cases—in negligence, contributory negligence does *not* negate liability (it only reduces it).

A defendant may also successfully avoid damages in strict liability by proving that the escape was caused by an "act of God" or by the acts of third parties.

Finally, where a statute regulates a dangerous activity, and the defendant complies with the statute, the defendant may have a defence called the **defence of statutory authority**.

defence of statutory authority
a defence to strict liability that is available where a statute regulates a dangerous activity and the defendant complies with the statute

VICARIOUS LIABILITY

The final subcategory of negligence that will be covered in this book is vicarious liability. Unlike strict liability, vicarious liability is argued fairly frequently, and sometimes successfully, in Canadian courts.

Vicarious liability, in a nutshell, is liability imposed on an innocent principal for the wrongful acts of the principal's agent in circumstances where the agency relationship makes it reasonable, considering public policy, to impose liability.

In simpler terms, vicarious liability makes one person liable for the wrongful act of another person.

Agency Relationship

An agency relationship is one in which one person, called the "agent," does something at the request and for the benefit of another person, who is called the "principal." The easiest example is an employer–employee relationship. The employee (who is the agent) does things for, and on behalf of, the employer, who is the principal.

There are other kinds of agency relationships, however. For example, when you hire a real estate agent to sell your house, he or she *is* your agent, and you *are* his or her principal, but you are not his or her employer. You have simply entered into a contract to buy his or her services.

A person who sells his or her services to others, whether on a one-time basis or an ongoing basis, is an "independent contractor." Many businesses like to purchase the services of contractors instead of hiring employees, because it means they do not have to pay benefits or pay for vacation and sick time. Finally, there are yet other kinds of agency relationships; for example, anyone who delivers a message on behalf of someone else is an agent (however briefly). And religious leaders, when they preach, consider themselves to be agents of God.

Vicarious liability is a form of strict liability in which the principal is made to pay for the wrongdoing of the agent.

Basis for Vicarious Liability

Why would the law make the principal pay?

Because often, when the agent does something wrong (for example, commits a tort), he or she does it in the course of doing something that profits or benefits the principal. Public policy dictates that "he or she who profits from a tort ought to pay" for the harm caused by the tort.

This situation is also better for victims, because the principal often is in a better financial position to pay damages.

Vicarious liability is not automatic; whether it is imposed depends on the facts. Increasingly, the courts are coming to view public policy/fairness concerns as the most important factor in imposing vicarious liability. But certain other factors come into it as well:

1. *Was the wrongdoer really an agent—did the principal profit from his or her actions?* If the principal did not benefit or profit, vicarious liability is less likely, unless the agent was an employee.

2. *Was the agent an independent contractor or an employee?* Employers are much more likely to be held vicariously liable for the actions of employees than for those of independent contractors.

   Regardless of what the parties *claim* the relationship to be, where the principal has control of not only *what* work the agent does, but *how* (where, when, according to what procedures, etc.) the work is done, the court may find that the relationship is an employment relationship.

   Where the principal has *little or no* control over how the work is done, and especially if the work is not an integral part of the principal's enterprise, the agent will likely *not* be an employee.

3. *If the agent was an employee, was the wrongful act done in the course of employment?* Wrongful acts done outside the normal course of employment—that is, not as an employer-sanctioned part of carrying out the job—do not *normally* lead to vicarious liability.

However, in a few cases, the court has held an employer liable in vicarious liability for the illegal acts of employees where the employer created an environment that was at high risk for illegal or tortious activity and failed to take appropriate steps to prevent that activity.

For example, several cases involved sexual assaults on vulnerable clients of a recreational program (children, people with developmental delays) by program employees. Although employers usually have no vicarious liability for their workers' illegal or malicious acts, in these cases, the employer was held to have created the risk (by putting vulnerable clients in the care of these abusers, in situations where there was one-on-one privacy) and to have failed to prevent the harm, for example, by not properly screening employees or by failing to establish protective policies and procedures. And so in those cases, the court felt that public policy reasons supported the imposition of liability on the employer.

LAW IN PRACTICE
Vicarious Liability or Not?

Consider the following examples:

- A temp who works "offsite" for a client is advised by the temp agency to overbill by 20 percent, and does so (liability likely).
- A pet store owner tells an exotic bird supplier, "I don't care where you get those parrots—don't tell and I won't ask," and the bird supplier purchases smuggled parrots (liability likely).
- A pizza delivery driver beats up a customer who does not tip (liability unlikely—acts of violence are usually considered outside the scope of employment).
- An employee sells OxyContin to co-workers in the lunchroom (liability unlikely).

CHAPTER SUMMARY

Within the broader field of negligence law, there are certain areas in which the law has developed specifically to address a certain kind or class of legal problem. These subcategories of negligence include occupiers' liability, product liability, professional malpractice or negligence, negligent misrepresentation, strict liability, and vicarious liability.

Occupiers' liability law developed under the common law but has since become codified into statute in many jurisdictions. The early law relating to occupiers imposed a very limited duty of care toward entrants, especially those who entered without invitation. The common law was heavily focused on categorizing entrants by type and tailoring the occupier's duty of care accordingly. Occupiers' liability statutes have simplified the regime somewhat. The most important distinction between entrants now is between those who enter with the intention of committing a criminal act or a tort and those who do not. The general standard of care toward entrants has been raised; the standard of care toward trespassers and criminals is lower. Special rules deal with the duty of care of an occupier of land that is not easily monitored.

Although purchasers of a product typically have a remedy under contract if the product turns out to be harmful, contract doctrine is not very useful for users of a product who are not the original purchaser. Product liability law, which is based on negligence, provides an additional cause of action for those harmed by products, whether or not they have a contract. Product liability can apply to producers, manufacturers, distributors, and retailers, and how liability is proved varies depending on whether the negligence occurred at the design stage, the manufacturing stage, or the distribution stage. A plaintiff harmed by a product may be entitled to a greater damages award by suing in tort than by suing in contract.

Professional negligence (or malpractice, as it is often called) is another subcategory of negligence. Because the public relies on the judgment and expertise of professionals, they are held to a higher standard of care than the general public with respect to their delivery of professional services, whether or not they are new to practice. Medical negligence is a common cause of action, and the law governing it is well developed. A key issue in medical negligence is consent; and whether a plaintiff chooses to sue in battery or in negligence is often determined by the absence or presence of consent.

Lawyers are also sometimes sued for malpractice; one of the obstacles in these suits is that the court must determine whether or not—or to what degree—the plaintiff would have succeeded at trial (or in the course of his or her legal dealings) had the lawyer met the standard of care.

Strict liability is a rare category of negligence that originated from the decision in *Rylands v. Fletcher*. Its application has been narrowed over the years; in general, to be successful in proving strict liability, a plaintiff must prove that the defendant was making an unusual and dangerous use of his or her land (or brought something unusual or dangerous onto the land) and that that thing escaped (through no fault of the defendant's) and harmed the plaintiff or his or her property. Where the plaintiff himself or herself, a third party, or an act of God intervened to cause the escape, the defendant will generally have a defence against strict liability.

Vicarious liability is a doctrine that permits plaintiffs to obtain damages in negligence, not against the party who committed the tort, but against another party: the principal. Vicarious liability usually applies where one party, in doing something on behalf of his or her principal and that benefits the principal (for example, paid or volunteer work), commits a tort. In these cases, public policy may dictate that the principal, who profited from the agent's activity, should bear the responsibility for the tort. In general, where the agent committed a criminal act that was outside the scope of the agency relationship, the principal will not be vicariously liable for the consequences of that act unless the employer created a situation in which the criminal act was likely.

KEY TERMS

attractive nuisance
defence of statutory authority
informed consent
negligent misrepresentation

occupiers' liability
pure economic loss
strict liability

REVIEW QUESTIONS
True or False?

1. Punitive damages may be available in a tort case based on product liability.
2. A property occupier cannot, using a waiver or by any other means, limit her liability for injuries to visitors to her property.
3. When a plaintiff consents to a medical treatment without understanding even the basic nature of the treatment, the plaintiff's consent is considered invalid and she can sue the physician in battery.

4. Employers can be held vicariously liable for the acts of paid employees, but not for those of volunteers.

5. Where a plaintiff was the purchaser of a product that turns out to be defective and to cause harm, the plaintiff probably can sue the producer of the product *either* in contract or in tort.

6. A defendant who brings something dangerous onto his land (for example, a venomous pet snake) will be liable for the harm the thing causes even if it escapes due to a natural disaster, like a hurricane.

7. Manufacturers sometimes "recall" a product because of their duty to act quickly, once they are informed of a design problem in the product, to communicate the problem to end users to prevent harm.

8. When a patient consents to medical treatment and the treatment is given incompetently, the patient can sue in battery.

9. The defining feature of an occupant is that he or she holds title to the property.

10. Ontario's *Occupiers' Liability Act* provides that "benign" trespassers are subject to a higher standard of care than burglars.

Fill in the Blanks

1. According to the _____ _____ rule, an occupier who built a big tree house high in a beech tree on his front lawn and did not effectively prevent access to it and/or shield it from view would be liable if children were attracted to it and were hurt.

2. Where a patient gives consent that does not constitute _____ _____, and the results of the treatment do not meet the patient's expectations, the patient may have a claim in negligence even if the treatment was competent and consistent with accepted practice.

3. _____ liability is tort liability that is imposed even though there was no negligence, nor any intentional tort.

4. _____ liability is liability imposed on an innocent principal for the wrongful acts of the principal's agent in circumstances where the agency relationship makes it reasonable, considering public policy, to impose liability.

5. Under the old scheme of occupiers' liability, there were four general classes of entrants to land: _____, licensees, invitees, and _____ entrants.

6. A court will find a product to have been _____ manufactured where the finished product is found to have deviated from the intended design and, as a result, to have harmed the plaintiff.

7. The Internet-based sale of prescription drugs is a modern context in which there is a high potential for negligent _____.

8. A plaintiff can establish that a defendant manufacturer is liable for the plaintiff's harm if the plaintiff can prove that the defendant was negligent, with respect to the product, at one (or more) of three distinct stages: product marketing/distribution, product _____, and product _____.

9. In all _____ cases, there must be a duty of care owed by the defendant to the plaintiff.

10. Under most occupiers' liability statutes today, there are two levels of duty of care to be considered: a general duty of care and an _____ for _____.

Short Answer

1. A plaintiff who brings an action in contract will often, where the facts allow it, add an additional claim in tort. Why?
2. Why does liability attach to the occupier of property and not necessarily to the owner?
3. Why do courts hesitate to hold the designers of new products automatically liable for any and all harm that the products cause?
4. Why does medical care lead to a disproportionately high percentage of professional negligence claims compared with other professional services?
5. What are the major difficulties with determining damages against a lawyer for negligence?
6. Which part of Ontario's *Occupiers' Liability Act* implicitly forbids the occupier of property to set traps against potential trespassers?
7. On what grounds are beginner practitioners of a profession not held to a lower standard of care than more experienced practitioners?
8. Describe the shift in our society's values concerning personal rights relative to property rights.
9. Explain the rationale for vicarious liability.
10. Why does negligent manufacture represent a lower total risk, from a liability perspective, than negligent design does?

EXERCISES

1. Two young couples arrived after dark at Lakeside Resort for a long weekend holiday. They drove to their cabin and parked and began excitedly unpacking. As they did so, they heard splashing and voices coming from the direction of a dock that could barely be seen in the darkness by the water's edge. Harry, one of the husbands, let out a whoop, kicked off his sandals, and ran toward the water. He ran to the edge of the dock. To avoid landing on the other hotel guests, who were swimming on the north side of the dock, he dove into the water on the south side.

Unfortunately for Harry, the water on the south side of the dock was only 1 metre deep. He hit his head on a rock and suffered a severe spinal injury. Harry is now suing 1405580 Ontario Limited, the corporate owner of Lakeside Resort, under the *Occupiers' Liability Act*.

The dock, in fact, did have a permanent sign, with black block letters on a white background, nailed to a post midway down the dock, reading "Danger, shallow water. No diving." However, since there are no lights on the dock, this sign was not clearly visible at night, when Harry's accident occurred.

a. Is 1405580 Ontario Limited an occupier under the legislation?

b. What duty did the occupier in this case owe to the plaintiff?

c. Did the occupier meet the standard of care required in attempting to prevent Harry's accident?

d. If the occupier did not meet the standard of care, will it be 100 percent liable for Harry's loss?

2. Natural Wonder, an herbal supplement startup, developed an herbal blend capsule that the company believed could reduce the body's absorption of alcohol. According to Natural Wonder, users who swallowed two capsules could, over the six hours following, drink three times their normal limit of alcohol before getting drunk. The individual herbs in the preparation had been tested for safety and were commonly available separately in health food stores. The combination and proportions, however, were Natural Wonder's secret recipe.

The company decided to promote its new product by distributing free samples in university "frosh week" swag bags. The sample blister packs were labelled with simple instructions: "Swallow two capsules with water an hour before imbibing," and bore the slogan "Party hard without paying the price."

Unfortunately, the product did not live up to its name. While it did promote alertness in many users, preventing them from feeling as drowsy as they normally would after overdrinking, 14 students who took the drug had to be hospitalized for alcohol poisoning, and a 15th suffered a fractured pelvis after she fell down a staircase.

Two of the users brought lawsuits against Natural Wonder.

a. Can the students sue the company even though they received the samples for free?

b. On what cause of action should the suits be based?

c. Will the lawsuits be based on negligent design, negligent manufacture, or negligent distribution?

d. Does the fact that all the components of the capsule were established to be safe and were readily available without a prescription individually limit the defendant's liability?

Glossary

A

absolute privilege
a defence against defamation for statements made in a court or parliament, or between spouses

absolute liability
liability that is imposed automatically (usually under a statute) when certain conditions are met, without reference to negligence or intent

abuse of process
malicious use of the court process for an improper purpose

accord and satisfaction
a means of discharging a contract whereby the parties agree to accept some form of compromise or settlement instead of performance of the original terms of the contract

acceptance
when there has been acceptance of an offer made by one party in the bargaining process, the parties are assumed to have reached an agreement on contract terms, and a binding contract exists from that time

accretion
slow accumulation over time

ad idem
see "*consensus ad idem*"

affidavit of execution
a sworn statement in writing, signed by the witness to a contract, stating that the witness was present and saw the person signing the contract actually sign it; the affidavit can be used to prove that a party to a contract actually signed it

aggravated damages
damages awarded where the defendant's flagrant actions caused severe harm

anticipatory breach
an express repudiation that occurs before the time of performance of a contract

apportionment
the practice of awarding damages based on the contribution of each negligent party

arm's-length transaction
a transaction negotiated by unrelated parties, each acting in his or her own independent self-interest; "unrelated" in this context usually means not related as family members by birth or marriage, and not related by business interests

assault
the intentional creation of the apprehension of imminent harmful or offensive contact

assignee
a party to whom rights under a contract have been assigned by way of an assignment

assignment
a transfer by one party of his or her rights under a contract to a third party

assignor
a party who assigns his or her rights under a contract to a third party

attractive nuisance
a dangerous condition of property that may arouse the interest of children

B

bailee
the party who holds or stores goods for another

bailment
an agreement between parties that one will store the goods of the other

bailor
the party who has handed over goods for storage to another

battery
any non-consensual physical contact or touching by the defendant to the plaintiff's physical person

beneficiary
a person who is entitled to the benefits of an agreement entered into between two or more other parties

breach of contract
failure, without legal excuse, to perform any promise that forms part of a contract

C

cause in fact
the factual link between one person's actions and another person's harm

cause in law
the proximity or remoteness of one person's
actions in causing another person's harm

cause of action
a set of factual elements that entitle a plaintiff to sue

chattels
possessions other than land

chose in action/thing in action
an intangible right of ownership in a tangible thing
that carries the right to take legal action on it—
for example, debts, insurance policies, negotiable
instruments, contract rights, patents, and copyrights

civil law
individuals' responsibility for pursuing
remedies for harms between them

civil procedure
established steps, rules, and procedures used
to administer civil (non-criminal) justice

class action
a lawsuit brought by one party who represents
many persons with similar claims

codified
written down and organized into topics

common law
a type of law developed in England,
based on previous judicial decisions and
common to all the people of a country

common mistake
both parties to a contract are mistaken
and make the same mistake

complex causation
multiple causative factors, including possible
contributory negligence on the part of the plaintiff and/
or conditions not caused by plaintiff or defendant

condition
an essential term of a contract, the breach of
which denies the innocent party the benefit of the
contract, or defeats the purpose of the contract

condition precedent
an event (or non-event) that must occur (or not
occur) before a contract can be enforced

condition subsequent
an event that, if it occurs, will
terminate an existing contract

consensus ad idem
when there has been acceptance by the offeree of an
offer, the parties have reached an agreement on terms,
and they have an intention to be bound by those
terms; they are said to have reached a *consensus ad
idem* (a "meeting of the minds"); sometimes a shorter
form is used, and the parties are said to be *ad idem*

consequential damages
secondary damages that do not flow from the
breach of contract but from the consequences
of the breach, such as loss of future profits

consideration
the price, which must be something of
value, paid in return for a promise

conspiracy
an agreement between or among parties to
deceive, mislead, or defraud others of their
legal rights, or to gain an unfair advantage

constitution
written and unwritten laws that set out
how a country will be governed

constructive trust
a trust created by the operation of law, as
distinguished from an express trust

contract
an agreement between private parties or
between a private party and the state

contract/agreement
an agreement made between two or more persons that
the law recognizes and will enforce; a binding contract

contra proferentem rule
a rule used in the interpretation of contracts
when dealing with ambiguous terms according to
which a court will choose the interpretation that
favours the party who did not draft the contract

contributory negligence
a partial defence that reduces the defendant's liability
on the basis of the plaintiff's own negligence

conventions
ways of doing something that have been accepted
for so long that they amount to unwritten rules

conversion
wrongful possession that includes exercise
of rights of ownership, preventing the actual
owner from exercising such rights

counteroffer
a response to an offer by an offeree that does
not unconditionally accept the terms of the offer
but proposes to add to or modify the terms

crime
an act or omission that is an offence under criminal law

Crown
the police and the government

D

deed
a written contract, made under seal by the
promisor(s); also called a formal contract

defamation
intentional harm to a person's
reputation in the community

defence
the collected facts and method adopted by a defendant
to protect against and counter a plaintiff's action

defence of statutory authority
a defence to strict liability that is available where
a statute regulates a dangerous activity and
the defendant complies with the statute

defendant
in civil law, the party being sued; in criminal
law, the party charged with the offence

denunciation
the formal or public expression of diapproval
(often on moral grounds and often on behalf
of civil society) of an act or omission

deterrence
a sanction imposed by the court upon a defendant
designed to reduce the likelihood of reoffence

detinue
wrongful possession of a chattel that belongs to another

direct intent
done with conscious purpose

discharged
released, extinguished; a discharge of a contract occurs
when the parties have complied with their obligations
or other events have occurred that release one or
both parties from performing their obligations

discharged
released, extinguished; a discharge of a contract occurs
when the parties have complied with their obligations,
or other events have occurred that release one or
both parties from performing their obligations

discoverability rule
a rule that allows plaintiffs to sue outside the
limitation period where the information needed to
support a suit was unavailable within that period

distress
a traditional remedy under which a person in
possession of the goods of another can seize and/
or sell those goods as compensation for a wrong

doctrine
journal articles, treatises, and other writing of legal
scholars on any legal subject, used by lawyers and
judges as an aid to interpreting or developing the law

doctrine of frustration of contract
a legal doctrine that permits parties to a contract to be
relieved of the contractual obligations because of the
occurrence of some event beyond their control that
makes it impossible for them to perform the contract

doctrine of laches
a common-law doctrine that states that the neglect
or failure to institute an action or lawsuit within
a reasonable time period, together with prejudice
suffered by the other party as a result of the
delay, will result in the barring of the action

due diligence
the attention and care that a reasonable
person would exercise with respect to his or
her concerns; the obligation to make every
reasonable effort to meet one's obligations

duress
an unlawful threat or coercion used by
one person to induce another to perform
some act against his or her will

duty of care
1. the legal obligation to exercise care in favour
   of a plaintiff and his or her interests
2. a legal obligation imposed on an individual to
   take reasonable care to avoid causing harm to
   another who might reasonably be affected and who
   ought to be in the individual's contemplation

E

equitable remedies
remedies developed by the court of equity
that are based on fairness instead of the
strict application of common law

estopped
stopped or prevented

exclusion/exemption clause
a clause in a contract that limits
the liability of the parties

expectancy damages
damages that are based on a loss of expected profits

express repudiation/express breach
the failure or refusal to perform the obligations
of a contract when they become due

express trust
a trust that arises as a result of an agreement,
usually in writing, that is created in express terms

extra-contractual
outside of contract

ex turpi causa non oritur actio
(Latin) "an action does not arise out of a shameful
cause"; a true defence that eliminates the defendant's
liability based on the action's illegality

F

fair comment
a defence against defamation used by individuals
and organizations whose mandate is the
dissemination of information to the public

false imprisonment
confinement within a fixed boundary of
a person against that person's will

fiduciary
a relationship where one person is in a position
of trust to another and has a duty to safeguard the
other's interests ahead of his or her own interests

force majeure
a major event that the parties to a contract did not
foresee or anticipate that prevents performance
of the contract and thus terminates it; such
an event—for example, a natural disaster or
war—is outside the control of the parties and
cannot be avoided with due diligence

formal contract
a contract that is in writing and sealed by any party
who is a promisor (which may be one or both parties);
formal contracts are also called "deeds," and in English
law are sometimes referred to as "covenants"

fraud
1. intentional misrepresentation that causes
   another to suffer damages; also called deceit
2. false or misleading allegations for the purpose
   of inducing another to part with something
   valuable or to give up some legal right
3. a tort and/or crime based on deception
   for the purpose of profit

fraudulent concealment
deliberate hiding, non-disclosure, or suppression
of a fact or circumstance with intent to deceive
or defraud in a contractual arrangement

fraudulent misrepresentation
1. a false statement that the maker knows is false,
   made to induce a party to enter into a contract
2. intentional fraud that causes another
   to enter into a contract

freedom of contract
the freedom of parties to decide contract
terms of their own choosing

fundamental breach
the failure to perform a primary obligation under a
contract, which has the effect of depriving the other
party of substantially the whole benefit of the contract

G

general damages
estimated damages unsupported by evidence of value

gratuitous promise
a promise made by someone who does
not receive consideration for it

guarantee
a promise by a third party to pay the debt of another
person if that person fails to pay the debt when it is due

guarantor
a third party who gives a guarantee to
the creditor of another person

I

implied repudiation
repudiation that is not express and must be
implied or deduced from the circumstances

inducing breach of contract
intentional incitement to terminate
a contract prematurely

informed consent
a legally capable patient's consent to a specific
medical treatment, in which the patient is
informed by the practitioner of the nature and
purpose of the treatment, its risks and benefits,
and the risks of not proceeding with it

injunction
1. a court order that prohibits someone from doing
   some act or compels someone to do some act
2. a court order intended to prevent future
   harm, enjoining a defendant to cease
   an activity or not do it at all

innocent misrepresentation
a false statement that the maker of the
statement does not know is false, made to
induce a party to enter into a contract

inquiry
questioning by the offeree as to whether the offeror
will consider other terms or is willing to modify the
terms of the offer; an inquiry does not constitute a
counteroffer and is not a rejection of the original offer

intellectual property
legal rights that result from intellectual activity in
the industrial, scientific, literary, and artistic fields

intent
the mental state (conscious action, malice,
carelessness, etc.) at the time of the act of
the person who committed the act

intentional infliction of mental suffering
an act or (false or misleading) statement that is
calculated to cause mental anguish, results in a
disturbance in the plaintiff's health, and is capable
of being diagnosed or confirmed by a physician

intentional tort
a tort that, once proved, is presumed to
have been deliberately committed

interlocutory/interim injunction
a temporary injunction granted by a court
before the final determination of a lawsuit for
the purpose of preventing irreparable injury

J

joint and several liability
the principle that all tortfeasors are collectively
and individually liable for the plaintiff's loss

judicial interventionism
an approach to the interpretation of law that draws on
social, economic, and political values in interpreting the
meaning and application of legal rules and principles

jury
a group of 12 (in criminal cases) or 6 (in civil
cases) citizens over the age of majority who
are convened to hear evidence, make findings
of fact, and deliver a verdict in a trial

L

lapse
the termination or failure of an offer through
the neglect to accept it within some time limit
or through failure of some contingency

legal codes
formal (usually written) collections of legal provisions

legal tender
notes (bills) issued by the Bank of Canada
and coins issued by the Royal Canadian
Mint, subject to certain restrictions

libel
making a defamatory statement by
publishing or broadcasting it

limitation period
a period defined by statute within which a
plaintiff must commence his or her claim

liquidated damages
damages that are easily determined from a fixed
or measurable standard or can be assessed by
calculating the amount owing from a mathematical
formula or from circumstances where no
subjective assessment has to be made

liquidated damages clause
a term in a contract that attempts to
reasonably estimate the damages that will
be suffered if the contract is breached

lost opportunity damages
damages that are based on a longer-
term loss of business

M

malicious prosecution
initiation of a criminal proceeding with malicious
intent for no reasonable or probable cause

mandatory injunction
an injunction that commands a
person to do a certain thing

material alteration
a change in a contract that changes its legal
meaning and effect; a change that goes to
the heart or purpose of the contract

material inducement
a statement made before a contract is struck that
influences a party to enter into the contract

material representation
a statement of fact, not opinion, made by
one party, of sufficient weight to induce the
other party to enter into a contract

mens rea
(Latin) "guilty mind"; the blameworthy
mental element in a criminal offence

merger
the discharge of one contract by its replacement
with, or absorption into, an identical contract

minor
at common law, an individual under the
age of 21; minority status has also been
defined by statute law, lowering the age of
majority to 18 or 19 in most provinces

mitigate
to take steps to minimize or reduce the damages one
will suffer as a result of another's breach of contract

mitigating factor
a defence available to a defendant who was provoked
into committing an alleged tort in which the court
still finds the defendant liable, but may reduce the
damages to reflect the plaintiff's share of fault

mutual mistake
both parties to a contract are mistaken
but each makes a different mistake

N

negative covenant
a promise in a contract to refrain
from doing a certain thing

negligence
1. an act committed without intention to
   cause harm, but which a reasonable person
   would anticipate might cause harm
2. a tort based on careless conduct or conduct that
   creates a reasonably foreseeable risk of harm

negligent misrepresentation
a careless representation made by a defendant while
having no reasonable basis to believe it to be true

nominal damages
a low amount of token damages awarded to
acknowledge the wrong done to the plaintiff

non est factum
(Latin) "I did not make this"; a defence used by one who appears to be a party to a contract but who did not intend to enter into this type of contract; in effect, the party is denying that he or she consented to this contract

novation
a requirement that the parties to a contract agree to substitute a new contract for an existing one, thereby terminating the existing contract

null and void
of no force, validity, or effect

nullity
nothing; something that has no legal force or effect

 O

occupiers' liability
the duty of care that those who occupy real property (through ownership or lease) owe to people who visit or trespass

offences
see "substantive criminal law"

offer
a promise to do something or give something of value to another person; if the other accepts the offer, a binding contract exists

offeree
a person to whom an offer is made during the bargaining process

offeror
a person who, during the bargaining process that precedes making a contract, agrees to do something for the other party; once the offer is accepted, the bargain is concluded and the parties have made an agreement

onus
the burden of responsibility or proof

option to terminate
a term in a contract that allows one or both parties to discharge or terminate the contract before performance has been fully completed

P

parol evidence rule
if a contract is in writing and is clear, no other written or oral evidence is admissible to contradict, vary, or interpret the agreement

passing-off
a defendant's false representation of its goods or services, made with the intent of confusing consumers that they are the goods or services of the plaintiff

past consideration
an act done or something given before a contract is made, which by itself is not consideration for the contract

penalty clause
a term in a contract that imposes a penalty for default or breach

persons under mental disability
a general term that includes persons who are delusional and insane so as to be a danger to themselves and others, and those who, while not insane and dangerous, lack the ability to manage their own affairs

plaintiff
in civil law, the party bringing the suit

positivism
an approach to the interpretation of law that states that the meaning to be given to the words in legal rules should be the ordinary, dictionary meaning without resorting to social, economic, or political values to aid in interpretation

precedent
a legal decision that is taken as a guide in subsequent cases; an essential doctrine of common law that requires judges to follow the rule in a previously decided case when that case deals with similar facts or issues to the case currently being decided and that case was decided by a higher court in the same jurisdiction or by the Supreme Court of Canada

presumption of law
an inference in favour of a particular fact; a rule of law whereby a finding of a basic fact gives rise to the existence of a presumed fact or state of affairs unless the presumption can be rebutted, or proven false, by the party seeking to deny the presumed fact

privity
the relationship that exists between the parties to a contract

prohibitory injunction
an injunction that directs a person not to do a certain thing

promisee
the party to a contract who receives the benefit of a promise made by another party to the contract

promisor
the party to a contract who undertakes to do something

promissory estoppel
a rule whereby a person is prevented from denying the truth of a statement of fact made by him or her where another person has relied on that statement and acted accordingly

provocation
a defence available to a defendant who was faced with a sudden act or an insult that would make a reasonable person lose self-control

psychological confinement
barrier-free confinement of a person against his or her will

punitive damages
a remedy awarded by the court for purposes beyond compensation, such as denunciation or deterrence

pure economic loss
the loss of money unrelated to injuries or to damage to goods or real property

Q

qualified privilege
a defence against defamation for statements made while fulfilling a duty

quantum meruit
an equitable doctrine that states that no one should unjustly benefit from the labour and materials of another; under those circumstances, the law implies a promise to pay a reasonable amount, even in the absence of a contractual term for price

R

representation
a statement made to induce someone to enter into a contract

repudiate
to renounce or reject an obligation

rescission
the cancellation, nullification, or revocation of a contract; the "unmaking" of a contract

rescission
the cancellation, nullification, or revocation of a contract; the "unmaking" of a contract

restitution
a remedy by which one seeks to rescind a contract; if granted, restitution restores the party, as far as possible, to a pre-contract position

restraint of trade
practices that are designed to artificially maintain prices, eliminate competition, create a monopoly, or otherwise obstruct the course of trade and commerce

restrictive covenant
a provision in a contract that prohibits certain activities or uses of property

revoke
to annul or make void by recalling or taking back; to cancel or rescind

S

self-defence
justifiable self-protection when a person reasonably perceives a threat and responds in a reasonable manner

self-help remedy
a remedy exercised by a wronged party without recourse to a formal system of justice

setoff
in an action for debt, a defence in which the debtor admits that he or she owes a debt to the creditor but also claims that the creditor owes a debt to him or her, and uses this reasoning to cancel or reduce the debt owed to the creditor

simple contract
a contract that can be oral or in writing and that is not a formal contract

slander
making an oral defamatory statement

slander of goods
false or misleading statements intended to decrease a competitor's market share

slander of title
false or misleading statements intended to deter another from entering into a transaction

special damages
damages that are known and described at the time of trial

specific goods
specific, identifiable chattels that have been singled out for contract purposes

specific performance
a remedy requiring the party who is in breach of a contract to perform his or her obligations under the contract

standard of care
1. legal criteria against which a defendant's conduct is measured to determine whether he or she has been negligent
2. how well, how carefully, or how thoroughly a person carried out the duty of care owed to another

stare decisis
(Latin) "to stand by the decision"; judges' practice of looking to precedent for guidance in deciding later cases

statement of claim
a document prepared and filed by a plaintiff in a lawsuit that initiates the court action

statute law
laws passed by legislatures

strict liability
liability that is imposed even though no negligence or intentional tort occurred

substantial performance
performance of contractual obligations that does not entirely meet the terms of the contract but nevertheless confers a benefit on a party

substantive criminal law
also called "offences," the crimes themselves

T

tender of performance
offering to perform that which the contracted
party is obligated to perform under a contract

term
a provision of a contract; terms are
either conditions or warranties

tort
a wrong between private parties or
between a party and the state

tortfeasor
the person who commits a tort

tortious
actionable in tort

transferred intent
intent to harm another party that
results in harm to a third party

trier of fact
the judge or jury in a trial

trust
a legal entity created by a grantor for a beneficiary
whereby the grantor transfers property to a trustee
to manage for the benefit of the beneficiary

trustee
a person who holds property in trust for,
or for the benefit of, another person

U

uberrimae fidei contracts
a class of contracts where full disclosure is required
because one party must rely on the power and authority
of another, who must behave with utmost good
faith and not take advantage of the weaker party

unconstitutional
in contravention of a constitution

under seal
bearing an impression made in wax or
directly on paper, or affixed with a gummed
paper wafer, to guarantee authenticity

undue influence
persuasion, pressure, or influence short of actual
force that overpowers a weaker party's judgment and
free will and imposes the will of the stronger party

unilateral mistake
one party to a contract is mistaken about a
fundamental element of the contract

unjust enrichment
a legal doctrine by which the courts sometimes award
compensation to a party in the absence of a contract,
or where the compensation is not contemplated by
the contract because it is equitable to compensate
the party who has enriched the other party with the
expectation of, but not the receipt of, financial reward

unjust enrichment doctrine
principle that a person should not be
permitted to inequitably gain a profit or
benefit at the expense of another

unliquidated damages
damages that cannot be fixed by a mathematical
or measured calculation but require information
from a source outside the contract

V

vicarious liability
the liability of a principal (an employer) for
the negligent or tortious acts of the principal's
agent (an employee) done within the scope
of the agent's authority or employment

vicarious performance
the performance of obligations under a contract by
a third party in circumstances in which the original
party remains responsible for proper performance

void ab initio
invalid from the beginning; no rights can
arise under a contract that is void *ab initio*

voidable contract
a contract that may be avoided or declared void at the
option of one party to the contract; once it is declared
invalid no further rights can be obtained under it, but
benefits obtained before the declaration are not forfeit

void contract
a contract that does not exist at law because
one or more essential elements of the contract
are lacking; an unenforceable contract

volenti non fit injuria
(Latin) "no harm is done to someone who
is willing"; a true defence that negates the
defendant's liability based on the plaintiff's
understanding and acceptance of the risks

W

waiver
1. a voluntary agreement to relinquish a
   right, such as a right under a contract
2. a form of express written consent

warranty
a minor term of a contract, the breach of which
does not defeat the contract's purpose

Index

Statute of Frauds, 66–69, 83
statutory assignment, 120–121
strict liability
    defences to, 315–316
    defined, 190–191, 314
    Rylands v. Fletcher rule, 314–315
substantial performance, 176
substantive criminal law, 7

T

tender of performance, 123–124
"thin-skull" rule, 271–272
tort law
    abuse of process, 224–226
    Charter of Rights and Freedoms, and, 6
    classification of torts
        nuisance, 191
        tortfeasor's intent, 186–191
    conspiracy, 223–224
    elements of a tort
        breach, 185
        causation, 185
        duty, 184–185
        harm, 186
    intentional torts
        as formulas, 199
        duty of care, and, 198
        intention, role of, 198
        proof of harm, and, 199–200
        standard of care, and, 198
    interference with business
        fraud, 219
        fraudulent concealment, 220
        fraudulent misrepresentation, 219
        inducing breach of contract, 220–221
        intimidation, 220
        passing-off, 222–223
        slander of goods, 221–222
        slander of title, 221–222
    interference with possessions
        conversion, 216–217
        detinue, 214
        trespass to chattels, 212
    interference with real property
        nuisance, 217–219
        trespass, 217
    interpersonal torts
        assault, 200–201
        battery, 201–202
        defamation, 206–212, 213
        false imprisonment, 204
        malicious prosecution, 205–206
        mental suffering, infliction of, 202–203
    overview, 184
    principles in statute law, 12–13
    tort, defined, 2

tortfeasor, 185
tortious, 6
trespass, 217
Trespass to Property Act, 217
trier of fact, 9
trust
    constructive trust, 119
    defined, 119
    express trust, 119
trustee, 119

U

uberrimae fidei contracts, 93
unclean hands, 171
unconscionability, 96–100
unconstitutional, 6
under seal, 43
undue influence, 95–96
unilateral mistake, 107–109
unjust enrichment, 24, 174
unjust enrichment doctrine, 24
unliquidated damages, 167

V

vicarious liability
    agency relationships, and, 316
    basis for, 316–318
    defined, 190–191
vicarious performance, 118
void *ab initio*, 72, 83
void contract
    defined, 32, 173
    minors, and, 77
voidable contract, 72, 173
volenti non fit injuria, 280–281

W

waiver, 126, 235
warranty, 138–139, 176
wrongful conduct, 254